Classroom Management for Middle and High School Teachers

Tenth Edition

Classroom Management for Middle and High School Teachers

Edmund T. Emmer
University of Texas, Austin

Carolyn M. Evertson
Peabody College, Vanderbilt University

PEARSON

Boston   Columbus   Indianapolis   New York   San Francisco
Amsterdam   Cape Town   Dubai   London   Madrid   Milan   Munich   Paris   Montreal   Toronto
Delhi   Mexico City   São Paulo   Sydney   Hong Kong   Seoul   Singapore   Taipei   Tokyo

Vice President and Editorial Director: Jeffery W. Johnston
Vice President and Publisher: Kevin M. Davis
Editorial Assistant: Marisia Styles
Executive Field Marketing Manager: Krista Clark
Senior Product Marketing Manager: Christopher Barry
Project Manager: Pamela D. Bennett
Program Manager: Janelle Criner
Operations Specialist: Carol Melville
Text Designer: Cenveo® Publisher Services
Cover Design Director: Diane Ernsberger
Cover Photo: Getty Images/Troy Aossey
Media Project Manager: Lauren Carlson
Full-Service Project Management: Thistle Hill Publishing Services
Printer/Binder: RR Donnelley/Harrisonburg South
Cover Printer: Phoenix Color Hagerstown
Text Font: Sabon LT Pro

Library of Congress Control Number: 2015952859

11 2021

PEARSON

ISBN 10:   0-13-402885-6
ISBN 13: 978-0-13-402885-9

To the many teachers who have taught us about classroom management.

E.T.E.

C.M.E.

PREFACE

Public scrutiny of our schools has never been more intensely critical than it is today. This concern is echoed in the public media along with both reasonable and impractical sounding proposals for what should be done to "fix" our schools and the poor achievement of our students. This attention has pressured schools and teachers for more accountability, more student testing, and particularly, more focus on the basic skills, where the United States seems to lag behind other countries. Media coverage of school violence quickly becomes breaking TV news, while at the same time most scholarly studies report that school violence overall has actually had a general downward trend across the past 20 years (National Center for Educational Statistics, 2014). The calls for better schools have nevertheless served to further various political agendas while heightening the public's concerns.

The effect of these political pressures might give the impression that our schools and classrooms are fundamentally different now from those in the past, that the task of managing classrooms has changed markedly and that more money and resources are needed to fix the problem. In fact, the basic principles for creating an effective learning environment remain the same. Regardless of conditions, teachers must still adapt the core ideas of effective teaching to the settings in which they now teach. This is a problem that every generation of teachers has had to address and solve as they encounter changing social and demographic conditions.

Students entering the nation's schools today come with vastly diverse backgrounds, capabilities, cultural norms, languages, and skills. Meeting their needs and finding the best learning activities requires care and skill and may sometimes seem overwhelming. Research has taught us that for effective teaching to succeed, one of our first and most basic tasks as educators is to develop worthwhile activities that support student learning. Establishing an effective classroom management system is also a first priority. Teachers who have developed such systems have taught us a great deal about the essential features of their classrooms and how they work to establish them.

We know that student academic success is built on a foundation of well-managed classrooms whose teachers have clear ideas of the classroom conditions and student behaviors necessary for a healthy learning environment. Moreover, effective teachers work very hard to create this foundation. This book describes what you can do to create a well-managed learning environment: first by planning in several key areas before the school year begins, then by implementing the plan from the beginning of the year, and finally by maintaining the management procedures throughout the year.

We have made these materials useful and practical by providing checklists, vignettes, case studies, and problem-solving exercises to help you imagine real classrooms as you organize your planning. These case studies and problem-solving scenarios focus on critical areas for managing student learning and behavior. You will find much here that is helpful as you plan and organize your own classroom.

Two helpful resources are handbooks compiled from the most recent research on classroom management: *Handbook of Classroom Management: Research, Practice, and Contemporary Issues* (Evertson & Weinstein, 2006) and the second edition of *Handbook of Classroom Management* (Emmer & Sabornie, 2015). In addition, this book is accompanied by a comparable text for elementary grades: *Classroom Management for Elementary Teachers* (Evertson & Emmer, 2017).

New to This Edition

This edition contains numerous additions, changes, and updates:

- A new chapter on developing positive classroom relationships has been added, including teacher–student and teacher–home relationships.
- Coverage of how management is affected by diversity, culture, and individual differences has been expanded.
- A new section in most chapters titled Who Will I Teach? explores how concepts from those chapters apply to diverse populations, including English language learners, students from diverse backgrounds and cultures, and students with special needs.
- New and updated research, readings, and more than 50 website links encourage readers to extend their knowledge of chapter topics and examine additional resources.
- Questions have been added to many vignettes to frame their content and encourage student reflection.
- Content has been added on the topics of teacher–student relationships, teacher–parent relationships, boundary issues, management in urban settings, room arrangement concerns, cultural influences, English language learners, inclusion, intervention strategies, Behavioral Report Cards, Response to Intervention (RTI), Positive Behavioral Interventions and Supports (PBIS), School-Wide Positive Behavior Supports (SWPBS), and Social-Emotional Learning (SEL).

New Digital Features in the Enhanced Etext with MyEducationLab®

The most visible change in this new edition (and certainly one of the most significant) is the expansion of the digital learning and assessment resources embedded in the etext. Designed to bring readers more directly into the world of K–12 classrooms and to help them see the very real impact that classroom management concepts have on learning environments, these digital learning and assessment resources also:

- Provide readers with practice using classroom management concepts in teaching situations

- Help readers see how well they understand the concepts presented in the book and the media resources
- Help readers think about and process more deeply the concepts presented in the book and the interactive media

Online resources in the Enhanced Etext with MyEducationLab include:

Self-Checks. At the end of each chapter, readers will find MyEducationLab: Self-Check Quizzes. These quizzes are meant to help readers assess how well they have mastered the learning outcomes covered in the chapter they just read. These self-checks are made up of self-grading multiple-choice items that not only provide feedback on whether questions are answered correctly or incorrectly but also provide rationales for both correct and incorrect answers. See the MyEducationLab box at the end of any chapter.

Application Exercises. Also at the end of each chapter and tied to specific chapter learning outcomes, these scaffolded analysis exercises challenge readers to use chapter content to reflect on classroom management concepts and principles in real classrooms. The questions readers answer in these exercises are usually constructed-response. Once readers provide their own answers to the questions, they receive feedback in the form of model answers written by experts. See the MyEducationLab box at the end of any chapter.

Classroom Management Simulations. In most chapters, readers will also be able to access interactive simulations that engage them in decision making about classroom management strategies. These interactive cases focus on classroom management issues teachers most frequently encounter on a daily basis. Each simulation presents a beginning challenge scenario and then offers a series of choices to solve each challenge. Along the way, users receive mentor feedback on their choices and have the opportunity to make better choices if necessary.

Acknowledgments

We extend our deep appreciation for the assistance of Inge R. Poole, Ph.D., Vanderbilt University, who served in many capacities, drawing from her more than 20 years as a classroom teacher and a trainer of teachers. Her help and her knowledge of programs and technology were invaluable.

We also thank the reviewers of our manuscript for their insights and comments: Marilyn Birnbaum, Rutgers University; Sara Cranford, George Mason University; Jo Beth Oestreich, Texas State University; Paula Joanne Politte, Concordia University, Portland; and Teri Walseth, University of South Florida.

BRIEF CONTENTS

CONTENTS

Shutterstock

CHAPTER 1

Introduction to Classroom Management

Classroom management is a broad concept that includes activities and strategies that teachers use to guide student behavior in the classroom. Its goals include fostering student engagement and securing cooperation so that teaching and learning can occur. Classroom management has both planning and interactive aspects. Planning aspects include such tasks as organizing the physical space of the classroom, identifying expectations for student behavior, developing incentives to encourage desirable behavior, arranging consequences to discourage inappropriate behavior, and organizing instructional activities to promote student involvement and engagement. Classroom management also includes a highly interactive, real-time set of teacher behaviors and strategies, including monitoring and interacting with students, providing support and feedback, intervening to redirect student behavior, and working with students to stimulate interest, involvement, and cooperation.

The many hours of our lives that we have spent as students have given the classroom environment a very familiar feel—so that it might not seem to take much effort to make the transition from student to teacher. But taking responsibility for teaching groups of 25 or more adolescents is a very different task than being a student in a classroom. As students, we observe teachers without being aware of the decisions they make or the planning that has gone into their teaching. Students enter an environment that has been arranged, participate in designed activities, and interact with peers and teachers without seeing "behind the scenes." For example, as students we probably observed teachers dealing with individuals who behaved inappropriately in

1

the classroom. Chances are we didn't identify alternate strategies for managing such behavior or what factors need to be considered when deciding what to do. One of the goals of this text is to provide insights into this behind-the-scenes world so that you're better prepared for your work as a teacher.

Many skills, attributes, and actions contribute to making a great teacher. The ability to design lessons that stimulate student interest and promote learning is certainly high on any teacher's list. Another important quality is establishing a connection with students so that they feel supported and motivated to learn. A great teacher also needs good communication skills in order to be able to work with diverse groups of students and their parents. Adding to this list of important competencies would be classroom management ability—not only because of its importance in fostering desirable student behavior but also because it facilitates the other desirable teacher traits and skills. And so, all these desirable teaching traits improve the general behavior of students and thus contribute to classroom management.

■ Classrooms Are Complex Places

It is important to learn about classroom management in order to simplify a complex environment. The idea that classrooms may be complicated workplaces has been recognized for a long time (Jackson, 1966) and is a persistent view (Brophy, 2006; Doyle, 1986, 2006). These observers and researchers have noted that classrooms have multiple actors with different agendas, that teachers have to plan for several activities, and that they have to make multiple, often rapid decisions. Events happen quickly and inexorably, giving teachers a limited amount of time to address students' needs and concerns. Moreover, much of what the teacher and students say and do is public, so everyone is constantly aware of and potentially reactive to events. To complicate matters further, teachers don't have a lot of time to think about what they're doing during an activity; things just happen too quickly for much on-the-spot reflection.

Teachers use a variety of strategies to help time slow down during teaching and to reduce the demand on their processing abilities. For example, teachers organize the classroom environment to facilitate activities and to prevent problems. They develop and install routines and procedures to guide their own and students' behaviors. They invite cooperation and encourage students to take responsibility for their actions, transferring some of the onus for managing behavior to the students themselves. Teachers also endeavor to be consistent in how they respond to students so that students learn what to expect from the teacher and so that the teacher doesn't have to mull over every action and decision. Teachers plan instruction to engage students, and teachers use their personal capital to influence students to follow classroom rules and procedures. All of these teacher actions promote order and regularity, freeing the teacher to focus on instruction and to help students learn.

■ Learning About Classroom Management: Two Vignettes

You have probably had the experience of trying to apply a new set of skills in a natural setting. Ideally, you were allowed to acclimate gradually to the new setting using a limited set of tasks. As your skills improved, you were given opportunities to apply the skills in more complex settings with greater demands. For example, when you first learned to drive a car, you weren't expected to drive on an unfamiliar road at high speed during rush hour. Instead, you were (or should have been!) provided opportunities to encounter different driving situations and develop more or less automatic responses to simple aspects of driving, so that as time went on, you could attend to more complex aspects of the task.

Learning to teach isn't the same as learning to drive, of course, but they do share some common features. Initially, you need help focusing on the basic features of the task. With time and practice, some of these basics become automatic, and you can react better to the more complex aspects. As you develop expertise, you integrate the skills, and the tasks appear less effortful.

Reading a book on classroom management will provide you with information about its basic features and a more integrated and complete perspective on the topic. But reading is not sufficient to become proficient. You need to apply the ideas in field settings whenever you observe in a classroom, assist a teacher, participate as an intern or student teacher, or reflect on your own work as a teacher. If you are conscientious about applying the ideas to actual teaching situations, you will soon begin to think like an experienced classroom manager and you will be well on your way to becoming a great teacher.

To illustrate key ideas and to make the content in this text concrete, we'll present short classroom vignettes based on actual classrooms (names and some identifying features were changed in order to maintain confidentiality). We'll begin by presenting two vignettes of teachers that illustrate a variety of management concepts and how they influence classroom behaviors. The vignettes will also show how good and poor practices can compound their effects over time. As you read these vignettes, try to imagine yourself as the teacher and reflect on what you would like to add to or avoid in your own teaching practice.

Vignette 1. Mark Smith is a middle school social studies teacher who genuinely cares about his students and wants very much to equip them with the knowledge and skills they will need for success in life. As the school year has progressed, however, he has felt increasingly frustrated with the general disorder that envelops many of his lessons. Like many teachers, he prefers to use nonconfrontational tactics to manage problems, and this stance has allowed him to avoid eliciting hostile responses or outright defiance from students he has had to discipline, while gaining a modicum of cooperation from many students. Nevertheless, significant amounts of time frequently are lost to non-academic activities, and students sometimes accomplish little in the way of learning. During some activities fewer than half the students are on task, and Mr. Smith finds it difficult to keep a majority of students fully engaged for more than a short time. Observations of some incidents in one of the classes reveal several problems that hamper his instruction.

- During a class activity that was well within their capabilities, several students left their desks to visit with other students. Mr. Smith initially continued to assist individual students, but eventually asked the wandering students to return to the task. His request was ignored, and an increasing number of students went off task.
- A knock on the door prompted three students to leave their seats to open the door for two tardy students. The teacher gave a reprimand, but the students argued that their friends needed to enter the class.
- During a 10-minute class discussion, four students read other material, three students at the back of the room chatted, and several others had their heads down. After hearing numerous irrelevant call-outs, Mr. Smith reminded students to raise their hands and wait to be called on. The call-outs continued, and only a few students participated in the discussion.
- Mr. Smith gave two students permission to go to the bathroom, prompting a flurry of requests to leave the room.
- At the beginning of a writing activity, half the students didn't have paper on their desks. Several boys called out loudly to one another across the room during the activity.
- During a whole-class activity two students moved to different seats to talk with friends as the noise level increased.

Following a suggestion from another teacher, Mr. Smith tried sending disruptive students to the office, but he sent too many, and the assistant principal asked him to limit use of this consequence. He tried writing student names on the board when they continued behaving inappropriately, with a detention consequence, but he didn't monitor carefully enough, and the system was soon overwhelmed. Students caught misbehaving, moreover, complained that others did the same things and didn't get caught.

Discussion. The general disorder in Mr. Smith's class has several sources. The evidence from the observation suggests that there aren't adequate routines or procedures in place to manage such common features of classroom life as beginning the class, expectations for talk and movement, contacting the teacher, and leaving and entering the room. Although Mr. Smith did communicate some expectations in the form of general rules at the beginning of the year, he didn't follow through. Initially, Mr. Smith thought all was well because there was no overt disruption, but the absence of specific procedures in many areas caused a gradual deterioration in student behavior. Because Mr. Smith tends to focus mainly on students with whom he is interacting, he doesn't monitor the whole class very well. The result is that problems escalate before he can deal with them effectively. Also, the activities don't seem to engage students and hold their interest; moreover, the constant interruptions interfere with the flow of the activities, causing even well-designed lessons to break down. As a result of these problems Mr. Smith feels unhappy and frustrated, and he finds it difficult to maintain an upbeat and positive demeanor.

Vignette 2. Down the hall, Sara Roberts teaches math to many of the same students that Mark Smith teaches. Her classes, however, are nearly free of troublesome behavior, and the general level of student cooperation is good. Ms. Roberts has a clear idea about what student behaviors are desirable in her classroom, and she communicated these expectations to students early in the school year. Her businesslike, brisk manner during teacher-led whole-class activities is tempered with a personal, familiar style with students on other occasions. She jokes with students, makes frequent eye contact, moves around the room, and she is animated and expressive as she talks. Observations of Ms. Roberts and her students reveal a well-functioning classroom.

- Ms. Roberts monitors the whole class during activities and limits off-task behavior by catching problems early. During group work and seat-work activities, she is constantly on the move around the room, checking on student work, giving feedback, and offering suggestions and encouragement.
- Students don't interrupt class activities. Procedures for participation, talk, movement, being ready for class, makeup work, and other key aspects of life in her classroom have been spelled out in a handout for students. These issues were reviewed early in the year, subsequent reminders are given as needed, and the procedures are followed consistently.
- Except for emergencies, Ms. Roberts won't allow students to leave her classroom during the period.
- The rare disruptive event is managed quickly. Students who persist in inappropriate behavior are assigned a lunchtime detention: "If I have to come find you, the penalty will be doubled," she says matter-of-factly, and she means it.

- She uses a variety of activities to engage students in the curriculum, including small groups, whole-class content development, individual assignments, and discussions based on some structured problem-solving assignments.
- Group progress is monitored and group composition is changed when students don't work well together. Students who are consistently off task lose the privilege and must work alone—a consequence Ms. Roberts rarely needs to administer because most students prefer to work together.
- Ms. Roberts emphasizes that students should give full effort—their "personal best"—and not be content to slide by. Not every student has been won over, but enough have so that a general norm of engagement and participation prevails.

Discussion. Students are engaged and participate more actively in Ms. Roberts's classes for many reasons. She took the time to think through the procedures that were needed to manage her activities, and she communicated them to her students. She also uses a variety of well-planned activities. Inappropriate behaviors are rare and are handled promptly. Because there are fewer inappropriate behaviors, there is less opportunity for activities to get off track; this, in turn, helps maintain momentum in the lessons and reduces the number of models for undesirable behavior. The clarity with which procedures and routines are understood and practiced by Ms. Roberts's students allows her to monitor students' behavior, and the lower frequency of departures from the norm makes it easier to deal consistently with problems when they do occur. In addition, Ms. Roberts's body language and expressive communication style focus student attention and reduce the likelihood of student disruption.

■ Classroom Management's Connections to Other Facets of Teaching

Good classroom management is not an end in itself. It's important because it establishes conditions that enable students to learn better and because poor classroom management creates conditions that interfere with desirable educational outcomes. A substantial body of evidence on the relationship of good classroom management to student learning has accumulated over several decades of research. It demonstrates that good classroom management consistently predicts desirable student outcomes (see reviews by Hattie, 2009; Wang, Haertel, & Walberg, 1993). It is a subject, therefore, that deserves our careful attention.

It is also important to be thoughtful about how management skills are applied. Although an orderly classroom with on-task students is desirable, we don't advocate a rigid, inflexible approach to implementing a plan. If a procedure doesn't work, it will need to be modified; if a student doesn't respond well to some intervention, then a new one must be found. Insisting on appropriate behavior is important; however, a "my way or the highway" attitude isn't an effective approach. To build a classroom community, the emphasis should be on cooperation, not just on compliance.

Working effectively with adolescents requires awareness of their motivations and interests. Researchers of student motivation have emphasized the need for teachers to create classroom systems that satisfy needs for autonomy, competence, and relatedness (Reeve, 2015; Ryan & Deci, 2000). Management strategies that are consistent with this motivational emphasis include providing students with opportunities to make choices, discussing the rationale for rules, giving students more responsibility, encouraging self-regulation, providing feedback that recognizes growth in skills and competencies, de-emphasizing comparisons among students, and using activities that promote student collaboration. Be sure to take motivation into account when designing your management system.

Developing good relationships with students is another significant corollary to effective classroom management practices. Research has shown that the connections students feel toward school are a significant factor in keeping students motivated (Battistich, Solomon, Watson, & Schaps, 1997; Pianta, 2006) and excelling academically (Hattie, 2009). There is, moreover, a reciprocal relationship: Teacher support of students tends to elicit student engagement and motivation, and students who show higher engagement tend to receive more teacher support (Skinner & Belmont, 1993). Thus, teachers need to work on building positive relationships with students, but they also need to manage "boundaries" in the development of their relationships; teachers should be supportive adults, not buddies or pals.

Good classroom management provides a structure within which students can participate in learning activities and make progress in their development of knowledge and mastery of important skills. As they provide the structure, teachers need to be aware of student interests and take them into account in their lessons and assignments. Often students are not intrinsically interested in many of the topics and objectives in the curriculum (Brophy, 2009; Renninger, 2009). Lesson content, activities, and assignments that appeal to the age- and grade-level interests of the students will be more likely to engage them and make classroom management easier. Similarly, having a well-managed classroom will make teaching easier, and it will give a teacher confidence to try out different activities and approaches that may appeal to student interests. In other words, just as with other teaching competencies, developing interesting lessons and establishing classroom management serve complementary purposes and enhance each other.

■ Overview of This Book

The content of this book is organized to reflect how teachers experience classroom management. Prior to the beginning of classes, teachers prepare their classrooms and plan their management system's key features, including expectations for behavior, classroom routines and procedures, consequences, physical layout of the classroom, and major academic activities. During the first weeks of the year, teachers establish their classroom system and help students learn appropriate behavior. As the year progresses, teachers work with students and respond to issues and problems, support student learning, and maintain a positive climate. Chapter 2 will address the important topic of relationships and how to make these effective for teaching. Chapters 3, 4, and 5 identify the features of the classroom environment that must be planned ahead of time so that you can be ready for the students when they arrive on the first day. Chapter 6 covers essential features of the first days of school, when you implement your system, and Chapters 7 and 8 address important concepts and skills that you will need to use as you engage students during academic activities. Chapters 9 and 10 take up the topics of how to maintain appropriate behavior and communicate effectively. Chapter 11 describes an array of strategies for responding to inappropriate and disruptive behavior if the preventive strategies and simpler approaches from the earlier chapters are insufficient. The final chapter considers the management of behavior arising from individual differences among students. Its position as the last chapter doesn't imply that it is the last thing that teachers consider; rather, the preceding chapters also apply to the management of individual differences, but this chapter adds some specific information pertinent to particular conditions or differences.

Each chapter has a number of common features. A section called "Who Will I Teach" follows the text of each chapter. In this section we extend the ideas and strategies in the chapter to some of the many individual differences that teachers encounter in their classrooms, such as students of different ethnic backgrounds, students who are English language learners, and students who have been identified as needing special education. The "Further Readings" section in each chapter provides resources, both printed and online, that can help explore and extend that chapter's content. A "Suggested Activities" section follows with opportunities for discussion and reflection. Finally, each chapter concludes with a reference to the MyEducationLab link available with this book.

■ Chapter Summary

Classroom management includes both preventive as well as interactive aspects; that is, teachers organize the classroom environment and prepare their students for appropriate behavior, and teachers must also interact constructively with students and respond as needed to refocus and redirect their behavior. Teaching is a complex task that requires continuing reflection and learning in order to progress from a student role to the teacher role. Two vignettes illustrated some characteristics of effective classroom management as well as problems that can result from poor management practices. Good classroom management has mutually supporting relationships with the effective teaching of content, the development of healthy student-teacher relationships, good communication, and a positive classroom climate.

■ Further Reading

Elden, R. (2013). *See me after class: Advice for teachers by teachers* (2nd ed.). Naperville, IL: Sourcebooks.

> *This humorous book addresses the concerns and answers the questions of new teachers. Providing good advice for problem-solving, the author helps readers access some of teaching's "common knowledge."*

Le Maistre, C., & Paré, A. (2010). Whatever it takes: How beginning teachers learn to survive. *Teaching and Teacher Education, 26,* 559–564.

> *In this essay, the authors discuss the common problems faced by novice teachers in comparison to novices in three other fields. The differences that novice teachers experience can be significant challenges. The authors suggest that experienced teachers mentor newcomers to help them cope effectively.*

McNally, J., I'anson, J., Whewell, C., & Wilson, G. (2005). "They think that swearing is okay": First lessons in behaviour management. *Journal of Education for Teaching, 3*(3), 169–185.

> *This article discusses the challenges beginning teachers (student teachers) encounter with behavior problems. The authors include quotes concerning new teachers' common struggles, coping reactions, and sense making of their experiences.*

■ Suggested Activities

1. Reflect on the vignettes of Mr. Smith and Ms. Roberts presented in this chapter. What are some important differences between their approaches to managing activities and students? How might students in these classrooms react to these differences over the course of a semester or year? What effects on students' learning, motivation, and attitudes might occur, and why?

2. Jot down some details of a classroom situation you remember as a student (e.g., field trip, daily activity, student misbehavior). With a partner, discuss what additional aspects may have been involved from the point of view of the teacher.

3. Describe a former teacher who you felt had great classroom management. What are some of the skills and strategies that were important to the teacher's success?

MyEducationLab *Self-Check 1.1*

MyEducationLab *Application Exercise 1.1*   Using what you've learned in this chapter, read and respond to this scenario.

MyEducationLab *Application Exercise 1.2*   Using what you've learned in this chapter, view the video and respond to the questions.

MyEducationLab *Classroom Management Simulation 1.1*   Engage with the Classroom Management Simulation *Creating an Effective Classroom Discipline Policy.*

Gino Santa Maria/Fotolia

CHAPTER 2

Building Supportive and Healthy Classroom Relationships

Relationships are fundamental to teaching. Teachers who have good rapport with their students get better cooperation and have a more positive classroom climate. When they ask students to do something difficult, these teachers find their students to be more amenable to making the effort. Maintaining order is less likely to be problematic, too, because good relationships make students more cooperative and less interested in disrupting an activity or supporting someone who is causing a problem. Relationships are also fundamental to learning. When good relationships are established, students know their teachers are receptive to their questions, concerned for their welfare, and supportive of their potential.

Your view of your role and your students' roles will have a major impact on the kind of relationships you will forge with your students. If you believe that relationships are an important foundation for your students' learning, you will be likely to work to establish and maintain them. Teachers can do many things to establish and maintain good relationships with their students. Some of these relationship-building activities and behaviors are illustrated in the following two vignettes.

Vignette 1. Mr. Sahedi is an active, energetic man who engages his middle school students as soon as they enter his classroom. "Come on in! Are you ready for some discussion? You're looking sharp today. How about that game!" he calls out to different students, using their names. Students, who are accustomed to Mr. Sahedi's exuberance, return his smile or offer a comment back. When the opening bell sounds, he begins class with the same energy. He engages students during class discussions, encouraging them by complimenting their answers and explanations and building on their ideas. "I love that answer," "That's fantastic," "This is a terrific discussion, so many good ideas," he says. His gentle critiques of students' work are couched in phrasing such as, "Here's another way to think about that," or "I liked how you began your answer, but I wonder if there's another conclusion that's possible," rather than simply contradicting them or calling on someone else. Mr. Sahedi tells students that he respects them and believes in them: "Work hard and don't let yourself down," he says. If students don't follow rules or if they slack off on their effort, Mr. Sahedi tries to deal with the problem unobtrusively and privately. When he confers with the student, he makes eye contact and expresses disappointment. "I know you have more respect for yourself and for me than you are showing. Can you take care of this problem? Is there anything I need to do to help you deal with this?"

Mr. Sahedi also uses classroom meetings to address problems and issues that affect the class. He has students meet in groups for 5 to 10 minutes to gather their thoughts before he conducts a class discussion about the problem. Students respond well to Mr. Sahedi's guidance; they trust him not to embarrass them and they value his opinions. In turn, Mr. Sahedi stays open to student input on many matters, though he insists that students follow the rules and treat each other with respect.

Mr. Sahedi engages students with his energy and enthusiasm—attributes that attract students. He also frequently expresses approval and liking for them and their work. His insistence on their working hard implies belief in their competence and ability to succeed. He tries not to embarrass them and he solicits their input on classroom concerns, which demonstrates respect for students as well as understanding their need to maintain self-image among their peers.

The second vignette describes a different teacher, whose approach illustrates other ways to build relationships.

Vignette 2. Mrs. Harrison, a high school English teacher, is not as demonstrative as Mr. Sahedi. Although she is typically somewhat reserved, Mrs. Harrison is pleasant as she greets students with a smile. Her demeanor is businesslike but cordial as she conducts classroom activities. "I want students to think of me as a friendly teacher, but as an adult. Some students will take advantage of overly friendly teachers," she shares. Nevertheless, Mrs. Harrison has developed good relationships with her students. One of her frequent assignments is journal writing, in which students are encouraged to write about topics important to them. This allows Mrs. Harrison to get to know her students, and helps her relate class activities and assignments to the students' important concerns and issues. "I've learned to listen to students when they come to me with a problem or issue. They appreciate that I usually can't solve their problem but I may offer a suggestion."

When students in class have a birthday or the teacher learns of a special event, she gives the student some personal and group acknowledgment during class. She also looks for opportunities to give recognition to students who are participating in school activities or community events, and to encourage others to find ways to become involved. Mrs. Harrison often attends both boys' and girls' athletic and other school events in which her students participate. Her contacts with parents at these events give her a conduit to parental concerns and to the community, as well as demonstrate her interest in her students. Mrs. Harrison also sponsors a lunchtime tutoring program that pairs students interested in getting help with schoolwork and those willing to provide it. In her classroom, Mrs. Harrison accommodates individual differences in language development, motivation, and interests by giving students choices and using multiple criteria for assessment. For example, students can choose among several project assignments, their grades are based on both oral and written reports, and Mrs. Harrison gives students oral feedback at an interim checkpoint. These features boost project performance and avoid failure that would drag down student morale. Students who have taken her classes express appreciation and liking for Mrs. Harrison; parents frequently request that their high school children be placed in her classes.

Mrs. Harrison uses a personal, individualized approach to build relationships with her students. By getting to know them, she forms a foundation for communication, and she demonstrates her caring in several ways. Her flexibility and her concern for helping students be successful are key attributes of her approach, as is her involvement in school activities and with parents.

The descriptions of Mr. Sahedi and Mrs. Harrison illustrate that there are many ways teachers build constructive and supportive relationships with their students. These methods will vary from teacher to teacher, depending on a variety of factors such as teacher temperament, personal preference, and availability of time. Student characteristics such as age, motivation, and interest may also influence how a teacher approaches the task of forming and maintaining relationships. However a teacher chooses to work on relationships, there is no escaping the fact that classrooms are social groups. And one of the defining features of social groups is the formation of relationships.

A substantial body of research and writing on teacher–student relationships exists. Many studies have looked at whether relationship-building teaching behaviors are associated with positive student outcomes, such as achievement and positive attitudes. One meta-analysis of over 100 such studies concluded that person-centered teacher behaviors including empathy, warmth, and encouragement were associated with desirable cognitive and affective student outcomes (Cornelius-White, 2007). Relationships can be described as having both positive and negative dimensions. An analysis of 92 articles that studied associations between positive and/or negative relationship dimensions and student outcomes was reported by Roorda, Koomen, Spilt, and Oort (2011). Examples of positive relationship factors included the teacher's expressions of closeness, support, empathy, warmth, relatedness, sensitivity, and involvement. Examples of negative relationship behaviors included neglect, rejection, negativity, anger and conflict. A moderate to strong association, on average, was found across the studies between positive relationship indicators and student engagement outcomes, and a moderate to low (but still positive) relationship was found with student achievement outcomes. Similar results were also found for the association of negative relationship indicators and student outcomes, but in a negative direction.

Reviews by Hattie and Anderman (2012), Eccles and Roeser (2011), and Klem and Connell (2004) also support the importance and impact of teacher–student relationships on student outcomes. A reasonable conclusion to be drawn from this extensive body of research is that it is critical for teachers to develop strong, positive teacher–student relationships. Doing so encourages student growth and engagement; ignoring relationship development may undermine the teacher's effectiveness.

Numerous researchers have noted that teacher–student relationships evolve reciprocally (Jerome & Pianta, 2008; Skinner & Belmont, 1993; Wubbels et al., 2015). Teachers no doubt have the primary effect on relationship quality at first, but students most certainly have an influence through their interactions with the teacher and their other classroom behaviors. Of special concern are students who exhibit "relational negativity" (Hamre & Pianta, 2001). Such children are more likely to have conflicted relationships with teachers, exhibit anger, and be at risk for poorer outcomes. Therefore, it is important to be concerned with both the nature of teacher strategies for relationship building as well as how the teacher reacts to students over time. In the rest of this chapter we will examine the meaning and types of classroom relationships, how these develop, and what strategies teachers can use to encourage constructive and healthy relationships. The goal is for you, the teacher, to be ready to establish supportive and constructive relationships and maintain them throughout the school year.

■ What Are Relationships?

Relationships can be defined as "the generalized personal meaning students and teachers attach to their interactions with each other" (Wubbels et al., 2015). A relationship develops over a series of interactions that are interpreted, summed, and eventually result in a general personal meaning. When a teacher critiques a student's academic work, the student might describe the teacher as "mean" if the student interprets the teacher's intent as hostile based on prior interactions, the specific wording of the critique, or the teacher's body language. Another student, who believes the teacher wants her or him to do well academically and who has a history of receiving encouragement, might describe the teacher as "helpful." Over time, the first student might withdraw from contact with the teacher, becoming less cooperative and receiving less positive teacher contact. The second student may tend to seek out contact with the teacher, strive harder, and receive more supportive teacher attention. The first student's relationship with the teacher is avoidant and not close; the second student's relationship with the teacher is closer and more positive.

It is common to hear the term *relationship* prefaced by different adjectives that describe a characteristic or quality, such as *supportive, caring, troubled, antagonistic, friendly, dependent, conflicted,* or *close*. Such descriptors reflect both the behaviors typical of interactions between parties in the relationship and the affective states they experience. Thus, we may think of the relationship between two individuals (e.g., teacher and student) as a mixture of shared experience, emotion, and viewpoint based on their history of interactions.

We can also describe relationships between teachers and their classes. Teachers spend a large portion of their time in classrooms interacting with the classroom *group*, and the relationship with this collective may be different than relationships with individuals. For example, it is quite plausible that a teacher could have generally friendly, supportive interactions with some individuals in a class, but be more distant and critical when addressing the whole class. As is the case with individual student–teacher relationships, whole-class relationships evolve as the result of a series of interactions and the interpretations made by the teacher and students over time.

Two fundamental dimensions make up the interpersonal behaviors that are the basis for describing relationships. These two dimensions have been given a variety of related labels, including agency and communion (Fournier, Moskowitz, & Zuroff, 2010), influence and proximity (Wubbels et al., 2006), or directivity and warmth (Dunkin & Biddle, 1974). We will use the terms *influence* and *affect* to label these underlying dimensions. The first dimension, *influence*, refers to the degree to which the interpersonal behaviors in the relationship exhibit direction, assertiveness, control, or leadership. *Influence* behaviors act on, direct, or control the behavior of others. The dimension of influence has high and low ends: higher-influence interpersonal behaviors include goal setting, giving information, explaining, expressing opinions, exerting control, and taking the lead. At the lower-influence end of the dimension are behaviors that reflect submissiveness, such as withholding opinions or feelings, withdrawing, avoiding confrontation, and giving in. Of course other interpersonal behaviors are more mid-range in *influence*, such as listening, watching, engaging in routine actions, and the like.

Affect, the second dimension that is needed to describe interpersonal relationships, represents the extent of sociability or connection present in the interaction. At one end of this dimension are behaviors that reflect agreeableness or positive affect; examples are expressing affection, reassuring, approving, encouraging, complimenting, and showing empathy. At the negative end of the dimension are disagreeableness, hostility, criticism, discrediting, disapproval, opposition, and sarcasm.

Combinations of these two dimensions produce interpersonal styles that characterize the relationship between a teacher and students. Teachers who frequently exhibit behaviors typical of high *influence*, but who are at the negative end of the *affect* dimension expect compliance to their directives but don't provide emotional support and acceptance. Students may comply but are less likely to show initiative and enthusiasm. Teachers who are high on both the *influence* and *affect* dimensions exhibit a style that is similar to a parenting style labeled "authoritative" (Walker & Hoover-Dempsey, 2015; Baumrind, 1971). Such teachers are "warm demanders" (Poole & Evertson, 2013). They provide direction and leadership, and they expect a lot, but they are also supportive and accepting; their relationships with students are more likely to be closer and friendlier than the more autocratic teacher, whose relationships with students are likely to be distant and guarded. Other combinations of *influence* and *affect* represent different styles. A teacher who is low on both *influence* and *affect* does not provide very clear direction for students and exhibits negative affect—a combination that produces poor relationships with students and inspires negativity on their part. Another interpersonal style is low on *influence* but more positive on *affect*. This style is labeled *uncertain/tolerant* (Wubbels et al. 2006); such a teacher's inconsistent classroom structure and expectations accompanied by tolerance and concern for students may lead to frequent testing of boundaries.

Most teachers want to have good relationships with their students, but it is clear that achieving this goal is not simply a matter of being a warm, supportive, and caring person, because that would address only the affective dimension of relationship behaviors. The classroom context and the teacher's role require establishing order so that 25 or more students can work together over a long period of time. To manage the behaviors of individuals and groups of students, the teacher's *influence* needs to be high; that is, the teacher will lead, direct, and organize students in a variety of classroom activities. It's not a passive role! The second dimension, *affect*, is also a critical feature of relationships. As noted earlier, most research agrees that teacher behaviors characterized as warm, supportive, accepting, and caring are associated with positive teacher–student relationships and desirable student outcomes.

Of course, not every interaction with students should be high in influence and affect. The context for the interaction will often dictate what is appropriate; many routine interactions that occur throughout the day are mainly neutral with respect to these dimensions. It is important to keep in mind that fostering good relationships with students will depend on an accumulation of interactions in which the teacher creates expectations, provides direction, and establishes boundaries, while at the same time gives students support and encouragement.

■ Self-Management as an Aspect of Building Relationships

Self-management is an important part of relationship development with students as well as the teacher's overall classroom management approach. All individuals project an image or identity to others. Common expressions, such as "making a good impression," "saving face," "keeping up appearances," "putting up a front," and the like, suggest how routine self-management is. The term *facework* is used by sociologists and communication specialists to describe the actions individuals take to manage their identities as they interact with others (Domenici & Littlejohn, 2006; Metts & Grohskopf, 2003). Facework, however, is more than establishing and maintaining a public identity; it also includes actions or communications that are sensitive to the "face" that others exhibit. In ordinary conversations, for example, it is typical to respond sympathetically to another's distress, nod approvingly when others talk about a subject that is obviously important to them, or communicate acceptance in response to a friend who appears to need support. Individuals may sometimes avoid sensitive topics when remarks might offend (and thus contradict the other's face) or seek to be tactful when disagreeing, thereby maintaining an identity as an honest, principled person while being respectful of the other's need to be considered seriously.

Facework is an integral part of relationships. When individuals are able to interact about issues or problems and to accomplish tasks in ways that are mutually protective of face or identity, the interactions are productive and healthy. But when face is threatened during interactions, relationships may deteriorate and communication may break down (Metts, 1997).

In classrooms, teachers have to be aware of how their interactions with students might enhance or tear down a student's self-image. Thus, teachers who want good relationships with students look for ways to build up their students' identities as competent, capable individuals who contribute to the class and who are making progress as successful learners. When student behavior needs correction, teachers address the student respectfully and as privately as possible, so that the student's public face is not threatened. When a public reprimand is required, the teacher needs to be mindful of the possible threat to the student's face and to correct the behavior without criticizing the character of the student. Respectful communication conveys to the student, as well as to all the other students in the audience, that the classroom is a safe place to live and learn.

■ Boundary Concerns in Relationships

Many teachers find that relationships with students must be balanced with other concerns, such as maintaining control, limiting emotional involvement, preserving instructional time, and school policies (Aultman, Williams-Johnson, & Schutz, 2009). For example, students could take advantage of a friendly relationship by trying to avoid focusing on academic tasks. Or a teacher might become so committed to helping a distressed student that it interferes with instructional time or the teacher's personal life. Teachers can find it difficult to deal with self-disclosures by students about personal problems and family issues or to manage their own emotions in such situations. Strategies for addressing boundary concerns evolve as teachers get to know their students and encounter relationship issues. For example, teachers can set time limits on off-task discussion or divert it to class meetings, they can refer serious student problems to a school counselor, and they can set aside specific times after school hours for their own personal time. Learning about resources at school (e.g., counselors) or in the community (e.g., medical clinics, child and family services) can provide an alternative when a problem exceeds the teacher's expertise or requires more personal resources than the teacher is willing or able to commit. Preventing some boundary problems is possible by planning how relationships will be accomplished and choosing from among the strategies described here those that are consistent with your view of the teacher's role.

■ Strategies for Building Relationships

We will now examine some specific strategies that teachers can use to foster positive relationships with students and their parents. As you consider these strategies, notice how they address either or both of the *influence* and *affect* dimensions of teacher–student relationships. Also worth considering is whether using the strategy is consistent with your view of the teaching role and if use of the strategy might affect instruction, available time, or other commitments.

Managing First Impressions

Relationships with students are developed during year-long interactions, but initial contacts will set the tone. Your role as teacher confers status, expectations, and influence. The relationships you establish with students are different from other relationships such as parent–child or adolescent–adolescent. In your students' view, you are their *teacher*, not a parent or friend. The initial impressions you make should convey your acceptance of that role, engaging in the actions expected of a teacher and doing them well. (We will have more to say about key aspects of beginning the year in Chapter 6.) At the same time that you exhibit your willingness to take the role of teacher seriously, you can communicate your positive regard for your students by doing the following:

- Welcome students with a smile and eye contact as they enter your classroom during the initial days of school.
- Use student names frequently during the initial class days as you learn names to help you establish positive early connections. Use seating charts to help with student names.
- Be organized and ready for all activities. This communicates your competence and promotes your influence.
- During the first several days of classes, you will be teaching students your everyday routines and procedures (e.g., hand raising, signals for attention, out-of-seat expectations, work procedures, and so on). Be sure to support students' appropriate behavior by giving recognition and positive feedback to the class as a whole. Be specific: "I appreciate how everyone stayed on task during our practice activity," or "Thank you for raising your hands and waiting to be called on during today's class discussion."
- Your body language also communicates a first impression. Persons high in *influence* are expressive with voice, face, and gesture. An instructional style that is dynamic and interactive captures student attention and contributes to establishing you as the class leader. Body language also conveys information about *affect*. Smiles, eye contact, and open body posture indicate acceptance and warmth.
- Making eye contact with students demonstrates your attention to and interest in students. Although you can't maintain eye contact with individual students very long during whole-class activities, you should scan the class frequently to monitor student activities and to communicate your awareness of students. Use group signals such as "Eyes to the front" or "Let me see your eyes" in order to re-establish eye contact and promote group attention during whole-class activities. When interacting with individual students during one-on-one conferences or conversations, eye contact helps establish a connection, but staring may be distracting and make students uncomfortable. For some Indian, Asian, and African cultures, extended eye contact is regarded as aggressive or rude (Burgoon & Bacue, 2003).
- When you introduce yourself to your students, share aspects of your personal life and preferences. You can decide what things to share ahead of time by writing down 10 or 15 items that help define your identity and likes/dislikes. From the list, choose items to share that your students might relate to, such as family, growing-up experiences, pets, food, experiences in school, favorite music, movies, and so on. Such sharing helps students connect their lives to yours. Some items from your life might be more appropriate to share during a particular activity—for example, when your students are struggling with some learning task, you might share with them the difficulty you may have had learning some task.

- Use a get-acquainted activity to set a positive tone and engage students personally. You can find examples of activities appropriate for middle school and high school grades at sites such as 712educators.about.com and scholastic.com.
- When you share information about yourself, students may ask personal questions that are inappropriate or that you are not comfortable answering (e.g., about romantic relationships). Be prepared to set boundaries; for example, you can tell students that the question is too personal. Remember that your students are adolescents who haven't fully developed social skills and that you need to help them learn what is acceptable in general as well as your limits.

Throughout the Year

Keeping a positive classroom climate throughout the year is important for maintaining good relationships with students. In addition to the behaviors and activities suggested in the previous section, you should consider the following strategies:

- Keep in touch with the interests of the age level you teach. Learn about the students' preferences for reading, television programs, movies, games, music, and websites. In addition to being useful for designing lessons, activities, and assignments that connect with students, such knowledge will add to your ability to have conversations with them.
- To the extent that your time and life outside the classroom permit, participate in school and community activities that bring you into contact with your students and their parents. Activities such as back-to-school night and parent–teacher conferences are a must, of course. But also consider such activities as eating lunch or breakfast in the school cafeteria with students or allowing students to bring theirs to your classroom as a special reward, or attending school athletic events or other performances, school-wide fairs, and other scheduled events.
- Look for opportunities to have conversations with students outside the classroom, such as in hallways and before or after school.
- Help students acquire life-long skills for working in groups, self-management, and effective communication. Students are still learning social skills, impression management, and politeness rules. Thus, they might say or do things that might offend, especially in conflict situations, when anxious, or under stress. Feedback to individual students about their behavior, especially at a quiet time when they are not as stressed, can help them understand the problem and learn a constructive way to deal with emotions and express feelings. Students may be unskilled in their use of social behaviors, but they are still sensitive to threats to their face. Such threats include public criticism and ridicule, especially those that run counter to the image a student is trying to protect. You will build trust and improve your relationships with your students when you are sensitive to such concerns. Be aware of the potential for embarrassing a student or causing him or her to lose face in group settings. A public power

struggle with a noncompliant student should be short-circuited (e.g., by having a private conference with the student, or asking the student to write out a version of the problem to discuss with you later). Sending the student to another location to cool off is better than a public struggle.

- A common problem in classrooms is dealing with public failure. Students are concerned about appearing stupid, inept, or foolish in front of peers, and will go to great lengths to avoid such displays. This type of impression management interferes with engagement and can seriously impede learning. Students can be helped to overcome such fears if teachers don't emphasize mistakes, but rather treat them as a normal part of learning. Students should be told that encountering difficulty is common and that frustration is part of the process. You might communicate that you admire students who work at learning until they get it. Tell them that doing so is a very valuable life skill. Teachers can describe struggles they had with learning some subject or skill and how it took hard work to overcome the obstacles. Teachers should also insist that no one should laugh at or think less of someone who has difficulty: "We should encourage those who are trying to learn; let's be helpful, not hurtful." Confirm that it takes courage to perform when a student is not sure about an answer, and that doing so is a good way to receive feedback and guidance. If you consistently support student effort and are fair in evaluating performance, students will learn to trust you and to feel safe in your class. Such trust is a foundation for maintaining positive student–teacher relationships.

- Students' beliefs about the causes of good and poor performance affect their willingness to persevere on difficult tasks. If they attribute success and failure to innate ability, they are less likely to be resilient when they encounter difficulty than if they attribute success or failure to hard work or effort. You will build more productive relationships with students when your feedback emphasizes effort. Also, tasks that are overly difficult must be anticipated and broken into do-able subtasks in order to foster persistence.

- Maintain a positive perspective when confronting a student about misbehavior and when following through with a consequence. Chapter 11 presents many strategies you can use to address problem behavior. How you handle such events will have an impact on your relationship with students. Remaining calm, making sure the student understands the problem, and enforcing rules consistently are important to maintaining relationships during conflict. Teachers should also emphasize that students have choices, and that they are making the decision about how to behave. Communicate that the student can learn from mistakes. After the problem has been settled, it's best if the teacher sets aside the negative emotions produced by the incident and keeps a positive tone in future dealings with the student.

Relationships With Parents

Good school–home relationships contribute to student engagement and learning, and also provide a helpful basis for classroom management (Walker &

Hoover-Dempsey, 2015). It is important, then, for teachers to develop links between classroom and home, and to foster mutually supportive communication.

- If your district has a grade-reporting website for parents to check their children's work, be sure to keep the data up-to-date.
- Communication skills, including active listening, empathic responding, and problem solving, are important to use when communicating with parents. Sometimes a communication between parent and teacher is only about information sharing, but the teacher always needs to be alert to the possibility of the relevance of these skills. The context and focus of the interaction will provide clues. Much more about the use of communication skills is presented in Chapter 10.
- Back-to-school night is a very important point of contact. It usually will be the teacher's first opportunity to form a relationship with parents, so warmth and openness in greeting and meeting are critically important. Naturally, teachers are interested in giving parents an overview of classroom activities and of the curriculum to be covered, but parents often are more interested in how well the teacher will connect with their child. So, providing a glimpse of what life in your classroom will be like for the students, your willingness to help them find areas of strength and interest, and your overall management plan will be useful topics to address. You also should plan time to interact with individual parents about particular concerns they might have for their child.
- Recognize student accomplishment and effort in your communications with parents. A tangible way to do so is to use recognition awards in the form of certificates for achievement, for good citizenship, improved performance, contributions to the class, and other desirable behaviors. Students love receiving such certificates to show their parents, so the awards do double duty by building relationships with both students and parents. You can find templates for certificates suitable for different grade/age levels at many teacher websites (e.g., teachervision.com/awards/resource6076.html, scholastic.com, and others).
- Parents may come from backgrounds very different from that of their teachers. Differences in language, country of origin, and socioeconomic status may be pronounced. These differences may lead to a variety of expectations, resources, attitudes, and beliefs that can hinder or help their children in school. Communicating clearly (without jargon) is very important. Likewise, your attitude of valuing and accepting differences will reassure parents who may be uncertain about how welcome they are and whether their children will be well-cared for in your classroom. A bulletin board display of contributions to your subject matter area made by individuals from a variety of cultural backgrounds will help convey an open and accepting perspective.
- A parent group email, a classroom website, or a classroom newsletter are all ways to provide information to parents throughout the school year. You can't count on such forms of communication to inform all parents, because not every message will be read. But these forms of generic information sharing will reach the majority of parents.

■ Teacher–parent conferences offer excellent opportunities for sharing information. Beginning with a description of some of the student's strengths is a good way for the teacher to set a positive tone for the conference. Areas needing improvement should also be identified, accompanied by work samples to aid in making recommendations concrete. Parents can give insight into their adolescents' attitudes, interests, and behavior outside of school that may be relevant for the your work with them. Parents who assist with schoolwork may have important insights to share. Not every parent feels competent to assist or has the time and energy to do so, but ways other than direct assistance are possible (e.g., providing a quiet place for homework, making sure the student completes the work, giving encouragement and showing interest). Discussing ways to promote learning and identifying appropriate support for that learning at home will contribute to a successful conference.

■ Some parents may be in a position to volunteer for different classroom activities, such as tutoring, reading with individuals or small groups, assisting in materials preparation and other clerical tasks, helping with technology, or updating a classroom newsletter. You'll need to be sure your procedures are consistent with your school and district guidelines for parent volunteers. You can ask for volunteers for specific activities, or you can ask parents if they have special talents or skills to share.

■ Contacts between the teacher and parents regarding discipline and behavior issues can contribute to problem resolution, but they also have the potential for disrupting relationships if not handled skillfully. When engaging parents about a problem, it's important to have a goal for the contact. Several are possible, such as alerting them to the problem, seeking information, involving the parents in identifying possible solutions, and/or carrying out a home-based consequence. The parents' experience can be very helpful in sorting out the situation and deciding on further steps, but not if the parents feel threatened and become defensive. Parents will be more cooperative if they believe that the teacher is supportive of them and their child, so it's important to assure the parents of your mutual interests in their child's progress and adjustment. Stick to behavior descriptions, avoid character judgments, and practice good communication skills. Describe your attempts to manage the problem and ask for the parent's suggestions. Keep the tone positive by mentioning some good features of the student's behavior. If a strategy is discussed, identify a timeline to evaluate whether it works and make a plan to follow up with the parent.

There are a number of effective ways to utilize technology in communicating with parents. For example, both software and mobile applications are available for quick texts to parents (e.g., Remind101). Also, a simple email listserv will allow your message to be sent to all your students' parents. Some teachers develop a class social media page for parents to join to increase communication. Others develop a class webpage for posting announcements (e.g., homework, study guides, field trips, etc.). Many districts have policies in place for the use of Internet-based technology.

In addition to following those policies, it is important for you to consider the following suggestions for representing yourself professionally:

- The communication you send is representative of you, your school, and your teaching ability, so double-check your message/posting for spelling, grammar, and appropriateness of expression.
- Digital communication is not assisted by facial expressions, so be careful with the words you use in your texts/messages/postings to avoid misunderstandings. Consider having a peer read your message before sending/posting to make sure the meaning you have intended is the one that will be received.
- The frequency of communication sends its own message. Consistent, timely communication helps establish a sense of trust with parents. For example, if you tell parents you will post weekly on your class webpage, they will learn to check it weekly when they see your efforts to meet that expectation.
- Not all parents/guardians may have access to the communication technology you select. Choose to be inclusive of all families as you communicate by offering a printed option of your postings/messages to students for whom access is an issue.

Relationships With Other School Personnel

In addition to the relationships you build with your students and their parents/guardians, there are several additional relationships within the school building that can be critical to your success in teaching. Think of yourself as part of a team that includes fellow teachers, administrators, and support staff. General civility is key to the quality of relationships you establish. Kindness, respect, and courtesy should all be important components of your communications with your colleagues. Learning names, listening to others, and being prompt in fulfilling your responsibilities are ways you can contribute to supportive team relationships. Doing so helps model healthy relationships to your students. In addition, these relationships may be of great help to you during the year (e.g., fellow teachers sharing ideas for lessons, administrators giving access to resources, custodians providing room maintenance, and so on).

■ Who Will I Teach? Teacher–Student Relationships in Urban Settings

Teachers working in urban settings know that good relationships are needed to create a strong foundation for student engagement. Compared to suburban settings, urban schools are more likely to draw their student populations from neighborhoods that have higher poverty levels, unemployment, single-parent households, immigrant populations, and crime rates (Clewell, Campbell, & Perlman, 2007; Milner, 2006). Certainly not all urban youth come from households with such characteristics, nor are all urban settings the same (Milner, 2015), but when teaching in settings whose populations evidence such characteristics, teachers need to be especially mindful of the relationships they create.

Urban teachers must give more attention to establishing trust, learning about their students' backgrounds and communities, and practicing good communication skills, such as empathy, assertiveness, and problem solving when dealing with classroom problems. Many teachers do not themselves have the same ethnic or cultural background as the urban students they teach. These background differences can limit teachers' awareness of the reasons for their students' classroom problems as well as teachers' empathy and communication effectiveness.

Promoting school engagement in secondary classrooms is especially important in urban settings because it acts as a buffer against long-term problems, including low achievement, poor motivation, dropping out, and disruptive behaviors. Urban students benefit from a well-managed classroom in which expectations for behavior are clear and enforced fairly and consistently. Students should also believe that their teachers care for them and support their efforts. Students need opportunities, within a safe and supportive classroom, to participate in decision making and to do meaningful work (Klem & Connell, 2004). In such classrooms good teacher–student relationships can flourish.

The research-based literature on teaching in urban settings has a number of useful recommendations that will help teachers establish good relationships within their classroom management structure (Delpit, 1995; Gay, 2006; Milner, 2015, 2006; Stairs, Donnell, & Dunn, 2012; Vavrus, 2008). Higgs (2014) also writes convincingly about relationships in urban schools. Although the recommendations in the previous sections, "Managing First Impressions" and "Throughout the Year," are also applicable in urban settings with diverse learners, additional recommendations are provided here.

- The first and most basic need is for teachers to learn about the students' community in order to inform their assessments of the students and their behaviors. Such knowledge will help the teacher understand the experiences, resources, and models that will be part of their students' daily environment beyond school. Such knowledge can aid the teacher's decisions about classroom activities and assignments, and help provide perspective when dealing with children and parents.
- Urban students are more likely to trust teachers who share something of their lives, interests, and values. Not all aspects of a teacher's life need to be on display, of course, but openness is desirable. Ideally, revelations will be on topics that intersect with students' lives. Students also want to know that their teachers are committed to their learning and will help them when they struggle with it.
- Teachers in urban settings need to show students that the teachers care about them individually. Caring can be shown in many ways: through careful listening, by being respectful of students when giving corrective feedback, and by giving personalized encouragement. It is particularly important to support students' efforts to learn and to recognize that learning usually proceeds imperfectly.
- Teachers may exacerbate the level of conflict when dealing with a student from a different cultural background. After being called out for misbehavior, instead of complying and responding politely a student might be defiant, noisy, or unruly. Or a student might withdraw and become uncommunicative. Such response styles may have been learned in the home and in the community. Rather than sending the student to the office with a disciplinary referral, the teacher can have the student go to a time-out area in the classroom until there is an opportunity to

discuss the incident with the student. In the former case, there is the risk of the student being labeled a troublemaker; in the latter case, there is a possibility of listening to the student's point of view and helping the student learn from the situation what is the right way and the wrong way to respond in a classroom.

- Scholars (e.g., Delpit, 1995; Gay, 2006) who have studied urban settings have noted the need for teaching practices that are respectful of students' cultures and that provide opportunities for students to participate in the decision-making process. Students should feel that their backgrounds and community knowledge are valued; they also need to learn what the larger society requires of them in order to be successful. Thus, it is recommended that teachers discuss with students the rationale for school rules, classroom rules, and other expectations. Also, clearly defining behavioral expectations and consistently using fair, reasonable consequences opens space for a teacher to give students opportunities for meaningful participation and decision making. Examples of things teachers can do include incorporating culturally relevant content into activities and assignments, giving choices in assignments, providing opportunities to volunteer for classroom responsibilities, and selecting classroom activities and projects that have varied roles for students to take.

■ Chapter Summary

Developing good relationships should be a key feature of the overall classroom management plan. Research links positive teacher–student relationships to many important student outcomes. Major dimensions that undergird relationships are *influence* and *affect;* the teacher role generally requires that higher levels of both dimensions be present in order to provide leadership in the classroom along with support for students. Relationships evolve, but initial impressions count; recommendations are given for starting the year, building relationships throughout the year, and forging good parent–teacher relationships. The final section of the chapter considers relationships in urban settings.

■ Further Reading

Aultman, L. P., Williams-Johnson, M. R., & Schutz, P. A. (2009). Boundary dilemmas in teacher-student relationships: Struggling with "the line." *Teaching and Teacher Education, 25,* 636–646.

Teachers were interviewed to determine the extent of "boundary" issues in teaching. Such issues are common and occur in a number of areas as teachers attempt to balance their caring for students with the need to manage behavior and cope with the many demands of teaching.

Higgs, C. (2014). Connecting with students: Strategies for building rapport with urban learners. Lanham, MD: Rowman & Littlefield Education.

This book provides many practical suggestions for relationship building in urban settings. The suggested strategies are consistent with the research literature on classroom management and are valuable for teachers whose classes are diverse and who want to work on establishing productive relationships.

Jerome, E. M., & Pianta, R. C. (2008). Teacher-student relationships. In T. L. Good (Ed.), *21st century education: A reference handbook* (Vol. 2, pp. 158–164). Los Angeles: Sage.

This article provides a succinct summary of research on teacher–student relationships. Many facets of relationships are examined, with an emphasis on development and attachment theory.

Wubbels, T., Brekelmans, M., den Brok, P., Wijsman, L., Mainhard, T., & van Tartwijk, J. (2015). Teacher-student relationships and classroom management. In E. T. Emmer & E. J. Sabornie (Eds.), *Handbook of classroom management* (2nd ed., pp. 363–386). New York: Routledge, Taylor & Francis.

The authors provide an authoritative summary of the literature on teacher–student relationships. Major theoretical positions are described along with research on the topic, including the authors' extensive program of studies in multiple countries.

■ Suggested Activities

1. Re-read the vignettes of Mr. Sahedi and Mrs. Harrison at the beginning of the chapter. What points of evidence do you have from their vignettes to identify them as high or low on both influence and affect?

2. Identify a teacher you had as a student who exemplified supportive and healthy relationships with students. What strategies did that teacher use to build these relationships? How did you benefit directly as his or her student?

3. Consider one episode of a TV show or a movie in which a teacher is featured. Analyze that individual's relationships with students according to the strategies listed in this chapter. Would you identify this example teacher as having boundary problems? If so, what caused the problems and how might they have been avoided? If not, what practices did the teacher put in place to keep healthy boundaries established?

4. Interview one or more secondary teachers in your content field. Find out what specific actions they take (at the beginning of the year and as the year progresses) to build productive relationships with students and their families.

MyEducationLab *Self-Check 2.1*

MyEducationLab *Self-Check 2.2*

MyEducationLab *Application Exercise 2.1*   Using what you've learned in this chapter, read and respond to this scenario.

MyEducationLab *Application Exercise 2.2*   Using what you've learned in this chapter, view the video and respond to the questions.

MyEducationLab *Classroom Management Simulation 2.1*   Engage with the Classroom Management Simulation *Developing Positive Teacher-Student Relationships With All Students.*

Noah Strycker/Shutterstock

CHAPTER 3

Organizing Your Classroom and Materials

Arranging the physical setting for teaching is a logical starting point for classroom management planning because it is a task that all teachers face before the school year begins. Many teachers find it easier to plan other aspects of classroom management after they know how the physical features of their classroom will be organized.

Effective room arrangement can help you cope with the complex demands of teaching 25 to 30 or more students at a time for five or more periods a day. During any given period, students will come and go; many activities will occur; and you and your class will use a variety of materials, texts, reference books, equipment, and supplies. Appropriate room preparation and arrangement of materials help activities proceed smoothly and conserve class time for learning, whereas inadequate planning may interfere with instruction by causing interruptions, delays, and dead time.

Before you begin to arrange your classroom, think about the following questions. The answers will help you decide what physical features need special attention. Prior to looking at your classroom, think about the kinds of learning you would most like to see there:

- What are your main types of instructional activities (e.g., small groups, whole-class discussions, teacher presentations, student presentations, individual assignments, group projects)? What physical arrangements will best support these activities?

- Will students be making extensive use of equipment (e.g., microscopes) or materials (e.g., science or math manipulatives)? Will these be shared among individuals or groups?
- Does your class include students with special needs that must be considered?
- Where are the areas of potential distraction (e.g., high traffic, animals, group centers)? Which students will need screening or distance from these areas?
- How much movement around the room will be necessary during the period? What areas of the room will be involved? Will students get their own materials, or will you have them distributed?
- What technology will be involved (e.g., SmartBoard, tablets)? How will these be powered/charged? Who needs simultaneous access?
- Will students need access to references, research tools, or trade books?
- How flexible or permanent will the arrangement be? Will you have to change it during a single day, for each new unit, or will it stay the same for months? Do you share your classroom with any other teachers?

Your room arrangement communicates to students how you expect them to participate in your class, and your philosophy of teaching and learning will influence how you arrange your classroom. Desks arranged in groups imply that interaction and collaboration among students are expected for at least some activities. Desks in rows indicate that the focus of the classroom is the teacher, the board or screen, or some other central point.

This chapter will help you make these and other decisions about room arrangement, equipment, and basic supplies. Each component is described, and guidelines and examples will help you plan.

■ Five Keys to Good Room Arrangement

The classroom is the learning environment for both you and your students. Although it may hold as many as 30 or more students each period, it is not a very large space. Your students will be participating in a variety of activities and using different areas of the room, and they will need to enter and leave the room rapidly when classes change. You will get better results if you arrange your classroom to permit orderly movement, few distractions, and efficient use of available space. The following five keys will be helpful as guidelines when you make decisions about arranging your room.

1. Use a room arrangement consistent with your instructional goals and activities. You will need to think about the main types of instructional activities that will take place in your classes and then organize the seating, materials, and equipment compatibly. Thus, if your main activities will be teacher-led discussions, demonstrations, and presentations, students should be seated so that they can easily see the main instructional area, and you will need nearby storage space and surfaces for materials. If you plan to use small work groups, however, you may need to arrange student seating and access to supplies quite differently than if your main instructional activities will be in a whole-class format.

2. Keep high-traffic areas free of congestion. Areas where many students gather and areas that receive constant use can be sites for distraction and disruption. High-traffic areas include group-work areas, the space around the pencil sharpener and wastebasket, doorways, computers, certain bookshelves and supply areas, student desks, and the teacher's desk. High-traffic areas should be separated and easily accessible. Be mindful of the traffic hazards that extension cords and surge protectors can pose as well as the regulations set by the local fire marshal.

3. Be sure students are easily seen by the teacher. Careful monitoring of students is a major management task. If the teacher cannot see all students, it will be difficult to determine when a student needs assistance or to prevent task avoidance or disruption. Therefore, clear lines of sight must be maintained between areas of the room that the teacher will frequent and student work areas. Be especially conscious of the placement of bookcases, file cabinets, and other pieces of furniture and equipment that can block your line of vision. Stand in different parts of the room and check for blind spots.

4. Keep frequently used teaching materials and student supplies readily accessible. Easy access to and efficient storage of such materials and supplies will aid classroom management by allowing activities to begin and end promptly and by minimizing time spent getting ready and cleaning up. If you or your students must stop to locate needed materials and supplies, you run the risk of losing student attention and engagement as well as instructional time and lesson flow (see Chapter 7).

5. Be certain students can easily see instructional presentations and displays. Check that the seating arrangements will allow all students to see the projector screen or board without moving their chairs, turning their desks around, or craning their necks. Don't put your instructional area in a far corner of the room, away from a substantial number of students. Such conditions do not encourage students to pay attention, and they make it more difficult for students to take notes. Double-check how well your students can see by sitting for a moment at desks in different parts of the room.

SHOE-NEW BUSINESS © MacNelly – Distributed by King Features Syndicate, Inc. World Rights Reserved.

Applying the five keys will help you design workable room arrangements. Some specific suggestions for achieving this goal are described in the next section. By attending to these areas, you will address all the important aspects of room preparation.

■ Suggestions for Arranging Your Classroom

Bulletin Boards and Walls

Wall space and bulletin boards provide areas to display student work, instructionally relevant material, decorative items, assignments, rules, schedules, a clock, and other items of interest. Ceiling space can be used to hang mobiles and other decorations. The following points should be considered when preparing these areas.

1. At the start of school, you should have at least the following displays for walls and boards: a decorative display to catch your students' interest such as a bulletin board with a "Welcome Back to School" motif or a display organized around a school-spirit theme ("Go Hippos!"), a place to list daily assignments, a calendar, and posted emergency escape routes.

2. If you are teaching in a middle school or if you are teaching ninth-graders in a high school, you should reserve some wall or bulletin board space for posting classroom rules. (At higher grade levels, you might post rules or you might handle the communication of expectations orally and/or via a handout—see Chapters 4 and 6.)

3. Other displays that many teachers find useful include an example of the correct paper heading to be used in your class and a content-relevant display such as one highlighting a topic that will soon be taught.

4. Covering large bulletin board areas with colored paper is an easy way to brighten your classroom. This paper comes on large rolls and is often kept in the school office or in a supply room. You can also trim the bulletin boards with an edging or border of corrugated paper. If you can't find these items in your supply room, they are usually available at a school supply center or variety store. You can also find books of bulletin board ideas as well as posters, cardboard punch-out letters, stencils, and other graphics for sale at such stores.

5. If you need ideas for decorating your room or for setting up displays, borrow some from other teachers or go online to a teacher site. Also, your departmental supply room may contain instructionally relevant display material. Ask your department chairperson for assistance if necessary.

6. Don't spend a lot of time decorating your room. You will have many other important things to do to get ready for the beginning of school. A few bare bulletin boards won't bother anybody. You can add displays later or allow your homeroom/advisory students to decorate a blank space for an art project. You can also reward a "class of the month" with the privilege of redecorating a bulletin board. Finally, don't overdecorate your classroom. Cluttered wall space is distracting and makes a room seem smaller. It will seem small enough when all your students are in it.

Floor Space

Arrange your furniture and equipment so that you can easily observe students from all areas in which you will work. Students should be able to see you as well as the projector screen and any board that will be used to give presentations to the whole class. Of course, you will have to adjust to whatever constraints exist in your assigned classroom. A classroom may be small or have inadequate or poorly located board space or electrical outlets. You should assess your space and determine whether changes can be made to accommodate whatever constraints exist. For example, if the classroom is small, be sure to remove unnecessary student desks or extra furniture or equipment; if you have inadequate storage, perhaps you can locate an extra file or supply cabinet.

A good starting point for your floor plan is to decide where you will conduct whole-class instruction. Decide where you will stand or work when you address the entire class to conduct lessons or give instructions. You can usually identify this area of the room by the location of the projector screen and/or board. This area should also have space for a table or desk where you can place items needed in presentations. You will also need an electrical outlet nearby for a computer, document camera, or any other electronic equipment you'll be using during class presentations.

As you read the following items, refer to Figure 3.1, which shows a floor plan for a secondary school classroom in which whole-class instruction and individual

figure 3.1 ■ An Example of a Workable Room Arrangement for Whole-Class Instruction

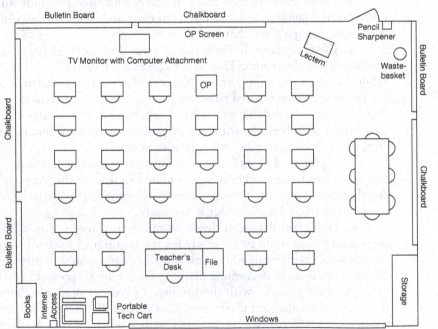

seat work are the main types of activities. Note how each item is addressed in this floor plan. Of course, this is just one of many possibilities. Consider how you might alter this floor plan to accommodate additional computer workstations, for example. Note that moving or removing the table on the right side of the room would open up space. The location of desks, work areas, and other physical features of the classroom depends on the size and shape of the room and how different parts of the room will be used.

Arrangement of Student Desks.   Many different arrangements of student desks are possible, but it's important to arrange desks so that all students can see whole-group instruction as well as the projection screen and the board without having to get out of their seats. Try to minimize having students face potential sources of distraction, such as windows, the doorway, an area where small groups of students will work, or eye-catching displays. Even if other arrangements are to be used later in the year, you might start the year with desks in rows facing the major instructional area. In such an arrangement, students are less likely to distract each other than if their desks are arranged in groups with students facing one another. In the example presented in Figure 3.1, the desks are arranged in rows and no student is seated with his or her back to the major instructional area. Thus, if the teacher puts a display on the projector screen, all students can see it easily and take notes when necessary. The following items may also be of concern:

- Because it is important to keep high-traffic areas clear, don't put desks or other furniture in front of doors, computers, the pencil sharpener, sinks, and so on.
- Be sure to leave ample room around student desks so that you can easily approach students when you are monitoring seat-work activities.
- Count the desks or chairs and make sure you have enough.
- Replace damaged furniture or have it repaired.

The Teacher's Desk, Filing Cabinet, Computer, Projector, and Other Equipment.   Your desk location needs to be functional. If you intend to use your desk to keep instructional materials used during presentations, the desk should be adjacent to the main instructional area or areas. If you plan to work at your desk at times during classes, you will need to locate your desk to facilitate monitoring: Sit facing the students, and be sure you can observe all of them from your seat. However, it is not necessary that students be able to see you from their seats, and some teachers prefer placing the teacher's desk at the back of the room rather than at the front (see Figure 3.1). Another desk location favored by many teachers is a front corner of the classroom. This location opens up the front of the room for instruction and keeps the teacher's desk within easy reach during whole-class activities. If you plan to work with individual students at your desk, you will have to consider traffic patterns. Student desks should not be so close to yours that students approaching your desk or working with you there create a distraction.

"Miss Marpole, I need to talk to you about your seating arrangement."

Reprinted by permission of George Abbott / *Phi Delta Kappan*

Access and function should be considered when locating other furniture, such as the filing cabinet and storage bins. A cabinet used for storing seldom-used supplies can be safely tucked away in a corner or hidden from view. Supplies that will be used frequently during class should be located near the area in which they will be used. All electrical equipment must, of course, be placed near an outlet and covered or otherwise secured.

The teacher's computer and printer are often kept on the teacher's desk or at a side table near the desk. While at the computer, the teacher should be able to monitor students, so lines of sight need to be kept open.

Computer Workstations. Your location choices for computers may be limited because of the need for wall outlets and Internet access, if wifi is not available. So, consider placing the stationary computer and/or printer workstations first and then arranging other centers and activity areas. Some schools have classroom sets of laptops on rolling carts that can be checked out. With this situation, you will have to consider the ease in getting them in and out of the room as well as charging them. Guard all electronic equipment technology by placing it away from dust, liquids, and magnets.

When arranging your room, make sure that computer monitors are positioned so that you can quickly scan them to be sure students are on task. This is especially important when students have Internet access. Check all equipment in advance of student use. Have on hand any necessary extension cords, cables, paper, printer cartridges, headphones, and other peripherals with the equipment, and store it safely.

Large groups around a computer can create a disturbance and lead to off-task behavior. Limit the number of students working on a computer to no more than three or four, and establish a policy that students who are using a computer have a purpose and a time limit so that the resource can be shared fairly. Teach students to save their work so that they will not lose it when they are unable to finish it in a session. Flash drives serve as a convenient storage tool.

Bookcases.   Bookcases should be placed where they will neither prevent you from monitoring students nor obstruct students' ability to see whiteboards or relevant displays. Tall bookcases perpendicular to a wall create hideaways that prevent you from seeing the students behind them. If a bookcase contains items that are to be used frequently, such as dictionaries or supplemental texts, it needs to be conveniently located and easily monitored. When a bookcase is used to store seldom-used items, an out-of-the-way place is best. If you have only one bookcase, store unneeded items in a cabinet so that the single bookcase can be used for materials in frequent use. Label doors on cabinets to identify materials or equipment stored there.

Work Areas.   In many subjects, such as science, engineering, industrial arts, home economics, and art, students will likely put in some time in a laboratory, shop, or other work area. For these or other subjects, students may spend time at computer stations or a computer lab. The work area may be in the same room or in another room adjacent to the classroom. Students may work individually or in groups. They might also work in small groups for discussion activities or for special projects in other subject areas as well. When arranging group-work or lab areas, follow the same principles you used when positioning student desks. Be sure you can see all students, keep traffic lanes clear, and avoid congested areas, especially near supply and cleanup areas. Provide clear lines of sight between students and any area of the room from which you will conduct instruction while students are in the work area. If you use bookcases for room dividers, be sure they don't obstruct your ability to monitor student activities.

Centers.   A center is an area where a few students gather to work on a special activity or to study some topic. Often, a center will have special equipment, such as an audio device with headphones for individual students. Other centers may be organized around a special study topic or around skill areas in a particular subject. In the latter case, the teacher might have a box of activity cards that students use to progress through a series of objectives as part of enrichment or remediation programs. Some teachers like to arrange a more informal area in their classroom. This area might include, for example, an area rug, bookcases, a small table, and comfortable seating. Such an area adds a homey, personal touch to the setting, and it can make a classroom more appealing to some students. Students might be allowed to use the area for special projects, group work, or during free reading activities. (You will need to develop procedures for when and how the area will be used; see Chapter 4.)

If you intend to use such a center, plan its location so that it won't interfere with or distract from other activities. Because this type of center requires quite a lot of floor space, you'll have to weigh its advantages against the loss of space for other activities and the crowding that will result, especially if you have a small room or large classes. If and when you do use a center, be sure to place it where you can monitor students easily. Also, be certain that all necessary materials and equipment are available at the center and in good working order.

Pets, Plants, Aquariums, and Special Items.   Special items can add interest and individuality to a room. However, the first week of school is itself quite exciting for students, so it is not necessary to introduce special features immediately. When you do bring in such items, place them where they won't be distracting, especially during whole-class activities. Of course, they should not impede movement about the room.

Storage Space and Supplies

After you have decided on your wall and bulletin board displays and have organized the space within the classroom, you can concentrate on obtaining supplies and providing for storage. Some supplies will be used frequently and thus will need to be readily accessible. Seasonal or infrequently used items can go into deeper storage.

Textbooks and Other Instructional Materials.   Identify the textbooks and supplemental materials (dictionaries, reference books, additional reading materials) that will be used in your class. Determine which books students are expected to keep in their possession and which must remain in the room. Then use easily accessible shelves in a bookcase for the everyday books and materials that will not be kept by students. If you do not know what supplemental materials are available or what the school policies are regarding these items, check with your department chairperson, the librarian, or another teacher. Also, find out what system is used for obtaining textbooks; often, it is a first come, first served policy. If so, get in line early to ensure that you obtain the books you need. Further information is provided in Chapter 6 concerning textbooks that are checked out to students.

Frequently Used Classroom Materials.   The necessary supplies that you and your students use will depend somewhat on the subject you teach. A basic set includes paper in varying sizes and colors, projector pens, rulers, scissors, dry erase pens (or chalk if you're teaching in an older building) and erasers, transparent tape and masking tape, stapler, and glue. These and any other supplies you need on a daily basis should be kept in a readily accessible place such as a worktable or shelf. Usually, students are expected to bring certain materials, including pencils, erasers, pens, notebook paper or spiral notebooks, a calculator, and a flash drive. Typically, schools post basic lists on their websites and make them available to local stores so that they can be purchased before the beginning of the school year. Because you cannot expect all students to have these materials at the beginning of the year, you should make sure you have an ample supply of items needed by students. Tell students and their parents if additional materials beyond the basic set are needed.

Teacher's Supplies.   You will receive some materials from the school office for your own use. These items, which should usually be stored in your desk, include pencils and pens, paper, extra chalk or dry erase pens, scissors, ruler, stapler, file folders, paper clips, and thumbtacks or pushpins. In addition, it's important to have the teacher's editions for all textbooks, and any school forms needed for attendance reports and for handling money. Set up a filing system that allows you to separate the notes, forms, papers, and other materials used in each class. Use different file folders for different periods, and color code them for added efficiency. For each class, keep frequently needed materials and forms separate from those needed only occasionally. You will also need passwords for any required online access (e.g., digital grade book, school email account). Ask about other supplementary books for your subject area. These items can usually be stored in your desk. Because some schools have budgets for paper, be sure to note any limitations for the year and abide by them.

Student Work.   You may prefer that students leave some of their work-in-progress in the room rather than take it home; examples might be journals, lab notebooks, portfolios, and project notes. Space is always at a premium for such items and it will usually be necessary to bring in storage containers. For example, plastic crates with dividers can contain a compartment for each student's work, journal, or folder. Some teachers usee file baskets for students' work. Students' computer-based work may also be saved on the desktop in named folders or on flash drives for future use (see also Chapter 7). Locate the supplemental storage in an area that makes it easy for students to gain access to their portfolios or other work. Also, consider if digital storage (e.g., photographs, scanned documents, videos) would be a viable tool for long-term storage.

Student-Owned Materials.   Occasionally students will bring in bulky personal possessions (musical instruments, large backpacks). When these items are too large to be stored at the student's desk or if their presence is likely to be distracting or to interfere with movement about the room, you can designate a storage location elsewhere in the room.

Other Materials.   In addition to the items supplied by the school, a number of other supplies will come in handy. If your room does not have a clock and a calendar, obtain them now. Both should be large enough to be seen from the room's seating areas. You may wish to buy a desk bell or a timer if you are going to use them as signals for starting or stopping activities. You might also add the following items: tissues, rags or paper towels, a bar of soap, bandages, scouring powder or liquid cleanser, and a small plastic bucket. Some teachers like to keep a few basic tools such as a hammer, pliers, and a screwdriver in case a minor repair needs to be made. Store all these items where they are accessible to you.

Equipment.   Check all equipment—including the projector, television, computers, calculators, headphones, electrical outlets, and pencil sharpener—to make sure everything is in working order. Necessary extension cords or adapter plugs may be stored either with the equipment or in a handy place. Check availability and access to electrical outlets, which may be limited, especially if you're teaching in an older school. Consider purchasing some power strips to increase accessibility if your students will need power frequently during class activities. Also, try to keep cords out of high-traffic areas and caution students to be careful when moving about the room when a large number of students are plugged in. You'll need storage space for peripheral computer equipment, such as cables, mouse, headphones, and so on. A drawer or box with labeled compartments for keeping equipment separated is ideal.

Seasonal or Infrequently Used Items.   Holiday and seasonal decorations, bulletin board displays, and special project materials are used only on some occasions, as are calculators, protractors, templates, special art project materials, and science equipment. Because you don't need to have ready access to these materials, you can store them at the backs of closets, in boxes on top of cabinets, or even out of the room if you have access to outside storage space. Check with your department chairperson about using a storeroom.

Special Project Materials.   In a few subject areas, such as industrial arts, science, home economics, and art, students may regularly work on projects. Occasionally these projects may become too bulky or awkward to store in lockers and must remain in the room. If that's the case, then you will need to provide special storage areas to which you can control access to safeguard the materials. You will be wise to avoid beginning such projects until you have arranged for adequate storage. Chemicals or potentially hazardous materials must be stored according to district or state standards.

To organize and keep track of your activities as you arrange your room and get your equipment and supplies ready, you will find it helpful to use the checklist at the end of this chapter. Each aspect of room arrangement has been listed, and space has been provided for noting what has to be done and for checking off each area.

■ If You Have to "Float"

At some point in their careers, many teachers have to share classrooms with other teachers. Sometimes teachers who are new to a school find that they have no classroom that they can call their own but instead have to "float," conducting their classes in several rooms during the day. Obviously, such a situation presents problems for classroom organization and management. If this is the situation you face, your ability to arrange and organize your classroom space the way you would like will be very limited. However, there are some things you can and should do before school begins.

Begin by conferring with the teachers whose classrooms you will be using. Inspect each room carefully so that you will know where everything is when school begins. In each room, try to arrange for the following:

- Access to the classroom's digital projector or document camera. Most classrooms should have some means of projecting DVDs or PowerPoints so that the only thing the floating teacher has to do is connect a laptop or plug in a flash drive to the classroom computer. If a document camera is available, you can have displays on paper to put under the "doc-cam."
- A designated space on a whiteboard or a bulletin board where you can post assignments or announcements for your class and leave them up for several weeks.
- One shelf, cabinet, or table, especially if your course requires a classroom set of materials that you cannot carry with you all day.
- A sufficient number of desks.

Plan to carry all essential teaching supplies with you each day or perhaps store them in one desk drawer or in a box in each room. Don't depend on other teachers for supplies. You will probably need dry erasers and markers, paper towels, chalk, extra pens and pencils, paper, paper clips, and tissues. File folders, large manila envelopes, and rubber bands will be useful for organizing and carrying student papers. Color-coded folders for each class will also help keep different classes' papers organized and separated.

If all your classes are on one floor, or if an elevator is available for moving to different floors, try to obtain a rolling audiovisual cart. A large sheet of tagboard taped to the front will provide bulletin board space and a little bit of privacy for your belongings.

Take your own laptop from room to room or request access to a computer for your use as needed for preparing materials. If you share a computer with another teacher, you will need to set up your own folder for storing your documents, and you should back up your information on a flash drive. To keep the flash drive from getting misplaced, attach it to a lanyard. Be sure to password protect any confidential documents on the flash drive.

■ Who Will I Teach? Considering English Language Learners

How will the classroom design and room arrangement content you have just read be affected by the kinds of students you teach? One very common situation in schools across the United States is the presence of increasing numbers of students for whom English is not their native language.

In some cases the students are recent arrivals and will be receiving supplemental instruction in English-as-a-language-learner (ELL) classes, or they may be placed in bilingual classes. In many instances the students will have moved past the early stage of English comprehension and use, but may lack the developed vocabulary or fluency of native speakers. Assume that your classes will have at least some such students. Because the fluency levels of your English language learners can greatly affect their ability to acquire knowledge as well as benefit from your instructional strategies (Hill & Miller, 2013; Carey, 2007), you'll make every effort to find out what you can about language skill levels.

You can make a number of key choices for room arrangement in anticipation of the needs of your English language learners as well as the rest of the students in your classes. For example, you should consider providing space for learning centers and/or for small-group instruction so that you can provide mini-lessons and extra support as students master content, especially for students whose English skills are at the beginning to intermediate levels. Depending on the subjects you teach, you may be able to obtain recordings of content-related material (e.g., literature, science programs, social studies content). Establishing a media center with computers and listening stations with video and audio capability will be very useful for supplementing your instruction. Such centers will also be helpful for native speakers of English who need supplemental instruction.

Assuming that you have a mix of language skill levels, including at least some students at the beginning level, plan your seating arrangement so that you can easily form pairs that have a more skilled student and a beginner together when you conduct "turn to your partner" or "think-pair-share" activities during instruction. Such pairings provide more scaffolding for the beginner.

You should also dedicate some wall and bulletin board space to visual displays that provide concrete illustrations of vocabulary on topics relevant to content in your lessons (e.g., labeled illustrations of the feudal system components for the study of medieval history or literature with ELL students). Students can help identify words to learn, contribute drawings, or locate video descriptions online. All students, not just your English language learners, will benefit from such resources. Another display should be dedicated to listing daily classroom activities so that students can anticipate what they will be doing (and called on to do) at different times. Whenever possible, create displays of assignments, vocabulary, and directions so that students whose listening skills are not well developed will have a visual alternative. If you run out of board space, try to obtain a roll of butcher paper or a tripod stand with a large pad of paper for additional surfaces. Also consider how you might utilize technology to help you store and project multiple displays as needed.

All students benefit from a welcoming classroom environment, of course, but students who come from an immigrant culture or whose family has limited financial means especially need to feel valued and welcome. Perhaps you can develop bulletin board and other visual displays that reflect and value the contributions and traditions of your students' ethnic groups (e.g., immigrant entrepreneurs, Latino/as in Congress) as well as meet your students' needs for access. As noted Chapter 2, working with your students to create a display of their names, pictures, and other information is a good way to personalize and create a welcoming climate.

In addition, you may need to provide access to materials or experiences in your classroom that students may not have received during prior years of schooling. Some students in your classes may have experienced years of opportunity gaps (Milner, 2010), such as not having eaten at a restaurant or not having a space at home to themselves. If the students have received their prior education at schools in another culture, they may not have received instruction in topics that are regarded as standard in your content area. Thus, building a library of printed and recorded materials that cover a variety of topics will give you a chance to tailor assignments and projects to special learning needs for such students. Also, providing a center with materials on special topics can help fill a gap in experience and exploration as well as vocabulary for *all* students in your classes.

■ Chapter Summary

Organizing the classroom, including space, materials, and equipment, is a major task at the beginning of the year. Five keys guide the placement of these items: (1) Use a room arrangement consistent with your instructional goals and activities, (2) Keep high-traffic areas free of congestion, (3) Be sure you can easily see all your students, (4) Keep frequently used teaching materials and student supplies readily accessible, and (5) Be certain all students can easily see whole-class presentations and displays. Additional recommendations are provided for teachers who teach in more than one classroom. Planning for students who are English language learners is also considered.

■ Further Reading

classroom.4teachers.org

> *This site provides easy-to-use tools for drawing a classroom layout. Just enter the room's dimensions and drag icons to try out different arrangements.*

designshare.com

> *This website for an international network of architects and educators includes school and classroom design photographs as well as a section, "Articles," with great breadth on design (including such topics as technology, autism, and crime prevention).*

Evertson, C. M., & Poole, I. R. (2004). *Effective room arrangement.* Nashville, TN: Vanderbilt University, Peabody College, The IRIS Center for Faculty Enhancement. iris.peabody.vanderbilt.edu

> *This website contains activities and case studies for accommodating students who have special needs. Click on "Effective Room Arrangement" for the cases.*

Lambert, N. M. (1994). Seating arrangements in classrooms. *The International Encyclopedia of Education* (2nd ed., vol. 9), 5355–5359.

This article provides a summary of research on classroom seating arrangements. Although it is only one factor, the way the teacher arranges student seating can have an important influence on a variety of student behaviors.

ncef.org

The National Center for Educational Facilities website offers a variety of resources for exploring classroom arrangements, including articles (e.g., Butin's "Classrooms") and reports (e.g., National Summit on School Design Excellence).

nea.org/tools/creative-classrooms-on-a-budget.html

Take a look at some ideas for room arrangement on this website. You can also follow links to other articles on the topic.

thecornerstoneforteachers.com/free-resources/organization/classroom-seating-arrangements

This collection of online resources includes photographs of a variety of classroom arrangements with comments on their relevant pros and cons.

■ Suggested Activities

The following activities will help you plan and organize your classroom space. Do as many of them as time allows.

1. Figure 3.2 shows a classroom with quite a few problems. See how many you can find and consider how each problem might be corrected. (A key for this activity is found in the Appendix.)

2. Two other room diagrams are shown in Figure 3.3. Discuss their advantages and disadvantages for different types of classes. With which of the Five Keys to Good Room Arrangement are they consistent? Would any rearrangements be helpful?

3. Make a scale drawing of your room, as in Figures 3.1 and 3.2, using a classroom setup tool from teacher websites such as scholastic.com. You can now experiment on paper or computer with furniture arrangements and the organization of space—a much simpler task than pushing the furniture around yourself. Try to evaluate your arrangement using the five keys to successful room arrangement presented earlier in the chapter.

4. Many short articles and examples of room arrangement and classroom design for K–12 can be found at www.learnnc.org, a website maintained by the University of North Carolina. Enter the phrase "room arrangement" or "classroom design" into the site's search tool. From this site, identify three tips for arranging your classroom that you plan to implement.

figure 3.2 ■ A Room Arrangement with Problems

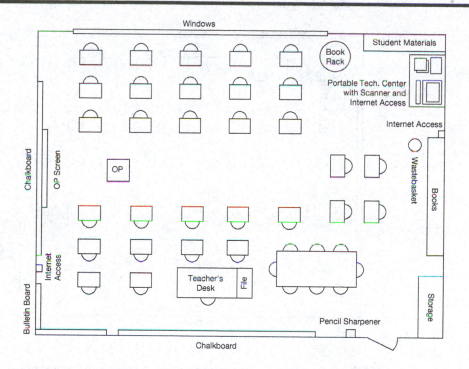

figure 3.3a ■ Two Room Arrangements for Discussion

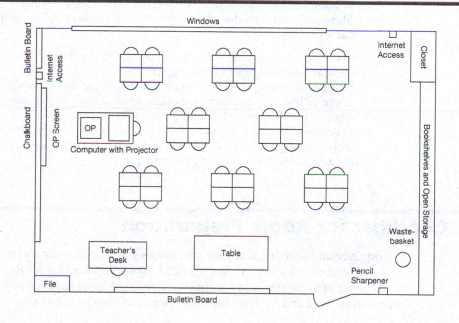

figure 3.3b

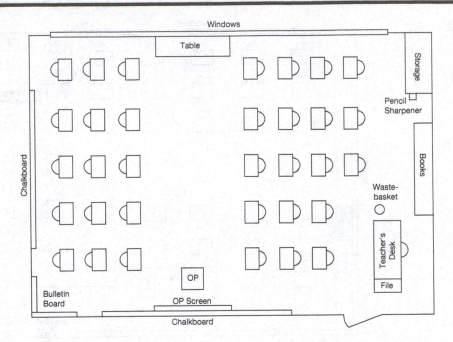

5. Visit other teachers' classrooms and examine their room arrangements. Use the items in the "Checklist for Room Preparation" at the end of this chapter and the five keys to room arrangement to guide your observation and analysis. If you are having a specific problem, ask several teachers for suggestions and see how they may have coped with the same problem.

6. After you have arranged the furniture in your room, test the traffic patterns, keeping in mind the recommendations in this chapter.
   a. Go to each instructional area and check it for your ability to observe all students wherever they may be during the instructional activity in that portion of the room. Also, be sure that needed materials are readily accessible.
   b. Now pretend you are a student. Enter the room; go to several desks; check for visibility, ease of movement to other parts of the room, and possible distractions. Alter the arrangement if you detect problems.

■ Checklist for Room Preparation

To organize and keep track of your activities as you arrange your room and get supplies and equipment ready, you will find it helpful to use this Checklist for Room Preparation. Each aspect of room arrangement has been listed, and space has been provided for noting things to be done and for checking off the area once you have it ready.

Room Preparation

Check When Complete	Subject	Notes
☐	A. Bulletin boards and walls	_____
☐	B. Floor space	_____
☐	1. Student desks/tables	_____
☐	2. Teacher's desk/equipment	_____
☐	3. Computer workstations	_____
☐	4. Bookcases	_____
☐	5. Work areas	_____
☐	6. Centers	_____
☐	7. Pets, plants, other items	_____
☐	C. Storage space and supplies	_____
☐	1. Textbooks	_____
☐	2. Frequently used materials	_____
☐	3. Teacher's supplies	_____
☐	4. Student work material	_____
☐	5. Student-owned material	_____
☐	6. Other material/supplies	_____
☐	7. Equipment	_____
☐	8. Seasonal items	_____
☐	9. Special project materials	_____

MyEducationLab *Self-Check 3.1*

MyEducationLab *Self-Check 3.2*

MyEducationLab *Application Exercise 3.1*   Using what you've learned in this chapter, view the video and respond to the questions.

MyEducationLab *Application Exercise 3.2*   Using what you've learned in this chapter, read and respond to this scenario.

Shutterstock

CHAPTER 4

Classroom Rules and Procedures

Now that your room arrangement planning has prepared the physical space of the classroom, you must consider how you will organize students' social space. An effective classroom has patterns and routines in place that make interaction and movement easy to organize and accomplish. For students to have a successful year in your classroom, they must understand and practice the behaviors you expect of them. Because you will want appropriate and cooperative behavior to become the norm in your classroom, think about how your students will learn about these expectations and follow them consistently. A carefully planned system of rules and procedures makes it easier for you to communicate your expectations to your students, and it helps ensure that the procedures you set up will be workable and effective.

■ Why Rules and Procedures Are Needed

Rules and procedures vary in different classrooms, but all effectively managed classrooms have them. It is not possible for a teacher to conduct instruction or for students to work productively if there are no guidelines for behaviors, such as when to move about the room or speak. Furthermore, inefficient procedures and the absence of routines for common aspects of classroom life—such as taking and reporting attendance, participating in discussions, turning in materials, and checking work—can waste large amounts of time and cause students' attention and interest to wane. Here is a brief example of a classroom with major problems in the area of rules and procedures.

When the tardy bell rang, only a few of Mr. Smith's third-period students took their seats. Two played catch with some pencils, while others congregated in small groups and chatted noisily. Mr. Smith had to shout over the din to be heard: "Get to your seats. I need to take roll." Some students moved to sit down, while others vied for places at back-row desks. After much prompting, most of the students were seated, and Mr. Smith began taking roll. Loud talking continued, abating only momentarily after Mr. Smith called repeatedly for silence. After 10 minutes, roll call was finally completed. Mr. Smith then asked students to get out their books and homework assignment. Loud protests ensued as students insisted that no assignment had been given. Furthermore, many students did not have their textbooks with them. Rather than allow a large number of students to go out into the hall to get their books from their lockers, Mr. Smith decided to conduct a review on the assigned lesson. By then, however, three students had already left the classroom to retrieve their texts. Attempting to get the activity under way, Mr. Smith called in vain for silence. He finally began to ask questions, but before he could select a student to respond, several others called out the answer. A chorus of comments greeted the responses. Mr. Smith tried to continue asking questions, but the noise from students' social talk made it difficult to hear.

Pause and Consider

1. How would you describe the social space (teacher–student, student–student interactions) of this classroom?
2. What are some things you feel could be adjusted to improve this social space?
3. Imagine you are a student in this class (select one of the following: student on time, student on task, student late to class, student without a text, student with limited interest in the class topic). Describe your surroundings and the impact this has on you and your learning.

Observers of this classroom might criticize Mr. Smith for allowing students to get away with so much misbehavior. "Be stricter," they might say. "Punish the misbehaving students," or "Develop more interesting lessons to capture student interest." Some might even suggest that Mr. Smith set up a reward system to encourage good behavior. Although these suggestions could be helpful under some circumstances, they do not address the fundamental problem in this classroom: The students have not learned the behaviors that are expected of them. These students almost certainly know that many of their behaviors would not be allowed in other classrooms, but the problem here is that Mr. Smith has not taught the students how to behave in *his* class. Areas in which this is evident in this example include (1) what to do when entering the room, (2) seating assignments, (3) bringing materials for class, (4) completing assignments, (5) out-of-room policies, (6) talking during discussions, and (7) responding to questions.

The fact that students know what is appropriate does not mean that they will behave that way. (For that reason, this book will not end with the present chapter!) However, a clear set of expectations about what constitutes appropriate behavior will be a major start in establishing a well-managed classroom environment.

The unique setting created by middle and high school organization makes it essential that you establish a clear set of rules and procedures for your classroom. You will likely be working with five or more classes of 25 to 30-plus students. Generally, you will be confined to a single room with limited space and materials; you will be responsible for teaching many cognitive skills to a diverse population of students; and, at the same time, you will have to handle administrative tasks, arrange for appropriate materials and supplies, and evaluate students. To do these things well, you need an orderly environment with minimal disruption or wasted time, leaving everyone free to concentrate on the critical tasks of learning. Carefully planned procedures help create this environment.

■ Preliminary Considerations

Definition of Terms

Goals are target aspirations not necessarily attained every day. However, long-term goals determine our daily actions. Carefully consider your personal goals and the goals you want your students to achieve during the year. Discussing goal setting with your students is an important way to establish common values regarding class activities. Keep in mind that your beliefs and the goals you set will influence the expectations you communicate to your students.

Expectations are desired behaviors or outcomes. Within a classroom, a teacher can make his or her expectations known to students, or the teacher can let students guess at the expectations. It is much easier for students to meet a teacher's expectations when they know what these expectations are. Teachers can make their expectations known to students by directly teaching the classroom rules and procedures, providing opportunities for students to practice them, and responding consistently to students' behavior. A teacher's consistent responses can include both positive consequences to reinforce appropriate behavior and negative consequences to deter inappropriate behavior.

Rules and *procedures* refer to stated expectations regarding behavior. A rule identifies general expectations or standards. For example, the rule "Respect other persons and their property" covers a large set of behaviors that should always be practiced. Rules may indicate behavior that is not acceptable, although teachers occasionally manage to write only rules that are positively stated ("We ask permission before talking in class"). In this example, the unacceptable behavior—talking without permission—is implied. In addition to general rules, many teachers will have a rule or two governing a specific behavior they anticipate being an issue or that they want to prevent (e.g., "No profanity" or "Gum chewing is not allowed"). Note that some teachers prefer to use the terms *policies* or *guidelines* rather than *rules*.

Secondary teachers use classroom rules to help communicate expectations for appropriate behavior. Based on interviews with high school students serving detention for school infractions, Thorson (2003) recommends that rules be positively worded, limited to a small number (three to five), and clearly stated. Similar suggestions have been made by many other researchers (e.g., Bicard, 2000; Boonstrum, 1991; Brophy, 1996; Evertson, 1994; Malone & Tietjens, 2000), who have also noted that student acceptance of the rules will be strengthened if they are presented positively and if their usefulness for maintaining a classroom environment conducive to participation and learning is emphasized.

Procedures (also called *routines*, especially when they combine several steps or procedures) also communicate expectations for behavior. They usually apply to a specific activity, and they are usually directed at accomplishing something specific rather than prohibiting some behavior or defining a general standard. For example, you will set up procedures or routines with your students for collecting assignments, turning in late work, participating in class discussions, leaving the room to go to lockers or the bathroom, and so on. Some procedures, such as the safe use of equipment or student notebook requirements, may be sufficiently complex or critical that you should post them on your class website and provide copies of guidelines for students to retain—or you may have students copy the procedures into their notebooks. However, many procedures are unwritten because they are very simple or because their specificity and frequency of use allow students to learn them rapidly.

Identifying School Rules and Procedures

School rules are usually expressed in a code of conduct that specifies desired and prohibited student behaviors. Often such codes of conduct will identify possible consequences for prohibited behaviors. In most schools, teachers are expected to enforce school rules; it is to the teachers' advantage to do so. A set of rules applied consistently in all classes and areas of the building is easy for students to learn. The rules also acquire more legitimacy in the eyes of some students because the rules are everyone's rules. In addition to rules and procedures that regulate student behavior, all schools have certain administrative procedures that every teacher must follow (e.g., keeping attendance records). You need to find out about your school's rules and procedures before the year begins so that you can incorporate them into your own classroom procedures. You can find school rules for students and administrative procedures for teachers at a school orientation meeting or from a teacher's handbook, a building administrator, or another teacher. A mentor teacher or another colleague can be a very useful resource for learning about school rules and procedures. We recommend that you ask such a person for feedback and suggestions as you plan your classroom procedures and policies. Pay careful attention to the following:

1. Note the behaviors that are specifically forbidden (e.g., running in the halls, talking or texting on a cell phone during class) or required (e.g., being in possession of a hall permit when out of the classroom during class time, bringing a note for absence).

2. Know the consequences of rule violations. Be aware of your responsibility for carrying out such consequences, such as reporting the student to the school office. If the school does not have a policy for dealing with certain rule violations, check with other teachers to learn about school norms. For example, if it is up to the teacher to deal with coming late to class or cell phone use, you must decide how to handle them yourself.

3. Follow administrative procedures that must be handled during class time. Some administrative tasks occur infrequently (e.g., assigning textbooks at the beginning of the year). Others occur daily, including recording class attendance, talking with previously absent students, or dealing with tardy students. You may have to collect money for special activities or from students in an advisory period or sponsored activity, so you will need a record-keeping system and a safe place to keep any money you may be handling. You will also need a procedure for allowing students to leave the room to go to other parts of the building. Procedures in these areas are usually established schoolwide. If standard procedures have not been adopted in some area, talking with experienced teachers about their procedures will be helpful.

"That's Miss Clamhouse. She runs a tight ship."

Tony Saltzman

■ Planning Classroom Rules

After you have information about school rules and procedures, you will be ready to begin planning for your own classroom. We will present guidelines for rules first, then for procedures. Note that some teachers prefer to call their rules *policies* or *guidelines*.

Many different rules are possible, but a set of around four to six is probably sufficient to cover the most important areas of behavior. Following are five general rules that encompass many classroom behaviors. These or similar rules are often found in well-managed classrooms, although we do not present them as a definitive list. You may decide to use other rules, such as one prohibiting some behavior or having more specificity. After each rule are examples of behaviors related to the rule. When presenting general rules to students, it is important to discuss your specific expectations relevant to each rule. During the discussion of the rules and related behaviors, it is best to emphasize the positive "do" parts of the rules rather than their negative counterparts. When you focus on the positive, you help students learn how to behave appropriately. You will have to be explicit about behaviors that are not acceptable when such behaviors might occur frequently (e.g., chewing gum, leaving one's seat, calling out). These may be incorporated into your set of rules or discussed when presenting procedures associated with specific activities. However, there is no need to recite a long list of forbidden behaviors during your initial discussion of rules.

The set of rules you choose will be used later in several ways. First, you will discuss these rules with your students on the first day or two of class. If you teach at the middle school level, you will post the rules in the room and/or make certain that students have their own copies. Some teachers also send a copy home to be returned with parents' signatures. In addition, you may also post your rules on your class website. Most schools have websites onto which teachers can insert content for student and parental access. Web pages should include, among other items, a course syllabus, an outline of what is being covered during the grading period, and information about assignments and grades. (These items are discussed in more detail in Chapter 5.) You can include a section with your class rules and major procedures in order to reinforce their importance not only with your students but also their parents.

A posted set of rules allows you to focus student attention on and create a strong expectation about behaviors that are very important to you. If you teach in a senior high school, posting rules is not mandatory, although it is definitely recommended for ninth-grade classes; these students will be less aware than older students of what behaviors are appropriate for the high school setting. At higher grade levels, you can provide students with a handout describing class rules, along with other information about the class. There is also some difference in how you should present the classroom rules to younger and older students, and this will be described in Chapter 6. Finally, you may refer to specific rules as needed to remind students of appropriate behavior during the year.

Note that your posted rules need not (and cannot) cover all aspects of behavior in detail; procedures for specific activities and perhaps some ad hoc rules will be needed. For instance, you may wish to keep your policies regarding student work separate from rules about general conduct. Examples of basic, commonly used rules follow.

RULE 1. Respect and be polite to all people. This rule is general; be sure to give sufficient examples and explanation so that both you and your students clearly understand its meaning. You should define *polite*, and give examples that emphasize the behaviors that are important for your classroom activities. You can also involve students in the discussion by asking *them* to give examples. Don't dwell on examples of lack of respect or impoliteness; as was stated earlier it's best to focus on the positive behaviors you want to encourage. You may also want to emphasize that "all people" includes *all* students as well as you!

RULE 2. Be prompt and be prepared. This rule includes guidelines that underscore the importance of schoolwork. *Prompt* may refer to the beginning of the class period, transition to group work, and moving to individual tasks. *Being prepared* acknowledges the importance of having the right materials, as well as the mental attitude, to be successful in schoolwork.

RULE 3. Listen and stay seated when someone is talking. This rule will help prevent call-outs and other interruptions. You can use the discussion of this rule to teach the students your procedure (e.g., raise a hand and wait to be called on) for asking a question or making a comment during a class discussion or other teacher-led activity. Note that this general rule will not be sufficient to deal with all aspects of student talk and movement, but it will be a start. Later you'll be able to clarify expectations for talk and movement that vary in other activities (e.g., small-group or independent work).

RULE 4. Respect other people's property. This rule encompasses such behaviors and guidelines as (a) keep the room clean and neat, (b) pick up litter, (c) return borrowed property, (d) use equipment carefully, and (e) get permission before using another person's materials.

RULE 5. Obey all school rules. This rule is useful because it reminds students that school rules apply in your classroom as well as outside it. It also suggests that you will monitor behavior in the areas covered by the school rules. Finally, including it in your rules gives you an opportunity to discuss whatever school rules are pertinent to your classroom (e.g., school policies governing use of cell phones).

Student Participation in Rule Setting

It is useful to involve students in rule setting to promote student ownership of the rules and student responsibility for their own behavior. Student involvement can take the form of a discussion of the reasons for having rules and clarifying the rationale for and the meaning of particular rules. For example, a discussion might begin with you making an analogy between society's laws and classroom rules and asking students what purpose these laws serve. Depending on the age level and sophistication of the students, typical responses might include ideas about protecting individual and group rights, preventing violence or destructive behavior, and permitting normal activities to take place. After this initial discussion, rules can be presented one at a time. You may first clarify the rule by describing (or asking students to describe) the area of behavior it covers. Students can usually supply concrete examples, although they will tend to give negative instances (e.g., "Respecting property means not breaking things or not stealing"). Consequently, you should be prepared to encourage students to state positive examples. The discussion of individual rules should also include a rationale for those rules whose justification is not obvious.

You can also involve students in a discussion of rules by asking for suggestions for specific behaviors it would be important for everyone to practice when the goal is to create a good climate for learning and in which all students feel comfortable about participating. Students might volunteer suggestions such as listen carefully, don't interrupt, no put-downs, and encourage others. After receiving a number of suggestions, you can organize the list into one or more general guidelines, such as "Respect others." If the goal is a rule that encourages effort and persistence, you can ask students for examples of behaviors that foster success and learning. Students will give examples such as turn in work on time, pay attention, ask for help when necessary, and do your own work. These suggestions can be summarized in a general guideline—perhaps "Always do your personal best." Student participation in such a discussion will demonstrate the reasonableness of the guidelines and their wide acceptance.

Another way of involving students in rule setting is to allow them to share in the decision-making process for specific rules. This is sometimes done at the school level by having student representatives or student council members participate in the identification of school rules. However, shared decision making is not commonplace in secondary classrooms for several reasons. First, the domain in which student participation is acceptable is limited. Schoolwide rules must be accepted as they are. Also, policies that are essential to managing instruction cannot be left to student discretion. Finally, secondary school teachers instruct five or more classes; if each class generates different rules, posting them may be a problem and remembering which rules are associated with which class could become cumbersome.

Some teachers permit student choice in particular activities or behaviors. For example, if chewing gum is not prohibited by a school rule, and if you do not find it objectionable, you could give your students a choice. (It would be a rare class that decided to prohibit it!) Another area in which an option may be available concerns whether seat work is to be done silently or whether quiet talking is acceptable. When students are given such choices, be sure they understand their responsibility for making the chosen procedure or rule work—and remind them that they will lose the privilege if their behavior warrants it.

Many effective managers do not provide for student choice in rule setting. Instead, they clearly present their rules and procedures to students and provide explanations of the need for such rules. These teachers strive to be reasonable and fair in their rules and procedures, knowing that teachers who act autocratically invite challenges from adolescents. However, a teacher who is authoritative, who establishes reasonable rules and procedures, who provides an understandable rationale for them, and who enforces them consistently will find the great majority of students willing to abide by them.

Consequences for Rule Violations

You should give careful consideration to the consequences for violations of your rules. One type of consequence is usually prescribed by school policy, such as consequences for tardiness and unexcused absences. Other consequences are often specified for fighting, classroom use of profanity, damage to property, and loss of books. You will have to familiarize yourself with these policies so that you can do your part in following through if rule violations occur and to be sure that your own classroom policies are consistent with those of the school.

Also, think about what consequences you will use to deal with classroom rules not covered by school policy. What will you do if a student ignores your rule for respecting others and chooses to interrupt your lessons by walking around the room to visit with friends? What consequence will you use if a student turns in an incomplete assignment? Planning consequences ahead of time is a good idea because it helps you use them consistently, and you will be more confident about using them. Also, you will be better able to communicate them to students. A basic system that works for many problems is (1) redirect, correct, or remind the student as a first response; (2) give a time-out or have a conference with the student if the problem persists; (3) call home if the first two strategies aren't successful; and (4) use a referral to an assistant principal or counselor as a last resort. There are many other options, however, depending on the situation, personal preference, the student, and your goals, so consider the basic system as a starting point and build on it. In particular, carefully consider the suggestions and strategies described in Chapters 9, 10, and 11 for communicating effectively with students and for dealing with problem behaviors.

Planning Classroom Procedures

If you have never analyzed the specific behaviors required of students in a typical secondary school classroom, you are going to be surprised by the complexity and detail in the following sections. Do not hurry through them, even though some items may appear trivial; these bits and pieces will combine to form the mosaic of your management system. Four categories of procedures are described: general procedures needed each class period, procedures for teacher-led instruction and seat-work activities, procedures for student group work, and miscellaneous procedures. The greatest emphasis is on the first two areas, although the third is very important if you're planning to use group activities, and the fourth category will contain a variety of procedures. A fifth area, procedures for managing student work, is presented in Chapter 5. As you read the sections that follow, you can note ideas for procedures on the Checklist for Classroom Procedures at the end of this chapter.

■ General Procedures

Beginning-of-Period Procedures

On five or more occasions every day, you will need to begin a class period. It is important to conduct this activity efficiently so that you will be able to begin content activities quickly. The following five items cover the things most frequently involved in getting the period under way.

Attendance Check.   In most schools, teachers are expected to file an attendance report during the initial part of every class period. To do so efficiently, prepare a seating chart for each class and use it to check attendance. Keep your seating chart along with attendance material, such as tardy slips, where you will take attendance. This location should provide an unobstructed view of all students. (*Note:* You may wish to call roll for the first few days of class and then use a seating chart after your class enrollment stabilizes and your students' seating arrangements are reasonably final.) Most schools use computerized attendance reporting, so you'll simply click on the names of students who are absent.

Students Absent the Previous Day.   Late-work policies should be described in your course syllabus and posted on your class website. As previously absent students enter the room, they can leave their absence slips at a designated location or give them to you. You can sign and return the absence slips while you are checking roll, immediately after, or during the first seat-work activity. To facilitate these students' obtaining handouts they might have missed, consider using a system of writing the absent students' names and the date on each handout and putting them in an absentee file. Direct returning students to the absentee folder for missed papers.

Keeping a record of daily assignments on your class website, on a posted calendar, and/or in an accessible notebook will allow previously absent students to identify work to be made up. An alternative procedure for assisting returning students is to use student helpers or assistants. Volunteers can take responsibility for keeping a set of handouts for each absent student, along with a list of missed assignments. The task can be rotated among volunteers on a weekly or monthly basis.

Tardy Students.   Most schools have a policy in this area, so be sure to follow it consistently. Teachers who begin to deviate from tardiness policies (e.g., letting students slip into the classroom if they are only a few seconds late) soon find that the rate of student tardiness will increase and that their beginning-of-class procedures will break down. Tardiness can become a nagging management problem if you allow it. In the rare case of a school having no specific schoolwide policy or consequences for tardiness, you will have to develop a procedure of your own. Some teachers assign detention during lunch or before or after school each time students are tardy without a valid excuse. Other teachers give a warning for the first incident and then provide detention or some other penalty beginning with the second occurrence of tardiness.

Behavior Expected of All Students. Students should be told what they are expected to do at the beginning of the period while you are handling your administrative tasks. They should know that they are expected to be in the room (some teachers require that they be seated at their desks) when the bell rings, or else they will be counted as tardy. When the bell rings, socializing should stop. Good managers often handle the beginning-of-class activity in one of two ways. Students may be given a regular activity that they are expected to perform at the beginning of every period. Some teachers use a warm-up in which several problems, a question, or some very brief assignment is displayed. The question or problems might, for example, review some aspect of the preceding day's content. An alternative to a work assignment is for the teacher to display an outline of the day's activities for students to copy in their notebook or on an assignment sheet. Another way to begin class is to tell students to use the time to get out any needed materials (headings on papers if needed, homework papers, textbooks, project materials, etc.) and to remain seated with no talking until you finish your administrative duties. This will work only so long as you handle these matters quickly and do not leave students in "dead time" for very long.

Leaving the Room. Occasionally students will need to leave the classroom during the period—to use the bathroom, to get a drink of water, to take medication, or to go to the library, the school office, or another area of the building. Schools always have policies for handling these matters, typically requiring the use of a hall pass signed by the teacher or by office personnel. Most effective managers discourage trips outside the classroom to the bathroom or water fountain except for emergencies. You can use a sign-up sheet (with time out/time back noted) and a "one-at-a-time" bathroom policy) to manage this behavior. Unfortunately, lax policies in this area frequently result in classroom (and school) management problems.

A second area that is sometimes troublesome concerns students returning to their lockers to retrieve materials during the class period. Frequently, teachers do not allow this at all and require that the students sit in class without materials or look at another student's text. In such a case, the student might receive reduced credit for work not brought to class. Another procedure is to allow the student to return to the locker to obtain the necessary materials but to impose a mild penalty or count the student as tardy. Whatever policies you establish, the overriding considerations are to minimize the number of students who go out of the room for noninstructional purposes and to follow your procedures consistently.

Use of Materials and Equipment

Your classroom will have a variety of materials and equipment. Identify those things that you expect students to use and indicate how these items should be operated and under what conditions. This should be done as soon as students are expected to use the equipment. There may also be a number of items in the room that you do not want students to use or handle. Identify them to the students and explain your rationale for keeping them off limits. If you have a class rule pertaining to respecting others' property, you can refer to it when you cover the procedures in this area.

Equipment and Materials for Students.   Items for student use include the pencil sharpener, student desks, tables, and special equipment such as computers, microscopes, globes, encyclopedias, dictionaries, and other room materials. You should establish procedures for the use of whatever items you have in your room. A common procedure for the pencil sharpener is to request that students sharpen pencils before the tardy bell rings, not during activities in which the teacher is presenting or instructing the whole class. If students need to sharpen their pencils during seat work, a common procedure is to allow only one student at a time at the pencil sharpener. If students have access to storage cabinets, bookshelves, or equipment in different parts of the room, you should identify how and when these areas and materials may be used. Consider posting directions for the use of these areas or equipment if they aren't obvious. Procedures concerning computer and media equipment may include the timing of their use, the number of students permitted in the area at the same time, and provisions for appropriate Internet use or email access.

Teacher Materials and Equipment.   This category includes your desk, storage areas, filing cabinet, and closet, as well as your personal possessions. You must make it clear to students that they are not to take things from your desk or use your supplies without permission. Older, more mature senior high students generally do not need to be told this procedure unless you observe students taking liberties with your materials. However, you should state the expectation to younger students, especially to middle school classes. Be pleasant when you explain it; the rationale for the procedure is so obvious that you need not dwell on it.

Ending the Period

Just as procedures are needed to begin a period, so too are routines helpful at its close. Two matters are of general concern: getting students and the room ready for the end of the period and dismissing class. Any room equipment or materials used during instructional activities must be returned to their storage spaces. Cleanup of materials and equipment should be completed before the end-of-period bell. Finally, you may wish to remind students of particular items needed for the next day or for future activities. To accomplish these objectives, you need to leave sufficient time at the end of the period to pull together any loose ends from the period's activities and for whatever cleanup and announcements are required. If students have been engaged in seat work with their own materials, only a short time (less than half a minute or so) may be needed to put materials away. You will have to judge the time needed and signal the students when to begin cleaning up. Sometimes students will stop work and get ready to go well in advance of the bell. If you tell students that you will let them know when they should begin to clean up or to put their materials away, they will be less likely to develop this habit. Be conscientious about giving students sufficient time before the bell rings; they have a limited amount of time to get to their next class, and it is not fair to them or to their next teacher to cause them to be tardy.

The second concern in ending the class is the signal for dismissal. Many teachers prefer to dismiss the students themselves rather than allow the end-of-period bell to be the students' signal. This allows the teacher to hold the students in their seats if the room is not yet properly cleaned up or if an announcement remains to be given. If you wish to use this procedure, you will need to tell students that you—rather than the bell—will dismiss them and that they should remain in their seats until you give a signal indicating that it is appropriate to leave. If you use this procedure, some students are sure to test it by leaving their seats when the bell rings. In such a case, you must be prepared to call them back to their seats. You can then dismiss all the students except those who left their seats early. These students leave last.

■ Procedures During Seat Work and Teacher-Led Instruction

Good procedures for teacher-led instruction and seat work are especially important because it is during these times that much instruction and learning take place. Good procedures will prevent or reduce the interruptions or distractions that can slow content development activities or interfere with student work.

Student Attention during Presentations

It is helpful to consider how students should behave when you or another student is presenting information to the class or while you are conducting a discussion or another teacher-led activity. Students are typically expected to listen attentively to the presenter and to other students (see Rule 3, p. 52). Teachers also expect that students should neither engage in social conversation with each other during such activities nor read unrelated materials or work on other assignments. The simplest way to enforce the latter requirement is to require that only books or other materials needed for the lesson be on the students' desks.

If you want students to take notes during your presentations, you must state explicitly that this is desired, and you will have to teach your students how to do it. Initially, many students may be unable to abstract key points from your presentations, so you will have to help them by telling them what they should record in their notes. You could also provide students with a partially filled-in outline, with directions to complete it during the presentation. If note taking is expected, show them how you expect their notebooks to be organized. This can be done by presenting an example of a properly organized notebook and periodically inspecting student notebooks. If students will frequently be working in groups and presenting the results to the whole class, mention the importance of attentiveness during group presentations. You should also reinforce this point when you discuss group-work procedures and behavior.

Student Participation

You will need to identify some procedure by which students can ask a question, contribute to a discussion, or receive help without interrupting you or other students during whole-class activities. During presentations and discussions, the simplest procedure is to require that students raise their hands and wait to be called on. (Some teachers occasionally have students call on the next contributor to avoid having all interactions channeled through the teacher.) Do not limit class participation only to volunteers. Call on all students and be sure that everyone has a response opportunity. In most circumstances it is not a good idea to allow students to call out comments or answers without raising their hands. Undesirable consequences of allowing call-outs include domination of participation by a few students, inappropriate comments, and interruptions of discussions and presentations. Teachers who rely on call-outs may get an inaccurate impression of overall understanding. Requiring that students raise their hands before commenting or asking questions gives all students an opportunity to participate.

Two exceptions to the "no call-out" procedure are reasonable. One occurs when teachers want students to provide a choral response—that is, a whole-class answer to a question. This can be handled by telling students at the beginning of the activity that they do not have to raise their hands. Also, many teachers use a nonverbal signal for a choral response—such as cupping one hand behind an ear—or a verbal signal such as prefacing the question with a cue word, as in "Everyone . . . ." A second exception may occur during activities in which hand raising might slow down or interfere with a class discussion. Again, students can be told that it is not necessary to raise hands during that particular activity. It is worth noting that such variations from a standard procedure generally should not be used early in the school year. Instead, follow a simple routine for several weeks until you are certain that students understand it. Then, if you choose to depart from the procedure, clearly communicate the difference to the students at the beginning of the activity.

Procedures for Seat Work

In many subject areas, students are frequently given assignments to be done in class. During such activities, the teacher usually circulates around the room, monitoring students and providing individual feedback. A number of procedural areas should be planned so that you will be able to direct student efforts while they engage in this activity.

Talk among Students.   Some effective managers allow no student talk at all during seat-work activities. They require that students work on their own, that they neither seek nor provide help to other students, and that they refrain from social conversation. Other effective managers allow quiet talking among students when such talk is content related. You will have to decide what your policy will be. The "no talking" rule is easier to monitor, and you may want to start with this procedure during the first month or two of the school year and then try allowing students to help each other on a trial basis. If you decide to allow students to talk to one another or to work together during seat-work activities, you will have to establish guidelines. For example, you might say that during certain activities quiet talking is allowed, but if it gets too loud, the privilege will be lost. Be specific about what you mean by "quiet talking"—for example, whispering, low-volume natural talking, or talk that can be heard no more than two feet away.

Obtaining Help.   When students are working at their seats and need help, you should have them raise their hands. You may then go to them or have them come to you one at a time. This procedure will avoid the formation of long lines of chatty students at your desk. It will also allow you to control where you give individual assistance. If you help students at a location other than their desks, choose one that allows you an unobstructed view of the rest of the class. Moving among students allows you to monitor their progress and helps keep them on task, so it's best not to rely on giving help from a single location for long periods of time.

Out-of-Seat Procedures.   To eliminate unnecessary wandering around the room during seat work, you can indicate when students are allowed to leave their seats. For example, students may sharpen pencils, turn in papers, and get supplies when necessary. Trash can be kept at each student's desk and discarded at the end of the period. A one-at-a-time rule often works well for movement during seat work.

When Seat Work Has Been Completed.   Sometimes one or several students will finish their seat work before the end of the period or before the next scheduled activity. This circumstance is frequently handled either by having students complete an additional, enrichment assignment for extra credit or by allowing such students to use the remaining time for free reading or to work on assignments from other classes. If you have enrichment activities that involve additional materials not in the students' possession, you must specify when these materials may be used, where they are kept, and what the procedures are for returning the materials to their proper place. Note that if many students frequently complete their work early, it may indicate that assignments are not challenging enough or that you have set aside more time than is necessary for seat-work activities.

■ Procedures for Student Group Work

Some teachers use groups extensively for a variety of tasks, such as short- or long-term projects, peer explanation and other assistance, and review of content learned in other formats. Other examples include laboratory assignments in science classes, the preparation of group reports or projects in social studies and English, home economics labs, and study groups organized to accomplish specific learning objectives or to prepare for an exam. To whatever extent groups are used, it is important for the teacher to develop efficient routines that support the learning objectives.

Routines are typically introduced to the students whenever groups are first used, and they are reinforced thereafter until the groups are working well. It is important that students learn appropriate group behavior, especially if the teacher intends to use groups extensively. Although the teacher can monitor group work, the fact that six or seven groups may be working simultaneously at varying paces using a variety of resources precludes the teacher from closely directing all group activities. Therefore, the procedures implemented for group work must be carefully chosen to encourage groups to work more or less independently toward the instructional goals, to promote desirable interaction among students in the group, and to support efficient use of time.

Johnson and Johnson (2013) recommend giving careful attention to teaching social skills to students who are going to work extensively in groups. First, students should be engaged in a discussion about the importance of each skill. Common types of desirable group behaviors include staying on task, contributing, listening carefully, and sharing and helping. Each skill needs to be carefully described. The Johnsons recommend discussing with students both what each behavior "looks like" and what it "sounds like" so that students have cues in more than one modality.

It may be especially helpful to middle school students if the teacher makes simple wall charts listing the desired behaviors. Besides communicating an expectation for these behaviors, teachers can give students feedback keyed to the desired behavior—for example, by engaging the whole class in a discussion about how well the groups are working and what could be done to improve them. It is helpful to stress each student's responsibility toward the common good. A recommended strategy is to ask students to critique their own group's performance—for example, "What are three things my group is doing well, and what is one thing that we need to improve?" To provide practice of desired behaviors, teachers can ask students to take various roles. Roles should be rotated to give each student an opportunity to practice all behaviors. A number of procedures that can help small-group activities proceed smoothly are described next.

Use of Materials and Supplies

Small-group activities, particularly those that are run as part of a laboratory, frequently require the use of a variety of materials and equipment. To avoid traffic jams, you must plan distribution stations carefully and use more than one if necessary. When possible, save time by placing some or all needed materials on students' desks or worktables before class starts. Be sure to check equipment for proper functioning ahead of time and have replacements on hand for use when needed. Student helpers may be assigned to distribute supplies and materials, to monitor supply stations, and to clean up work areas. When students need to bring special materials for group or project work, they should be told far enough in advance so that they can obtain them, and you may have to locate safe places for materials to be stored while work is in progress. If any equipment poses a potential hazard to students or can be easily damaged by careless use, you must identify safety routines and plan appropriate demonstrations.

Assignment of Students to Groups

Attention to assignment is important for two reasons. First, students who do not work well together should not be placed in the same work group. Second, a group composed mainly of poorly motivated students is not likely to accomplish much. If each person's grade is based partly on the individual's accomplishments and partly on the group's accomplishments, everyone in the group has a stake in what everyone else does, and the chances for a successful experience are increased. To obtain groups that are well balanced, to discourage excessive social talk during the assignment, and to save time in forming groups and getting started on the task, the assignment of individual students to groups should be determined ahead of time by the teacher. Later in the year you can consider rotating group assignments or allowing some student choice in group membership.

Student Goals and Participation

Students should be told what they are supposed to accomplish in their small-group work and taught how to go about the task. It is a good idea to assign specific roles and to discuss with students ahead of time the different roles they will take in the group work (e.g., reader, recorder, reporter). Preparing a list of steps that should be followed and providing it on a handout can help students monitor their own progress. You might even discuss or suggest time allotments for accomplishing each step.

Other areas of behavior such as out-of-seat movement and contacting the teacher can be managed using the same procedures identified for seat-work activities. Obviously, quiet talk must be permitted, but the noise level may become a problem. Impress students with the importance of keeping talk focused on the task. During the activity, monitor the groups carefully and stop inappropriate behavior quickly at the individual or group level before it spreads to the whole class. You may want to identify a signal you will use to warn the class that the noise level is too high.

Cooperative Learning

An instructional method that makes extensive use of groups, called *learning teams* or *cooperative learning groups* (Johnson & Johnson, 2009; Slavin, Karweit, & Wasik, 1994), has been applied widely in many subjects and grade levels. Typical practices are for teams to be formed heterogeneously and to work on academic tasks requiring interdependent action. Evaluation criteria reward the group for individual achievement, thus encouraging cooperation; teams may compete against each other and be rewarded on the basis of group performance. Procedures for learning teams incorporate many of the factors described in the preceding sections on the use of small groups, but they also have unique characteristics. Suggestions for the management of cooperative learning groups are presented in Chapter 8.

■ Miscellaneous Procedures

A few other procedures merit mention. Although not all of them will be of concern to you, you may find it helpful to consider them.

Signals

A signal is an action, behavior, or physical prop used to obtain student attention or to indicate that some procedure or behavior is called for. If you always begin instruction by moving to a specific location in the room where you stand facing students, they will learn that you are giving them a signal that instruction is about to begin. Some teachers like to have a readily identifiable signal to notify students that seatwork or group-work activity is about to end and that another activity will soon begin. Examples of such signals include turning the lights off momentarily, ringing a bell, or clapping while counting down. Any signals that you intend to use should be explained to the students; they should not have to guess what you are trying to accomplish.

Public Address Announcements and Other Interruptions

It is important that you and your students hear public address (PA) announcements. Therefore, you should explain that during such announcements there is to be no talking, and students should not attempt to ask questions or leave their desks. You should also listen during these announcements; it shows respect for your own rules. Other interruptions, such as visitors, office workers seeking information or forms, and loud noises in the hall may be a frequent distraction in your school. You can reduce their effects by teaching your students a procedure to handle interruptions. A simple one is to indicate that whenever you are interrupted, students should sit quietly with no talking if they have no assignment, read a book, or continue working if they already have an assignment. Be sure to have at least one set of handouts ready as a backup assignment in case the interruption is very long.

Special Equipment and Materials

When you have special equipment or materials that are likely to capture students' immediate interest (e.g., live animals), decide on policies for access and use and communicate them to students right away. For most special equipment, learning centers, and special materials, however, wait until the first time they are to be used to give a demonstration and instructions. You can also post a list of specific instructions.

Fire and Disaster Drills

Learn the procedures that are followed in your building. Because most secondary students know the basic procedures, a few timely sentences during the first week about the procedure for leaving the room (e.g., by row) will be sufficient. You should post a map showing where students are supposed to go. Eventually, a schoolwide rehearsal will be held.

Split Lunch Period

Tell students whether they should clear their desks or leave their work out when they are dismissed for lunch. Tell them whether it is safe to leave personal belongings in the room. Show or tell the class what route they should take from your room to the cafeteria and remind them of school areas that are off limits and of proper hallway behavior. Be specific as to the time class will resume and stick to it; otherwise, you will find students wasting 5 or more minutes every day.

■ Who Will I Teach? Considering Student Cultural Backgrounds

Consider the possibility that your class may contain students from cultural groups that are unfamiliar to you. For example, students might be immigrants, from another ethnic group, or living in a household with little access to financial resources and thus belong to a "culture" of poverty. Persons who don't have direct experience with such cultures tend to make false assumptions about them (Gorski, 2013; Higgs, 2014; Stairs, Donnell, & Dunn, 2012). For example, it might be assumed that parents don't care very much about the children's education or that they are lazy. Such stereotypic views might be reinforced by encountering individuals who fit the stereotype or by media reports, when, in fact, data strongly indicate that, for example, education is highly valued by immigrants, minority ethnic groups, and the poor, and that most such parents work very hard when jobs are available. A lack of familiarity with a cultural group's norms and practices may cause a teacher to misinterpret the way a student responds to classroom activities or procedures. If that misunderstanding is combined with a negative stereotype, then there is more potential for an overreaction to the student and a setback in the student's adjustment to the classroom and the teacher's ability to form a constructive relationship.

> *Jim rarely speaks in his ninth-grade class and never volunteers an answer. Even when called on, he gives limited answers. His teacher considers him unmotivated and lower achieving. In actuality, Jim's Navaho background causes him to value group accomplishment and to downplay asserting individual achievement when in a large group setting. His culture emphasizes community knowledge whereby the individual responding would be seen as boastful.*

There are other possibilities for a disconnect between common classroom practices and procedures and the cultural backgrounds of students. Consider the examples shared here and your view of them. For example, some cultures insist on a young person making eye contact with the adult in charge when they are being admonished. Others require a child to look down, out of respect to the adult. What do you expect? Similarly, handshakes, high-fives, fist bumps, and other limited and brief physical contact are successful ways to encourage student participation with expected procedures. However, in some cultures, physical contact with a nonrelative of the opposite sex is forbidden. How do you interpret a smile? In some cultures, smiling is seen as encouraging; whereas in others, it is seen as a sign of ignorance or lack of focus. Some teachers might use a paper-passing procedure to quickly and efficiently distribute work to students, but some students may see the teacher's efficiency as a sign that the work is not personally connected to them (and therefore not of value to complete). Would you lean on the side of efficiency or seek to hand papers directly to each student? If you discover a cultural norm that conflicts with your procedural practices, you have options. You can modify or drop the teaching practice (e.g., touching) when interacting with the affected student, seek advice from others (including the student's parents), or explain to the student that expected behavior in school is not always the same as at home or in the neighborhood.

In order to best prepare the social space of your classroom for the students you will teach, you will want to get to know them and their families. In advance of that opportunity, you can read recommendations in books such as Cary (2007), Gay (2010), or Higgs (2014). Perhaps you already know that your class will have students from a culture that is unfamiliar to you. If so, find a teacher or another person who has experience with the cultural group and discuss your classroom management plans. You could also do some reading about the group, with a view toward anticipating the issues that might arise.

■ Chapter Summary

Teachers communicate clear expectations to help students understand what they need to do in order to be successful in a classroom. A system of procedures and rules puts into place the details of those expectations. Thus, a significant planning task at the beginning of the year is to think through the set of expectations that will guide student behavior in general as well as in particular activities and instructional formats. A comprehensive set of suggestions is given in this chapter. Case studies provide additional concrete examples. Strategies for communicating the system to students, including soliciting the students' participation, are discussed. The "Who Will I Teach" section examines the possible influence of cultural factors.

■ Further Reading

Bicard, D. F. (2000). Using classroom rules to construct behavior. *Middle School Journal,* 31(5), 37–45.

This article does a good job of describing how rules are part of a comprehensive plan for establishing and maintaining appropriate behavior. Implementation involves teaching, monitoring, praising, and correcting.

Charles, A. S. (2012). Cell phones: Rule-setting, rule-breaking, and relationships in classrooms. *American Secondary Education, 40(3),* 4–16.

The prevalence of technological devices, including cell phones, ipads, and laptops, and the certainty of continuing innovation and new instructional applications make it complex to establish and enforce school policies and classroom procedures for their appropriate use. This article shows how different teachers and students constructed boundaries and adapted their usage practices.

Fenning, P. A., & Bohanon, H. (2006). Schoolwide discipline policies: An analysis of discipline codes of conduct. In C. Evertson and C. Weinstein (Eds.), *Handbook of classroom management* (pp. 1021–1039). Mahwah, NJ: Erlbaum.

The authors describe characteristics of schoolwide codes of conduct, including their history, purpose, and uses. Using a code of conduct to support positive student behaviors is emphasized—rather than setting up a system of punishments that increases expulsion or suspension rates.

Fenwick, D. T. (1998). Managing space, energy, and self: Junior high teachers' experiences of classroom management. *Teaching and Teacher Education, 14,* 619–631.

This study found that teachers think about their work in terms of classroom management, with three dominant aspects: managing classroom space and objects within it, managing persons and teaching practices, and managing themselves. Teachers organize space and behavior using routines that provide structure and help them manage student activity and energy.

pinterest.com/weareteachers/classroom-rules-that-work

Pinterist allows individuals (and, in this case, groups) to pin examples of resources they would like to return to or promote to others. When exploring the resources within this site, consider how the example fits with your developing philosophy of teaching as well as the students with whom you work. This particular group also includes pins for classroom organization (Chapter 3), classroom jobs (this chapter), lesson plans in specific instructional areas, and other topics.

Rubie-Davies, C. (2008). Teacher expectations. In T. L. Good (Ed.), *21st Century education* (vol. 1, pp. 254–264). Los Angeles: Sage.

The rules and procedures teachers establish for their classes convey a set of expectations to students. This chapter examines research on teacher expectations and provides a thoughtful basis for reflection on goals.

■ Suggested Activities

1. If you are currently working or participating in a school, identify the schoolwide rules and procedures teachers and students are expected to observe. Note any for which compliance seems to be an issue and why.

2. Conduct an Internet search using the descriptors "classroom rules and procedures" or similar terms. You'll find many websites developed by teachers who have posted their classroom systems. Review some of them and consider which ones can be useful for your classroom.

3. Read Case Studies 4.1 and 4.2 on the following pages. They illustrate classroom procedures and rules for most major areas, and they will be helpful as you develop your own system of management.

4. Reconsider the vignette of Mr. Smith at the beginning of the chapter. Work with a partner to describe five procedures this teacher could put in place to have a smoother, more orderly classroom.

5. Make a copy of the checklist at the end of the chapter. Observe a middle or high school classroom for 30 minutes (or find an online classroom-observation video of similar length). Fill in as many blanks as possible in the checklist to describe the procedures in this classroom. Which procedures were most helpful to the lesson's progression? Were there any additional procedures you would recommend to better support students' learning and behavior? Which procedures would you incorporate into your own classroom?

6. Develop a list of four to six classroom rules. Be sure they emphasize areas of classroom behavior that are important to you and to the functioning of your classroom. Compare and contrast your policies with those of colleagues. Discuss reasons for differences.

■ Case Study 4.1

RULES AND PROCEDURES IN AN EIGHTH-GRADE CLASS

The classroom rules in Ms. Ashley's English class were simple: Be prompt, be prepared, and be polite. When the tardy bell rang each day, students were expected to be in their seats copying the plan of the day shown on the overhead screen. This plan usually included the topic, objectives, and materials for the day's lesson and the assignment for homework. Thus, the beginning class routine for students consisted of putting away other materials, getting out their spiral notebooks, recording the date, and copying a daily plan. While students did this, the teacher checked roll. If students were tardy to class, they immediately signed a tardy roster on a table by the door and took their seats. The penalty for unexcused tardiness was 30 minutes of detention after school. Students who had a valid excuse checked the "Please excuse" column on the tardy roster and left their "tardy excuse form" in a tray next to the roster.

The "Be prepared" rule required that students bring their materials and completed homework assignments to class each day. Students were not allowed to return to their lockers. Unexcused late papers were not accepted, but incomplete work was accepted for partial credit.

The "Be polite" rule required that students not interrupt the teacher or other students when they were speaking to the class. To avoid interruptions and to give everyone an opportunity to speak during whole-class discussions or instruction, students were required to raise their hands to get permission to speak. However, the teacher did not limit questioning only to volunteers; any student could be called on at any time. This rule also covered listening carefully when the teacher or another student was addressing the class and being respectful when commenting or disagreeing with someone. Students were not to use the pencil sharpener or do other distracting things during discussions or other interactive activities.

Ms. Ashley's students were allowed to leave their seats to turn in work at designated trays or to get supplies of materials from shelves without permission from the teacher, but if individuals wandered and bothered other students, they lost their privilege and had to raise their hands for permission. When seatwork began, the teacher circulated among students, checked progress, and gave individual feedback and/or instruction. She later sat at a worktable from which she could monitor the class easily while she helped individuals or small groups. Students raised their hands for permission to come to the table. Sometimes the table was used for peer tutoring.

Consequences of breaking class rules or not following procedures were related to a schoolwide system of demerits. Demerits resulted in detention after school and in contacting parents. Ms. Ashley emphasized communication with parents about student behavior and work. She called or emailed students' parents with good news as well as bad. Each grading term she presented awards to students who had very good attendance and behavior records, as well as those who did outstanding work and those who improved their work during the term.

Each day, Ms. Ashley used the last few minutes of class for cleanup and announcements. If students were working on individual assignments, she had them stop, get their supplies ready to go, return materials to shelves, and check around their desks for papers and trash. Then she made announcements of upcoming events and reminded students of any unusual supplies they would need to bring the following day. After the bell rang, she dismissed her students.

■ Case Study 4.2

PROCEDURES FOR SMALL-GROUP WORK/ LABORATORY ACTIVITIES

The day before her science class had its first laboratory assignment, Ms. Davis discussed procedures and rules for group work and use of the laboratory facilities. The policies she discussed included the following:

1. Work with your assigned partner(s). Participate, do your share of the work, and be polite and considerate.

2. Raise your hand for assistance from the teacher. Don't call out.

3. All talk should be quiet and work related.

4. Stay at your group-workstations unless it is necessary to get supplies. Don't wander or return to your desk until the teacher tells you to do so.

5. Read instructions on the board or worksheet, and listen to the teacher's instructions.

6. When you finish work, check your worksheet to be sure it is complete and neat. If there is extra time, ask the teacher for more lab instructions. If there are none, read the references listed for the day's lesson.

7. The teacher dismisses the class. The class will not be dismissed until the laboratory area is clean.

8. Report broken equipment quietly and quickly to the teacher.

9. Obey laboratory safety rules: Never turn on gas jets unless instructed to do so; never put anything in electrical outlets; never drink from laboratory faucets; stay out of the laboratory storeroom; keep your hands away from your mouth and eyes; wash your hands after laboratory activities; no horseplay.

Students in this class worked in pairs for most laboratory activities. Partner assignments were changed several times during the year, not at every lab session. On the day of a lab, Ms. Davis began activities by quickly going over the objectives of the lesson, the grading criteria, and the procedures listed on the lab worksheet. If the laboratory activities consisted of several major parts, she suggested time allotments for each part to help students pace themselves. The teacher also had a list of some references in the text and from other sources in the room for students to read for background information if they completed their worksheet early. New words or terms used on the worksheet were defined. If the laboratory work involved many procedures, the teacher helped students divide the work. For example, jobs for Partner A and for Partner B were listed separately, either on the chalkboard or overhead screen. Two separate supply stations were often used to avoid congestion.

During lab activities, the teacher circulated and answered the questions of students who raised their hands. Ms. Davis gave several reminders about time, providing a 10-minute, a 5-minute, and a 2-minute warning before cleanup. She allowed plenty of time for cleanup (usually at least 5 minutes before the end of the period). To make sure the class did not run overtime, she used a kitchen timer. Immediately after cleanup, the teacher had all students return to their desks. There, she discussed any common procedural or academic problems. This information was helpful to students in future lab sessions and in filling out or correcting their worksheet for the day.

Sometimes Ms. Davis used work groups for discussions, problem-solving sessions, or test review. For these activities, she decided on group assignments ahead of time and listed names of students in each group on the overhead screen, along with specific responsibilities within groups (e.g., discussion leader, recorder, reporter, supplier). Tables and/or groups of desks were numbered before students arrived, and students were told to sit in the group indicated on the list. In arranging seating beforehand, the teacher spread these groups as far apart as possible in the classroom. Then, as soon as class began, Ms. Davis went over the objectives, procedures, and grading criteria for the activity before letting students begin work. Especially at the beginning of the year, she reminded students of the classroom rules for group work. As students worked in groups, she carried a clipboard so that she could note participation easily. At the end of group discussion activities, students always filled out self-evaluations on how well their group had met the objectives of the lesson, how well they had followed the small-group activity rules, and how well they, individually, had met their responsibilities to their group.

■ Checklist: Classroom Procedures

Check When Complete	Area	What Is Your Procedure in This Area?
	General Procedures	
☐	A. Beginning of period	_____
☐	1. Attendance check	_____
☐	2. Previously absent students	_____
☐	3. Tardy students	_____
☐	4. Expected student behavior	_____
☐	B. Out-of-room policies	_____
☐	C. Materials and equipment	_____
☐	1. What to bring to class	_____
☐	2. Pencil sharpener	_____
☐	3. Other room equipment	_____
☐	4. Student contact with teacher's desk, storage, other materials	_____

☐   D. Ending the period   _____

Seat-Work and Instruction Procedures

☐   A. Student attention   _____

☐   B. Student participation   _____

☐   C. Seat-work procedures   _____

☐   1. Talk among students   _____

☐   2. Obtaining help   _____

☐   3. Out of seat   _____

☐   4. When seat work has been completed   _____

Student Group Work

☐   A. Use of materials and supplies   _____

☐   B. Assignment of students to groups   _____

☐   C. Student participation and behavior   _____

Miscellaneous

☐   A. Signals   _____

☐   B. Behavior during interruptions   _____

☐   C. Special equipment   _____

☐   D. Fire and disaster drills   _____

☐   E. Split lunch period   _____

MyEducationLab *Self-Check 4.1*

MyEducationLab *Self-Check 4.2*

MyEducationLab *Application Exercise 4.1*   Using what you've learned in this chapter, view the video and respond to the questions.

MyEducationLab *Application Exercise 4.2*   Using what you've learned in this chapter, read and respond to this scenario.

MyEducationLab *Application Exercise 4.3*   Using what you've learned in this chapter, view the video and respond to the questions.

MyEducationLab *Application Exercise 4.4*   Using what you've learned in this chapter, read and respond to this scenario.

MyEducationLab *Classroom Management Simulation 4.1*   Engage with the Classroom Management Simulation *Creating Classroom Behavioral Expectations.*

Diego Cervo/Shutterstock

CHAPTER 5

Managing Student Work

When we presented a set of procedures for establishing an orderly classroom setting in Chapter 4, we indicated that additional procedures would be needed to help manage student work and learning. In this chapter, we describe the additional procedures that are aimed at encouraging students to complete assignments and to engage in other learning activities. Ultimately, the goal of a system for managing student work is to help students become independent learners; thus, your procedures should give as much responsibility as possible to the students themselves rather than depend on either you or parents to see that assignments are completed.

As we discuss student work procedures, it is easy to focus on the products students will create: completed assignments, test scores, and so on. These are the tangible, measurable outcomes of the activities you will engage in with students each day. It is important, nevertheless, not to lose sight of your goal as a teacher: to facilitate student learning. Your system for managing student work should lead you and your students to examine their learning and the learning process in which they are engaged.

In all academic core subjects and in many others, students are given assignments or projects frequently, perhaps even daily. Projects, written assignments, problem sets, and a variety of other academic tasks are typical of the secondary school curriculum. Sometimes these assignments are done in class, at other times they are given as homework, or perhaps both. Assignments are important for learning and retention because they provide systematic practice, application, and repeated exposure to concepts. Consequently, your management system supports learning when it supports consistent and successful engagement in these assignments.

71

However, when procedures for managing student work are not working well or when students are not held accountable for their performance and learning, many problems can occur. Consider the following vignette.

Toward the end of the first grading period, Ms. La Rosa noticed several disturbing signs of lack of student interest in completing written work in her social studies classes. The deadline had passed for students to turn in their first major project of the year—a report on their state's water resources—and fewer than half the students had met the deadline. The teacher then extended the due date by one week. But even with the extension, one quarter of the reports were not turned in. Those reports that were completed were disappointing because many consisted mainly of pictures of water scenes clipped from magazines or downloaded from Wikipedia or another website. Ms. La Rosa had suggested the Internet as one resource—not as the sole source of information. Many of the reports looked as though they had been thrown together the night before they were due. With a sinking feeling, Ms. La Rosa realized that if she graded strictly, many students would do poorly. Because she had intended to use the report for a major portion of the students' grades, some students were in danger of failing.

To make matters worse, numerous students had not been completing recent shorter assignments, and many of those that were completed were of poor quality. These had not been demanding assignments, and they were well within most students' capabilities. The activities included completing worksheets and answering questions listed at the end of the text chapters. Ms. La Rosa typically had students do two or three such assignments each week and place them in their notebooks. She collected them every three weeks and assigned a grade to the notebook. Of the students who did complete all assignments, quite a few did them poorly, with sloppy or partially completed work. The teacher felt herself caught in a dilemma. If she graded strictly (or just fairly), many students would fail, and she might face great resistance from both students and their parents. However, if she relaxed her grading standards, students would learn that they could get away with not doing their work.

Pause and Consider

Discuss with a partner your responses to the following questions:

1. What are some of the difficulties students are experiencing with this project?
2. What are Ms. La Rosa's expectations?
3. What are some of the issues preventing the project from matching these expectations?
4. How might a written description of the project look?

Discussion

It is clear that many students in Ms. La Rosa's classes do not feel accountable for completing work carefully or on time. The basis for absence of effort and the middling work can be determined from answers to the following questions.

- Do students know how each assignment contributes to their overall grade?
- Are requirements for assignments clear with respect to standards for quality, amount of work, and due dates?
- Is student progress being monitored frequently enough?
- What kinds of feedback do students receive about their progress as well as about their completed work? How immediate is the feedback?

In each area, Ms. La Rosa could have done several things to encourage students to complete assignments promptly and correctly. This chapter text focuses on aspects of classroom procedures that communicate the importance of work assignments, enabling students to understand what is expected of them and helping them make desired progress. Critical procedures for which you must plan include your grading system, monitoring and feedback, and communicating assignments and work requirements. Each of these areas is discussed here. The Checklist for Managing Student Work at the end of this chapter will help organize your planning in these areas, and case studies at the end of the chapter will provide further help.

■ Your Grading System and Record Keeping

At the end of each grading period, you will have to record a report card grade for each student. How you determine this grade has important implications for classroom management. Grades are very important to most students (and to their parents) because they are tangible evidence of student accomplishment. It is therefore important that your grading system accurately reflect the quality of student work. In addition, you will want to use your grading system to help ensure that students complete their assignments by the due dates.

The first thing you should do before deciding on a grading system is to determine whether your department, school, or district has any policies that you must follow. Usually, a school or district will have established a numerical standard for grades (e.g., 90–100 = A, 80–89 = B, etc.). If so, you will have to become familiar with the policy and adapt your grading system to it.

After determining the relevant school policies, you should identify the components of your grading system. Most secondary teachers use several factors in grading students. Academic achievement is the most important one, of course, but effort, participation, homework, and improvement are also given weight by many teachers

(McMillan, 2001). High school teachers are more likely to use major exams than are middle school teachers.

Remember that the most accurate assessment of performance will generally be based on frequent evaluation of all aspects of student work, not on a few test scores or a major project grade. Consider your grading system carefully. Avoid systems that give very large weights to single tests or assignments. Also, realize that using 0 for missing assignments results in "catastrophe" grading (Carifio & Carey, 2009) in which one or a few such scores makes a failing grade inevitable. The grading system should permit students to stumble occasionally but still be able to recover sufficiently to succeed overall. A system incorporating a daily or weekly grade that contributes significantly to an overall grade allows for frequent evaluation and feedback and keeps students accountable for their everyday work; it is an important aid to the academic success of many students. In subjects that have individual projects extending over several days or weeks (for example, industrial arts, home economics, science, social studies, or writing projects in English), a teacher can still examine student work daily and record a grade or note satisfactory or unsatisfactory progress.

In addition to daily assignments, frequently used components of grading systems are tests, papers, projects, workbooks, quizzes, performance, quality of participation (as in discussions), and extra-credit work. Many teachers include student notebook grades in their grading system. Students are required to keep all their work organized in a notebook, which is graded periodically for completeness and neatness. Often, students must make corrections on all graded work before putting it in their notebooks. If you want students to keep notebooks, be explicit about what should be placed in the notebook and how it should be organized. (It is a good idea to include this information in a course syllabus.) The notebook should include a table of contents and/or a list of assignments. Also, a sample notebook can be displayed so that students can see what is required. These practices encourage students to be organized and help them keep track of materials they need to study for exams. In planning your grading system, be sure that you can manage the bookkeeping aspects and remember that you will have to evaluate 25 to 30 or more students in each class. Finally, note that students' grades and other personal information are confidential. Protect your grade book, printed summaries, and/or passwords to maintain data security.

HI & LOIS © Distributed by King Features Syndicated, Inc. World Rights Reserved.

After you have identified the components of your grading system, decide what percentage of a student's grade each component will represent. Once you have decided on your system, you can post it on your class website, where it will be available to both students and their parents. You can also prepare a handout with this information for students to take home for a parent or guardian to sign. This procedure has several virtues. For one thing, it makes very clear to students what criteria will be used to determine the grade. It also informs the parents, who may then be of assistance in monitoring progress or assisting their child. Having provided this information to the parents, you may find it helpful later in the year to refer to it when discussing their child's progress in your class.

If your grading system contains unusual features, the recommendations in the preceding paragraph will be especially important. Posting the information on your website or providing it in written form helps signal its importance, and it might prompt students to seek clarification if they don't understand some aspect. Also, parents apprised of your system may be more supportive than those who learn of it only after some problem has occurred.

Perhaps your school will provide software (e.g., Blackboard, GradeSpeed) that will allow you to record student performance data and calculate report card grades. If not, you may purchase such software or even download freeware from the Internet. Well-written programs contain features that construct seating charts and compute grades based on various weighting methods. These features can make grade calculation more efficient, but data entry can be time consuming if the grading system includes daily grades or other multiple components that are frequently recorded. Teachers who have such systems sometimes choose to maintain a traditional grade book for daily grades and transfer a summary score into the computer for use in calculating a report card grade. Because the information entered into such programs is confidential, the program needs to be used securely with password-protected access. A backup copy of the files is essential to prevent a loss of student grade information. Determine whether your school's computer system automatically backs up information in each teacher's classroom computer. If it does not, be certain to do so yourself and/or maintain a paper copy of grade book information.

■ Feedback and Monitoring Procedures

Good monitoring procedures are essential to providing quality feedback to students, and regular feedback is more desirable than infrequent feedback because it offers students more information and reduces the amount of time they spend making errors. If you give daily assignments, you will almost certainly wish to involve students in checking them because your time will be too limited to check 125 to 150 assignments every day. Of course, you cannot expect students to check complex assignments calling for advanced levels of knowledge (e.g., essay scoring). However, many daily assignments are of a more routine nature and can be checked by students. The following procedures should be kept in mind:

1. Students can be allowed to check some of their own assignments. You can reduce the temptation to be dishonest by requiring that a different color pen (or pencil) be used for checking. When students do check and correct their own work, you must monitor them closely and at least occasionally collect and spot-check the papers yourself.

2. Describe and model to students how you want the checking done; for example, mark or circle incorrect answers, put "graded by" and the name in a specified place on the paper, put the number missed or correct or the grade at the top of the first page, and so on.

3. If a student feels that his or her paper was marked incorrectly by another student, a simple system is to have the student write a note to that effect on a designated part of the paper. You can then verify the work when you examine the papers.

4. We do not recommend the practice of recording grades by having students call them out. If you do not wish to collect an assignment after checking, a simple procedure is to have students leave the work on their desks so that you can record grades as you move from student to student. This can be done during a later seat-work or classwork activity to avoid leaving students in dead time while you record their grades.

When you have students working on long-term projects, it is important to help them make satisfactory progress. Break the assignment into parts or checkpoints and then set deadlines and goals for each part. A term paper, for example, might have intermediate checkpoints established for (1) a description of the topic and thesis statement, (2) a list of sources and an outline, and (3) a rough draft. It is not necessary (or efficient) to collect the interim products; instead, circulate around the room to check each student's work and give feedback. You might assign a letter grade for satisfactory progress at some major checkpoint, though most teachers who use checkpoints assign a simpler "satisfactory/unsatisfactory" assessment. For a construction project, a plan or description of the project or major stages in its completion can be evaluated as an intermediate check.

SHOE-NEW BUSINESS © MacNelly – Distributed by King Features Syndicate, Inc. World Rights Reserved.

Group projects require special attention to feedback and monitoring. Identifying a timeline for progress checkpoints (e.g., proposal, mid-project progress report, group presentation) will help you and the students stay on course. Discuss the criteria for evaluation and then solicit the students' input to encourage awareness and commitment to high standards. Teachers often use such discussions to develop a rubric—that is, a set of outcomes and perhaps rating scales for evaluating important outcomes. Students can be encouraged to use the rubric for monitoring their own group's progress. More material on managing student work in groups is presented in Chapter 8.

Some teachers utilize peer review of first drafts of written products or project plans. Peer feedback from such reviews can stimulate new learning and promote student reflection, thereby improving the quality of student products. Peer review is usually done in a small-group format (e.g., pairs), so the teacher should prepare students for the activity by, for example, conducting a discussion of the types of feedback and comments that are desirable and most likely to be helpful.

Monitoring Student Work in Progress

Monitoring student progress helps you identify students who are having difficulty and enables you to encourage other students to keep working. After you have given students an assignment, pay careful attention to their work. Seat-work activities need a guided beginning. If you immediately begin to work at your desk or go to help one student without first checking to see that all are working, some students may not even begin, and others may proceed incorrectly. Two simple strategies will help avoid this situation. First, you can assure a smooth transition into seat work by beginning the assignment as a whole-class activity; that is, have everyone take out papers, worksheets, or other materials, and then answer the first question or two or work the first few problems together as a group. Ask the first question, solicit an answer, discuss it, and have students record it on their papers. Not only will this procedure ensure that all students begin working, but immediate problems with the assignment can be identified and solved.

A second way to monitor student involvement in the assignment is to circulate around the room and check each student's progress periodically. This allows corrective feedback to be given when needed and helps keep students responsible for appropriate progress. Avoid going only to students who raise their hands for assistance; otherwise, you will never note the progress of students who may be reluctant to ask for help.

Monitoring the Completion of Assignments

Consider how you will collect work. When all students are turning in materials at the same time, one efficient procedure is to have papers passed in a given direction until you have all papers in your hands. Bulky materials such as notebooks or journals might be collected by designated helpers and stacked in a particular spot. Papers or assignments turned in by students at varying times can be placed in labeled baskets, trays, or plastic containers. Having students identify their papers by an assigned number corresponding to their alphabetical order makes sequencing papers a fast task for easy recording. Locate drop-off spots away from congested areas or areas that might be distracting to students. If students are submitting assignments online, consider setting up an email account for that sole purpose so students' work does not get overlooked or lost by intermingling with other messages. Let students know the procedure you expect them to use. Following it consistently saves time and prevents confusion.

There may be occasions when you will prefer not to collect work, but you do wish to retain some record of it. A simple procedure is to have students place their work at a designated corner of their desks so that you can easily identify the work as you move about the room. This procedure is especially useful for checking work in progress or a mid-project milestone.

Long-Range Monitoring

Be sure to monitor completion rates and performance levels on assignments. The first time a student fails to turn in an assignment, talk with him or her about it. If the student needs help, give help, but require that the work be done. If the student neglects two assignments consecutively or begins a pattern of skipping occasional assignments, call the parent(s) or send a note home or an email notice immediately. Be friendly and encouraging, but insist that the work be done. Don't delay making contacts with the parents, and above all don't rely on using only the grade at the end of the grading period to communicate that a student's performance is below par. By then, a pattern of poor performance may have developed from which the student will find it difficult to recover.

Parents can also access their children's grades via teachers' online grading records as well as check attendance in their child's classes and assignment due dates and requirements. The school's grading software program may also allow parents to set grade and attendance triggers that will send them an email when their child's grade drops below whatever number the parent has set or if the student misses a class. Of course, not all parents have access to the Internet, nor will all parents necessarily use it to keep track of their child's progress. For those who do, however, these systems provide an efficient basis for parent–teacher communication.

Managing the Paperwork

Keeping up with all the paper generated by student assignments can be overwhelming. One way to avoid mountains of "back papers" is to look over, grade, record, and return assignments quickly. Not only is this timely feedback for your students, but it also helps you to spot students who are "fading" and to diagnose areas needing whole-class remediation. Be realistic about your grading capabilities. Try not to get overwhelmed. If you are behind in grading six sets of papers and are planning to assign essays due in two days, rethink your plans. Allow yourself enough grading time to do the job well—on the last paper as well as the first. Try making a grading schedule to distribute a huge task into manageable segments rather than plowing through until you are exhausted. Instead of collecting, checking, grading, and returning each assignment, try another routine: Go around the room to check each student's work. Record a grade or note completion as you move to each student's desk. This type of checking is fast, personal, and efficient and is especially effective for written assignments that require holistic assessment. Remember, not every problem in the textbook needs to be assigned, nor every problem completed be graded. Decide, and communicate clearly to both students and parents, when assignments are being assessed for completion and when they are being assessed for accuracy or demonstration of mastery.

■ Communicating Assignments and Work Requirements

Students need a clear idea of what their assignments are and what is expected of them. This means that the teacher must explain all requirements and features of the assignments. However, that alone will not be enough. Not all students will listen carefully, some students may be absent when the assignment and requirements are discussed, and the assignment itself may be complex. In addition, there is more to completing assignments than doing the work accurately; standards for neatness, legibility, and form should be considered. Although we do not want to encourage an overemphasis on form to the neglect of content, some standards in these areas must be set. After all, good work habits, neatness, and careful attention to detail are valued attributes in most occupations. The following three areas should be considered.

Instructions for Assignments

In addition to making an oral explanation of the assignment requirements, you should post the assignment and important instructions. Use the procedure of requiring that students copy the assignment into a notebook or onto an assignment sheet. Consider posting an assignment calendar or keeping an assignment notebook available. Such a record will be helpful to students who have been absent.

The grading criteria and requirements for each assignment should be clear and explained to students. If the instructions are complex, as for a long-term project or portfolio, it is best to post the requirements on your class website and/or have students copy the instructions into their notebooks. If in-class performance is to be evaluated—as in a group project report, drama and speech class activities, or science lab—tell students exactly what you will be rating (e.g., following correct laboratory procedures, working quietly and cooperatively, cleaning up) and how much weight (or how many points) each factor will carry.

Information about developing criteria for assignments, projects, reports, and so on can be found at rubistar.4teachers.org. This site allows you to search for examples of teacher-created rubrics on a wide variety of topics. Ideas for alternative criteria may be helpful when you create your own rubrics, and you may be able to quickly tailor an existing rubric to the assignment you are giving to your students.

Standards for Form, Neatness, and Due Dates

You'll have to decide whether students may use pencil or pen and what color or colors of ink are acceptable. If students may complete written work on a word processor, what size and style of font is acceptable? Also communicate to students what type of paper and notebook are to be used in class and whether students should write on the backs of pages. A policy for neatness should also be determined. Students need to know whether you will accept paper torn from a spiral notebook, how to treat errors (e.g., draw a line through them, circle them, erase), and how stringent you are about legibility. You should think about the consequences for students who do not complete work properly. Will you deduct points or reduce the grade on the assignment? Because some students may turn in incomplete work, you must decide whether you will accept it and grade only what is done, subtracting the part not done from the grade, or whether you will accept late papers only when complete and assess a late penalty.

"Oh no, not homework again."

Arnie Levin/The New Yorker Collection/The Cartoon Bank

Decide on a heading for students to use on their papers. Post a sample heading, have students make copies to keep in their notebooks, and go over it with students the first time they are to use it. You may have to remind them of this heading several times during the early weeks of school.

Finally, due dates should be reasonable and clear; exceptions should not be made without good cause. Tell students your policy for turning in work on time, and follow it consistently. If you regularly extend the due dates for assignments, students may learn that they can negotiate for extra time and may not use their time well. In general, insist that work not done on time be completed at home or after school. This assumes, of course, that students possess the necessary knowledge or skills to do the work on their own. When possible, post due dates online for easier student and parent access.

Procedures for Absent Students

When students are absent from classes, they miss instruction, directions for assignments, and assistance they may need in getting work under way. Establishing routines for handling makeup work can be very helpful to returning students. Routines will also help prevent these students from milling around your desk asking questions about missed assignments and from interrupting you to obtain directions for makeup work. Consider the following items:

1. Post the daily and long-term assignments on the class website and scan essential handouts. Doing so regularly will give absent students easy access to them and may even allow students to complete some of the makeup work prior to returning to school. Using the class website, students who don't have home access to the Internet can obtain their makeup assignments on a classroom or library computer following their return to school. You can also keep an assignment folder or calendar for each class, allowing previously absent students to refer to it.
2. Decide how much time will be allowed for making up work (e.g., one day late per absent day). For students who are absent for lengthy periods, it would be a good idea to meet with them and/or contact parents to identify what assignments must be made up and when.
3. Set up a place where students can turn in makeup work and where they can pick it up after it has been checked (e.g., baskets or trays labeled "Makeup work" and "Graded"). The "Graded" basket will also provide a place where students can pick up any graded work that was distributed while they were absent.
4. Establish a regular time, such as 30 minutes before or after school, when you will be available to assist students with makeup work. Also, you can use student volunteeers who will be available at particular times of the class period (usually during seat work) or out of class to help students with makeup work.
5. Determine how students who have missed group work will make it up. Assist groups in planning for the inclusion of absent members and in helping those members catch up when they return.

■ Who Will I Teach? Students Frequently Absent

Sometimes when envisioning what our classrooms and students will be like, we overlook the likelihood that one or more of our students may frequently be absent. Chronic absence, defined as missing 10 percent or more of school days, affects, on average, around 1 in 10 primary grade students and somewhat fewer in later elementary grades. At the high school level, chronic absenteeism varies across types of schools and communities, but an average rate of around 6 percent is typical (Sheldon & Epstein, 2004). There are many reasons for frequent absence, including homelessness, transitional living arrangements (e.g., between various family members or juvenile system/foster home placements), and severe or chronic health problems. Other contributing causes may include inflexible employer schedules, parental or caregiver neglect or illness, school refusal, and bullying in and out of school (Chang & Romero, 2008). In all of these instances, the students' intermittent access to resources and/or lowered attendance will play a role in managing their work.

Chronic absence has negative effects on the student for obvious reasons: Instruction is missed, opportunities for practice and feedback are diminished, and peer relationships at school are disrupted. Chronic absence may also be a prelude to dropping out of school. Along with these issues, the student must somehow cope with the problem that has caused the absences in the first place, be it an illness, a family crisis, or poverty. Chronic student absence also affects teachers' work; it takes time to provide make-up instruction and arrange assignments; instructional activities can also be affected by slow-downs if a previously absent student does not understand instruction and needs remediation.

Absences due to illness can be lengthy, including when a student experiences frequent intermittent absences because of treatment and/or associated travel. In such cases, teachers are usually informed of the situation by a parent or the school counselor's office. A special teacher may work with the student in a hospital or at home to assist in keeping up with assignments. After conferring with parents, the teacher can encourage students in class to send cards or notes, email, or other electronic messages of support in order to maintain peer contact. To prepare for the transition back to the classroom, helpful guidance for the teacher may be provided from the student's medical team and parents or school nurse regarding possible effects of medications on the child's behavior or learning. Also discussed should be what information would be appropriate to share with classmates. To assist in the transition back to class, it might be helpful if the school nurse, counselor, or a parent is involved.

Sexson and Madan-Swain (1993) offer helpful suggestions for working with a student during the transition back into the classroom:

Avoid teaching at a frustration level.

Help the student to structure tasks so that he or she can proceed step by step.

Be firm. Do not allow the student to escape a task he or she is currently capable of completing.

Allow the student freedom to take breaks and move around. (pp. 117–118)

If a student's absence is more than occasional and *not* health-related, then one of the other previously mentioned causes must be suspected. Your school may have a policy that a staff member will phone a parent/guardian anytime a student doesn't come to school. This procedure has been found to be effective in reducing absences (McConnell & Kubina, 2014). It's also a good idea for the teacher to call as well, in order to get information about what is keeping the student away, to make arrangements for making up work, and to encourage the caregiver to make arrangements to get the student to school.

Developing home–school relationships in addition to contacts about absences appears to be linked to improving attendance across a number of school sites (Sheldon, 2007). Strategies for communicating with caregivers include describing ways to support their child's efforts to learn at home and in school, providing information about the student's progress, giving ideas for ways to help with assignments, and inviting the parent to attend school functions. Parents working several jobs to make ends meet, whose housing arrangements are transitional, or who are experiencing other stressors will usually appreciate your efforts at communication even if they are not able to fully participate. At least you will gain some knowledge about the student's situation and what steps might be taken next.

In the classroom, an important teaching task with students whose disrupted connections are related to poverty or family crises will be to build a productive relationship to nurture a sense of safety and belonging. A good relationship will help encourage the student to want to come to school, to keep a more positive attitude, and to persevere during difficult times. More than likely, these students may not have consistent meals outside of school or resources for completing schoolwork. Often such students will not have access to school supplies. Your principal, school counselor, or school social worker should be contacted to help you determine how these issues can be addressed. Typically, your school will have a fund that can be used to assist with the student's expenses. In addition, motivation and capacity to learn may be lagging for students when the lack of sleep, food, health, and/or the presence of chronic stress come into play.

Students in these situations may have deficiencies in some content areas. Depending on their needs, you can keep a folder of past assignments and select from those that will help the students understand the basics they will need for their work. Also, you can assign one or two peers to help with assignments and to understand how things are done in your class. Be ready to help direct them if you see them floundering. It may be necessary to set individual goals for progress, and the student may be aided by having concrete outcomes to work toward, such as completion of specific assignments with an opportunity to redo work to reach a standard. Here are a few more ideas to consider:

- Keep an assignment book so that students can find what they are missing and catch up.
- Designate in-class helpers who will assist the student. Be sure to tell the student to ask the "buddy" for assistance.
- If you regularly use small groups to organize activities in your classroom, be sure to place the student with a group that has students likely to be helpful.

You can talk to your group about the student's situation in general terms: "_____ is going through some struggles this year with health [or family or living arrangements] and will need our help to get through this. I know _____ doesn't want anyone to do his [her] work, but I know he [she] would appreciate some help with keeping track of assignments and getting work completed. I'll talk with you about what needs to be done. . . ."

- You might need to individualize some assignments in order for the student to keep up and to avoid being overwhelmed by all the work that has been missed. A student who returns from a 2- or 3-week hospital stay or who is spending nights in a shelter may not have the ability to complete assignments after school hours.
- If the student has one or more good friends in class (you can ask the student or the parent/guardian), the friend(s) may be willing to assist after school hours.
- If your school has a volunteer program, enlist a volunteer's help to work with the student.

■ Chapter Summary

Student work provides teachers with an opportunity to see what the students are learning and where they may need additional instruction. Managing the ebb and flow of student work requires teachers to communicate clearly what is being assigned, how to do it, when to do it, and where to turn it in, as well as how to make up the assignment if a student is absent. In addition, students need teachers to monitor the students' progress on assignments to check instructional clarity and to assist students with learning in the process. Managing the student work after it is completed means maintaining accurate, up-to-date records; providing timely feedback to students; and teaching students how to reflect on their own work. A final section considers effective procedures for helping students who are chronically absent.

■ Further Reading

Bambrick-Santoyo, P. (2010). Driven by data: A practical guide to improve instruction. San Francisco, CA: Jossey-Bass.

This practical text provides descriptions, directions, and examples of data-driven instruction in classrooms. The author provides reteaching strategies, scripts, and advice for data meetings for teachers and schools to strive for high achievement with all students.

Eilam, B. (2001). Primary strategies for promoting homework performance. *American Educational Research Journal, 38,* 691–725.

> *This study provides details about the reasons some students experience great difficulty completing homework satisfactorily, including not keeping track of assignments, not organizing their work, and having limited understanding of the task. The research highlights the importance of teaching students to record assignments, to be able to locate the record, set deadlines, organize their work, and know how to proceed with the task on their own.*

Guskey, Thomas R. (Ed.). (1996). *Communicating student learning.* Alexandria, VA: Association for Supervision and Curriculum Development.

> *This ASCD Yearbook contains chapters on many aspects of communicating student learning, including grading of students with special needs, reporting methods for different grade levels, alternatives to traditional grading, and the use of technology.*

Kuhn, D. (2007, June). How to produce a high-achieving child. *Phi Delta Kappan, 88*(10), 757–763.

> *In this short article, the author considers what schools are and should be doing to provide meaningful learning experiences for students. She describes key research and makes several clear recommendations for focusing instruction in ways that motivate students to know the hows and whys as well as the whats of subject matter.*

Shores, E., & Grace, K. (2005). *The portfolio book: A step-by-step guide for teachers.* Upper Saddle River, NJ: Pearson Prentice Hall.

> *This work provides portfolio assessment techniques in easy-to-manage steps covering several major features in one book: portfolio assessment, practical applications, usable forms, emphasis on family involvement, and teacher reflection.*

www.apa.org/education/k12/classroom-data.aspx

> *This site shares the teaching module Using Classroom Data to Give Systematic Feedback to Students to Improve Learning, providing some dos and don'ts of managing student work for the purpose of improving learning.*

www.ascd.org/publications/educational-leadership/dec07/vol65/num04/Feedback-That-Fits.aspx

> *Susan Brookhart discusses "Feedback That Fits" by considering feedback delivery, content, and effectiveness. She includes examples of potential feedback with evaluative statements for their appropriate use.*

■ Suggested Activities

1. Choose a subject and grade you will teach, then identify the kinds of products or performances (daily assignments, papers, tests, projects) you will use to show evidence of student learning. Use the checklist at the end of this chapter to organize your plan for managing different types of student work.

2. You can obtain additional ideas for managing student work at the website atozteacherstuff.com (click on the link for "Tips") as well as other sites for teachers such as scholastic.com or 712educators.about.com. Use these sites to identify alternative procedures for managing different aspects of student work. As part of a group discussion activity, compare your procedures to those developed by other group members.

3. Reread the vignette that introduced this chapter. Based on the suggestions made in the rest of the chapter, identify some procedures or actions this teacher might have taken to prevent the problems she is facing.

4. Read Case Studies 5.1, 5.2, and 5.3, noting positive examples and ideas you might apply to your own classroom.

5. In Activity 1 you assumed a particular grade or age level of the students. Now assume that you will teach a class several grades above or below that level. How would such a change affect the procedures you use to work in the new setting? Discuss the rationale for any changes in your plans.

■ Case Study 5.1

MANAGING STUDENT WORK IN A MIDDLE SCHOOL ENGLISH CLASS

Ms. Clark posted on her class website a weekly chart listing daily activities and showing the maximum number of points students could earn for each activity (a possible 100 points for daily work and tests per week). The students kept a copy of that weekly chart in their notebooks, recorded the points they earned beside each assignment, and had the sheet signed by their parents each week. Students also kept a list of books and materials to bring to class each day.

In addition to the weekly chart, the teacher listed daily activities on the front whiteboard. Her lessons followed the order on the list, and at several times during each class period she pointed out to students their progress on the list. When describing seatwork assignments, Ms. Clark told students how much time they would have to complete each assignment; she then actively monitored students as they worked, circulating and providing assistance. During class discussions, she made sure that all students participated by calling on nonvolunteers as well as volunteers at least once and by keeping a checklist to be sure everyone responded.

Students who had been absent were expected to find their assignments on the weekly list, confer with the teacher before or after school, and file makeup work in a special folder. Students picked up papers that were handed back in their absence from an "Absent" basket. The first few times the teacher placed an absent student's paper into this basket, she reminded the class whose responsibility it was to get the paper.

Ms. Clark was consistent in her procedures for checking student work. She had students check their own work with red pen or pencil. She always collected papers afterward. Sometimes she had students turn papers in for checking and grading. Students recorded their points on their weekly assignment sheets when the papers were handed back. All papers for the week were handed back by the end of class on Friday. Students were expected to record their grades on their assignment sheets and have them signed by a parent.

■ Case Study 5.2

MANAGING STUDENT WORK IN A MATH CLASS

An important tool in Mr. Richard's system was a notebook he required his students to maintain. On the first day of class, he introduced it by showing a sample notebook. In addition to daily assignments and tests, the notebook included a grade sheet that was sectioned for recording homework grades, test grades, pop quiz scores, and a notebook score. Students recorded their grades on this page each marking period, calculated an average, and compared their computations with the teacher's to verify their grades. Major tests were put in the notebooks after having been signed by parents. The notebook also had a section for the class notes that students regularly took during presentations. Mr. Richard collected and assigned a grade to student notebooks a week before the end of the grading period. The notebook grade was given a weight equal to a major test grade in determining the student's course grade. Although he did not collect the notebooks until late in the grading period, Mr. Richard circulated around the room to check notebooks several times before collecting them. The first time he checked the notebooks, shortly after the beginning of the first grading period, Mr. Richard simply looked for correct form and made sure that each student had begun using a notebook. Several weeks later, he verified that the students were including the appropriate material and continuing to follow correct procedures.

Each day's assignment was written on the front board. Beginning on the fourth day of school, students did warm-up problems immediately after entering the room. These problems were displayed on a screen using a doc-cam, and students handed in their work after the teacher finished checking roll. The daily exercises were always graded and returned to the students either at the end of the period or on the following day.

Homework was always checked and had to be completed on time. Mr. Richard explained to students that it would not be fair to those who completed their homework promptly for others to have more time or perhaps the opportunity to copy answers from another student's completed paper. When grading a homework assignment, students were given explicit instructions on how to mark it. When work was checked by students, Mr. Richard frequently asked who had missed a particular problem. If many students had difficulty, he explained the problem to them in detail. After the papers were checked, he told students how to determine the grade. Points were deducted if a student failed to use pencil or did not write out each problem. When calculating their weekly homework average, students were allowed to drop the lowest grade for the week. At least once a week, Mr. Richard collected students' homework papers and checked them himself.

■ Case Study 5.3

MANAGING LONG-TERM ASSIGNMENTS

In Ms. Curry's science class, students completed two multimedia research projects during the year. Ms. Curry had carefully planned the procedures to help students achieve success on these assignments. For the first project, she assigned topics rather than allowing students to choose their own. An assigned topic made it easier for students to begin quickly and allowed the teacher to make adjustments in the difficulty of the assignment for different ability levels of students. When she introduced the first project, Ms. Curry gave her students two handouts describing requirements. One contained a description of the topic and a list of cards or PowerPoint slide categories the presentation should include; the other handout, the same for all students, outlined general requirements for the project, a calendar of checkpoints, due dates, and information about how the project would be graded. Ms. Curry also posted these requirements along with due dates on the class website for interested parents.

Following an initial multimedia presentation she had prepared as an example, Ms. Curry reviewed all of the directions and requirements with the students, using PowerPoint slides from her presentation as examples. One requirement was appropriate color selections of backgrounds and text to ensure that the presentation could be read by an audience when displayed. Additionally, Ms. Curry included a written admonition for students to save their work frequently and in two places: both to the school network and to their own flash drive. Another requirement concerned references and the bibliography, including sample citations for both text and Web-based references. Students were to use at least four references, one of them being Web based. A specific requirement set the minimum number of slides in the presentation, and at least one of the slides had to include a sound or video file rather than written text.

Ms. Curry provided a printout of her example presentation with notations for transitions and actions she had included. She also indicated the days the class would be scheduled to work in the library and computer lab, and provided a sign-up sheet for using the classroom computers during classwork time or study hall.

The checkpoints for the research project included an initial approval of the list of references identified by each student. Ms. Curry examined the students' notes or sketches. At both checkpoints she gave students feedback about the appropriateness of their sources or work. Ms. Curry gave two grades: one based on the project and the other based on the oral presentation of the project to the class. Before the project was due, students received a check-sheet they could use to determine whether they had met all of the requirements before submitting their work. Before the oral presentations, Ms. Curry gave students copies of the check-sheet she used to evaluate each presentation and discussed each item with them.

■ Checklist: Managing Student Work

Check When Complete	Area	Notes
	Your Grading System	_____
☐	A. What are your school's policies about grading?	_____
☐	B. What will be your grading system's components?	_____
☐	C. How will you weight the components?	_____
	Feedback and Monitoring	_____
☐	A. What procedures will you use to monitor student work in progress?	_____
☐	B. What records of their work will students keep?	_____

Check When Complete	Area	Notes
☐	C. When and how will you monitor student classwork?	
☐	D. How will you monitor projects or longer assignments?	
☐	E. What records of student work will you retain?	
☐	F. What kinds of feedback will you provide, and when?	
☐	G. How will you encourage students to reflect on their own progress?	
☐	H. What will you do if a student stops doing assignments?	
	Communicating Assignments and Work Requirements	
☐	A. Where and how will you post assignments?	
☐	B. What will be your standards for form and neatness?	
☐	C. What will be your policies for late or incomplete work?	
	Procedures for Absent Students	
☐	A. How will previously absent students identify the assignments they must make up?	
☐	B. How will they obtain handouts or other material?	
☐	C. What procedures will you use to provide assistance (e.g., classroom helpers, time before/after school)?	

MyEducationLab *Self-Check 5.1*

MyEducationLab *Self-Check 5.2*

MyEducationLab *Application Exercise 5.1*   Using what you've learned in this chapter, read and respond to this scenario.

MyEducationLab *Application Exercise 5.2*   Using what you've learned in this chapter, view the video and respond to the questions.

MyEducationLab *Application Exercise 5.3*   Using what you've learned in this chapter, read and respond to this scenario.

MyEducationLab *Application Exercise 5.4*   Using what you've learned in this chapter, view the video and respond to the questions.

Amy Walters/Shutterstock

CHAPTER 6

Getting Off to a Good Start

The beginning of school is a critical time for classroom management because your students will learn attitudes, behavior, and work habits that will affect the tone of your class for the rest of the year. It is in the first few weeks of school that students learn the behaviors expected of them and how to accomplish school tasks successfully. They also learn in what ways these tasks are meaningful to them and why success is worth pursuing. Much of this meaning is communicated simply by how you treat your students and what you expect of them from the very first day. Careful planning for the beginning of school sets the stage for the rest of the year.

Your major goal for the beginning of the year, then, is to strengthen each student's belief that school tasks are worth doing and that he or she can be successful. One key way to support this goal is to build productive relationships with students (see Chapter 2). In addition, in order to conduct instructional activities effectively you must obtain student cooperation in two key areas: following your rules and procedures and engaging successfully in all learning experiences. Establishing good relationships and obtaining cooperation will make it possible for you to create a positive climate for learning throughout the year.

Getting off to a good start requires careful attention to how you will communicate your expectations to your classes, introduce your course to the students, plan lessons and assignments, and decide on the sequence and amounts of time for various activities. This chapter addresses these topics and considers special problems encountered during the first week or so of classes. In addition, two case studies of beginning-of-year activities in secondary school classrooms are presented along with a checklist that will help organize your planning for the first weeks of school.

Creating Positive Teacher-Student Relationships

Having a good management plan when the school year begins is essential, but its long-term effectiveness will depend on the presence of a positive classroom environment. Your goal is not to be the ruler of a classroom kingdom, but to be the designer and facilitator of an interactive classroom community. The foundation of a positive climate starts with good relationships between teacher and students. A positive environment encourages students to be excited about learning and to feel free to explore, to be challenged, and to engage the content.

Recall from Chapter 2 that relationships have two fundamental dimensions: *influence* and *affect*. *Influence* refers to the degree to which the interpersonal behaviors in the relationship exhibit direction, assertiveness, and control, or provide assistance and leadership. *Affect* reflects the degree of sociability or connection present during interactions, as evidenced by expressing approval, exhibiting warmth, reassuring, or giving encouragement.

At the start of the school year the *influence* aspects of relationship behaviors are especially salient. This is because students need to learn so much new information about class requirements and become acclimated to their new school and classroom environments. Teachers are therefore in a prime position to provide key information to students, to guide their behaviors, and to help them be successful. By having well-structured classrooms, by being prepared, and by being available to students, teachers give direction and exhibit leadership, and thus establish positive influence in their relationships with students. The *affective* aspects of relationship development are also important, of course. Teacher warmth, acceptance, enthusiasm, and encouragement make students feel supported and more likely to give second effort when difficulty is encountered. Positive teacher affect is also more likely to elicit a positive, reciprocal response from students, contributing to an overall positive climate. As you read the next section, "Perspectives on the Beginning of the Year," consider how the two dimensions of relationships—*influence* and *affect*—manifest themselves in the principles.

Perspectives on the Beginning of the Year

Several principles should guide your planning for the beginning-of-year classroom activities.

1. Resolve student uncertainties.   When your students arrive on the first day, they will not be sure of your expectations for behavior or of your course requirements. Although previous experiences in other teachers' classrooms will have given them general expectations about what constitutes acceptable or unacceptable behaviors in school, they will not know what *you* expect. Should they raise their hands if they want to comment or ask a question? May they leave their seats without permission? May they speak to each other during seat work or at other times? Moreover, the students do not know how consistently you will enforce your procedures and rules or what the consequences will be if they do not follow them. In addition, they will be unfamiliar with your system for grading and other procedures for managing student work. Because of these uncertainties, you will be in a very good position at the beginning of the year to help students learn appropriate behavior by providing a specific, concrete description of your expectations for behavior, course requirements, and standards for work. If you do not take advantage of this opportunity, however, students may begin to behave in ways that interfere with good instruction and learning. You will then face the more difficult task of eliminating unacceptable behavior and replacing it with more appropriate behavior.

Take the necessary time during the first few days of classes to describe carefully your expectations for behavior and work. Do not be in such a hurry to get started on content activities that you neglect to teach good behavior. Rather, combine learning about procedures, rules, and course requirements with your initial content activities to build the foundation for the whole semester's or year's program.

2. Help students be successful by planning uncomplicated lessons.   Your content activities and assignments during the first week should be selected and designed to ensure maximum student success and engagement. Give students support and encouragement as they work on their initial assignments and take advantage of chances to acknowledge good effort and performance. Your goal is for students to feel secure and optimistic about their ability to do well in your class.

3. Keep a whole-class focus.   Plan activities for the first week or so that keep a whole-class focus. This means that your instruction and directions will be made to the entire class at the same time and that students will work on the same tasks or assignments. You might still plan for small-group work during this time, but the groups should work on the same task or assignment, and you should give initial instructions to all students at once. Unless it is necessary, you should not individualize instruction or assignments during the first week or so, nor should you have groups engage in activities or projects that require you to work extensively with individuals or a group while the rest of the class waits. You might wish to prepare some extra-credit, enrichment assignments, problems, or questions to challenge students who complete seat-work assignments early.

One reason for emphasizing a whole-class focus is that it will keep your classroom procedures simpler and therefore easier to implement with a new group of students. Another reason is that complex activities are often difficult to monitor; thus, inappropriate behavior will be more likely to go uncorrected, giving it a chance to take root. After your classes are running smoothly and students have learned correct behavior, you can introduce more complex activities.

4. Be available, visible, and in charge.   It's important that students learn to look to you for information about procedures and behaviors. Even if you're careful to state your expectations clearly during the first several days, questions will arise regarding appropriate behavior in domains that weren't explicitly covered. Students will experience uncertainty because guidelines or rules are often general and require a context to be understood. Moreover, students may have learned that teachers don't always follow through, and they will check your limits to see how much "give" is in your system and to establish the boundaries between acceptable and unacceptable behaviors.

Make yourself available during seat-work time or group-work activities rather than retreat to your desk to finish paperwork. Circulate around the room, monitoring student progress and providing assistance when needed. Your physical proximity to students will encourage appropriate behavior and work habits. Keep visual contact with students as much as possible during whole-class activities. For example, use a doc-cam projector rather than write on a whiteboard with your back to the class. Scan around the room often, rather than focus on one area. Also, avoid becoming so involved with one or a few students that you stop monitoring the rest of the class.

Teacher Authority

Teacher authority refers to the teacher's right to set standards for student behavior and performance and to the likelihood that students will follow the teacher's lead in their decisions and behaviors. When students do as the teacher expects, they are vesting the teacher with the authority to lead them. When they intentionally engage in behaviors contrary to the teacher's wishes, they are disputing the teacher's authority.

Teacher authority can be derived from multiple sources (Pace, 2003; Spady & Mitchell, 1979). Under *traditional* authority, students are expected to behave because the teacher is the adult in charge, much as children are expected to obey their parents. Teachers who rely exclusively on this form of authority will find dealing with adolescents problematic when their authority is challenged. *Bureaucratic* authority derives legitimacy from the teacher's ability to use grades to reward effort and performance and to use prescribed consequences for desirable and inappropriate behaviors. *Expert* or *professional* authority is based on teacher knowledge and skills; thus, students may accept a teacher's decisions about curriculum and academic tasks because of the teacher's expertise in the subject matter. Finally, some teachers have *charismatic* authority; they are expressive and outgoing, or they engage students with their interactive style and good communication skills. Students follow these teachers' lead because they like and are attracted to them.

Pace (2003) found that teachers derive their authority from several sources rather than relying on just one. For example, a *charismatic* teacher might use *bureaucratic* and *traditional* authority with students who don't respond positively to his or her interpersonal style.

Mention of teacher authority can make some persons uncomfortable because the term suggests "authoritarian," and thus evokes an image of repression and arbitrary governance. But there are several forms of authority, and they are not all repressive. Furthermore, society depends on authority for organizing its social and work groups. In the same way, schools depend on student acceptance of legitimate authority in order to create a safe setting in which teaching and learning can occur.

Another perspective on authority makes a distinction between *authoritarian* and *authoritative* leadership. *Authoritarian* teachers don't provide reasons for rules, try to control students through threats and punishment, and use consequences arbitrarily. In contrast, *authoritative* teachers explain the basis for their actions and decisions, give students more independence as they demonstrate maturity and the willingness to behave responsibly, and administer consequences fairly and proportionately. Regardless of the style of teacher authority or combination of styles, authoritarian behavior invites challenges and resistance, whereas authoritative leadership invites cooperation.

You will find it useful to pay attention to how students react to your use of authority and then to consider ways to adjust your approach when necessary. Some students may be less likely to accept your authority if it relies on a different source than they have experienced in the past. For example, students who are used to traditional forms of authority at home and in school may need a long transition period before they will be comfortable with less adult-centered approaches. Students in the middle and high school grades, however, may be responsive to expert or professional authority, especially if their families or previous teachers have utilized nontraditional authority sources. You won't be able to turn a specific style of authority on and off, of course, but if you are aware of your tendencies, you can at least anticipate your students' reactions to your leadership and adapt your approach to best effect. It may be comforting to remember that teachers have multiple sources of authority to draw from in their work with students.

It's a useful exercise to pay attention to how students react to your use of authority and then consider ways to adjust your approach when appropriate. No single approach is best in all circumstances, so try to be flexible and open to feedback.

■ Planning for a Good Beginning

Before you plan classroom activities for the first week, you need to have your room and materials ready and have your rules, procedures, and consequences identified. If you have used the checklists and suggestions in Chapters 3 through 5, you are ready to consider a few final items.

Procedures for Obtaining Books and Checking Them Out to Students

Learn what procedures veteran teachers use in your school to obtain books, and have on hand any needed forms to record book numbers and names of students. If there is no special form, you can record book numbers in your grade book. Be sure to wait until students have been assigned their lockers before you check out textbooks. If you are teaching in a school district in which students are expected to cover district-issued books, have an adequate supply of covers on hand. Instead of paper copies of book records and locker assignments, your school may use computer-based record keeping. If so, find out how to use the system so that you can keep up with these administrative tasks.

Many teachers check out textbooks by the second or third day of classes and do so during a content activity. A common procedure is to distribute the textbooks to students at the beginning of the activity, indicating whether the books need to be covered and providing any other relevant information, such as the cost of the book if lost. Later, after students have begun the seat-work portion of the lesson, they can be called to the teacher's desk one or two at a time so that the teacher can record their book numbers and note any damage to used books. An alternative procedure is to move from student to student while they cover their books, recording book numbers and noting any damage. Using a name stamp to record the teacher's name on the inside front cover facilitates the process and increases the likelihood that lost books will be returned. If you don't have a name stamp, have the students print your name legibly.

Required Paperwork

Have all forms on hand. If you have a homeroom or advisory class, there may be forms specific to that period. Examples of forms for one or all classes include book cards, office passes and hall permits, parental consent forms for field trips, health and emergency care forms, statements of having read the student handbook, computer-use agreements, parking permit requests, locker release forms, and forms for recording collected money. Use file folders and desk drawer compartments to keep these materials separate and organized.

Class Rosters

Be sure you have class rosters organized by period. Note any special students who have unique conditions that must be taken into account in seating or who require medication. You will probably be told whether you have such students by a special education teacher or counselor. These professionals are also a useful source of suggestions for working with such students in your classes.

Besides using roster printouts, another way to keep records until classes stabilize is to use a set of three-by-five-inch cards for each class. Have one card for each student and record on it the student's name, book number, and attendance and grades for the first two weeks. This not only makes it easier to move student records from period to period as schedules are finalized, it also provides a set of name cards for use throughout the year to make sure all students are called on. Some teachers have students write their own names, parents' names, telephone numbers, and other useful information on these cards.

Seating Assignments

Plan to assign seats during the first week of classes. Assigned desks allow you to make a seating chart from which you can learn student names and check attendance quickly. There is little point in assigning seats on the first day of classes unless you are quite sure that very few changes in your class rosters will occur. By the second or third day, however, class rolls may stabilize enough for permanent seating. Your computer-based grade book should allow you to create seating charts from class rosters. Subsequent changes in your class rosters and seating charts then can easily be made.

Some differences in seating assignment practices are observed between middle schools and senior high schools. It is more common at the middle school level for teachers to assign seats, often alphabetically. (An advantage of alphabetical seating is that assignments can be collected in the same order that you will record them in your grade book, thus saving you some time. Multiplied by five classes, the gain in efficiency is significant.) At the senior high level, some teachers assign seats, whereas, especially in upper grades, other teachers allow students to choose their seats. In the latter case, the chosen seat is the permanent one; that is, students usually are not allowed to move around at will. Also, teachers reserve the right to reassign students to different seats if necessary. Whatever the grade level, you can change seating arrangements later in the year to accommodate work groups, to move students who need close supervision to more accessible seats, or just to provide a change.

First-Week Bell Schedule

Find out how much time is available for each period during the first week. Some class periods may be shortened to accommodate extra-long advisory or homeroom periods. If so, find out which periods are affected and how much time will be available for each class.

Tardiness During the First Days of Classes

Most teachers do not attempt to enforce their tardiness policies during the first few days of classes; students are still trying to find classrooms, and the time for passing between periods is not always predictable. By the third or fourth class day, however, it is usually reasonable to expect all students to arrive at your classroom on time. Tell them the day before that you will begin to count students tardy unless they are in your room or in their seats before the bell begins to ring (or whatever your policy is). Then enforce the policy the next day and thereafter.

Administrative Tasks

If you have not already done so as part of Chapter 4 activities, be sure you know what special administrative tasks are required during the first week. If you have a homeroom or advisory class, be sure to keep its forms and materials in separate file folders.

Rules

You'll need to discuss your expectations for behavior with your students on the first day you meet with them and as many times thereafter as needed. This means that you'll need to have your rules ready to present at the start. You can list rules or guidelines on a large chart and post it on a bulletin board or a wall, or you can include them on your course website or in a course syllabus. Or perhaps you will decide to distribute copies of rules or display them on a board or screen and have students copy them into their notebooks.

Course Requirements

During the first week of school, you will need to discuss course requirements with your students. Outline the major requirements, such as tests, pop quizzes, a notebook, projects, and homework, and indicate how they contribute to the students' grades. You do not have to list each requirement in detail, but you should indicate the major features. It is a good practice to provide students with a copy of your requirements—perhaps on the same sheet as your classroom rules. Some teachers have students take it home for parents to sign. If you have a class website, you can post your course requirements along with other information.

A Beginning-of-Class Routine

Decide what standard routine you will use to open each period. The routine should enable students to make the transition into your classroom in an orderly manner, ready for instruction. It will also allow you to check attendance and perform other administrative tasks quickly and without interruption. If you have not yet decided on a beginning-of-period routine, you should review the relevant section in Chapter 4. Whatever your opening routine, it is reasonable to expect students to complete it without talking and to remain seated and quiet until you are ready to begin instruction.

Alternative Activities

It is a good idea to prepare interesting academic activities for occasions when extra minutes are available and students have nothing to do. This is especially likely to occur during the first week or two of classes, when the bell schedule may be altered unexpectedly. Examples include worksheets, puzzles, and logic problems related to your subject. You can find books containing such activities among the supplementary materials in your department's storeroom, in a bookstore, in a teachers' supply store, or from teachers' supply catalogs online. Search for ideas on websites such as www.education-world.com and www.712educators.about.com. A section of enrichment or supplemental exercises, questions, or problems might be found in the teacher's edition of your text and can be used either as a seat-work assignment or as a whole-class recitation topic.

Another possibility is to allow individuals who complete work early to have free reading time while they wait for the next activity to begin. You can keep a shelf of books and magazines for such times. We don't recommend that you give students access to computers or special equipment as enrichment activities during the first week; wait until you have used them in an activity and have established procedures for their use. You can add them later, as appropriate, after you've established the basic routines in your room.

Communicating with Parents or Guardians

Parent involvement has long been recognized as a positive factor in student academic and social growth (Walker & Hoover-Dempsey, 2006, 2015; Jeynes, 2005). Current research suggests that parent involvement may make an important contribution through its influence on student beliefs and behaviors that lead to achievement (Hattie, 2009). When parents find significant ways to participate in schooling, they model for their children the importance of education and help bring together the cultures of home and school.

Establishing Formal and Informal Communication.   One of your first steps at the beginning of school will be to establish some means of formal communication with parents and guardians, including sending a letter containing essential information about your class that has not already been covered in school handouts. This beginning link with families opens the door to further contact. If your school is organized into subunits or teams, your team may send a single letter. Otherwise, you should write one of your own and send it home on the first or second class day. Depending on your school's population and demographics, you may want to consider bridging possible language barriers and include a translation of your letter in the predominant language. Items you can address in the letter include the following:

- A brief introduction of yourself
- Any special materials or supplies students need to bring to your class
- Your conference times and how parents may contact you
- Brief overview of curriculum you will teach during the semester or year
- Special events for families, such as a back-to-school night
- Information about your class website, homework, class requirements, and special assignments
- An invitation to visit their child's class
- An invitation to contact you regarding special issues or problems concerning their child

Your letter should be cheerful and friendly, but above all, it must be grammatically correct and free of misspellings. It is easy to be overwhelmed at the beginning of the year with the abundance of tasks and to let this letter be rushed. But you have only one chance to create a good first impression, and you will want it to be professional and competent. Ask a friend to proofread it to be sure it is clearly written, accurate, and easy to read.

Technology adds additional considerations for communicating with parents. The privacy of students and the confidentiality of their records require that teachers be cognizant of how they and their students use technology. For example, parental permission must be sought in writing to post any student work, name, likeness, or photograph online. Note your school district's policies that govern online posting about students and follow them. It is also helpful to know your district's email policy for communications with parents. Know how to phrase and format text so that it is courteous and professional. Keep in mind that all documents and communications written from a district-owned computer are considered public and are accessible to administrators in the course of their duties, and to the public via an open records request or a subpoena.

Teachers also need to remember that not all families have home computers or email access; therefore, it is important to retain communication using other sources (e.g., written notes home and phone calls). Furthermore, teachers need to be sensitive to the possibility of causing embarrassment to students or their families through calling attention to noncomputer use or by having the students self-identify publicly as not having home access (Seiter, 2007).

This first letter to parents is an important contact with families, but it is only a first step—a one-way formal communication wherein you provide them with information. Your ultimate goal is to establish a dialogue between home and school and to invite constructive contact during the year. Consider implementing some of the following measures in your subsequent contacts with parents.

- Encourage classroom visits.
- Engage in brief conversations and exchanges on occasions such as school programs and events.
- Make and encourage phone calls.
- Post curriculum and activity updates for parents on your class-linked website.
- Reply promptly and courteously to email and other notes and messages from parents.

■ Activities on the First Day of Classes

For class periods of normal or nearly normal length, your first-day activities will generally include administrative tasks, introducing your course to students, communicating your course requirements and expectations for student conduct, and an initial content activity. For shortened class periods, some of the discussion of course requirements can be postponed, and the content activity can be shortened or eliminated. First-day activities are described here in a commonly used sequence. Where significant variations in the activity or sequence may occur, they are noted in the discussion.

Before Class Begins

Before the bell rings, stand near or immediately outside the door. Help students find the correct room and prevent groups of students from congregating nearby and blocking your doorway. Students will have an easier time finding your room if you post a sign with your name outside the door. Usually, students enter quickly and quietly on the first day; however, should some students enter in an unacceptable manner, you can have them repeat their entrance properly or tell them that they are expected to enter quietly and without commotion in the future.

Greet students pleasantly, smile and make eye contact, but do not start long conversations. Tell students that they may choose their seats for the day, and when most students have arrived, enter the room. When in the room, help students with seating, stay in prominent view, and monitor student behavior. When the period begins, tell students your name and the course title (this information should also be displayed ahead of time) and ask students to check their schedules to be sure they are in the correct room. Look around the room frequently, making eye contact with all students.

Administrative Tasks

Have all necessary materials close at hand so that you can begin quickly. You will first need to check attendance. When you do, have students raise their hands (rather than only call out) when you call their names so that you can begin to associate names with faces. Using this procedure conveys the idea that hand raising is more desirable than call-outs. Pronunciations and preferred names can be noted on the class roster at this time. If students must complete forms or class cards, or if you must take care of other administrative matters at this time, tell students what needs to be done and what behavior is expected of them; for example, "After you fill in the class cards, hold them at your seat until I call for them to be passed in." To facilitate the completion of class cards or other forms, write the needed information on the front board or display it on the overhead screen.

Introductions

Take a position front and center in the classroom. Look around while speaking and make eye contact with students. Smile and try to present a friendly, confident, businesslike demeanor. Tell students your name and something about yourself, such as your interests, hobbies, family, or why you enjoy teaching your subject. If many students do not know each other, you can use a brief get-acquainted activity. You can also have students complete a short questionnaire identifying interests, hobbies, or experiences related to your subject. Afterward, give students an introduction to your course, including an overview of topics to be covered. Try to emphasize the course's importance, interest, challenges, and applications. Mention some activities that will be of interest to the students so that they can begin the year looking forward to taking the course.

Discussion of Class Rules

During your presentation of the class rules, discuss your expectations for student conduct. Refer to the rules (some teachers prefer to call them *guidelines*) you have posted, displayed on a screen, or made available on a handout. Read each rule and explain it, giving examples when needed. Describe the rationale for each rule and any penalties associated with breaking it. You can involve students in this discussion by asking them for examples or reasons for particular rules. (See also Chapter 4 on student participation in rule setting.) Because students are often reserved in their class behavior on the first day or two of school, don't expect eager participation in this discussion. If you intend to use special incentives, you can introduce them now—or you might save this discussion for later in the week.

If your rules do not already incorporate major procedures, you should discuss your expectations in these areas at this time. Students should understand what is acceptable with respect to student talk, how to contact the teacher for help, when movement about the room is permitted, and how to ask questions or volunteer an answer or comment. In addition, your procedures for tardy students and beginning the period should be explained. Do not go over procedures for activities that you aren't going to use right away; you can discuss them when they are needed. Unless particular school rules are relevant for your classroom, you do not have to include them in your discussion; they will probably be discussed by a building administrator on the public address system or in a general assembly, or teachers may cover them during a homeroom or advisory period. If such a presentation has not occurred, you should go over the rules briefly during your first-period class for the benefit of students new to the building.

Some senior high teachers, particularly in the upper grades, prefer a less explicit approach to class rules. They do not identify expectations as "rules," nor do they post or otherwise provide copies of rules. They limit their discussions of expectations for conduct to a few major areas such as tardiness and student talk. This does not mean that such teachers have no expectations in other areas of behavior—they are quick to give feedback when students' behavior is not acceptable. For example, if such a teacher is presenting material to the class and students leave their seats, the teacher will use the incident to tell the class that students should remain in their seats during presentations. The advantage of this approach is that it invites cooperation by recognizing that many older senior high students are well acquainted with prevailing school norms and will behave acceptably with no prompting. The disadvantage of this approach is that it places a considerable burden on the teacher's ability to monitor students' behavior so that initial deviations from expectations can be detected. If they are not detected and corrected, students may believe that the behavior is acceptable; consequently, more inappropriate behavior may occur. Note that the less explicit approach to rules is the practice of only some senior high teachers. Other good managers at this level are more systematic in their presentation of expectations for student conduct. Finally, we note that the less explicit approach should not be used at the middle school level or for ninth-graders; these students benefit from the structure provided by an explicit set of rules and expectations for major procedures.

When you present and discuss your rules and procedures with students, you should set a positive tone, emphasizing the benefits to all: "These rules are intended to help us have a class atmosphere that is appropriate for learning. We all know that a classroom will work better when everyone's rights are respected"; or "An orderly class helps everyone by giving students a good chance to listen and learn and to do their work without being bothered or distracted." If some procedure or rule will be difficult to follow, you might acknowledge the students' feelings as you discuss it: "I know it isn't easy to remember to raise your hands before speaking during a discussion, but doing so will give everyone opportunities to participate"; or "It will be hard not to start using the new equipment right away, but we need to wait for directions so no one is injured." Such expressions of empathy when presenting rules that may appear arbitrary have been found to help students to exhibit more self-control.

A Get-Acquainted Activity

Some teachers like to use a get-acquainted or icebreaker activity. If your school uses block scheduling, you should have enough time to use this activity on the first day. Be careful with the time allocated to it, because it can eat up a period quickly and not leave enough time for other essential matters. Also, because it is the first activity with extensive student participation, be sure to set the tone by telling students what behaviors are expected. The purpose of this activity is to promote positive relationships and participation, and for you and the students to learn some basic information about each other; in other words, to build some positive connections. Many adolescents are uncomfortable about divulging personal information in public, so pick an icebreaker activity that isn't too risky. You can find examples of age-appropriate get-acquainted activities at websites that provide resources for middle and high school teachers.

Presentation of Course Requirements

Describe briefly the major course requirements and indicate how they will contribute to the course grade. It is not necessary to go into detail about grading procedures or other course requirements unless some aspect of them will be used immediately. For example, you do not have to go over test or homework procedures at this time, but you should describe in your syllabus and list on the board or PowerPoint slide those materials that students should bring to class each day. If you plan to give students a handout listing rules and major procedures, you can include on it a list of materials and major course requirements. If you don't have a handout with this information for students, then you should have them copy it into a notebook. When periods have been shortened, or to conserve time for a content activity, you may limit discussion of course requirements to the absolute essentials and wait until the next class day to fill out the picture.

An Initial Content Activity

Choose an initial activity that students can complete successfully with little or no assistance. This will leave you free to handle other matters and to monitor students. The activity should be an interesting one that will involve your students. Look in the teacher's edition of your textbook for ideas. Possibilities include a review worksheet based on content from earlier grades, a subject-related puzzle, and a worksheet activity. You could also conduct a short demonstration or present an experiment, essay, story, description of an event, and so on, which you might then use as the basis for a short discussion. This could be followed by questions for which students write answers. Available time is a critical factor, so use an activity that can be continued the next class day if the period ends before the activity. It is best to collect unfinished classwork at the end of the activity rather than to assign it as homework on the first day. You can then return it to students to be finished on the second day instead of relying on students to return it themselves—they may not yet have lockers, and some students probably will not have notebooks or other containers for papers on the first day.

Use the initial content activity for teaching important procedures. Begin the activity by stating what procedures students should follow. If the activity is a presentation or a discussion, let students know what to do if they want to speak; for a seat-work assignment, inform students how to contact you to get help. Teachers who allow students to work together on seat-work assignments usually wait a week or more before beginning the procedure. That allows the teacher to become better acquainted with students' work habits and to judge how much responsibility students can be given.

When you introduce a procedure for the first time, follow these steps: (1) Explain the procedure by telling students exactly what they are expected to do, (2) Use a PowerPoint slide or use the board to list the steps in the procedure if it is complex, and (3) Demonstrate the procedure whenever possible. Then, the first time students are expected to use the procedure, watch them carefully and give corrective feedback about their performance. For example, you will probably have students use a specific heading on written assignments. To teach this procedure, introduce it when the first assignment is given. Display a sample heading, go over its parts, and then have students head their own papers. You could either check the students' headings at that time or wait until you circulate around the room after the seat-work assignment has been given.

Some teachers give a pretest at the beginning of the year to assess students' readiness for instruction. We prefer to wait a day or two before administering tests. An interesting content activity sets a more positive tone on the first day and is a better motivational tool than a test. It may also take a day or two for enrollments to stabilize, so it makes sense to hold off initial assessments.

In general, on the first day, avoid using small groups, projects, individualized instruction, or any other format that requires complicated procedures, extensive student movement, or materials that students may not have with them and that you cannot supply. Help your students learn whole-class and seat-work procedures before you try more complex activities.

Ending the Period

You should establish an end-of-period routine that helps your students get ready to leave the room as they found it and in an orderly manner. Make every effort to dismiss the class promptly to enable them to be on time for the next class. Shortly before the dismissal bell (the amount of time depends on how much cleanup needs to be done), signal your students that it is time to clean around their desks and put their materials away. If you consistently give students ample warning, you can prevent their stopping work too early.

Some teachers prefer to dismiss the students themselves. They tell students, "Please do not leave your seats when the bell rings because I may have an announcement to make, or I may need to give you materials before you leave the class. I will tell you when you can leave the room." Such a procedure allows the teacher to wrap up any unfinished business at the end of the period and to hold students until they have cleaned up the room properly. Some students may challenge this procedure by getting out of their seats as soon as the bell rings, so be prepared to call them back and have them wait.

■ The Second Day of Classes

If your first day's class periods are very short, you may not be able to do much more than introduce yourself and your course and present rules and procedures. If so, you should begin the second day with a review of major class procedures and follow the first day's plan, beginning with a discussion of course requirements.

If your first day's class periods are of normal or nearly normal length, you may follow this outline of activities on the second class day:

1. **Identify new students and get them seated.** Have them fill out class cards or any other forms from the first day. If the forms are time consuming to complete or require extensive directions, you can wait until the rest of the students are engaged in a seat-work activity before having the new students complete them.
2. **Remind students of the beginning-of-class routine, and use it to start the period.** Perform your administrative chores, such as attendance check, at this time.
3. **Review your major rules and procedures.** Provide new students with a copy of the rules and procedures.
4. **If you did not discuss course requirements on the first day, do so now.** If students will keep a notebook or folder for your class, this is a good time to go over its organization and contents.
5. **Present a content activity.** Many teachers distribute textbooks, conduct a lesson, and then give a seat-work assignment from the text. If for some reason students cannot be assigned textbooks at this time, you can still distribute the textbooks and collect them at the end of the period. Alternatives are to provide lesson

materials, such as worksheets, or to give students a pretest or some assessment of readiness for the first unit of the course. Readiness assessment is an especially good idea if you have not previously taught the subject, the grade level, or students with backgrounds similar to those of students in your classes. If you are teaching in a school that uses a block schedule format, you will teach fewer classes per day but your class periods will be longer than if all classes meet each day; consequently you will have to plan for more instruction per period. See Chapter 7 for suggestions about time allocation for longer periods.

6. **Close the period.** Use the procedure you introduced the first day.

After the Second Class

Continue using the procedures you introduced on the first two days of each class, adding new procedures as needed. Monitor student behavior carefully. Review your procedures and give students feedback when their behavior does not meet your expectations. By the third or fourth class day, you should be giving regular assignments to be done in class and at home. Check work promptly and begin using your grading procedures at once so that students receive feedback about their work and are held accountable for it.

Who Will I Teach: Students Who Arrive After the School Year Has Begun

It's the end of September and Mr. Hahn's classes have settled nicely into their routines. At the beginning of the day on Tuesday of the fourth week, Mr. Hahn receives notification from his grade level counselor that his first period class will have two new students, Adele and Dmitri, who have transferred from other school districts. They will arrive sometime during the period, as soon as the counselor finalizes their schedules and transfer paperwork. At the beginning of that day's class, Mr. Hahn informs his students of the imminent arrival of Adele and Dmitri. "I'd like to let you know that we have two new students arriving today. Their names are Adele and Dmitri and they likely won't know any of us because they're from another district, so let's make them feel welcome." Mr. Hahn uses students who have volunteered to assist with various tasks such as homework and absence helpers. He says, "They'll need some help figuring out how our class works, so I'm going to ask Desirae and Donte to be mentors this week for Adele and Dmitri. Also, it's not easy to start over in a new school, so everyone can help by being friendly toward them and making them feel welcome."

Pause and Consider

What initial impression will other students have of Adele and Dmitri based on Mr. Hahn's comments?

1. Can you anticipate some strategies that Mr. Hahn could use that would help a new student?
2. What are some concerns that a student might be expected to have when entering a new classroom?
3. How might students in the class help a new student?

It is quite common for new students to arrive after the school year has begun. When such arrivals occur during the first week or so of school, it's relatively easy to accommodate them because the teacher is still in the process of organizing content activities and teaching procedures and routines. When arriving later in the year, new students take more effort and planning to accommodate. Unfortunately, new students sometimes arrive without much notice, so it's a good idea to have some procedures in place to accommodate them when it happens. It's also a good idea if, like Mr. Hahn, teachers project a positive attitude about the new arrival and enlist their students' support of the effort. The following items are useful strategies to prepare for late arrivals and to manage their transition into the new classroom:

- Keep essential handouts and materials in clearly marked folders. Then you will be able to give copies as needed to late arrivals. Note that these folders will do double duty for absent students.
- Use volunteers to choose mentors for new students. Student mentors can show a new student around the school, help learn your classroom routines, and be lunch partners during the first week.
- Make copies of rules and major procedures so that new students have another way to learn about classroom routines.
- Assign the new student to a nearby desk or table for easy monitoring during the first week or so. You can reassign different seating later, if necessary, after the student has become more acclimated.
- Contact the student's parent(s) or guardian as soon as possible to welcome them to the school and to your classroom community and to begin to establish a working relationship.
- Check with the student from time to time during the next week or so and provide assistance as needed to help with the transition.

Some students change schools several times during their school years, so some who arrive later in the school year may experience this phenomenon multiple times. Several factors can cause student mobility, including changes in parents' employment, divorce or other relationship problems, poverty, and associated housing issues.

Research indicates that multiple school changes have a negative impact on a student's achievement and attitudes toward school, and are linked to a higher probability of dropping out of school before graduation (Rumberger, 2003). Research also indicates that *teacher support* and *peer acceptance* have a positive impact on the academic performance of children who change schools (Gruman, Harachi, Abbott, Catalano, & Fleming, 2008). This mitigating effect was noted even after controlling for other possible predictors of the student's at-risk status. It is therefore important to give special attention to students who arrive later in the school year and to monitor their progress and integration into the school environment. Following are additional recommendations that may prove helpful for such students (Popp, Grant, & Stronge, 2009; Rumberger, 2003):

- Assess relevant skills in your subject as soon as possible so that you can be sure instruction is provided at the proper level. Also review any records that accompany the student's transfer materials to get more information about the situation at home.
- Plan to meet with the student before or after school or during lunch and other open times to get to know the student and provide some orientation to your class.
- Keep extra school supplies available in case the student needs them.
- Pair the new student with another student for assistance in catching up with some content.
- When you use groups, be sure to assign the new student to a group whose members are likely to be helpful and welcoming.
- If you have volunteer tutoring assistance available for your class, consider assigning someone to this student if remediation is needed.
- Pay attention to these new students. Give positive feedback for their effort when they work hard, and provide support when they struggle.

■ Chapter Summary

The beginning of classes is a critical time for establishing classroom management. It is especially important for the teacher to be organized and prepared in order to help students get off to a good start. This chapter presented principles that are the basis for good management practices, along with a comprehensive set of guidelines and concrete suggestions. The tasks that must be attended to at the beginning of the year were described, and ideas for conducting those activities were presented. Also discussed were teacher-student relationships, teacher authority, contacts with parents, presentation of course requirements, how to discuss rules or behavior guidelines, and administrative tasks. Case studies at the end of the chapter will illustrate how different teachers begin their classes.

■ Further Reading

Capizzi, A. M. (2009). Start the year off right: Designing and evaluating a supportive classroom management plan. *Focus on Exceptional Children, 42*(3), 2–12.

> *A comprehensive strategy for beginning the year is summarized, with examples drawn from a variety of grade levels and classrooms. The article includes ideas for planning for students with special needs. A worksheet to help organize preparation is included.*

Emmer, E. T., & Gerwels, M. C. (2006). Classroom management in middle and high school classrooms. In C. Evertson & C. Weinstein (Eds.), *Handbook of classroom management* (pp. 407–437). Mahwah, NJ: Erlbaum.

> *This chapter provides a review of research on classroom management at the secondary level. The research base described here is extensive and well worth examining.*

Evertson, C. M., & Poole, I. R. (2008). Proactive classroom management. In T. Good (Ed.), *21st century education* (pp. 131–139). Thousand Oaks, CA: Sage.

> *The research base, rationale, and examples of planning for classroom management are included in this chapter. It highlights several areas of special importance to consider before school begins in order to create a positive classroom environment.*

Good, T., & Brophy, J. (2008). *Looking in classrooms* (10th ed.). Boston: Allyn and Bacon.

> *Research-based and informative, this book offers many insights and ideas about classroom teaching. Several chapters provide a good foundation for beginning the school year by planning important classroom routines, activities, and instruction.*

Mackenzie, R. J. (1997). Setting limits in the classroom. *American Educator, 21*(3), 32–43.

> *Reducing uncooperative attention-seeking, oppositional, and disruptive behavior requires that teachers use effective limit-setting strategies. Doing so helps students learn about the consequences of their actions.*

http://712educators.about.com

> *This website for middle and high school teachers has numerous links to articles helpful for beginning the school year.*

teachersnetwork.org

> *Sponsored by the New York Teachers' Network, this website has lesson plans, activities, model parent letters, videos, and other resources for teachers. Users can select grade level and subject areas.*

www.teachervision.com

> *This website provides a variety of topics and tips helpful in planning for the start of classes, as well as the remainder of the year.*

■ Suggested Activities

1. Use the checklist at the end of the chapter to be sure you have planned all aspects of the beginning of the year.

2. Read Case Studies 6.1 and 6.2. They describe teachers beginning the year in quite diverse settings. These cases can be used for individual analysis or group discussion. Consider the following questions:
   a. To what extent are the principles described in this chapter in evidence in each case?
   b. Can you identify critical beginning-of-year planning and preparation activities for each case?
   c. What similarities are apparent between the teachers in their beginning-of-year activities or approaches? Which one(s) would you be most likely to use? Why?

3. Read Case Study 6.3, which depicts a teacher facing escalating disorderly behavior. What teacher actions or omissions contributed to the problem? Suggest strategies for improving the situation.

4. What do you think your students' goals and concerns are or will be at the beginning of the year? How can a classroom management plan accommodate them?

5. Talk with teachers who have had several years' experience in a subject and at a grade level you would like to teach. Ask them what activities they use during the first few days and how they sequence them. Teachers are often willing to share handouts and ideas. You might also ask someone to look over your lesson plan for the first day and give you suggestions.

■ Case Study 6.1

BEGINNING THE YEAR IN A FIRST-YEAR ALGEBRA CLASS USING COOPERATIVE LEARNING GROUPS

First-Day Activities

Activity	Description
Before the bell	Desks are clustered in seven groups of four or five each. The teacher, Mrs. James, collects a folder for each group of desks from the previous class, replacing it with another folder of a different color, marked with the period and group number. As students enter, Mrs. James tells them they may sit wherever they choose today but that seats will be assigned later in the week.

(continued)

First-Day Activities

Activity	Description
Initial greeting (4 minutes)	The teacher smiles and states her name. She introduces herself, telling students about her family and some out-of-school interests. She tells students that she is a hard worker and she expects them to work hard. She says that she will be in her room an hour before classes begin and will stay in her room until 4:30 each day so that students can come in for help if they need more explanation or assistance. "The most important thing in this class is *trying*. We will all make mistakes and get stuck, but by working together, we will be able to solve the problems and learn a lot of new things."
Introduction (10 minutes)	Mrs. James notes that students have all had an introduction to algebra in earlier grades but that she is curious about whether they know how important and useful it is. She leads a discussion in which she elicits their ideas about how algebra and other math might be useful. She asks students to raise their hands and wait to be called on before speaking during this activity. During the discussion, Mrs. James comments on the origins of the subject, the Arabic basis of its name, and some of its applications in science, business, and everyday math. She calls attention to a bulletin board that has several colorful posters highlighting math applications.
	During the discussion, the teacher thanks students on several occasions for raising their hands and for listening well. When a couple of students call out, she reminds them to raise their hands so that she can call on them.
	Mrs. James comments on the grouping of desks. She explains that in her classes students work in groups much of the time and that this activity can be very helpful in learning. She states that they won't always work in groups; students will keep an individual notebook and take tests by themselves. For many assignments, however, they will be expected to work together and to assist each other in understanding the content and solving problems. Mrs. James points out that students often find this not only a good way to learn but an enjoyable way. A student asks if she can choose her group. Mrs. James responds that she must reserve the right to arrange the groups. Because group membership will change at different times, however, students will have an opportunity to work with a variety of other students. The teacher also emphasizes that because this high school draws from many feeder middle schools, many students do not know each other, so working in groups with others is a good way to get to know other students.
Initial presentation of procedures (6 minutes)	Mrs. James thanks the students for raising hands before speaking. She says that she has a few other procedures for the class to run smoothly and that she will go over some of them now, saving the others for when they start group work. She tells her students that during class, when she is talking or when a student is presenting something to the whole class, they are to remain in their seats. If they wish to comment or ask a question, they should raise a hand and wait their turn. At other times, when they are working in groups or on individual assignments, they may talk if it is to someone in their group and it is about the work. If they need to sharpen a pencil or get some materials during work times, they may do so without permission as long as they do not disturb other students.

First-Day Activities

Activity	Description
Administrative activity and an initial group task (8 minutes)	The teacher tells students that she would like them to fill out a class card and make a name card to be used in class to help her and other students learn their names. She then designates students in each group as Chair 1, Chair 2, Chair 3, and Chair 4. She tells them that when they work in groups, different chairs will have different roles and that the roles will be rotated so that each student gets a chance to do different things. Then Mrs. James requests, "Chair 1, please open the group folder on the desk and look in the right-hand pocket. Take out a yellow card and a class card for each student."
	She has Chair 1 distribute these items in each group. Mrs. James then has students make name cards for their desks and fill out class cards. While students work on this task, she returns to her desk for a couple of minutes to attend to administrative matters. She then asks Chair 1 to collect the cards.
Description of procedures (10 minutes)	Mrs. James asks Chair 2 to look in the left-hand pocket of the folder and to take out the blue sheets listing classroom policies and procedures for each group member. She tells students that everyone will need a three-ring binder for this class and that this page should be the first one in it. The teacher then reviews the classroom and school policies regarding absence and tardiness, leaving the room, makeup work, tests, and detention for violating rules. Mrs. James explains that if she gives a warning to a student and it's ignored, she will assign a lunch detention, and the student must bring lunch to the room at noon and eat it there. She says, "If I have to come find you, you will serve two lunch detentions."
End of period	Mrs. James notes that time is almost up. She tells the students that she'll explain her grading policies and class activities the next day. Then she says, "Chair 3, if there is a new student in class assigned to your group tomorrow, would you please be responsible for helping her or him get a copy of the class policies, name card, and class card?"
	As the end-of-period bell rings, she asks the students to return their cards to the folder and to remain in their seats until she dismisses each group, which she does when materials have been returned to the folder and each group is seated and quiet.

Second-Day Activities

Activity	Description
Before the bell	Mrs. James collects folders from each group from the preceding period, replacing them with the next period's folders. She greets students as they enter, asking them to take seats with yesterday's group. She directs a few new students to join groups.

(continued)

Second-Day Activities

Activity	Description
Beginning the period (3 minutes)	The teacher greets the students warmly as soon as the bell rings. She reminds students that they are in groups and that they have a designated number, which will be the same as yesterday's number. She reminds those designated Chair 3 of their responsibility to help new members of the group.
Diagnostic test (15 minutes)	The teacher states, "Before we get started on today's lesson, I'd like you to answer some questions. This assignment is not group work; it must be done by you individually. This will not be for a grade, but I would like you to do your best. Your answers will help me understand what topics need review and also help me make group assignments. If you complete the work early, you should check it over, and then you may sit quietly and read." Mrs. James then distributes the diagnostic test and tells students to show their work. She monitors as students do the work. When the time is up, she asks those students who have been designated as Chair 4 to collect the papers in each group and bring them to her.
Description of procedures and grading policies (8 minutes)	The teacher reviews talk and movement procedures in groups. "Use group voices, please. Talk loudly enough to be heard by others in your group, but not so loudly that groups near you will be disturbed. Like this." (She demonstrates.) Mrs. James gives students a one-page handout describing grading policies. She explains these policies in detail and asks students to place this handout in their notebooks.
Preparation for group activity (4 minutes)	Mrs. James then announces the first activity. She explains to students that this activity will help them learn about working in groups and teach them some math concepts. She asks students to volunteer ideas about what it takes to be a good group member. Stressing positive examples, Mrs. James supports especially the ideas of sharing, helping, listening, encouraging, and working hard.
Math lesson (20 minutes)	The teacher shows students a balance scale and relates it to the idea of an equation. She points out that if something is added to or subtracted from one side of the balance, it must also be added to or subtracted from the other side to preserve the balance. She asks for volunteers to come up and demonstrate how to put the equation in balance if an operation is performed on one side. Then she demonstrates how to add and subtract quantities to determine the value or weight of an unknown item. She gives the class similar problems to work in groups, stating that there are several ways to solve the problem and that they should use the materials in their group folder. Then Mrs. James requests that Chair 4 opens the folder and distributes the materials. She says she will ask someone in each group to report on the group's solution to one of the problems. After the groups have worked for a little while, the teacher calls on one person from each group to report on a problem; she prompts students as needed while they demonstrate the process of arriving at a solution using the scale.

Second-Day Activities

Activity	Description
End of period (5 minutes)	Mrs. James asks students to comment on their roles in their groups. She also asks for suggestions about what works best for various roles. She praises the students for their creativity in developing solutions to the problems and for their efforts. About a minute before the end-of-period bell, she announces to the students that they may put away their materials and get ready to leave. She asks those designated as Chair 1 to return the materials to their group's folder. When the bell rings, Mrs. James dismisses the class by groups after materials are put away and the group's desks are properly arranged.

Third-Day Activities

Activity	Description
Before the bell	Mrs. James tells students to check the name list at each group of desks to find their group.
Group activity (5 minutes)	The teacher tells the students that they will stay in their groups for several weeks. She assigns chair numbers to the group members and asks students designated as Chair 1 to open the folder and distribute a blank card so that each student can make a name tag. Then she has students play a quick name game for introductions within each group.
Textbook checkout (12 minutes)	Mrs. James has one student from each group distribute texts from several piles at the back of the room. While students cover their books, the teacher records book numbers.
Content activity and a new teaching strategy (15 minutes)	The teacher reviews concepts from yesterday's lesson with the balance scale. She has Chair 2 distribute materials from a box in each group. Students use the materials to work along with the teacher as she demonstrates various ways to solve several problems. Then Mrs. James tells the students that they will work in pairs in the next activity, and she writes "Think-Pair-Share" on the chalkboard. Students will first think about how to solve a problem, then work in pairs on it, and then take turns explaining the solution or demonstrating the steps to each other. "It's not enough just to work out a solution. Each of you must be able to explain to your partner how you did it," she adds. Afterward, Mrs. James has volunteers come forward to demonstrate and explain their solutions using the scale.
Group work (17 minutes)	Students are now given problems to solve as a group. These problems are somewhat more difficult, involving several steps. Mrs. James asks each group to work together to solve the problems. She asks Chairs 3 to be recorders of the solutions and Chairs 4 to be moderators. Based on yesterday's discussion, the teacher reviews briefly what these roles entail.

(continued)

Third-Day Activities

Activity	Description
	As the groups work on the problem, the teacher moves from group to group, checking on progress. She has several groups report back to the class. Afterward, students are given an assignment, due the next day, which they work on for the remainder of the class. They may work together on problems but are expected to show their own work on the assignment.
End of period (5 minutes)	With about 5 minutes remaining in the period, the teacher asks students to put away their work. She says that unfinished problems should be completed as homework. Mrs. James then initiates a short discussion about helping; she asks students what it feels like not to understand something. She also asks about ways they might react when they're in that situation. "Everyone will experience those feelings and do some of those things, especially if they're made to feel dumb. In this class, though, we will learn from our mistakes, and no one should be embarrassed by not understanding something. Also, helping other students is a great way to gain in understanding. I certainly understand math much better now that I have taught it than I did when I was a student."
	Mrs. James explains that everyone will have opportunities to explain problems and answer questions in her class. If there is something they don't understand, they should ask for another explanation. She and the class then discuss how to explain in ways that are most helpful. The class is dismissed at the bell.

■ Case Study 6.2

BEGINNING THE YEAR IN A HIGH SCHOOL BIOLOGY CLASS

First-Day Activities

Activity	Description
Before the bell	As students enter the room before the bell rings, Ms. Holly greets students at the front of the room near the doorway and tells them to take a seat near the front of the room.
Introduction (1 minute)	When the bell rings, the teacher moves to the front of the room and introduces herself. She tells students how to check their schedules to make sure they're in the right room. She gives her name and its spelling, announces the room number and course number, and tells students what abbreviations to look for on their schedule cards. Then she pleasantly welcomes them to her class.

First-Day Activities

Activity	Description
Roll call (3 minutes)	Before the teacher begins to call roll, she explains to students the procedures she wants them to use. She expects them to raise their hands when she calls their names and to tell her the name they would like to be called. After roll call, she records the names of two students not on her roll after checking their class schedule cards.
Course overview (6 minutes)	Ms. Holly begins by giving an introduction to the course. She lists seven major topics to be covered during the semester. She then describes each of the items on the list and mentions several of the activities and goals relating to each topic. Students listen quietly and ask a few questions when the teacher invites them to respond.
Presentation of classroom behavior policies and rules (12 minutes)	Ms. Holly distributes copies of procedures and requirements for the class. She tells the students to put their name, the date, and the period at the top, and to keep these sheets at the front of their class folders at all times. The information sheet contains three sections. The first outlines eight areas of classroom procedures and rules. The second describes the notebook that is a major requirement for the course, and the third describes the grading system that will be used in the course. The teacher discusses each of the items in the procedures section in turn, and the students listen and follow on their sheets. Next, Ms. Holly covers policies for being on time to class and consequences for tardiness, the importance of daily attendance, procedures for making up work after absences, turning in classwork on time and consequences for late work, keeping all papers in the science notebook and replacing lost papers, and routines for ending the class period and dismissal. The teacher displays the school handbook for students and tells them that they will go over the handbook and laboratory procedures in greater detail in class later during the week.
Discussion of grading and notebook requirements (10 minutes)	Ms. Holly then describes the system that she will use for determining grades in the class. One of the major requirements will be a notebook for all student work. She explains the requirements for this notebook: the type of folder, the importance of keeping papers in the proper order, the heading for papers, the table of contents, and the requirement that all papers in the notebook be completed and/or corrected before the notebook is turned in. After answering student questions about the notebook, the teacher describes the grading system. (Tests in the class count as 40 percent of the grade. Daily work is also 40 percent, and the notebook is 20 percent. There will be two or three unit exams during each six-week period.) The teacher also mentions extra-credit projects, which can be done later in the grading period.

(continued)

First-Day Activities

Activity	Description
Filling out information cards, checking out books, and covering books (12 minutes)	After this presentation of procedures and requirements for the course, Ms. Holly asks students to fill out information cards. She shows a model card on the projector screen and goes over the items with students. Then she explains to them the procedure they will use for checking out books and covering them. Because students have been assigned their lockers, the teacher passes out textbooks, directing students to check through them for damage and write their names inside the front cover. The teacher has the name of the text and the information that students are supposed to write in their book displayed on the whiteboard, along with instructions for recording the number neatly on the class card, covering the book, and information about the cost of the book. The teacher passes out book covers, and students cover their books after completing their information cards.
Discussions of textbook reading assignment (8 minutes)	Ms. Holly then asks students to look at a page in their text, and she introduces them to its format. She leads a discussion on how students can find the chapter objectives and use chapter titles and subtitles, along with the glossary and index, to guide them in their reading. The teacher briefly discusses their reading assignment (written on the chalkboard).
Seat work (5 minutes)	Ms. Holly distributes assignment sheets and gives directions for answering questions on the sheets as part of the homework assignment. This assignment is a simple introduction to using various parts of the textbook to locate information. Students begin work on their reading or homework assignment while the teacher confers with one student about registration. When the bell rings signaling the end of class, the teacher reminds students of what to bring tomorrow and dismisses them.

Second-Day Activities

Activity	Description
Seat work, roll, and other administrative matters (6 minutes)	As soon as the tardy bell rings, Ms. Holly distributes a sheet for students to work on. This task is an extension of the students' classwork assignment from the previous day—an easy assignment in which students used the table of contents and book index to locate specific information. While students work on the assignment, Ms. Holly calls roll and takes care of two new students.
Discussion of homework and seat-work assignments (12 minutes)	The teacher calls for the students' attention and begins asking questions from the previously assigned worksheets. Students volunteer answers, and the teacher leads a discussion. Students check their own papers during this discussion.

Second-Day Activities

Activity	Description
Presentation and discussion of textbook chapter (30 minutes)	Ms. Holly distributes an outline of the chapter that students were to have read for homework. The outline gives the main points and allows students room to fill in additional information from the presentation. The teacher also has a copy of the outline displayed on the projector screen. Students take notes as Ms. Holly discusses the content.
End of period (2 minutes)	The teacher ends discussion of the first chapter and explains requirements for a short homework assignment. She then reminds students that each day they are to get ready to leave class by checking their work area for neatness and making sure they have all their belongings and materials ready.
	Ms. Holly shows them where the homework assignment will be written each day on the front board, along with the list of what they will need to bring to class the next day. Students are told to be sure to check this every day. The teacher answers several questions from students and leads an informal discussion until the bell rings. Ms. Holly then dismisses the class.

■ Case Study 6.3

CONDUCT PROBLEMS IN A HISTORY CLASS

When the school year began, Mr. Davis told his American history classes that he had just one major rule for conduct: the Golden Rule. "If you'll treat others as you want to be treated, then we'll get along fine," he said. Then he added, "Just be sure to respect each other's rights, and that includes mine, and we'll all have a good year." Mr. Davis also told his students that he expected them to behave maturely because they were in high school and that if one of them got out of line, he would be quite willing to send that student to the school office to be dealt with by the assistant principal.

The classes did, indeed, function without major disruptions for several weeks. Gradually, however, almost imperceptibly, Mr. Davis began having difficulty getting students settled down to start the daily lesson. And once begun, presentations and class discussions seemed to be conducted with an undercurrent of noise as students whispered, joked, and socialized. Mr. Davis found himself interrupting the lessons more and more often to call for quiet or to remind students of what they were supposed to be doing. Problems were occurring in each class period but were worst in the last period of the day. By the end of the fourth week of classes, the teacher had sent two students to the office for persistent talking during class, including talking back to him when he asked them to be quiet. Behavior was better for a day or so afterward, but students were soon back to being noisy and inattentive. The following description of the class a few days later is typical.

At the beginning of the period, Mr. Davis wrote a discussion question on the front board. While he checked roll and returned papers, students were supposed to write a paragraph answering the question in preparation for a class discussion. However, only about half the class actually did the work; other students talked, several sat doing nothing, and two students were out of their seats. The teacher asked one student to sit down, but the student didn't. When he told a particularly noisy girl to "close your mouth," she responded, "I can't." During the discussion, students who were talking at the beginning of class complained that they did not understand the question. A few students raised their hands to volunteer responses during the discussion, and Mr. Davis called on them; other students called out responses, sometimes silly ones. Later, he assigned questions for the end of the chapter to be turned in the next day. Most students worked on this assignment in class, although some played with electronics or talked. Three students passed notes back and forth. The noise level built up. Ten minutes before the end of the period, most students had stopped working and were conversing.

What might Mr. Davis do to establish better behavior in his classes? Compare your answer to the key in the Appendix.

■ Checklist: Getting Off to a Good Start

Check When Complete	Item	Notes
☐	1. Are your room and materials preparations complete? (See Chapter 1.)	_____
☐	2. Have you decided on your class procedures, rules, and their associated consequences? (See Chapters 3, 8, and 10.)	_____
☐	3. Are you familiar with the parts of the building to which you may send students (library, bathrooms, etc.), and do you know what procedures should be followed?	_____
☐	4. Have you decided what school policies and rules you will need to present to students?	_____
☐	5. Have you prepared a handout for students or a bulletin board display of rules, major class procedures, and course requirements?	_____
☐	6. Do you know what bell schedule will be followed during the first week?	_____
☐	7. Is your lesson plan for the first few days of school ready for each class?	_____
☐	8. Do you have complete class rosters?	_____
☐	9. Do you have adequate numbers of textbooks, desks, and other class materials?	_____

Check When Complete	Item	Notes
☐	10. Have you decided on the procedures you will use for checking out textbooks to students?	
☐	11. Have you prepared alternative activities to use if the period is extended?	
☐	12. Do you know whether any of your students have a physical condition that should be accommodated in your room arrangement or instruction?	

MyEducationLab *Self-Check 6.1*

MyEducationLab *Self-Check 6.2*

MyEducationLab *Self-Check 6.3*

MyEducationLab *Application Exercise 6.1*   Using what you've learned in this chapter, view the video and respond to the questions.

MyEducationLab *Application Exercise 6.2*   Using what you've learned in this chapter, view the video and respond to the questions.

MyEducationLab *Application Exercise 6.3*   Using what you've learned in this chapter, read and respond to this scenario.

MyEducationLab *Application Exercise 6.4*   Using what you've learned in this chapter, read and respond to this scenario.

MyEducationLab *Classroom Management Simulation 6.1*   Engage with the Classroom Management Simulation *Helping All Students Believe They Can Achieve.*

CHAPTER 7

Planning and Conducting Instruction

Let's assume that your classroom is organized, you've developed and taught your rules and procedures, and you have systems in place to manage student work. It is at this point that management and instruction meet. Well-planned lessons with a variety of appropriate activities support the positive learning environment that your carefully considered management decisions have begun to create. Interesting, well-paced lessons are a key to holding students' attention; unimaginative or confusing lessons with limited opportunities for student participation are boring or frustrating to students, and they will create the conditions for discipline problems to develop.

This chapter describes how to plan and conduct instruction in ways that support the kinds of learning you want for your students. When you plan for instruction, you will need to identify the activities you will use. Therefore, we will examine the key aspects of the many types of activities that form the basis for instruction at the secondary level. We will also consider how to arrange these activities and how to get the most out of them, including provisions for feedback to students, technology use, clarity, effective activity management, and efficient transitions. Although this chapter is not intended to substitute for the study of specific methods of teaching particular subjects, some of the tasks of planning, organizing, and conducting instruction are basic to all content areas. Consequently, the ideas presented here should be helpful regardless of the secondary subject you teach.

■ Planning Classroom Activities

The term *activity* describes organized behavior that the teacher and students engage in for a common purpose. Typical activities in secondary classes include presentations, discussions, recitations, group work, classwork, independent seat work, and checking, among many others. Furthermore, activities are not always content based. For example, beginning-of-period activities may be mainly procedural.

Activities are an important aspect of instructional planning—they consume time, and time is a precious commodity. Unless your school uses block scheduling, class periods are usually less than an hour long, so activities must be limited accordingly. If your school uses block scheduling, your class periods will be longer, but (depending on the type of blocking) you may meet only every other day. Regardless of the length of your class periods, you will need to be efficient in order for your students to have enough time to accomplish your curriculum's learning objectives.

You will engage in several levels of planning, both long range (by the year or semester) and short range (weekly and daily), and each level of planning should be coordinated. Thus, you can divide the semester plan into units of instruction, and within units, into weekly and daily plans. This type of organization allows you to coordinate the daily activities to produce a cohesive course focusing on the main objectives and goals. Without a master plan, daily activities can appear unrelated to one another and to long-range objectives.

In addition to their potential for helping students reach learning objectives, activities are selected in part for their potential for maintaining students' involvement throughout the period. For this reason, multiple activities—rather than a single long one—need to be planned for most class periods. Activities that allow student participation or that provide each student with an opportunity to practice or apply lesson content are also desirable; they help students learn the content, and they promote higher levels of involvement in the lesson compared to only sitting and listening.

Even though much of your daily planning for classes will focus on organizing activities, you should keep in mind the broader perspective: your course as a whole. You need to know what knowledge and skills students are expected to develop and what units, topics, or textbook chapters are typically included in the course. Many outcomes are determined by state or local curriculum guidelines or by mandated testing. Examine the teacher's edition of your textbook and preview each major section, noting statements of overall objectives and the scope and sequence of content. Identifying reasonable expectations for your grade level will be helpful when you decide on course objectives and determine adequate coverage of topics. Other useful sources of information about appropriate content and reasonable expectations for students in particular age and grade levels may be found in school district or state education agency curriculum guides, courses and books on instructional methods in your subject, and yearbooks of national teachers' organizations in your academic field. Finally, your department chairperson, your instructional coordinator or supervisor, and other teachers in your subject area can provide helpful suggestions on course scope and topical sequence.

Types of Activities

Some of the most frequently used types of classroom activities are described in the following sections. Think of them as building blocks for constructing your class periods.

Opening and Closing the Period.   The chief concern of the *opening* activity is to help the students make an orderly transition into the classroom and be ready for the rest of the period, while the teacher handles administrative tasks such as the attendance check and takes care of previously absent students. In Chapters 4 and 6, we described alternatives for structuring the opening, including the use of either academic warm-ups or an administrative routine with stated expectations for student behavior.

The goal of the *closing* activity is to bring the period to an end in an orderly manner, with students ready to move on to the next class, leaving your room in good condition for the next period. Teachers usually give students a warning before the end of the period so that they have enough time to put materials away and get their own things ready. Other procedures for the closing activity were discussed in Chapter 4.

Presenting New Content.   In this activity, the teacher presents new information, elaborates or extends a concept or principle, conducts a demonstration, shows how to perform a skill, or describes how to solve a problem. During content development, the teacher takes an active role in helping students think about the new content, relate it to what they know, and apply it. One chief management concern is making sure that students are *active* rather than passive. Therefore, you will have to find ways to involve them in the development of the lesson. Teacher questions are used for this purpose, allowing the teacher to check student understanding and to encourage students to contribute to steps in problem solving, to apply concepts or principles, and to analyze ideas. In addition to questioning for comprehension, it is often a good idea to obtain work samples or other student demonstrations of the skills being taught during content-development activities. Doing so allows the teacher to gauge how well students follow the presentation and also helps engage students.

As you present a lesson, stay with the planned sequence unless an obvious change is needed. Avoid needless digressions, interruptions, or tangential information. Inserting irrelevant information into a lesson only confuses students about what they are expected to learn. Displaying key concepts, new terms, major points, and other critical information on a screen or board underscores their importance.

Presentations should be as focused and concrete as possible. Use examples, illustrations, demonstrations, props, charts, and any other means of adding substance and dimension to abstractions in the lesson. Avoid the vague expressions and verbal time fillers that, at best, communicate little information and make presentations difficult to follow. Then allow students time and opportunity to process the information.

Discussion.   In most secondary school classes, discussions are conducted as teacher-led, whole-class activities. The purpose of using discussion is to encourage students to evaluate events, topics, or results; to clarify the basis for their judgments and opinions; and to become aware of other points of view. Discussion questions usually elicit student judgments and opinions, and teachers avoid evaluating the students' responses directly. Instead, students are encouraged to examine their opinions and beliefs and to understand other perspectives. Students may respond to each other rather than to the teacher alone. The teacher's role then becomes one of clarifying and using student ideas rather than evaluating their correctness.

Management of a discussion activity calls for a number of skills, including warmth or friendliness (to promote security); listening skills (to invite participation); conflict resolution; and encouraging expression of divergent points of view (to foster acceptance and openness). Although it is common for some students to contribute more to a discussion than others, the teacher should not allow a few students to monopolize the discourse. Asking reticent members for their opinions or views of what has just been discussed is a good way to do so. Giving students opportunities to paraphrase, clarify, and elaborate on their own or other students' remarks is a useful way to keep a discussion moving along and on target, perhaps allowing the teacher to transfer some of the responsibility for discussion maintenance to students. Getting students to listen to each other, rather than treat the discussion as a dialogue with the teacher, is sometimes difficult. It's important, then, to emphasize that students should respond to each other—not only to the teacher's questions and comments.

When using a discussion format, plan your questions carefully. Students should be made aware of your ground rules for participation (raise hands, listen carefully, respect each person's right to self-expression). Some secondary classes, especially at the middle school level, have difficulty sustaining a discussion for very long, so plan short ones (e.g., 10 to 15 minutes) until you have an idea of what you and your classes can handle. After students have acquired good discussion skills, the length of this activity can be increased as appropriate.

Checking Classwork or Homework.   In this activity, students evaluate their own work. The activity is appropriate only when a judgment as to the correctness of the work can be made easily. Student checking provides quick feedback to students and allows the teacher to identify and discuss common errors on assignments. If performance on the assignment is given a grade, monitoring during checking may be needed to prevent cheating. Some teachers discourage cheating by requiring that checking be done with a pencil or a pen of a different color than was used for the assignment. Collecting and examining student papers will give you a good idea of comprehension of the assignment content.

Remember that you must teach students the appropriate procedures for checking (e.g., make no mark if the answer is correct; neatly mark an X before the item if it is wrong). A uniform checking procedure helps students complete the activity efficiently; it will also be easier for you to review the students' work when you collect it if all students use the same set of marks and symbols.

Recitation.   This activity, sometimes called a *drill*, is a question-and-answer sequence in which the teacher asks questions, usually of a factual nature, and accepts or corrects student responses. This sequence of question/answer/evaluation is repeated frequently, with many students being asked to respond until a body of content has been covered. In effect, a recitation is a form of oral checking. It can be used to provide practice, quickly review content, or check student understanding of a previous lesson or assigned reading. It can also be used to review spelling words, vocabulary definitions in any subject, or other recall of facts.

When using recitation to check student understanding, it is important to distribute questions to all students, not only to the volunteers. Develop a way to determine systematically who gets a turn to answer, perhaps by using a checklist or name cards. Sometimes teachers do not allow students enough time to respond, which reduces opportunities for students who are slow to answer. Some experts recommend a "wait time" of several seconds before giving a prompt or calling on another student.

Instead of asking only individual students to respond, the teacher can ask for a "choral" response; that is, all students are expected to respond. This provides for greater student involvement and may encourage more reluctant students to participate. It is also a good pacing strategy because it avoids the slowdowns that occur when individual students are unable to answer the question. Most recitation questions should be easy, by definition, because they review content and are factual. Frequent wrong answers are a sign that reteaching is needed or that more student practice should be provided.

Classwork.   *Classwork* is a set of exercises, problems, or assignments worked on by students while in a whole class, teacher-led format. The teacher asks questions, poses a problem, or asks students to complete an exercise, usually following a presentation. All students are expected to engage in the task, which the teacher actively monitors and provides feedback and clarification, as needed. Classwork is used to check students' understanding of the content and to identify any additional instruction needed before asking the students to work on the assignment independently or in groups. It is commonly used as a bridge or transition activity between a teacher presentation and independent student work.

Independent Work.   Often teachers give students assignments that build on previously presented material. *Independent work* (sometimes called *seat work*) is that portion of the assignment completed by individual students, generally while the teacher moves through the class to check their progress. Often, the portion of the independent work assignment not completed in class becomes a homework assignment, unless the material or resources needed to finish it are available only in the classroom.

Good management of independent work activities has several components. First, adequate content development must precede the independent student activity so that students can work productively on their own. Next, the teacher must clearly communicate the requirements and objectives of the students' work and arrange for access to needed materials or resources. A good strategy is to begin the independent work assignment only after it has been preceded by a similar classwork activity (e.g., by working several of the exercises, problems, or questions together in whole-class format). This gets students started, gives them an opportunity to ask questions, and enables the teacher to observe and correct common problems in a whole-class format rather than having to deal with the same problem with several individuals. Subsequently, the teacher should actively monitor the students' work to detect problems early and provide corrective feedback.

Independent work activities are best used for consolidating or extending prior learning rather than for acquiring new content. Therefore, be careful not to overuse independent work. A rule of thumb is to devote at least as much time to content development as to independent work. Moreover, student engagement is harder to maintain in lengthy independent activities. If you do find yourself assigning long periods of time to individual assignments, try breaking the activity into smaller segments and having a discussion or review between them. The change in lesson format will help refocus student attention, and it will give you an opportunity to check student comprehension and clear up problems.

Small-Group Work.   The small-group format can achieve many objectives. For example, to promote greater comprehension and facilitate retention of important content, pairs of students can explain concepts to each other or describe how they solved a problem. Group work can also be used for completing laboratory observations or other assignments, drilling on spelling words or new vocabulary, reviewing for a test, or generating different ways to solve a problem. Small groups can be used for gathering the information needed to prepare a project, planning a group report, or discussing an issue or topic.

Small groups are used as an integral part of such teaching methods as cooperative learning, reciprocal teaching, and project-based learning. In cooperative learning activities (see Chapter 8), students work together to complete group and individual assignments. In reciprocal teaching, students take turns as small-group leaders during discussions of text material in order to practice summarizing, questioning, clarifying, and predicting. In project-based learning, students work collaboratively to develop solutions to "ill-structured" problems; that is, problems having multiple possible solutions or unknown aspects, or that require judgment and evaluation.

Small groups work best when objectives are clear and when steps or procedures for achieving them are understood by the students. Careful monitoring of the groups is helpful in keeping them focused and on track, although the teacher's role depends in part on the nature of the group task (Cohen, 1994). When students are working on a closed-end objective in which the outcome is clear and a course of action to achieve it is apparent, specific teacher direction—along with close monitoring, prompting, and redirection, when necessary—is an efficient management approach. If the task outcome is not well defined, however, and the approach to the task is divergent, a hovering teacher can reduce the likelihood that a group will take responsibility for developing its own approach or achieve optimum results. To maximize student involvement in such group tasks, it's best to give groups more latitude in determining how to develop their ideas while still providing direction about acceptable behavior. Management of small groups is discussed extensively in Chapter 8, so we will not pursue it here.

Test Administration.   Administering tests or quizzes is a common activity in middle and high school classrooms. Presenting directions on a PowerPoint slide or transparency helps make certain that all students know what is expected of them. Your planning for this activity should include what early finishers may do while waiting for the rest of the class to complete the exam. Teacher monitoring during exams reduces the likelihood of cheating, so it's best not to engage in activities that distract your attention from the students.

Student Presentations and Demonstrations.   In this activity students give a report, demonstrate a procedure or skill, or summarize work done on a short- or long-term project. Presentations may be made by individual students or by groups. You will find that presentations go better when students are allowed time for planning and when presentation guidelines are given in advance. It's also useful to discuss with students the kinds of audience behaviors that are desirable. A good opener for a discussion of procedures is to ask students for suggestions about how they want others to behave or participate when it is their turn to give a presentation.

■ Organizing Activities

The center stage of instruction is often occupied by teacher presentations because they are a major vehicle for new learning. However, all class periods include other activities, so an appropriate sequence must be planned. Here is one commonly observed sequence of activities in secondary school classrooms:

1. Opening routine
2. Checking of previous work
3. Presentation of new content
4. Class work
5. Independent or group work, or discussion
6. Closing

Advantages of this sequence are that it has a minimum number of transition points, it allows checking and feedback of previous work, it provides for the presentation of new material, and it has a practice or an application activity.

A disadvantage of the same sequence is that it does not easily allow for the presentation of different topics within the same period, and it requires that the content be amenable to presentation in a single segment. Also, it may be difficult to sustain student engagement if the teacher presentation or independent work activities are lengthy, as will occur in an extended block period. A variation of the sequence that accommodates more than one type of content or more complex content is this:

1. Opening
2. Checking
3. Presentation
4. Class work and/or independent work
5. Presentation
6. Class work
7. Independent or group work, or discussion
8. Closing

This sequence or a similar one can be used when two different types of content must be taught within the same period, and the teacher wants to provide a period of practice or consolidation following each content development activity. Beginning teachers whose schools use block scheduling, in which classes meet for "double" periods, report that planning for the longer periods is challenging, in part because the teachers don't plan enough content to fill the time and find it difficult to keep students engaged (Zepeda & Mayers, 2001). The second activity sequence described, with its shorter but more frequent activities, would usually be a better way to organize instruction for longer periods. The sequence can also be used when a complex lesson is divided into two phases of content development, each followed by short periods of student work either alone or in groups. Subdividing new content into two parts with an intervening practice activity helps students consolidate learning from the first part before they are asked to contend with the new learning required in the second part. It also allows the teacher to check student understanding and provide prompt feedback. A possible problem with this sequence is that it produces more transition points and thus greater potential for student disengagement. These transitions can usually be managed without difficulty, however, because student movement, new materials, or change in lesson focus are not required in the teacher presentation–class work–independent work cycle. Thus, the various activities blend together, usually without conspicuous transitions.

Of course, not all whole-group lessons fit either of the activity patterns just described. For instance, a science or social studies lesson may consist of a relatively long period of active student exploration or problem solving in small groups, followed by a whole-class content development discussion. Ongoing projects may entail long segments of individual seat work or small-group work interspersed with short segments of whole-class or small-group instruction. Nevertheless, the two common patterns described here provide useful frameworks for building many teacher-directed lessons.

■ Planning for Technology in the Classroom

Using technology—whether for content development, research, or practice—requires awareness and planning. Few classrooms have as many computers as teachers would like, but almost all have at least one. Develop strategies to make technology a productive tool in helping students reach their academic goals. Your school may have a computer lab, your classroom might include computer stations, and/or your class may have access to individual laptops or tablets. As noted in Chapter 6, each type of technology access requires procedures for its use. In addition, you may want to train one or more student "computer experts" who can assist quietly while you continue with whole- or small-group instruction. This responsibility can be rotated among students so that everyone has an opportunity to become an "expert" at different times. Parent volunteers may also provide helpful classroom assistance.

Internet access at school gives students ready and convenient access to information. Unfortunately, not all of it is appropriate; therefore, certain precautions must be taken when including Internet use in your lessons. Some school districts have developed fair use policies for the technology they provide that include required signatures of all staff agreeing to supervise student online access. Most districts utilize Internet filters. If a school district requires that parents give written permission before their child is allowed on the Internet, teachers will need alternatives for students without permission. Students should be cautioned not to give their last names or any personal information over the Internet.

Visit websites (or use software) in advance so that you know the expected screen displays and can anticipate any student difficulties. Monitor students frequently as they access information on the Web. By giving them specific information to find and a limited time in which to find it, you can avoid many hazards. It is a good idea to set up guidelines for use at the beginning of the year. For example, have the students sign a contract that states "I will use the Internet for school use only. If I knowingly search for inappropriate materials, I will lose the privilege of using the Internet for the remainder of the grading period." To eliminate the argument that a site was accidentally found, teach students to click the "back" button on the browser and get your attention immediately if they access an inappropriate site by mistake.

When you plan an activity that integrates technology with instruction, it's important to preview software, test equipment, and check Internet accessibility to avoid problems that can interfere with the activity's momentum. For example, if students need to Skype™ or connect to an online site, technical problems may cause slowdowns or stop the activity altogether. Having a backup assignment or alternate online sites would be possible, of course, but preventing the problem is the most desirable course.

■ Kounin's Concepts for Managing Group Instruction

A central theme in managing activities well is the idea of activity flow, the degree to which a lesson proceeds smoothly without digressions, diversions, or interruptions. Lessons with a good flow maintain student attention and are less likely to offer opportunities for deviance because most of the cues for students are directed toward behaviors appropriate for the lesson. When lesson flow is jerky, with frequent interruptions and side trips, there is more competition for student attention from cues external to the focus of the lesson and therefore a greater tendency for students to go off task.

A classic series of classroom research studies by Kounin and his colleagues (Kounin, 1970; Kounin & Gump, 1974; Kounin & Obradovic, 1968; see also Johnston, 1995; Perron & Downey, 1997) identified several concepts that contribute to the effective management of interactive group activities such as content development, discussion, and independent work. In Kounin's studies, classroom lessons were videotaped, and teacher behaviors were analyzed to determine which ones predicted classrooms with high amounts of student involvement and low levels of deviant behavior. The concepts that emerged from this research provide a rich source of ideas about conducting instruction.

Activity flow is maintained through three types of teacher behaviors: preventing misbehavior, managing lesson movement, and maintaining group focus. Within each type of behavior are two or three related skills. These skills are defined and examples of them are given in Table 7.1, accompanied by a discussion.

Preventing Misbehavior

Classrooms are complex settings. Many events can take place at the same time, and one cannot always anticipate what will occur or when. New teachers especially are at risk of focusing too closely on single events or on selected areas of the classroom, thus overlooking developing problems until they have spread or become disruptive. Understanding two of Kounin's concepts, withitness and overlapping, helps to prevent this mistake.

Withitness is the degree to which the teacher corrects misbehavior before it intensifies or spreads; it also targets the correct student. A teacher who is not very "withit" fails to stop a problem until it has escalated and may require a major intervention to bring it to a halt, or else the teacher fails to catch the perpetrator and instead targets either the wrong student or a Johnny-come-lately. Underlying aspects of withitness include good monitoring and the prompt handling of inappropriate behavior.

Overlapping refers to how the teacher handles two or more simultaneous events: For example, a visitor comes to the door in the middle of a lesson; a student leaves his seat without permission while the teacher is leading a discussion; several students get into a squabble while the teacher is busy helping other students across the room. A teacher who has good overlapping skills handles both events without

table7.1 ■ How Effective Managers Maintain Activity Flow

Issue	Skill	Definition	Example
Preventing misbehavior	Withitness	General awareness of the classroom and students; prompt and correct identification and correction of misbehavior	The teacher makes eye contact with a student who is about to "shoot a basket" with a wad of paper. The student puts the paper away. A student behind him, who has seen the interaction, decides he's not likely to get away with shooting a basket either.
	Overlapping	Attending to two or more simultaneous events	The teacher is leading a class discussion when a student comes in late. The teacher nods to him, continuing the discussion. Later, when students have begun a seatwork assignment, she attends to him and signs his tardy slip.
Managing movement	Momentum	Keeping lessons moving briskly; planning carefully to avoid slowdowns	The teacher notices that the explanation of a relatively minor concept is taking too long and distracting attention from the primary focus of the lesson. The teacher makes a mental note to go more deeply into this concept in a separate lesson the next day and moves on.
	Smoothness	Staying on track with the lesson; avoiding digressions and diversions that can lead to confusion	While being responsive to student interests, the teacher avoids comments that tend to draw attention away from the key points of the lesson.
Maintaining group focus	Group alerting	Engaging the attention of the whole class while individuals are responding	Each student has a number that was drawn from a hat on the way into class. The teacher draws numbers and uses them to call on students during a fast-paced review.
	Encouraging accountability	Communicating to students that their participation will be observed and evaluated	At the end of discussion and practice of a new skill, students are told to turn to a neighbor and explain the process to him or her.
	Using higher participation formats	Using lessons that define behavior of students when they are not directly answering a teacher's question	While some students work problems at the board, students at their desks are instructed to check them by working the problems on paper.

dropping one to handle the other or ignoring the second event. To manage a long interruption, a teacher might tell students to get out some work; after they have done so, the teacher might then deal with the interrupter. The squabble away from the teacher might be handled by eye contact or a brief verbal directive while the teacher stays in contact with the original group.

A teacher who is "withit" and exhibits good overlapping skills is able to insulate lessons from the intrusions that student misbehavior or external interruptions might cause. Furthermore, by reacting promptly to problems (but not overreacting), the teacher can often use simple measures (eye contact, redirection, a quiet desist) that do not interfere with ongoing activities or distract students. If a teacher is not very "withit" or does not overlap when needed, lessons may be interrupted by student misbehavior and subsequently by the teacher's more visible and tardy reactions.

Managing Movement

Whereas withitness and overlapping are accomplished by handling external interruptions and student intrusions into the flow of the lesson, movement management is accomplished by avoiding teacher-caused intrusions or delays. (Note that "movement" in this context refers to lesson pacing and flow, not physical movement.) Good movement management is achieved through momentum and smoothness.

Momentum.   *Momentum* refers to pacing, and it is evident when lessons move along briskly. Teachers can slow momentum by dwelling too long on individual parts of a lesson, directions, or skills and by breaking an activity into too many parts. For example, students should be taught a standard heading for assignments that can be used routinely rather than having various forms that must be explained repeatedly. Another example is that teachers should avoid overdwelling on topics during presentations.

Smoothness.   A lesson that exhibits continuity rather than jerkiness epitomizes the concept of *smoothness*. A smoothly flowing lesson keeps students' attention; one that is jerky can be distracting. Teachers cause jerkiness by inserting irrelevant topics into a presentation or discussion, by deviating from the lessons, by starting an activity and then interrupting it, or by intruding into an activity (e.g., independent work) unnecessarily. In contrast, a smoothly managed activity is organized and free from diversions.

Maintaining Group Focus

Classroom instruction involves teaching students in groups, often a whole class at a time. The teacher should be conscious of the group influence on instruction. Like a conductor leading an orchestra, the teacher must elicit the performance of individuals yet still provide signals and directions that keep the whole class together. Group focus can be maintained through several techniques.

Group Alerting.   *Group alerting* means taking an action to engage the attention of the whole class while individuals are responding. It can take the form of creating suspense by telling students they might be called on next; calling on them randomly; asking students to listen carefully because they might be called on to add to the answer; or using a visual aid, display, or attention-capturing strategy. In contrast, examples of poor group alerting are engaging in a dialogue with one student or calling on a student before asking a question so that the rest of the class feels no need to pay attention to the question.

Encouraging Accountability.   *Accountability* occurs when the teacher lets students know that their performance will be observed and evaluated in some manner. It does not require a letter grade or a score (although it might); it only communicates some degree of teacher awareness of how individual students are performing. For example, the teacher might ask everyone who knows an answer to raise a hand and then call on one or more of those students; or the teacher could have all students write down answers, perform, or display work and then circulate to check it.

Higher Participation Formats.   Lessons that cue or program the behavior of students when they are not directly involved in answering a teacher's question have a higher built-in rate of participation than do lessons that merely assume that students will sit and watch when other students respond. *Higher participation formats* occur when students are expected to write answers, solve problems, read along, manipulate materials, or perform some other task during instruction.

Some activities lend themselves more to one type of group focus than to another. When teachers are planning instruction, it is helpful for them to consider which of the three aspects to use. For example, it might be difficult to use a high participation format during a demonstration that involves expensive materials, but group alerting might be easy to incorporate into the lesson.

Kounin's concepts are an important addition to a teacher's repertoire for understanding how to engage students during instruction. Not only do they help identify key aspects of effective teaching, but they can also be used to diagnose instructional problems and identify possible solutions. For example, if lessons seem to drag and student response is unenthusiastic, there may be a problem with group focus; a solution may be to work on alerting or accountability or to increase the degree of participation. Activities that take too long and that seem to go off track constantly might have a problem in the area of movement management; perhaps this teacher should check for the incidence of slowdowns and jerkiness.

■ Transition Management

The interval between any two activities is a transition, and the beginning and ending of periods are transitions. The goal of a transition is to bring the preceding activity to a successful conclusion and begin the next one without undue delay. Several management problems can occur at these times, such as long delays before starting the next activity or high levels of inappropriate or disruptive student behavior that can spill over into the next activity. Arlin (1979) found that the amount of off-task behavior increased during transitions, but when teachers structured transitions, off-task behavior was substantially reduced. Also, classrooms populated by students with learning and attention disorders are more susceptible to transition problems (Marks et al., 2003). The causes of transition problems include a lack of readiness by the teacher or the students for the next activity, unclear student expectations about appropriate behavior during transitions, and faulty procedures. Consider now several examples of transition problems and the suggestions for correcting them.

Transition Problem	Suggested Solution
Students talk loudly at the beginning of the period. The teacher is interrupted while checking attendance, resulting in a delay of the start of content activities.	Establish a beginning-of-period routine with clear expectations for student behavior. Have a content activity ready for students to begin at once.
Students talk too much during transitions, especially after an independent work assignment has been given but before they've begun working on it. Many students do not start their work activity for several minutes or at all.	Be sure students know what the assignment is; post it where they can see it easily. Work as a whole class on the first several exercises so that all students begin the lesson successfully and at the same time. Then walk around the room, check students' work, and give corrective and/or encouraging feedback.

Continued

Transition Problem	Suggested Solution
Students stop working long before the end-of-period bell; they then engage in excessive talking and leave the room a mess.	An end-of-period routine should be established: Students work until the teacher gives a signal, then they clean up around their desks or work areas before being dismissed.
Whenever the teacher attempts to move students from one activity into another, a number of students don't make the transition but continue working on the preceding activity. This delays the start of the next activity or results in confusion.	The teacher should establish a routine. Give the class notice a few minutes before an activity is scheduled to end. When it ends, students should put away materials from the first activity before getting out new materials for the second. The teacher should monitor the transition to make sure that all students complete it.
A few students always seem to be slow-pokes during transition, delaying the rest of the class.	Don't wait for one or two students and hold up the rest of the class. Go ahead and start, but be sure to monitor to find out why those few students are having trouble. It may help to move closer to these students during the transition.
Students frequently leave their seats to socialize, come up to the teacher to ask questions, attempt to get a bathroom permit, go to the wastebasket, or wander around the room during transitions.	Define appropriate behavior during transitions and explain the rationale for limiting student behavior during these times. Monitor students and be sure procedures are established to handle out-of-seat behavior.
The teacher delays the beginning of activities to look for materials, finish attendance reporting, return or collect papers, or chat with individual students while the rest of the students wait.	The teacher needs to have all materials ready. Once a transition begins, the teacher should avoid doing anything that interferes with his or her ability to monitor and direct students.

Instructional Management

Planning

Organize the parts of your lesson into a coherent sequence. If the lesson is complex, write down the main components. Be sure to review the unit and lesson in the teacher's edition of your textbook(s) and pay careful attention to suggestions for lesson development and activities. Study the exercises, questions, or problems provided in the textbook and decide which items would provide appropriate review of lesson objectives. Note examples, demonstrations, and key questions and activities to use in developing the main concepts. If some items in the independent work assignment go well beyond your lesson's scope, don't assign them as classwork or homework until you can teach the necessary content. If the content is not essential and you do not plan to teach it later, assign such items for enrichment or for extra credit.

Try to anticipate problems students may encounter in the lesson or assignments. Check for new terms and be ready to define them and present examples. It will benefit you to do some of the classwork or homework assignment yourself to uncover hurdles students will face; you can then build into your lesson some helpful hints or extra emphasis in these areas.

Consider what interest the lesson is likely to have for students. Will you be enthusiastic about teaching this material to your classes in this way? Your enthusiasm about the lesson is contagious and signals to students how you feel about its importance. If you find it interesting and exciting and you communicate this excitement to your class, students will probably respond with interest. However, if you are unenthusiastic about a lesson, chances are that your students will share your feelings. Consider changing your approach in some way to put a little more spark in the activities.

Presenting New Content Clearly

Either at the beginning of or during the presentation of new subject matter, explain to the students what the lesson objectives are. If the lesson is complex, provide an outline; displaying the topical sequence helps organize the content for students and provides a road map to keep them on course.

When students are expected to understand content from silent reading, viewing a film or tape, or completing an Internet search, provide a content outline with a few items filled in and spaces for students to supply the rest. This task focuses attention and provides motivation for careful reading or viewing.

As you present a lesson, stay with the planned sequence unless an obvious change is needed. Avoid needless digressions, interruptions, or tangential information. Inserting irrelevant information into a lesson only confuses students about what they are expected to learn. Displaying key concepts, new terms, major points, and other critical information on a PowerPoint slide or writing them on the board will underscore their importance. If students are required to take notes, the display will guide the information the students record.

Your presentation should be as focused and concrete as possible. Use examples, illustrations, demonstrations, physical props, charts, and other means of providing substance and dimension to abstractions in the lesson. Avoid vague expressions and verbal time fillers that communicate little information and make presentations difficult to follow.

SHOE–NEW BUSINESS © MacNelly – Distributed by King Features Syndicate, Inc. World Rights Reserved.

Monitoring Understanding

Student understanding should be checked during instruction, not only as a part of formal evaluations such as tests and assignments. Doing this allows the teacher to reteach essential content as needed. It also helps the teacher gauge when to adjust instruction.

Comprehension and skills can be checked at the beginning of, during, and at the end of instruction. The amount of informal assessment that is feasible depends on the available time and the importance of the information. Informal assessments are made by obtaining samples of oral, written, or other performance and using them to judge the degree to which students possess the desired knowledge or skills. Examples of checking for understanding include the following:

- At the beginning of a presentation, the teacher asks several students to define basic concepts that were covered previously and that will be needed to comprehend the presentation.
- During a presentation, the teacher asks students to write their answers to a pertinent question. She then moves among the class to read students' answers.
- Students, seated in groups, are given a problem to discuss and solve. Then the teacher asks one student in each group to summarize its solution.
- Halfway through a presentation, the teacher conducts a recitation on the lesson's main ideas up to that point.
- At several times during a lesson, the teacher displays on the overhead screen a multiple-choice question on a critical point. After students record an answer, she asks for "hands" to indicate response choices.
- During a content development activity, the teacher looks around the room frequently, observing student behavior; she or he also moves among the students as they work on a short classwork exercise, looking for evidence that students can perform the task.

In these examples, pertinent information was obtained from several students. In addition to providing potentially useful information about student comprehension, the strategies also allow a more active student role than simple listening and thus may encourage student involvement in the flow of the lesson.

■ Who Will I Teach? Coteaching in an Inclusive School

Marissa Higgins, newly hired to teach eighth-grade social studies at Zavala Middle School, is on her way to meet the other teachers on her team. The team consists of teachers from the content areas of math, science, social studies, and English language arts; a special education teacher; and a teacher certified in teaching English as a second language (ESL). In addition, a full-time teacher's aide is available to assist teachers across classes. When the principal, Mrs. Darcy, interviewed Marissa for the job, she explained that the school is organized into grade-level teams of 125 to 140 students each, and that scheduling of core classes is done within teams, although students may take elective classes out-of-team. "We think it's best for students if there is a core group of teachers working with the same group of students; having teams encourages collaboration on interdisciplinary units and it also promotes communication among teachers about their students," Mrs. Darcy explained. "In addition," she said, "since our school operates on an inclusion model, students who require special education are part of the student body taught by the team."

When Marissa asked about the number and kinds of students with special education status, she was told there are around 15 to18 on the team and that most have learning disabilities in language or math, but that some have ADHD. One student has an autism diagnosis, another student has significant hearing impairment, and yet another student has cerebral palsy and needs a wheelchair and a special computer to do his assignments. The principal added, "Around a third of the students you will teach come from homes where Spanish is the first language. Even though most of these students converse fluently in English, many still struggle in content subjects, so we place an ESL teacher on teams to work with these students and their teachers."

Pause and Reflect

1. How might the presence of these different kinds of students affect instructional planning and the management of instruction?
2. What roles will the teachers on this team take—that is, how will they work together and how will they work with the students?
3. What are some things that Marissa will need to address as she plans her work with the special education teacher and the ESL teacher?

Marissa Higgins will teach students in five different classes, and among the students in her classes will be both those who are second language learners and others who have an individualized education plan and are eligible to receive special education. Note that the school uses an *inclusion* model for delivering special education services. This means that most students requiring special education will receive their instruction in regular classroom settings, unless doing so will not be beneficial to them. Thus, Marissa's responsibility will be to *all* her students, including those who are eligible for special education services and the students who are English language learners. She will, however, have help!

Marissa will need to find out how instructional responsibilities are divided among members of the team. The most likely arrangement will be coteaching, with Marissa and the other content teachers taking a lead role, and the special education and ESL teachers acting in a supportive capacity during instruction. It would be possible for roles to change on occasion; for example, the special education or ESL teacher might take the lead in a lesson on study strategies in the content area, or a class might be split and each teacher could work with a group, or one teacher might lead one group while the other teacher works with the rest of the class (Villa, Thousand, & Nevin, 2004). However, because the special education teacher, the ESL teacher, and the aide will work with the classes of all four of the content teachers, they will have to rotate their time across classes; this arrangement thus favors a lead-teacher, support teacher arrangement. Other roles for the support teacher include circulating and assisting individual students during independent work (note that the support teacher may work with any student, not just special education or ELL students), team teaching, giving alternative assessments, and guiding a group of students through supplemental enrichment or classwork exercises (Dierker & Hines, 2014).

In addition to coteaching, other important considerations for collaboration include avoiding practices that cause problems for students who have special needs, such as overreliance on whole-class presentation and a "one-size-fits-all" approach to assignments and assessment (Cook, McDuffie-Landrum, Oshita, & Cook, 2011). The presence of a second teacher makes it more feasible to use differentiated instruction via small groups, to better monitor academic progress, and to use alternative forms of assessment. Similarly, ELLs have a better chance of receiving targeted literacy instruction and timely interventions as the result of collaboration between the regular education and the ESL teacher (Allison & Harklau, 2010). Students who are English language learners will benefit from vocabulary development in the content field as well as learning skills such as highlighting, taking notes, organizing information from multiple sources, and preparing a report or oral presentation (Mariage & Englert, 2010). Instructional modifications that may prove useful are structuring assignments to give credit for daily work and breaking more complex assignments into smaller segments for feedback and credit. Of course, all students in the class may also benefit from these modifications and competencies.

As she prepares to teach her classes, Marissa will need to learn about the special needs of her students. The special education teacher will be able to supply crucial information as well as to identify technology that is available for the students with hearing impairment, cerebral palsy, and learning disabilities. The ESL teacher will also be able to provide specific information about the language levels of students and will suggest ways to make instruction comprehensible to them.

Other areas for collaboration can be worked out over time, including coplanning, deciding on responsibilities for assessment and grading, maintaining communication with parents, and building a teamwide discipline plan. Having adequate time for group planning, evaluation, and reflection will be crucial to team functioning. A principal supportive of this approach is a great benefit to the teachers.

■ Chapter Summary

This chapter described concepts and strategies used during instruction that will help keep students engaged and actively learning. Appropriate design and arrangement of instructional activities was emphasized. Concepts developed by Kounin, such as withitness and movement management, gave insights into strategies that teachers can use to keep students engaged and prevent behavior problems from developing. Instructional planning, technology use, transition management, and presentation skills were also described.

■ Further Reading

Borich, G. (2014). *Effective teaching methods* (8th ed.). Upper Saddle River, NJ: Pearson Prentice Hall.

Practical yet theoretically substantive, this book provides teachers with effective teaching practices. Attention is given to instructional topics, including lesson and unit planning, teaching strategies, and technology integration.

Bransford, J. B., Brown, A. L., & Cocking, R. R. (Eds.). (1999). *How people learn.* Washington, DC: National Academy Press.

This research-based examination of learning emphasizes applications for schools and teachers. It's very readable, and it's packed with good ideas for instruction.

Feedback for Learning [Special Issue] (2012, September). *Educational Leadership, 70*(1).

This special issue includes multiple articles on providing effective feedback to students. Articles review the research, provide classroom examples, and offer practical suggestions for feedback (e.g., timing, impact, technology, and student response).

Johnston, B. D. (1995). "Withitness": Real or fictional? *The Physical Educator, 52,* 22–28.

This article reports a study of 31 middle school PE teachers who were videotaped responding to misbehaviors. Interventions that were accurate and prompt were successful in returning students to the task around 80 percent of the time, compared to 45 percent for interventions that targeted the wrong students or were late. Clearly, withitness makes a difference!

Price, K. M., & Nelson, K. L. (2013). *Planning effective instruction: Diversity responsive methods and management* (5th ed.). Belmont, CA: Thomson Wadsworth.

This work provides excellent descriptions of a variety of instructional methods, including steps in how to plan for their use with a variety of students.

Smaldino, S. E., Lowther, D. E., Mims, C. D., & Russell, J. D. (2014). *Instructional technology and media for learning* (11th ed.). Upper Saddle River, NJ: Pearson.

Focused on helping teachers maximize the use of technology for the benefit of student learning, this text utilizes the ASSURE model of lesson planning to enhance teaching.

www.apa.org/education/k12/classroom-data.aspx

This module, "Using Classroom Data to Give Systematic Feedback to Students to Improve Learning," was designed by the APA Task Force on the Applications of Psychological Science to Teaching and Learning to maximize teachers' use of formative assessment to build toward student understanding, application, and appreciation.

www.lessonplanspage.com; www.712educators.about.com; www.teachervision.fen.com

These websites for educators contain a variety of materials, including thousands of sample lesson plans for all subjects (PreK–12).

■ Suggested Activities

1. Case Studies 7.1, 7.2, and 7.3 describe difficulties three teachers are having with instruction. After reading each case, review the relevant sections of this and earlier chapters and decide what strategies would be helpful in overcoming the problems. You might use each case as a basis for a group discussion and generate a list of possible solutions or strategies. Case Studies 7.4 and 7.5 provide further opportunities for review of and practice in applying concepts from this chapter.

2. How many examples of Kounin's concepts can you find in Case Study 7.4? Compare your list with the key in the Appendix.

3. Analyze the lesson in Case Study 7.5 by first identifying the sequence of activities used by the teacher and then discussing what occurred within each activity. Where problems are evident, describe alternative approaches or strategies that might be used. Compare your answers with the keys in the Appendix.

4. If you have access to a secondary classroom for observation, watch a class period and note how transitions are managed. Observe which students seem to lose their way during transitions and how the teacher brings them back to the next activity. Note any structure supplied by the teacher, such as signals or routines. Also note how the teacher uses proximity, movement, monitoring, and eye contact during the transition.

5. Observe a couple of lessons with different formats of instruction (e.g., whole-group content development, group work, discussion, testing). Respond to the following questions: What types of lesson formats did you see? How did these formats differ in arrangement, procedures, and advance planning? What management techniques did the teacher use across these differences?

6. Answer the following questions in conversation with a partner: How do you think students learn? How do you know when someone is learning? What is your own preferred style of learning? How will these beliefs affect your choice of teaching strategies?

■ Case Study 7.1

OVER AND OVER

In Ms. Liu's class, there are almost always some students who don't understand presentations or assignments and who need a lot of re-explanation. While she is lecturing, students continually ask questions about what they should write in their notes. When an in-class assignment is made, Ms. Liu finds herself answering many questions about information she has just covered in the lecture. Sometimes she has to re-explain parts of the lesson to the whole class. As a result, there is often not enough time to complete activities before the end of the period. In an attempt to avoid the problems associated with note taking, she decides to write important information on the chalkboard during the lecture. What else can Ms. Liu do?

■ Case Study 7.2

TRANSITION PROBLEMS

Mr. Miller feels that too much time is wasted in his ninth-grade class while students get settled at the beginning of the period, get supplies ready, or move from one activity to another. While the teacher deals with students' problems, makeup work, or questions at the beginning of class, students talk, play around, or wander. It then takes some time to get their attention and begin class. When activities change during the class period, students sometimes delay activities while they sharpen pencils or borrow supplies. Trading papers to check work in class usually results in some confusion.

Mr. Miller has already spoken with his class about the problem and has reminded them of the procedures for sharpening pencils immediately after arriving and taking seats before the bell. He tries to enforce these procedures, but he is also required to monitor the hall. What else can he do to cut down on wasted time?

■ Case Study 7.3

PROBLEMS WITH SMALL-GROUP AND DISCUSSION ACTIVITIES

Ms. Jackson's middle school science class is usually on task and well behaved during whole-class, teacher-led presentations and during seat-work assignments (when students work independently). But whenever Ms. Jackson begins a small-group activity or tries to lead a whole-class discussion, behavior problems emerge: Many students waste time, lose focus, and engage in off-task chit-chat. No sooner does Ms. Jackson address the problems with one group of students than problems surface elsewhere. What are some possible sources of these problems, and what are some strategies for dealing with them?

■ Case Study 7.4

KOUNIN'S CONCEPTS

As his fourth-period class begins, Mr. Case makes eye contact with two students who are exchanging notes; the students quickly get out their class materials. "Let's begin by working some of the exercises at the end of the chapter; you'll need your notebooks." As students begin to get out their materials, Mr. Case calls out, "Oops, I forgot to tell you to bring money tomorrow for the field trip. How many of you will be going?" After a brief discussion, students finish getting out their materials. Mr. Case says, "We'll go through these exercises orally, but I also want you to write the answers in your notebooks as part of today's classwork. I'll come around and check on your notebook work later in the period. Now, who can answer the first question? Hands please. Tyrone?" Mr. Case conducts the lesson by calling on various students, some with hands up, others seemingly at random from the nonvolunteers.

About halfway through the exercises, a student enters the room and says that he is new to the school and has been assigned to the class. Mr. Case goes to his desk, sits down, and says, "Okay, come here. I'll check out a text to you. I wish the school office wouldn't send people in the middle of a period. Where are you from, anyway?" After giving the student a syllabus and a text, Mr. Case leaves his desk and says to the class, "Now where were we? Oh yes, question seven. Hey, where did Kim and Lee go? I didn't give them permission to leave." After several more minutes, Mr. Case calls a halt to the activity and says, "Now I'd like us to discuss the test coming up this Thursday. Let's make sure that you are all clear on what will be on the exam and what you will need to study to get ready for it." After a pause, he adds: "I almost forgot. Get out your questions from before and look at the next to the last one. We need to add an important point that was left out." After finishing the item, Mr. Case turns the topic back to the upcoming test: "Now, where were we? Oh, yes. I need to show you some items that will be similar to those on the test. Here's one." He writes it on the board, then pauses: "Well, I don't want to give away the test, do I?" Without discussing the test further, he turns to another topic: "Just wait until you hear about the program we will be viewing tomorrow. I borrowed it from another teacher, and she said that her students thought it was one of the most thought-provoking, exciting stories they had ever seen!"

What examples of Kounin's concepts can you find in this description of Mr. Case and his class?

■ Case Study 7.5

A SCIENCE LESSON

After checking roll, Ms. Grant tells students that the day's activity will be their first lab assignment and that they will work in groups. "The purpose of the lab work is to get practice with the scientific method," she says, and she lists the stages: observation, formulation of a hypothesis, gathering evidence, analysis, and conclusions. Ms. Grant tells students that they must work together in an assigned lab group, and she calls out the group assignments, forming six groups of four or five students each. Students are then told to arrange their desks according to groups. Students are very noisy as they do so, with much playing and talking occurring. Ms. Grant has to speak very loudly to regain the students' attention and give directions for a lab sheet that she distributes to each student. Standing at the front of the room, the teacher reads the directions on the lab sheet while several students continue to converse. Two groups at the back of the room do not pay attention to the teacher's presentation of directions. Ms. Grant tells students that each group will get a box with something inside and that they should try to determine what it is. They must work together as a group. Having said that, Ms. Grant distributes to each group a small box wrapped in construction paper. Students immediately treat the boxes as noisemakers, causing more commotion. Ms. Grant yells above the din, "Be sure to fill in three guesses at the bottom of the page."

During the ensuing activity, only one group discusses what possibilities exist and how they might determine what the box contains. The other groups mainly record the first three guesses that are offered by group members. The teacher observes the groups from a stool at the front of the room. After 4 minutes, she says, "List the tests that you performed. Then put down your three best guesses." After 6 minutes, four of the groups are finished, and students put the boxes back on the teacher's desk. Two groups continue to work on the problem, while the remaining students sit idly or talk. One boy calls out, "When are we going to start?" The teacher responds, "Soon, when everyone is ready." After 2 more minutes, the teacher says, "Listen up. We are ready for the group reports." Some students are still talking while Ms. Grant gives directions for each group's oral report. One student from each group will give the group report, which is a statement of each guess and the reasons for it. The teacher also reminds students to follow class rules for listening when other students talk and for not leaving their seats during discussions. "If you can't keep your mouths shut, we won't be able to do activities like this," she notes. While giving reports, students speak softly; it is difficult to hear each report because of talking and fooling around by a number of students. The students' reports are short, and the teacher's comments are limited to brief evaluations and indications of acceptance, such as "Okay," "Good," or "Good observation." Ms. Grant does not record or compare group observations or guesses, but she occasionally asks for clarification, such as, "What makes you guess that?"

After about 10 minutes, each group report has been given, although many students have not paid attention to any report except the one from their own group. Ms. Grant tells students, "You used a lot of good observations, like the last group that distinguished between round objects and objects with flat sides. Most of the groups were close, and tomorrow I'll tell you what was in each box. Please pass your papers in." After papers have been collected, Ms. Grant asks two students to distribute a classroom set of books. She tells the class to begin reading a chapter on molecules for the next day. After several minutes of commotion, students settle down and read silently for the remaining 13 minutes of class.

What problems are evident and what changes would be appropriate?

MyEducationLab *Self-Check 7.1*

MyEducationLab *Self-Check 7.2*

MyEducationLab *Self-Check 7.3*

MyEducationLab *Application Exercise 7.1* Using what you've learned in this chapter, view the video and respond to the questions.

MyEducationLab *Application Exercise 7.2* Using what you've learned in this chapter, read and respond to this scenario.

MyEducationLab *Classroom Management Simulation 7.1* Engage with the Classroom Management Simulation *Effectively Handling Transitions.*

CHAPTER 8

Managing Cooperative Learning Groups

Cooperative learning is a form of instruction in which students are organized into groups to complete assignments and projects collaboratively, to assist each other, to solve problems, to share materials, and to participate in discussions. Teachers who use cooperative learning groups do so because they believe that the method increases student learning and involvement. Many teachers also value the increased student independence from the teacher's direction that results from an emphasis on group planning, assistance, and decision making. Such teachers often describe their role as that of facilitator rather than director of group activities. Finally, teachers value the social skills and problem-solving abilities that are enhanced through frequent group work. These important life skills will serve students well in many work and social settings that they encounter in or out of school. The following are examples of cooperative learning activities in different subjects and grade levels.

Students in a blocked English and history class complete a "diary project" in groups of three or four. Each group selects a historical person and prepares a diary written from their subject's perspective. Diaries consist of a description of the era, a persuasive essay, an advertisement for a product the person might sell or endorse, and several daily "diary" entries detailing reactions to events of the era. Students complete the project over a two-week period, which includes library research, computer searches, and in-class writing sessions. Group presentations and written products are utilized.

In an English class, students work in pairs to rewrite fairy tales using the style of a selected author. Although each student is responsible for his or her own version, students assist each other when identifying the features of the author's style they wish to incorporate into the rewritten tale and when outlining their versions. Students also edit each other's work and give suggestions for revision.

In an engineering design class, tenth- and eleventh-grade students work in teams of four to design an automated device to separate recyclable materials. Over a several week period, each group develops different design solutions and eventually builds a device, using materials obtained from a common pool available to all groups. Students keep individual design notebooks, and the group submits interim reports that include design sketches and descriptions of alternatives considered. Each group also submits a final design and a report.

Students in a middle school social studies class work in groups of three or four on an "explorers" assignment. In each group, students read text materials, discuss them, and write answers to questions about an explorer's life, actions, and impact. At a designated time, students change seats to go to new groups, where they share their information with other students who incorporate it into their reports.

In a math class, students explore different ways to solve a problem to discover a preferred approach. Each group is responsible for generating at least two approaches to the solution and then deciding which approach it prefers and why. After about 10 minutes, the teacher extends the problem by changing one of the conditions. Groups discuss the effect of the changed condition on their choice of a solution.

In a world geography class, students work in groups of four or five to prepare a computer-based report on a South American country. Different students assume responsibility for assembling information about their group's country, such as physical geography, economics, government, climate, culture, and customs. Individual student roles in the group include producer, technical director, and researchers.

In a middle school science class, groups of four students work together to identify characteristics of three samples of sand and dirt plus an additional "mystery" sample. Each student is responsible for completing a lab report on the samples' characteristics, and the group will submit a separate report summarizing its investigation of the "mystery" sample.

Pause and Consider

What are some of the similarities in these examples? How might the use of groups vary by subject? desired outcome or product?

Vignette Reflection

Please discuss your responses to the following questions with a partner: What would students find attractive about the lessons depicted in these vignettes? What should the teacher do to ensure they are effective? How are these lessons different from whole-group instruction? How might whole-group instruction be involved in these lessons?

These examples illustrate that cooperative learning is much more than simply having students work in groups to complete an assignment. It usually involves a common task or group product, and students need to interact and work together in order to accomplish the group's goals. Groups may be used in self-contained lessons or in longer-term projects in a wide variety of subjects and at any grade level. Using cooperative groups does require some changes in traditional managerial routines. Although a number of the procedures described in earlier chapters for managing student work and behavior in whole-class and individual formats will continue to apply to cooperative groups, some of the *talk* and *movement* procedures need to be modified. In addition, the teacher's managerial tasks of *pacing* activities, *monitoring*, and *giving feedback* to students become especially important. The process of introducing cooperative groups is also crucial and deserves careful consideration. In particular, your focus will be on *teaching students the skills* necessary for working effectively in groups.

The term *cooperative learning* is used in this text in its broadest sense, to indicate students working collaboratively in groups of two or more to accomplish an instructional goal, instead of referring to a specific form of group learning. The defining features of cooperative groups vary somewhat depending on the particular application (Cohen, 1994; Johnson & Johnson, 2013; Putnam, 1998; Slavin, 1995), but common elements among these variations include group goals or task interdependence, some degree of individual accountability, and good group interaction processes. The management strategies presented in this chapter apply to group activities that utilize these generic features rather than to any one model of group work. It should also be noted that cooperative learning is only one type of instructional format available to you as a secondary teacher. Teachers should not depend on cooperative groups for all their content-development work. Whole-class presentations, demonstrations, and discussions will continue to be essential formats for delivering and applying content, and seat-work and class-work exercises will continue to be important formats for consolidating individual student learning through practice. Cooperative learning activities do, however, add a very useful methodology to more traditional instructional approaches.

■ Research on Cooperative Learning

Substantial research on cooperative learning has focused on its effects on achievement and other outcomes of importance, such as interpersonal relations, motivation, and student attitudes toward learning (Gillies, 2015; Gillies & Ashman, 2003; Johnson &

Johnson, 2013; Slavin & Lake, 2008). Explanations of the positive benefits of cooperative groups usually point to the students' increased engagement with the content as an important factor. Compared to large-class or individual work formats, collaborative small groups result in increased student academic achievement (Hattie, 2009). With small-group work, there is greater potential for participation, feedback, and mutual construction of meaning among students. The group format encourages students to become active participants rather than passive recipients of information. Other explanations suggest that lower-achieving students profit from their peers' explanations, and high achievers benefit from constructing explanations for other students. All students can develop interpersonal skills and relationships through group tasks with a common goal. Furthermore, all can benefit from the support they receive in a cohesive group. Such support can help create positive norms for achievement and learning.

Although cooperative groups can improve learning and other outcomes for students, such results are by no means assured simply by the use of groups. Research has shown that student achievement is promoted by helping behaviors such as giving and receiving explanations (Nattiv, 1994; Webb & Farivar, 1994; Whicker, Bol, & Nunnery, 1997), but such assistance does not occur automatically. Students who need help do not always ask for it, nor do they necessarily receive assistance when they do. Moreover, helpers might simply give a correct answer or share a solution rather than engage in constructive dialogue. Without feedback and instruction on how to collaborate, higher-achieving students may retreat to a less advanced level of cognition (Tudge, 1992). More frequent use of group activities promotes positive outcomes when the quality of group interaction is high, but when group interactions are of low quality, outcomes may be negatively affected (Battistich, Solomon, & Delucchi, 1993). Students with disabilities especially need supportive, positive partners, and teachers must be proactive about arranging group membership, teaching group behaviors, and monitoring to promote successful participation in group activities (O'Connor & Jenkins, 1996).

Research has identified a number of strategies that you can use to promote the effectiveness of cooperative groups (Emmer & Gerwels, 2002; Gillies, 2007; Lotan, 2006). Such actions include teaching students how to work in groups, practicing the role of facilitator, carefully choosing and pacing academic activities, and promoting interdependence along with individual responsibility within a group context. Characteristics of more effective cooperative group lessons also include some form of daily accountability (versus later or no evaluation of individual or group performance), teacher monitoring of and feedback to groups, and the use of manipulative materials (Emmer & Gerwels, 2002).

The importance of these and other skills will depend in part on your goals and the nature of group-based academic tasks. Some teachers use groups as the primary means of instruction and develop projects and an integrated curriculum to deliver much of their academic content. Other teachers use groups primarily as a supplement to whole-class and individual instruction, relying on groups during the classwork portion of lessons to provide short practice activities. Whichever approach you adopt, you will find the skills described in the remainder of this chapter helpful. You will, however, need to tailor them to your own application.

■ Strategies and Routines That Support Cooperative Learning

Beginning to Use Cooperative Learning Groups

Whether you begin to use groups at the start of the year or wait until later, you should address several matters. It is important that the physical arrangement of the classroom supports the use of groups, especially if you intend to use them extensively. You should also teach the desired procedures for the groups as initial group tasks because you want a successful experience to set the stage for subsequent group activities. Group composition is important; students must be able to work constructively with each other and aid each other's learning. Additionally, you must plan how to teach the group attention signals needed for effective communication mid-lesson. Finally, it is critical to balance building group interdependence and simultaneously developing individual student accountability.

Room Arrangement.   If you plan to make extensive use of groups, it will be advantageous to arrange student seating in groups rather than have students move to group seating each time the format is used. Some classrooms are equipped with tables; to facilitate monitoring, they should be arranged to permit your unrestricted movement among them. In the absence of tables, desks can be pushed together to form groups.

In some classrooms it will be necessary to move from whole-class seating arrangements to small groups. Plan ahead to speed these transitions. Mark on the floor with masking or colored plastic tape the location of tables or desks in each arrangement. Then, when it is time to make the transition, show students where to place desks and how to move to groups, just as you would teach any other classroom procedure.

Teachers often begin group activities with pairs of students rather than larger groups, but seating arrangements can still accommodate larger numbers; for example, when using table groups of four, divide the larger groups into pairs.

When group work involves using materials or equipment, a supply station or materials center may need to be created. Try to locate it in an accessible place in the room, away from student desks or other high-traffic areas. Some teachers place a small box or bin in the middle of each table or group of desks for materials to be used by everyone in the group. A common materials center in each group eliminates the need for borrowing these supplies from other students, and it reduces the need for trips to out-of-group storage areas.

Talk and Movement Procedures.   Don't assume that because students follow the rules during whole-class and independent work activities, they will automatically do so during group work. Instead, be prepared to teach students your specific expectations for talk and movement during group work. Teachers often report that when they begin using groups, the increased noise level bothers them. After a while they get used to it and are less anxious when they realize that the noise is coming from engaged, involved students. Nevertheless, to prevent excessive noise, teachers should discuss this issue with the class and develop guidelines. Common guidelines are to use "six-inch" or "twelve-inch" voices, or to speak quietly enough so students in nearby groups can't hear or aren't distracted. "Whisper voices" does not work well as a guideline because groups usually can't work efficiently and conduct discussions while whispering. If noise becomes excessive, you can use a group attention signal (discussed next) to restore it to an acceptable level.

Movement will not be a major problem if students are already seated in their groups, although it may be useful to provide a guideline such as "Stay with your group" or "Take care of out-of-group business promptly" to limit unnecessary wandering and visiting. Some movement will be necessary, of course, when students must obtain materials. Assigning a "materials manager" role in each group will help take care of such business efficiently.

Some teachers change group composition for different activities, resulting in student movement during the transitions. Such transitions can be real time-wasters and make it difficult to start the next activity. An efficient routine is to announce the beginning of the transition, state the expectation, and tell students how much time they have to get ready ("Everyone bring materials and be in your group in one minute."). Continue to monitor throughout the transition to cut down on stragglers ("Thirty seconds left, . . . fifteen seconds, . . . Everyone should be in her or his group now"). You can also state your expectation about what the students are to do when they arrive at their group's location ("Sit in your seat and put your supplies—book, paper, pencil, etc.—on the table/desk" or "Start work on your project right away").

Forming Groups.   At the beginning of the year, before you know your students very well, it may be instructive to allow students to choose partners for a few initial activities. Limit the length and scope of these activities, and monitor closely to make sure that no student is left out. Your initial use of groups may involve pairs only, having the students simply check each other's work or discuss a question or problem. You might also use pairs to work on a class exercise or to practice spelling words or number facts. When pairs are used in such straightforward ways, most students do not have to move to new locations, and the activity is brief, placing fewer demands on the students and on you.

As groups are used more extensively, frequently, and with increasing levels of accountability, group membership becomes more critical. Teachers usually form groups ahead of time and seat students accordingly. When assigning students to groups, a main consideration for most teachers is to represent in each group a range of achievement in the subject. A second concern is often to place an appropriate leader in each group (see the section on leadership skills later in this chapter). Teachers also try to avoid personality conflicts. Students who are argumentative often work best in groups that have a student with good leadership abilities, including social skills. Gender, English language fluency, artistic ability, and other traits can also be used to vary group composition or to match the group task assigned.

Some teachers avoid placing in the same group those students who are at extremes in achievement levels in the content area. For example, they would not place a very high achiever and a very low achiever in the same group, instead seeking less variation and pairing a mid-range achiever with a very low achiever. The concern is that the pace of work and the discourse patterns in the groups with high-achieving students may be inappropriate for and intimidating to the lower-performing students, resulting in their withdrawal and task avoidance. In groups having mid-range achievers, the pace and vocabulary are more likely to encourage the lower achievers' participation. This principle obviously depends on the degree of social and explanatory skills various students possess.

No hard-and-fast rules can be stated about how long groups should stay together. Some teachers change group membership frequently, as often as every few weeks. Most leave students in the same groups for longer times but shift membership at least a few times each year. Some teachers allow students to form their own groups for special activities or projects or as a change of pace, but rarely do they allow self-selected groups for an extended time, except for a special project. An alternative grouping technique is to group the students by interest. Place several topics or types of activities on the board. Have the students write down their first, second, and third choices. Collect the choices, and assign students to groups based on their first or second choice.

After groups are formed, they should be monitored for signs of conflict. Don't be too quick to step in with a solution, but do ask groups to address such problems. Giving students responsibility for dealing with group problems can create an opportunity for learning. As students acquire group skills and experience success in working together, conflict usually diminishes. When conflicts cannot be resolved in a reasonable time within a group, most teachers choose to move antagonistic students to new groups. Later in the year, when such students have become more adroit at cooperating, they might be given an opportunity to work together again.

Group Attention Signals.   When your students work in groups, you may need to stop their work to provide additional directions or to make a transition to another activity or task. You may also need to provide feedback to the whole class, modify some aspect of the assignment, or provide additional instruction. In addition, noise may rise to unacceptable levels, requiring you to intervene. In all of these cases, you will be faced with the task of interrupting students who are engaged in a task or interacting with each other, making it difficult to gain their attention. The solution to this problem is to use a signal.

Efficient signals for group attention require that students make some overt response, which interrupts whatever else they may be doing. When teaching middle school students, you can give a verbal signal such as "Raise a hand if you can hear me," "Fold your hands if you can hear me," or "Clap if you can hear me." These signals gain students' attention by requiring that they substitute a behavior, thus effectively stopping their activity. Verbal signals are especially useful when students are working with manipulatives that might distract them from attending. Another common signal, appropriate for any grade level, is to turn off the lights or turn on the projector and at the same time request, "Eyes to the front, please." Because you are interrupting the students, capturing their attention will not be instantaneous; you may find it useful to pace the transition by counting down: "Five, four, three, two, one . . ." and then begin the next activity promptly.

When students are not as interactively engaged, you can use a less dramatic or intrusive stimulus to get their attention. Ringing a bell and giving a simple verbal direction such as, "Stop, look, listen," "Eyes to the front," or "Eyes on the teacher" will often suffice. It's a good idea to teach several signals to students to avoid over-working one of them and to give you some options. Finally, avoid unnecessary inter-ruptions. Try to present information or directions ahead of time, or post them on a board or display them on a screen to minimize the need to break into ongoing stu-dent activities.

Be sure to teach the students about your signals ahead of time. Explain what signal(s) you will be using and why. There's no point in leaving them guessing about why you're turning off the lights or counting down!

Promoting Interdependence Within the Group

When either the group's product or the performance of individual group members is enhanced by the actions of other group members, positive interdependence has occurred. In addition to improving group and individual performance, interdepen-dence builds group cohesion and helps create group norms that support learning. Interdependence can be fostered in a number of ways.

- Assignments or projects can require varied skills and abilities, such as draw-ing, organizing data into charts, using computers, giving oral presentations, and making constructions, in addition to the more traditional skills of reading, writing, and computing. Such variation in tasks gives more students the oppor-tunity to contribute to the final group product.
- Each student can be responsible for contributing a unique component to the group's product. For example, students might do research on different aspects of a topic for a group report.
- Each student chooses a specific part of a topic to teach to the rest of the stu-dents in the group. Or, in groups of four students, pairs work together to pre-pare information for the other two students in the group.
- In groups of two, students work as drill partners to help each other learn.
- The teacher assigns roles to students (e.g., reader, checker, recorder, materials manager) to ensure that each student makes a contribution to the group's activity.
- Group assignments (projects, reports, performances, constructions, oral group presentations) can be given a group grade, recognition, or points.

Individual Accountability

Although interdependence is important, students must also feel individually responsible for their learning. This is not much of a problem when students are expected to complete assignments as individuals with group support. When group assignments are the outcome, however, establishing group accountability—for example, by giving the group's product a grade or by asking the group to report orally—may not be sufficient for some students, who may be content to loaf or ride other students' coattails. When that's the case, then it may be necessary to give individual grades in addition to the group grade. Individual accountability in the context of a group-based assignment may be increased in several ways.

- Require that individual students perform an identifiable portion of the group assignment.
- Ask groups to turn in a list identifying each student's contribution to the final product.
- Use peer evaluation of group members' participation and contributions.
- Ask students to record observations in individual notebooks that you will collect and grade at various times.
- Have students turn in individual work—even if it is just their class notes—along with the group's product.
- Require students to keep a daily record of their own work in notebooks.
- Let students know that when their group reports to the class, each student should be ready to explain its work. Better yet, require that each student be responsible for some part of the group presentation.
- Have selected students report individually on their group work.
- Give students a quiz based on the group assignment.

You can also foster individual responsibility when you set expectations: Stress to students that even though they are working on a group assignment, each of them is responsible for learning the material. Tell students that it is important for the members of a group to help each other understand what they are learning and for each person to contribute. Finally, when you monitor student work in groups, note participation by individual students. If particular students are not contributing, try to determine why not and take corrective measures, such as redirecting them. When simple interventions don't work, teachers often ask the group to help solve the problem, or they may have a conference with the student to try to assess the situation and work out a solution.

Maintaining individual responsibility in a group setting is not always easy. Adding individual assessments on top of group assessments may increase the amount of time the teacher must spend on planning and preparation as well as evaluation. Focusing on individual accountability, moreover, may deflect attention from group outcomes. Procedures for accountability, therefore, should be planned carefully and amended as necessary until there is a balance between accountability needs and the available time and energy.

■ Group Tasks

Initial Group Tasks

Students who don't have much experience working in groups need to develop their skills in uncomplicated tasks rather than in complex projects. Holubec (1992), a pioneer in the development of cooperative learning groups, describes a number of simple, easy-to-implement activities for beginning group work. Her suggestions include:

Drill partners. Use this for practicing material that must be memorized.

Reading buddies. Students read to each other. This activity can be built on by asking students to summarize or make up a question for the partner.

Checking. Students compare answers and resolve discrepancies. Each student should be able to explain the answer.

Reviewers. Students review for a quiz or test or prepare for an oral report by working together to develop questions or by asking and answering each other's questions.

Turn to your partner. Ask students to explain something or compare answers to a problem or exercise. Students might also choose the next step or add to an answer. As the students gain experience, this format can be used for problem solving.

Another format similar to "Turn to your partner" is the "think-pair-share activity." The teacher poses a problem or asks a question and asks students to think about the solution or an answer. Then, after a minute or two, students discuss their thoughts with a partner; afterward, the teacher asks different pairs of students to share with the class. A variation of this format is to have students write their responses (i.e., write-pair-share).

It is important not to rush into complex group work until you build a foundation of skills through practice. Teaching group-work skills is easier in simpler formats with uncomplicated procedures. After your students have had success in the initial group tasks, they will be ready for more complex group formats and assignments.

Teaching Effective Group-Work Skills

To work effectively in a group, students need to practice a number of group-work skills. They include *social skills*, such as active listening, sharing, and supporting; *explaining skills*, which convey understanding and meaning in academic tasks; and *leadership skills*, such as planning and demonstrating initiative and enthusiasm.

Social Skills.   Active listening includes listening to others without interrupting and being able to summarize others' ideas, incorporating them into the ongoing discussion and using them constructively in completing the group's assignment. Sharing materials and taking turns are also necessary for effective cooperation. Another social skill is giving support, which includes accepting differences, being friendly, and encouraging others. Students who lack social skills may insist on doing things their way, argue frequently, ignore or put down another student's contributions, or not participate in the group's work.

The ability to work in a group depends on good social skills, so teachers usually emphasize their development. One way to do this is to teach students what skills are needed for group work when group activities are first introduced and later as the need arises. Teachers may even teach certain phrases for students to use when summarizing, asking questions, and expressing disagreement. Another way to promote social skills is to assign roles that require their use. For example, students can be assigned the role of encourager (makes certain that each group member has an opportunity to contribute to the group's work and interaction and gives positive feedback to others when appropriate) or summarizer (helps keep track of ideas and progress).

Mrs. O'Neal focused on one group skill a week until her seventh-grade English Language Arts class developed an effective repertoire by the end of the first 6 weeks of the school year. During the first week, she emphasized participating during group work; during the second week, she focused on remaining on task. Subsequent weeks were devoted to cooperating, encouraging, explaining, and active listening. Mrs. O'Neal introduced each skill in a whole-class discussion, soliciting examples, suggestions, and a rationale from her students. During the first week, she displayed on the overhead a five-point rating scale for "participating" and indicated what she would be looking for as students worked in groups. At the end of several group-work activities that week, she engaged students in a discussion about the skill, asked them to review their performance, and then shared her assessments with the groups. In each subsequent week, Mrs. O'Neal added a new scale so that groups received feedback about their progress in acquiring the skills.

Pause and Consider

What group work skills did Mrs. O'Neal choose to feature and in what order? What other group work skills might she want to practice with her class across the next six weeks? Would you change the skills or procedures for a different grade or content area?

Students need feedback about their use of group skills. Mrs. O'Neal's use of scales is one way to focus students on specific components of group work. Another way is to conduct whole-class discussions about group-work activities. Such a discussion can begin with a request that students evaluate an aspect of their group's work, indicating what went well and what could be improved, or they might be asked to describe how someone in their group performed one of the group skills effectively. Students might also be asked to describe what makes it difficult to perform a particular skill and how that problem might be overcome. Getting students to talk about their group experience is an excellent way to help them develop good monitoring and self-regulation skills.

Explaining Skills.   Explaining skills are an important aspect of group work, and they are critical to the development of academic outcomes. Indicators of explaining skills are student comments that describe a problem, assignment, or goal. Student comments might also identify steps to be accomplished or followed to complete a task as well as reasons for the steps. Students might summarize the work they have done or plan to do. When a group assignment includes answering questions, students could give their answers and describe how they obtained them.

Another important component of the explaining process is seeking explanations from others. This may involve students describing what they do and do not understand and asking for help from other group members. Seeking such help is unlikely to occur unless other students in the group practice good social skills. To encourage seeking help, the teacher might say, "No one knows everything. If there's something you don't understand, it's smart to ask for help from the group. And if someone asks for help, be a friend and give a good explanation."

Student interactions concerning content are essential to the process of constructing meaning. Interactions enhance comprehension and are the basis for learning. Most students will need encouragement to engage in these behaviors because conversations about content are not a natural part of their interactions. Some ways to do this include:

- Assign the role of summarizer and rotate the role among students.
- Have students turn to a partner and explain something; then have the partner "explain back."
- Model key explanatory behaviors such as summarizing and clarifying, using available text material. Then ask students to practice in pairs, alternating the roles of explainer and listener.
- Have each student in the group write one question; members of the group then answer it.
- Lead a discussion about how to give a good explanation and how to ask for help.
- Conduct role-plays of asking for help and explaining.
- Have students write their group's ideas on a chart and present them to the class.
- Give the groups one question to answer and have each member record or restate other members' contributions.

Leadership Skills.   When a group has someone who steps up and says, "Let's figure out what we need to get this job done," it has someone who is practicing a leadership skill. Desired attributes include demonstrating initiative, planning, and enthusiasm.

Good social skills also complement this repertoire, as does basic competence in the content relevant to the group's task. Many teachers value these skills highly and try to form groups that have at least one student who exhibits them "naturally."

Although leadership skills are developed over time and students will possess them in varying degrees, all students can make some progress toward acquiring or improving them. You can help develop leadership skills by assigning roles, such as presenter or discussion leader, which give students the opportunity to demonstrate initiative and gain confidence. You can also identify various student leadership actions, such as planning steps for the group to reach a goal, encouraging and supporting other group members, finding alternative ways to complete the group's assignment, and volunteering for a difficult job. Discuss these behaviors with the class, perhaps making a list to which students could refer. Give positive feedback to students who engage in these and other leadership activities. Opportunities to practice leadership skills are especially important for the quiet though competent students who might not otherwise be noticed and who need encouragement to develop these skills.

■ Monitoring Student Work and Behavior

Good monitoring of group work is essential. Typically it requires you to walk among the groups, scanning the rest of the class from time to time. Try not to spend too much time with a single group at the expense of keeping abreast of the activities of the rest. Goals for monitoring include keeping track of individual performance and growth in academic areas, group skills, and individual behaviors. A complicating factor is the extent to which individual performance needs to be distinguished from group performance.

How you keep track of student work in groups will depend on the nature of the group activity. When individual assignments are used and the group's function is to support individual learning, monitoring academic performance is not much different than in classrooms in which whole-class and independent work are the primary formats. You can circulate among the groups and note individual student performance, and you can also collect the individual assignments and check them. Critical to the effective use of groups to support individual learning is the quality of interaction among students. It is important to note the degree to which students provide explanations and demonstrations for one another instead of giving answers alone or ignoring peer questions. A good way to encourage quality interaction is to ask students to be sure that *everyone* in the group—not just one or two students—can explain the ideas or concepts.

One effective monitoring technique is the use of a clipboard or tablet with the students' names and space to record ratings or notes about performance and behavior during group activities. This technique encourages teachers to record information about all students, not only the visibly active ones. The information can later be used to give feedback to groups and individuals or to add to performance evaluations. Use of this strategy as seldom as once or twice a week can add important information about individuals and supplement other types of monitoring. If you let students know what you are looking for when you monitor, a side benefit is that it will improve the identified behaviors.

When group assignments are used, the focus of monitoring shifts to the group's collective progress, along with individual performance. If you provide checkpoints, reminders, and time limits, you will not only give yourself monitoring milestones, but you will also help students self-monitor. Asking groups to report to you on their progress, plans, or difficulties will also provide information about comprehension that you might not obtain through observation alone. As we noted in the section on individual accountability, it may be beneficial to include an individual component to a collective assignment. Not only will such data increase your information about each student's achievement, but the procedure itself will improve individual accountability.

Teachers use various indicators to determine satisfactory group functioning. Because students usually have a specific task to perform in the group, it is not difficult to determine whether students are engaged in a suitable activity. When students are talking with each other about the task and performing behaviors needed to complete an assignment such as writing, assembling materials, practicing, or constructing, teachers can easily identify appropriate on-task behavior. Teachers also watch for signs that individual students may be uninvolved or disengaged. Momentary off-task behavior can usually be ignored, but if it is prolonged, some form of intervention may be needed. Another indicator is the level and nature of emotion exhibited by students. Teachers should take note of students in a group when they exhibit tense, angry, or hostile behaviors. Such emotional reactions suggest frustration or potential conflicts that could escalate and therefore call for an early intervention to prevent the development of more serious problems. Occasionally, a student will exhibit very oppositional behaviors in a group, refusing to compromise or share in the work. Intervention by the teacher will then be required to help divert the group's focus away from the negative behavior and toward constructive action.

■ Interventions for Groups

Interventions are closely related to the monitoring features just described. The most common interventions are simple ones—easy to use and brief. Individual students and groups who are off task may be verbally or nonverbally redirected to the task. Students who persist in inappropriate behaviors can be given a short time-out (1 or 2 minutes initially) or sent to work alone for a longer time if they don't respond to milder interventions. Other interventions for individuals are described in Chapter 11.

When interventions are needed for noncompliance or misbehavior that the group is not able to resolve for itself (e.g., repeated distraction from the group task, exclusion of other group members), a conference can be used. Conferences with students can be used more readily during group time than during whole-class activities because other students will be occupied with their group tasks. Conferences are typically brief—less than a minute or so—and consist of listening to concerns and providing feedback to the student or group, along with redirection and a plan for changing the behavior. Such an approach is more effective than a simple reprimand because it offers an alternative behavior. A brief conference also allows the teacher to provide feedback on the spot rather than delaying it so long that it would prove ineffective.

Teachers also engage groups in a conference when a group process has broken down. Examples include groups in which students don't ask for or give assistance constructively, make poor progress toward the group's goal, or encounter a problem they aren't able to overcome. Teachers often describe their role as that of *facilitator* or *mediator* in this type of conference. Although the teacher may provide feedback about the problem and a reality check for the group's perceptions, students are encouraged to solve the problem themselves. Strategies teachers use to facilitate a solution include asking students to identify the problem and suggest alternatives, asking for reactions and comments, and calling for the group to select and try a different approach. As a last resort, teachers may offer a solution or change group membership if the problem proves intractable.

■ Who Will I Teach? Encouraging Participation in Diverse Classes

Mr. Esquivel is a new middle school social studies teacher. His seventh- and eighth-grade classes each consists of as many as one-third of the students who are English language learners, including several with learning disabilities in reading. In addition, there are one to three other students in each class who have a learning disabilkty (LD) diagnosis. Intending to stimulate participation, Mr. Esquivel began the year with collaborative groups of four students for project-based content. Nine weeks into the school year, he had to rethink his approach. During the initial group project on climate and its effects on society, he observed that lower-achieving students and some of the students with limited English proficiency did not participate fully. Other students were more dominant during group discussions of content and were much more likely to contribute during planning activities.

After consulting with another teacher who used groups extensively, Mr. Esquivel decided that he needed to provide more structured interaction in smaller groups to encourage all students to participate and to develop group-work skills. He also wanted students to develop better reading comprehension skills because he had noticed that poor understanding of written materials limited many students' participation. One structured group activity chosen by Mr. Esquivel was a 30-minute reading and discussion activity done in pairs. Students were matched so that their reading levels were not too disparate and they read to each other from climate materials in 5-minute turns. In different turns the students took the roles of reader or listener/helper, and they practiced clarifying, questioning, summarizing, and predicting skills.

Mr. Esquivel also began using a variation of think-pair-share (Cooper & Robinson, 2000; Lyman, 1992) during his whole-class lessons. He would pose a question or problem, and then students were asked to think about the question or problem for a minute before discussing their thinking with a partner. Initially, Mr. Esquivel would ask for volunteers to share their ideas with the class, giving him opportunities to provide support for good listening and feedback about content. After a week of this activity, Mr. Esquivel had students share their ideas in their project groups after the think-pair portion of the activity. Similar to the reading comprehension activities, the use of think-pair-share provided a structure for all students to participate in pairs. Work in pairs also encouraged students to listen to their partners' ideas, setting the stage for fuller participation in the four-student groups.

Finally, Mr. Esquivel provided students with individual and group "learning log" forms on which they could keep track of work in their four-student project groups. At the end of each group work session, students had 5 minutes to write about what they had learned and worked on during that day's activity. Once each week, students in the group discussed their group's progress on their project and a student "recorder" wrote a brief summary using the group's "learning log."

Pause and Consider

What value did Mr. Esquivel place on his observations of student interactions? Why might he emphasize smaller group (paired) interactions after these observations? How might the strategies Mr. Esquivel implements resolve the issue he has noticed?

Many of Mr. Esquivel's students needed group-work activities with structured participation formats to develop their confidence to participate in open-ended activities. The reading comprehension activities conducted in pairs provided needed vocabulary development in the content area. They also produced opportunities to respond in multiple ways, similar to group-based learning activities such as Reciprocal Teaching (Palinscar, 2013; Palinscar & Brown, 1988) and Peer-Assisted Learning Strategies, or PALS (Saenz, Fuchs, & Fuchs, 2005), which have been found to be effective for diverse student populations that include English language learners and students with learning disabilities. An advantage of these activities is that they allow each student to be both helper and receiver, or tutor and tutee. To manage these activities for maximum success, teachers need to choose reading material for the pairs at appropriate levels, and students need instruction and feedback so that student skills in explaining and helping are reinforced. This example also illustrates that there are multiple group formats for cooperative learning that can benefit language learners (McCafferty, Jacobs, & DaSilva Iddings, 2006).

Individual accountability and group interdependence are more important in the four-student group project activities. The use of "learning log" forms for individuals and the group will promote these characteristics. On the individual form, each student will summarize what he or she has done in different topical areas important for learning. The group "learning log" form can be completed as a group self-evaluation activity. The rubric for the form along with examples can be discussed with the whole class. Setting aside some time and asking each group to self-evaluate its processes and progress toward a goal (e.g., a group report or product) is an excellent way to encourage interdependence.

■ Chapter Summary

Arranging students in groups for instructional and work activities has become a common format in middle and high schools. This chapter described management practices that will facilitate the effective use of groups. Basic components of group management include arranging the setting, identifying appropriate talk and movement procedures, using appropriate signals for student attention, planning for interdependence and accountability, monitoring students' work and behavior, and intervening as needed. Ways to help students develop skills for working in groups were presented, along with suggestions for beginning the use of groups. A case study of using group-based activities to accommodate individual differences was provided. A checklist of topics for planning the use of groups concludes the chapter.

■ Further Reading

Gillies, R. M. (2007). *Cooperative learning: Integrating theory and practice.* Los Angeles: Sage.

The author presents a thorough description of cooperative learning and strategies for implementation. Numerous case studies are included.

Gillies, R. (2015). Small-group work: Developments in research. In E. T. Emmer & E. J. Sabornie (Eds.), *Handbook of classroom management* (2nd ed., pp. 261–280). New York: Routledge.

This chapter considers recent research on how best to structure groups to facilitate student learning and interaction. Strategies that promote student discourse in groups are highlighted.

Johnson, D. W., & Johnson, F. P. (2013). *Joining together: Group theory and group skills* (11th ed.). Boston: Allyn & Bacon.

A broad, integrative overview of group dynamics is presented in a well researched, readable, and experiential format.

Vermette, P. (1994). Four fatal flaws: Avoiding the common mistakes of novice users of cooperative learning. *The High School Journal, 77*(3), 255–260.

Based on extensive observation, the author recommends that teachers assign students to groups, use group assignments that have a high chance of success, and have students perform group work in class so that the teacher can readily monitor and give feedback to groups. Other recommendations include providing a rationale for group work and discussing group processes with students.

www.co-operation.org

This website for the Cooperative Learning Institute gives detailed information about cooperative learning and how it is accomplished.

www.teachervision.com/cooperative-learning/resource/48649.html *and* https://ethemes.missouri.edu/themes/1746

These sites have basic information about teaching with groups. Links are given to information about different approaches to group learning and lesson plans.

■ Suggested Activities

1. Observe a class using cooperative learning. As you do so, note room arrangement features and routines that support group learning. Use the checklist "Planning for Cooperative Groups" at the end of this chapter as an observation guide.

2. Choose a lesson (from observation, online, or a teacher's edition) that was designed for an individual or whole-class instructional format. Decide how you might use cooperative learning groups to teach the lesson. Discuss the modifications you would make to incorporate concepts presented in this chapter.

3. In a group, discuss (a) problems associated with fostering individual responsibility in a group-based task and (b) how to give feedback to individuals about academic performance and individual behaviors in the group setting. What are some workable, efficient strategies for enhancing responsibility and providing feedback?

4. Reread Case Study 6.1, which illustrates one teacher's approach to introducing cooperative groups at the beginning of the year.
   a. Note concepts described in this chapter that are evident in Mrs. James's procedures and strategies. What functions do the associated procedures and strategies serve?
   b. Are any areas discussed in this chapter not present in Mrs. James's classroom during the first three days? Would you suggest introducing them? Why or why not?

5. Review plans for cooperative group lessons by going to the Web (e.g., www.internet-4classrooms.com/training/cooperative_learning.htm), or to find examples, type "sample cooperative group lesson plans" in a search engine. Share a favorite lesson plan with colleagues. What management issues could arise if you were to teach this lesson? Get feedback from others in your group.

■ Checklist: Planning for Cooperative Groups

Check When Complete	Item		Notes
	Room Arrangement		
☐	A.	How will student seating be arranged?	_____
☐	B.	How will group materials/ supplies be stored and accessed?	_____
	Routines and Expectations		
☐	A.	What are your expectations for student movement to, from, and during group work?	_____
☐	B.	What expectations about talk will you communicate to students?	_____
☐	C.	What group attention signals will you use?	_____
☐	D.	How will you form groups?	
	E.	Will students have assigned roles?	_____
☐	F.	What group skills need to be discussed, modeled, or practiced?	_____

(continued)

Check When Complete	Item		Notes
	Monitoring, Accountability, and Feedback Procedures		
☐	A.	When will group work have individual products, group products, or both?	_____
☐	B.	How will individual or group work be assessed?	_____
☐	C.	How will you monitor student behavior and work during group activities?	_____
☐	D.	How will students receive feedback about individual and group performance?	_____
☐	E.	How will students receive feedback about their behavior in groups?	_____
	Interventions for Groups		
☐	A.	How will you encourage good group skills?	_____
☐	B.	How will you redirect struggling groups or individuals?	_____

MyEducationLab *Self-Check 8.1*

MyEducationLab *Self-Check 8.2*

MyEducationLab *Self-Check 8.3*

MyEducationLab *Application Exercise 8.1*   Using what you've learned in this chapter, read and respond to this scenario.

MyEducationLab *Application Exercise 8.2*   Using what you've learned in this chapter, view the video and respond to the questions.

MyEducationLab *Application Exercise 8.3*   Using what you've learned in this chapter, view the video and respond to the questions.

Michelle D. Bridwell/PhotoEdit, Inc.

CHAPTER 9

Maintaining Appropriate Student Behavior

As we have seen in the preceding chapters, good classroom management depends on the very careful planning of classroom organization, rules, procedures, and instruction. This planning and preparation will pay large dividends when the students arrive. Readiness alone, however, is not sufficient to sustain good behavior throughout the year; you cannot assume that students will behave appropriately just because you carefully taught them what was expected of them. Instead, you will need to be actively involved in maintaining student cooperation and compliance with classroom rules and procedures.

Do not be lulled into complacency by the good behavior of your students during the first few days of school. Most classes are cooperative initially even when the teacher does not pay careful attention to maintaining good behavior. But a class that seems to begin very well may ultimately become disruptive and difficult to control. Behavior problems can have a gradual onset, developing over several weeks or even months. It is possible to avoid these problems, but doing so depends on your understanding why they occur and what to do to prevent them. Because problems often develop gradually, the causes are not always apparent to the teacher or even to an observer unfamiliar with the history of the classroom.

Teachers who are able to maintain a high level of cooperative, appropriate student behavior often share a number of characteristics and skills. One of them is the observant monitoring of students. Teachers who have a greater awareness of classroom events and behaviors are better able to detect and treat problems and help students who are having difficulty. Another characteristic of good managers is consistency in the use of rules and procedures and in their dealings with students who do not follow them. A third attribute is the prompt management of inappropriate behavior before it escalates or spreads. Finally, good behavior is maintained by creating a positive classroom climate, with an emphasis on encouraging appropriate behavior. This chapter discusses how these concepts can be implemented.

■ Monitoring Student Behavior

To be an effective monitor of classroom behavior, you must know what to look for. Two categories of behavior are especially important.

1. Student involvement in learning activities
2. Student compliance with classroom rules and procedures

Student involvement is indicated by many behaviors, including attention during presentations and discussions, and progress on seat work and other assignments. Students' compliance with classroom rules and procedures will be easy to monitor if you have a clear set of expectations for student behavior, and you communicate them to the class.

Monitoring student behavior during presentations requires that you stand or sit so that you can see the faces of all the students and that you scan the room frequently. Actively monitoring a class by walking among students tends to increase student attention. Some teachers are not very good monitors of student behavior during whole-class activities because they focus their attention on a limited number of students, especially those seated in the middle rows and at the front desks. Other teachers "talk to the board." In neither case does the teacher have a very clear perception of overall student response to the presentation or of what may be occurring at the periphery of the class. During your presentations, therefore, try to move

SHOE-NEW BUSINESS © MacNelly – Distributed by King Features Syndicate, Inc. World Rights Reserved

around and develop "active eyes." If you notice commotion involving several students and you have no idea what is going on, it may be a sign that you have not been monitoring closely enough.

When students are working on individual assignments, monitoring should be done by circulating around the classroom to check each student's progress periodically. You will, of course, help students who request assistance; however, if you just "chase hands," you will not be aware of the progress of all students. One way to prevent having to chase hands is to establish a procedure by which students can ask questions of or receive assistance from members of their group or their neighbors. This can free you to work with other students.

It is difficult to monitor student progress on assignments from your desk or from any other fixed location, so spend as little time as possible at one place. If you must work at your desk or computer for a time, get up periodically and check on students' progress, making sure that directions are being followed correctly. If you must spend more than a minute or two helping an individual student, avoid doing it at the student's desk unless you can monitor the rest of the class from that position. (If the student's seat is in the middle of the room, half of the class will be behind you.) In such a case, call the student to your desk, to the front of the room, or to some other location from which you can easily see all students. Finally, if for some reason you must work at your desk or at any other location, don't let students congregate around the area. They will obstruct your view of the class, and they may distract students seated nearby. Instead, call students to you one at a time.

A technique for monitoring at the beginning of independent work that is effective in getting everyone started is to begin the work as a whole-group, classwork activity. Have students get out the necessary materials, head their papers, and then do the first exercise or answer the first question or two under your direction. Check and discuss this work with the class. This makes it easy for you to scan the room to be sure that everyone has begun and to determine whether students understand what to do.

A critical monitoring task is checking assignments. Collect them regularly and look them over even when students do the checking in class. Keep your record of grades current so that you will be able to detect students who are doing poor work or who skip assignments. If you give a long-term assignment, be sure to check progress regularly. You may even wish to give a grade or assign points toward a grade at the progress checkpoints. To encourage self-monitoring, you can have students keep their own checklists of assignments.

In addition to planning technology for student use, consider how technology might assist you in monitoring student involvement (e.g., www.getkahoot.com), student understanding (e.g., www.socrative.com), and student volume level (e.g., www.toonoisyapp.com). You can select apps that allow you to stay focused on the teaching and learning at hand, allow you to collect quick data points, and provide you with information or reports to share with students and parents as needed.

■ Consistency With Procedures and Consequences

Consistency means retaining the same expectations for appropriate behavior at all times and for all students. If students are expected to work silently during independent work activities on Monday, the same procedure is in effect for all students on Tuesday, Wednesday, and so on. Penalties should also be applied consistently. If the penalty for tardy arrival is detention, the teacher makes sure that all tardy students receive the penalty and that this procedure is followed even on days when it is inconvenient to administer it or in spite of the pleading of a student that an exception be made. Obvious inconsistency in the use of procedures or in the application of penalties usually leads students to test the limits by not following the procedure or by repeating whatever behavior was to have evoked the penalty. These events can escalate rapidly and force the teacher either to abandon the procedure or to tolerate high levels of inappropriate behavior. Because neither outcome is desirable, it is best to avoid the problem by resolving to be consistent in the first place.

Of course, it is important to recognize that there will be occasions when the most reasonable course of action is to make an exception to a rule or procedure. If a student's individualized education program stipulates a particular way to handle rule violations, the plan must be followed even if you might respond differently to other students who commit the same infraction. Or a deadline for an assignment may be extended when a student has a valid reason, or some procedure might be changed to accommodate a special event. Procedures used routinely for some activities but not for others will not be perceived as inconsistent if you give an explanation to the students. For example, you may stipulate that students should remain in their seats during discussions or presentations but that during independent work they may get materials, sharpen pencils, or turn in papers as needed without permission. As long as you differentiate between the activities when you explain the procedures to the students, no problems should occur.

Maintaining a consistent policy for student talk can be complicated by the need for student interaction during some activities. During small-group activities, on-task student-to-student interaction is needed and encouraged, but in some independent work assignments it is undesirable. During other independent work activities, talking may be allowed so that students can assist each other. Such an inconsistency, even though it is required by the goals for particular activities, can confuse students. One way to manage varied expectations for talking is to introduce the activities gradually and explain clearly what talk is appropriate for each activity type. For instance, the teacher might begin the year with a "no talking" procedure for seat work; when the students are acclimated to the activity, they can be introduced to independent work activities with on-task talking allowed. Teachers who have varying expectations for student talk can provide a signal that identifies which procedure is to be used. For example, a procedure used by some teachers is to post a sign listing the names of common activities (groups, independent work, study pairs) and the varieties of talk permitted (on-task talking, quiet voices, silent work) and use movable arrows to indicate the appropriate talk level.

Undesirable inconsistency usually arises from three sources. First, the procedures or rules are not reasonable, workable, or appropriate. Second, the teacher fails to monitor students closely and does not detect inappropriate behavior. This gives the appearance of inconsistency when the teacher *does* detect the behavior and tries to stop it. Finally, the teacher may not feel strongly enough about the procedure or rule to enforce it or to invoke the associated penalty. If you find yourself caught in an inconsistency that is becoming a problem, you have these alternatives:

1. Reteach the procedure. Take a few minutes to discuss the problem with the class and reiterate your desire that the rule or procedure be followed. Then enforce it.
2. Modify the procedure and then reintroduce it.
3. Abandon the procedure or consequence and perhaps substitute another in its place.

The alternative you choose depends on the circumstances and on the importance of the component to your classroom management system. *Note:* Options 2 and 3 don't apply in the case of schoolwide procedures and consequences, which must be enforced by all teachers to be effective.

■ Prompt Management of Inappropriate Behavior

Prompt handling of inappropriate behavior helps to prevent its escalation. Behaviors of concern include lack of involvement in learning activities, prolonged inattention or work avoidance, and obvious violations of classroom rules and procedures. Effective managers have a high degree of "withitness"—that is, they are so attuned to the class that they are able to detect off-task behavior and stop it before it escalates (see Chapter 7 for the discussion of withitness). It is not a good idea to ignore persistent off-task behavior because prolonged inattention makes it difficult for the students both to learn and to complete assignments. Violations of rules and failure to follow procedures create many problems we have already discussed. These behaviors should be dealt with directly but without overreaction. A calm, reasoned tone or approach is more productive and less likely to lead to confrontation. The following alternatives are recommended.

Four Simple Ways to Manage Inappropriate Behavior

We will assume that the classroom tasks are within the capabilities of the students. If not, the first priority in addressing problem behaviors is to provide suitable instruction or to modify the tasks. When the suitability of the task is not at issue, the following simple strategies are often effective. Note that the underlying goal in using these strategies is to keep the pace of the activity flowing with as little interruption as possible while redirecting the student to appropriate behavior.

1. Make eye contact with or move closer to the student. Use a signal, such as a finger to the lips or a head shake, to prompt the appropriate behavior. Monitor until the student complies.
2. If the student is not following a procedure correctly, a simple reminder of the correct procedure may be effective. You can either state the correct procedure or note other students who are doing what is expected.
3. When the student is off task—that is, not working on an assignment—redirect his or her attention to the task: "Robert, you should be writing now" or "Rosa, the assignment is to complete all of the problems on the page." Check the student's progress shortly thereafter to make sure that work is continuing.
4. Ask or tell the student to stop the inappropriate behavior. Then monitor until it stops and the student begins constructive activity.

The four procedures just listed are easy to use, cause little interruption of class activities, and enable students to correct their behavior. If a student persists in the behavior, however, another alternative must be used. If the rest of the class is working and does not need your immediate attention, a brief talk with the student may be sufficient. If that doesn't settle the matter, or if an immediate conference isn't desirable or feasible, stop the student's behavior, and assess whatever penalty is appropriate. Some teachers use a time-out desk or chair as a separate space for erring students. Note that these four response options apply to relatively minor forms of misbehavior. Additional measures for dealing with more disruptive problem behaviors are described in Chapters 10 and 11.

■ Building a Positive Climate

This chapter has emphasized maintaining appropriate behavior by applying procedures and rules consistently, handling problems promptly, and using nonintrusive interventions when possible to maintain activity flow and student involvement in lessons. We now want to emphasize the importance of keeping a positive perspective and avoiding overdwelling on student misbehavior or inadequacies. Sometimes teachers get caught in the trap of seeing only faults and problems and overlooking the better features of students' behavior. Instead of rejoicing when 29 students are involved in learning, we complain about the one student who is off task.

Mr. Acerbic's ninth-grade physical education class could do no right. Although most of the students initially participated willingly in the class activities, students never seemed to perform quickly or well enough for their teacher. "Come on, you horseflies, quit buzzing and listen up," he would yell when he heard talking. "Laps" around the gym were given for even slight infractions such as inattention; there always seemed to be three or four students making the rounds at any given time. Instead of feedback about good performance, criticism was usually given for inadequacies. Although students took the constant carping in stride, they displayed little zest for the class.

Pause and Consider

What are the results (short-term and long-term) of Mr. Acerbic's approach? How might students interpret his actions?

Vignette Reflection

Discuss with a partner your responses to the following questions: Why might Mr. Acerbic be focused on the negatives? What might improve the situation? How might teachers avoid being trapped by the negatives?

Although poor performance should not be ignored—students need specific, corrective feedback to know what to improve—it is important that the climate for learning be positive. Students should look forward to a class; they should expect to learn and to receive assistance when they encounter difficulty and should feel supported in their efforts. Such a climate can be fostered by communicating positive expectations to students, providing them with opportunities to contribute to the management of the class, praising good performance, and at times using additional rewards.

Teacher expectations can be communicated in a variety of ways, some obvious and others subtle. Teachers can:

- Identify appropriate instructional goals and discuss them with students so that they are clear about what is expected.
- Communicate acceptance of imperfect initial performance when students struggle to achieve new learning.
- Insist that students complete work satisfactorily.
- Refuse to accept excuses for poor work.
- Convey confidence in the students' ability to do well.
- Display an encouraging, "can do" attitude that generates student excitement and self-confidence.
- Avoid comparative evaluations, especially of lower-ability students, that might cause them to conclude that they cannot accomplish the objectives.

By communicating positive expectations, teachers lay the foundation for students to attempt new tasks and reach new goals. When students know that their teacher believes them to be capable, they are more likely to work harder. (For further discussion of communicating expectations, see Chapter 2 in Good and Brophy, 2008.)

Giving students classroom jobs that help in the management of the class can promote responsibility and pride and leave you with more time to work with students. Possible jobs include recording assignments and collecting handouts for absent students; helping such students when they return; organizing, distributing, or collecting materials; welcoming and providing orientation for new students and classroom visitors; and caring for classroom plants and animals. Freiberg (1999) recommends developing, perhaps with students' help, a large number of "one-minute jobs" and letting students apply for them. Or you may assign jobs to volunteers, rotating them for variety and to allow full participation.

A positive climate for learning is also created by appropriate teacher praise. When used well, teacher praise can be uplifting and provide great encouragement to a student. The most powerful type of teacher praise provides the student with information about what aspect of student performance is praiseworthy and also demonstrates that the teacher is impressed with the quality of the student's work. In other words, effective praise provides both informative feedback and genuine teacher approval. It can also accompany suggestions for improvement (constructive criticism) without loss of effect.

Public praise that focuses on student *accomplishment* works better than praise for student effort alone. When the teacher praises only for working hard, students may assume that the teacher thinks they aren't very able. When you know that a student put forth considerable effort and you want to acknowledge it, be sure the praise includes an emphasis on the student's achievement. "Desirae, all your hard work paid off because your project was beautifully done. The organization of ideas and the extra details in the descriptions were outstanding!" However, lavish public praise of a student for success on an easy task can communicate to the rest of the class (and the student who was praised) that the teacher believes he or she has little ability.

It is a good idea to look for private ways to provide praise. Written comments on papers, tests, and other assignments offer excellent opportunities for quality praise. Private conversations, conferences with parents, emails and notes home, and informal contacts also offer opportunities for praising students. Private praise avoids some of the complications of public praise and permits the teacher to include a greater variety of performances and behaviors as its focus. Further discussion of the uses of teacher praise can be found in Emmer (1988), Brophy (1996), or Burnett (2002).

■ Improving Class Climate Through Incentives or Rewards

Extra incentives or rewards can help build a positive climate. The improvement in class climate occurs because the incentives add interest or excitement to the class routine while directing attention toward appropriate behavior and away from inappropriate behavior. When students are rewarded rather than punished, they are more likely to respond positively to the teacher, thereby contributing to a mutually supportive pattern of interaction.

Before introducing an external incentive, you should consider several factors that might affect its appropriateness and effect. Check your school or district policies because sometimes the use of incentives is restricted; you would not want to promise a field trip or party only to find out that it was prohibited by school board policy.

Your rewards should target the behaviors you would like to encourage. Rewards too easily earned or too difficult to achieve lose their motivational effect. Also, you should be concerned about whether the use of a reward takes too much class time for record keeping or related administrative tasks. Avoid using complex systems that distract you and your students from a focus on learning. Start with simple procedures and add to them as needed.

Be careful not to set up incentives that only the most able students can achieve. Systems that encourage excessive competition for scarce rewards will discourage students who don't have much chance. The examples in this section and in the case study at the end of the chapter include a variety of types. Combine these ideas with those of other teachers and your own experience to develop alternatives for use at various times of the year. Many different types of rewards, including symbols, recognition, activities, and materials, can be used with secondary students. Each type is described, with examples, in the following sections.

Grades and Other Symbols

The most prevalent form of incentive is the letter or numerical grade, although other symbols such as checks or stars are sometimes used with students in middle school classes. Good grades are a powerful incentive for most students when they are perceived to be a direct reflection of their achievement and competence. Therefore, it is important to tie as many facets of student work to grades as possible. In addition, you should make clear to students the basis for determining grades to help them know what they have to do to achieve good grades. Identifying criteria for grading and communicating them to students have been discussed earlier, in chapter 5 (pp. 73–75 and 86–87).

One caveat is worth noting. Occasionally, teachers react negatively to the grading system because they feel that too much emphasis is placed on grades and not enough on learning. This feeling may cause the teacher to project a casual attitude about grades and to be vague about the grading criteria. This is a mistake; the teacher is still required to assign grades, and the students are left with less control over their fate. A more constructive reaction would be for the teacher to work hard to make the grading criteria reflect the course's learning objectives.

Recognition

Recognition rewards involve some means of giving attention to the student. Examples are displaying the student's work; awarding a certificate for achievement, improvement, or good behavior; sending positive notes or emails home; giving compliments and also nonverbal responses such as thumbs-up; and verbally citing the

SHOE-NEW BUSINESS © MacNelly – Distributed by King Features Syndicate, Inc. World Rights Reserved

student's accomplishments. Some adolescents are embarrassed by being singled out for attention, so giving public recognition to several students at the same time is a better strategy. Privately given recognition is also a good alternative. At a school, team, or grade level, recognition awards are often given at the end of the year or semester, with teachers nominating the recipients. If this is the case in your school, be sure to find out what awards are commonly given. Then tell your students about them (e.g., awards for attendance, achievement, improvement, honor students, hard work, conduct, good citizens) early in the year. Early discussion of these awards may motivate your students to work toward them. A similar procedure is to establish and display an honor roll (all-star list, honor society) to reward students at the end of each grading term. Certificates, stickers with designs appealing to teenagers, or treats can be used in conjunction with the awards, especially for younger secondary students. It is a good idea to spread the honors around to include a good portion of your students. Don't give awards only for outstanding achievement; have awards for improvement, excellent effort, good conduct, and so on.

Activities as Rewards

Granting privileges such as working with a friend, free computer or reading time, choosing where to sit for the day, visits to the school library, a homework pass, or helping to decorate a bulletin board are examples of activity rewards. A more elaborate activity reward would be a field trip or a party. Because school policy may affect your use of the latter activities, check the rules before announcing activities to your classes. Be certain to describe clearly what students need to do to receive any privileges.

Teachers who use activity rewards as incentives for the whole class can permit students to participate in their identification and selection. A list of potentially desirable (and acceptable) activities can be presented to a class or solicited from students during a discussion; either way, the class can vote on whichever one it wishes to seek. Some whole-class activities that might be used include 15 minutes of free time, playing games, listening to music, having a popcorn party, or no homework. A group activity reward should be made contingent on specific desirable behaviors; if the group cooperates, students will receive the incentive. If not, they will lose some or all of the time in the activity. Because the purpose of an activity reward is at least in part to promote positive climate building, it is important not to let one or two students spoil the fun for the rest of the class. A chronically uncooperative student or two can be invited to participate, but if they persist in noncompliance, the teacher may exclude them from the activity. In most cases, positive peer pressure encourages such a student to cooperate without the teacher having to resort to exclusion.

Finding a supervised place for the excluded student during the activity is a drawback to using this incentive. Sometimes teachers solve the problem by arranging ahead of time for the student to go to another teacher's classroom, where he or she will complete assigned independent work during the period.

Material Incentives

Material incentives include the awarding of objects of value to students. Examples are food, discarded classroom materials, games, and books. In addition to ascertaining school policy, you must consider your own financial circumstances before deciding to use such rewards. Because you will have a large number of students and limited resources, your use of material rewards will be restricted at best.

When you consider what types of rewards to use in your classes, several factors should be kept in mind. Your rewards should be related to the student behaviors that are most important to you, such as satisfactory completion of assignments, participation in academic activities, and attainment of learning objectives. For these student behaviors, grades are effective and relevant rewards. Another set of important student behaviors are those related to following rules and major procedures. For these behaviors, recognition and activity rewards can be used effectively. Some teachers hold competitions among their classes, rewarding the class that has the best behavior record, punctuality, or homework completion rate for a grading period. With the cooperation of other teachers and administrators, good student behavior can be rewarded by a party, a movie, or a field trip at the end of the semester for all students who have stayed off the detention list and maintained good attendance records. An incentive on such a grand scale requires much planning and effort and the cooperation of many people.

Using candy or other foods of little or no nutritional value as rewards is not recommended, because it encourages habits that contribute to obesity. An extensive list of alternatives to food can be found at cspinet.org/new/pdf/constructive_classroom_rewards.pdf or at healthymeals.nal.usda.gov/hsmrs/Connecticut/Food_As_Reward.pdf.

Individual and Group Incentives

Technology offers multiple tools for acknowledging appropriate behavior. Consider, for example, the Class Dojo® app (www.classdojo.com) that allows teachers to implement a point system for recognizing students (or use with penalty points as well) via multiple devices. Students have individual avatars and can log in to keep track of their individual or group points. Parents can also utilize this tool for more complete school-to-home communication.

Caution in the Use of Rewards

Some researchers (Deci, Koestner, & Ryan, 2001) have urged caution in the use of extrinsic rewards, especially tangible rewards, pointing out that under some circumstances their use may reduce students' intrinsic motivation to engage in the rewarded activity. Rewards that are expected, tangible, and unrelated to the quality of task performance may interfere with the process and quality of learning. In general, these rewards have a negative effect on a student's intrinsic motivation and cause a shift of attention away from the content to be learned, the challenge to a student's natural curiosity, and a desire to be competent. Explanations of this dampening effect on motivation usually focus on the thinking processes that occur when individuals are given rewards: "This must be an unpleasant or boring task because I'm being offered a reward to get me to do it." Or the student may feel as though the reward is being used to control behavior rather than to encourage learning. Frequent use of these types of rewards may result in passive learning and undermine creativity instead of supporting the teacher's goal of developing self-regulation, deep understanding, and appreciation of knowledge and skill.

Teachers need to differentiate between rewards given to control or shape behavior and those designed as feedback to student competence or that support a sense of mastery (Reeve, 2006; Reeve, 2015). If the teacher's objective is to control student behavior through prizes or other extrinsic rewards, students may comply with specific standards. They may not, however, develop a sense of self-regulation or an appreciation of the need for competence.

Not all rewards are perceived to have this dampening effect. Cameron (2001) noted, "In fact, few teachers set up incentive systems for tasks in which students already have a high level of interest" (p. 32). Awards tied to progress, competence, or a sense of mastery increase inner motivation by validating a student's sense of

CALVIN AND HOBBES © 1989 Watterson, Dist. by UNIVERSAL UCLICK. Reprinted with permission. All Rights Reserved.

personal ability. Praise, symbols, or prizes should be tied as specifically as possible to positive behavior. The informational aspect of the reward, or feedback, is important and nurtures students' inner motivation.

The most reasonable application of the research results for classroom use of rewards is to be thoughtful about their use. No purpose is served by rewarding students for participating in activities that are already interesting to them; the evidence suggests that doing so may actually reduce intrinsic motivation. However, many classroom tasks are not highly interesting, especially during the extensive repetition that is needed to produce skilled performance and learning. When student motivation flags, external incentives help to maintain engagement. In fact, the use of incentives is much more desirable than lowering expectations and accepting poor performance or using punishment and threats to attempt to keep students working. When rewards are used, they should support students' engagement and self-management rather than emphasize teacher control over student behavior (Reeve, 2006). The message the student receives should be "You did a great job!" rather than "Do it my way or you don't get a reward."

Finally, the teacher can counteract the potential for negative effects on intrinsic motivation by pointing out the usefulness of the skill to be learned, by choosing materials and activities that have high potential for sustaining student interest, by describing long-term outcomes of value to the students, and by modeling and demonstrating personal interest and enthusiasm for the task.

■ Using School-Wide Positive Behavior Support to Maintain Appropriate Student Behavior

Although the techniques and strategies in this text are research-based, appropriate, and effective, they are not the only means for maintaining appropriate student behavior, nor are they limited to working in isolation from other approaches. Our approach is typically defined as an ecological one (Bear, 2015). Additional theories of classroom management and lines of research have provided alternate ways of cultivating positive student behavior and contributions. The following brief description is an overview of one prominent alternative: School-Wide Positive Behavior Support (SWPBS). A second approach, social-emotional learning, is described in the Who Will I Teach section that follows.

School-Wide Positive Behavior Support is a research-based, data-driven systems approach. It is classified within behavioral theory (Bear, 2015), although its applications incorporate aspects of other approaches (e.g., ecological). A SWPBS system is based on establishing shared expectations for behavior across the school environment, along with multiple levels of intervention (Lewis, Mitchell, Trussell, & Newcomer, 2015). Obtaining broad support from teachers, staff, students, and parents is essential. Strategies to support appropriate behavior are organized into three tiers. The first tier is considered to be the universal (Tier I) support strategies applicable to all students and consists of preventive approaches that encourage appropriate behavior (e.g., promote safe classroom and school environments, establish clear expectations, provide consistent support to students). Another level of strategies (Tier II) addresses problem behaviors that occur in spite of the first tier's preventive and supportive approaches. The goal of Tier II strategies is to respond promptly to problems to minimize their effects on the classroom and school climate and to redirect students to desirable behavior. When interventions beyond the universal or Tier I supports are required for individuals or small groups of students (e.g., students who have received several office referrals, or who are chronically tardy), they are identified through data collection at the classroom and school levels. The selected strategies continue the universal supports and simultaneously refine the student's/ students' understanding of and ability to meet the stated expectations. Tier III strategies focus on identifying and treating students who are not responsive to Tier I or Tier II approaches. If a student demonstrates serious, risky, or chronic inappropriate behavior, interventions are individual and function-based to target the cause of the inappropriate behavior. Again, data determines the need, intervention, monitoring, and success at the Tier III level (Sugai & Simonsen, 2015).

The three-tiered conceptualization of prevention-intervention is often depicted as a triangle of participation. At the base of the triangle, 100% of the students are exposed to the Tier I components in all classrooms and throughout the school. Many of the strategies described in this text would be considered Tier I (or universal), because they are preventive and focused on teaching desirable behavior, promoting success, and preventing problems. Depending on a variety of factors, perhaps 10 to 15% of the students in a school may not respond adequately to primary prevention, and thus they need support at the Tier II level. Such supports might include instructional modifications, anger or stress management training, daily monitoring of work completion or other behaviors accompanied by reinforcement plans, mentoring, peer problem-solving groups led by counselors, or supportive contacts with parents. A smaller number of students will require even more monitoring and intervention (Tier III) because of high rates of office referrals, aggression, and antisocial behavior. In this book, strategies that could be incorporated into Tier II or Tier III plans can be found mainly in Chapters 10, 11, and 12.

School-Wide Positive Behavior Support emphasizes a team approach to managing behavior throughout the school. Teachers, staff, and administrators work together to develop a school-wide system to support desirable student behavior and to prevent problems. If you teach in a school that has adopted a SWPBS plan, expect to work with other teachers and school personnel to identify goals for school and classroom management. You may be part of a planning team and thus will have input into the decisions that are made, and you will benefit from the collective wisdom and support of your colleagues. You will also be expected to help with efforts to gather data to document the effectiveness of specific strategies and interventions. Participation may take some of your time, but the potential payoff is that you'll have fewer discipline problems and your school will be a safer place and a better environment for student learning. See www.pbis.org and the Further Readings section of this chapter for specific references if you are interested in deepening your understanding of SWPBS.

■ Who Will I Teach? Providing Students With Opportunities for Social Emotional Learning in the Classroom

Social-emotional learning (SEL) can be defined as "the process of gaining competencies and intrinsic motivation for emotional self-awareness and self-regulation, for safe and responsible behavior and for assertive, empathic, and skillful social interaction" (Schwab & Elias, 2015, p. 95). Thus, SEL is concerned with the individual's knowledge about his or her own and others' emotions, and with skills for managing emotions and emotion-related behavior. The knowledge and skills of the SEL process support the maintenance of appropriate classroom behavior because they are a strong foundation for individual adjustment as well as positive social interaction. Consider the following example (adapted from Schwab & Elias, 2015, p. 97):

> *Suppose someone tells a ninth-grade girl that several classmates have been spreading rumors about her. Will she exert self-control or will she retaliate? How she handles the information depends largely on her emotional competence. If she does not attend to her emotional state, then she may react in an unacceptable way such as by spreading counter rumors or attacking. If she does attend to her emotions and label them accurately (e.g., anger, hurt, disbelief) she may be able to regulate them and develop a plan for responding to the situation constructively (e.g., remaining calm, talking to an adult, asking the classmates for an explanation). The girl's skills in managing relationships also will be important competencies for resolving the situation; if she knows constructive ways to handle conflict she will be more likely to address the problem and resolve it. Lacking those skills, she may internalize the comments or overreact.*

This example is just one of many emotion-laden events that might happen to a student throughout a school day. Here are some more examples and possible accompanying emotions.

- Difficulty in completing assigned work may cause frustration.
- Feeling unprepared for a test might result in anxiety.
- Noticing other students performing well elicits envy.
- Being bumped and jostled can cause anger.
- Being threatened by other students causes fear.
- Receiving a low grade produces sadness.
- Being rejected by classmates causes loneliness.

Lack of self-understanding and the absence of skills to deal constructively with emotions can disrupt an adolescent's life, spill over into classroom behavior, and adversely affect others. Although teachers are not therapists, they do have many opportunities to help their students learn about emotions and related skills. For example, learning about emotions can be integrated naturally in many content areas such as literature, language study and language arts (e.g., vocabulary and writing), science, history, and other social studies. Information about emotions and related topics, such as other persons' feelings or self-management strategies, can be incorporated into discussions. Lessons that deal with local, national, and world events and issues also provide venues for considering the role of emotions and related behavior. Regardless of subject matter taught, conversations with students about appropriate behavior, following rules, respecting other students, or participating in the classroom community can incorporate content about feelings, self-management, or taking responsibility.

An organization called Collaborative for Academic, Social, and Emotional Learning (CASEL) has done substantial work in developing curricula addressing emotions, including self and social awareness, self-management, relationship skills, and responsible decision making. You can read about this organization, its curriculum, and related research at www.casel.org. Many SEL programs use ideas drawn from CASEL's pioneering work in the field. An example of a middle school program that teaches SEL skills is *Second Step* (http://www.cfchildren.org/second-step/middle-school), which has 13 to 15 lessons for each grade (6, 7, and 8) organized into units on empathy and communication, bullying prevention, emotion management, problem solving, and substance abuse prevention. Individual lessons can be taught as part of a course, or they can be incorporated into weekly homeroom or advisory periods over a semester or year. At the high school level, an example of an application of the SEL approach is *School-Connect: Optimizing the High School Experience* (http://www.school-connect.net). The *School-Connect* program consists of four modules (Creating a Supportive Learning Community, Developing Self-Awareness and Self-Management, Building Academic Strength and Purpose, and Resolving Conflicts and Making Decisions); each contains 10 lessons to build SEL skills. One use of this curriculum is as a basis for a semester-long class for ninth-graders, in order to assist them in the transition from middle to high school and to prevent course failure, discipline referrals, and dropping out. In some schools in participating school districts, only identified ninth-grade students take the class; in other schools all ninth-graders enroll.

When schools or school districts adopt an SEL curriculum, then teachers are provided with training and curriculum materials. In addition to the training provided to teachers, advantages of schoolwide implementation are greater consistency of application throughout the school and common terminology. For teachers not directly involved in teaching SEL skills, the fact that their students will have been exposed to the content and will have developed skills allows teachers to reinforce the emotional learning in other classes and activities. For example, in one participating high school, the athletics department made a deliberate effort to utilize the ideas to emphasize teamwork and problem solving. Even if your school has not adopted an SEL-based program, you can still incorporate some of its features into your classroom management plan and content activities. You may examine in more detail one of the SEL-based curricula cited earlier in this section. Also, in this book, Chapters 2, 8, and 10 include information relevant to content and skills for promoting social-emotional learning for your students. Those chapters, combined with an organized sequence of topics and activities adapted from an SEL curriculum, will provide a good foundation for your teaching in this area.

■ Chapter Summary

Once good classroom management has been established, it must be maintained on a daily basis. Four areas help sustain good student behavior: monitoring behavior and academic progress; consistency; addressing problems promptly; and building a positive, supportive classroom climate. Incentives and rewards have a role to play in the system of positive behavioral supports, but should be used thoughtfully. School-Wide Positive Behavior Supports (SWPBS) and social-emotional learning (SEL) are described.

■ Further Reading

Akin-Little, K. A., Eckert, T. L., Lovett, B. J., & Little, S. G. (2004). Extrinsic reinforcement in the classroom: Bribery or best practice. *School Psychology Review, 33*, 344–362.

> *The authors review the history of research on the use of rewards, with special attention to the debate over their effects on motivation. Their conclusion is that detrimental effects are minimal and that the use of extrinsic rewards should not be equated with bribery. The authors provide suggestions for the appropriate use of rewards in educational settings.*

Hansen, J. (2010). Teaching without talking. *Phi Delta Kappan, 92*(1), 35–40.

> *In this brief article, the author encourages teachers to consider their nonverbal communication being extended to students. She offers suggestions for utilizing these interactions in supportive, nondistracting ways to encourage student participation and learning.*

http://712educators.about.com/od/classroomhelpers/tp/student-rewards.htm

> *Ideas for rewards at the middle and high school levels are given on the site.*

Jennings, P. A., & Greenberg, M. T. (2009). The prosocial classroom: Teacher social and emotional competence in relation to students and classroom outcomes. *Review of Educational Research, 79*, 491–525.

> *The authors propose a model of classroom climate that emphasizes the role of the teacher's social and emotional competence. They provide a literature review that supports connections of student social, emotional, and academic outcomes to effective classroom management, healthy student–teacher relationships, and teacher social–emotional competence.*

Mueller, C. M., & Dweck, C. S. (1998). Praise for intelligence can undermine children's motivation for performance. *Journal of Personality and Social Psychology, 75,* 33–52.

> *In a series of six studies, the authors demonstrate that students who receive positive feedback based on their effort continue to exert effort in learning. These students associate struggles with a lack of effort and ability, and therefore may not make further attempts. Students who receive positive feedback based on their intelligence seek to continue looking smart and may choose activities with less challenge.*

Reeve, J. (2015). Rewards. In E. T. Emmer & E. J. Sabornie (Eds.), *Handbook of research on classroom management* (2nd ed., pp. 496–515). New York: Routledge.

> *The author provides a comprehensive review of research on the use of rewards, with an emphasis on providing classroom structure along with supporting student autonomy and engagement rather than behavior control. Effects of rewards in the brain and principles for the appropriate classroom uses of rewards are described.*

Wentzel, K. R., & Brophy, J. E. (2014). *Motivating students to learn* (2nd ed.). Hillsdale, NJ: Erlbaum.

> *This very readable book addresses teachers directly and offers strategies and principles to use in motivating students to learn. Helpful examples and applications are provided with an eye toward the complexities of the classroom setting.*

www.interventioncentral.org/behavioral-interventions/rewards/jackpot-ideas-classroom-rewards

> *This webpage is part of a larger free website (Intervention Central) to support teachers with their student interventions. This specific page highlights a range of potential rewards for supporting students' appropriate behavior.*

■ Suggested Activities

1. Discuss with a partner: What does "appropriate" behavior mean to you? Imagine your own classroom. When students are behaving appropriately, what will it look and sound like? How much movement and talk do you find acceptable?

2. Review the checklists at the end of Chapters 4 and 5 and identify any individual or group rewards you intend to use with major conduct and work procedures. By planning ahead, you will be better able to explain these incentives and be consistent in their use.

3. Interview a practicing teacher on maintaining student behavior. Include in your conversation questions about school and/or district policies that affect that teacher's use of rewards, as well as how faculty consistency across a school affects schoolwide procedures.

4. Read Examples 9.1 through 9.6, and consider how you might adapt these descriptions of incentive systems to your own classroom. Analyze each example using the following questions as the starting point:
   a. Is the system primarily intrinsic or extrinsic?
   b. Is the system cooperative or competitive?
   c. What kind of classroom environment is the system likely to foster?

■ CASE STUDY 9.1

EXAMPLES OF INCENTIVES AND REWARDS

Example 9.1 Awards and Recognition   An attractive award certificate was designed by a teacher and used for individual students at different times during the year. The certificates were especially impressive because each was signed by the principal as well as the teacher. Students were recognized for outstanding effort, along with improvement or accomplishment. To save time, the teacher made many copies of the blank certificates before school began and asked the principal to sign them all at once. She filled them in as needed with students' names and accomplishments. The certificates were awarded both publicly and privately, according to the student and the accomplishment. (*Note:* Blank achievement/appreciation certificates can be purchased from school supply stores or downloaded from suitable web sites.)

Honor roll systems are common. Generally, these schoolwide systems have incentive value for better students and don't provide much motivation for the less academically successful. One teacher who taught several classes of low achievers in a school that used ability grouping developed an in-class honor roll that was more accessible to his students. At the end of each grading period, students who had improved their performance or who had participated well in class activities were named to a "Best in the West" honor roll. Their names were placed on a bulletin board honor roll, and they received attractive stickers to display on their notebooks or textbook covers.

Example 9.2 Competitions   For some subjects, long-range incentives are available in the form of city, regional, or statewide competitions (e.g., spelling or composition contests, science and math fairs). Other competitions can be conducted within a school, with classes competing against one another, or they may even be limited to the classes taught by one teacher. The teacher can establish a reward for the best projects or for the class in which all students complete the project first. Within-class rewards can also be offered. One teacher posted spelling grades by class on a bulletin board display. The class with the highest overall score at the end of each month received a special prize or treat.

Teachers who use some form of cooperative groups may use group competitions. Members of winning groups may receive a reward such as extra time in desirable activities (free reading, computer use, library passes), recognition, certificates, appreciation notes sent home, or bonus points. Competitions can be based on average test scores of students in the group, performance criteria for projects or assignments, desirable group behavior, or improvement on some criterion. When using group competitions, it's best to have a fairly short time frame (group-of-the-week rather than group-of-the-semester awards).

Example 9.3 Encouraging Improvement.   One of the defining characteristics of the mastery learning approach is the opportunity to retake tests and redo assignments until a predetermined criterion, such as 80 or 90, is reached. Even if mastery learning is not adopted *in toto*, some teachers allow students to redo incorrectly done assignments to improve their grade. Students might be allowed to earn enough points to bring their grade up to a B level, for example.

Example 9.4 Extra-credit assignments   Extra-credit activities are frequently popular with students, and the extra credit earned toward improving a grade is an important incentive for most students. One teacher kept an extra-credit logic problem on the side board, changing it every week or two depending on its difficulty. She also had extra-credit puzzles and worksheets on a front table. These puzzles covered material currently being studied by the class, and students were encouraged to work on them after they had finished their required work. They could also copy them and work on them at home. This teacher had students keep their completed extra-credit problems in a special section of their notebooks, where they were checked when the teacher graded the notebooks. Each correct problem was worth one point and was added to the notebook grade at the end of the grading period.

A science teacher kept a list of extra-credit projects for students to work on individually or in groups. Along with the list of projects was a description of the requirements for each project, its complexity, a deadline for completion, and the number of points earned toward a report card grade. English and social studies teachers frequently have book lists from which students may choose extra-credit reading. A form for students to use when reporting on the book should also be available.

Sometimes bulletin boards are used to display extra-credit work. One math teacher had a picture of a mountain, with math problems relevant to current lessons at each of several elevations. Beneath the mountain were lines for 10 student names. The first 10 students (from all classes) correctly completing the problems had their names posted under the mountain. When the tenth name was posted, the teacher taped a piece of gum beside each name for the student to remove.

Example 9.5 Combined Incentives   Allowing students special privileges or permitting them to participate in desired activities is a commonly used reward, and it is often combined with another kind of reward such as recognition. For example, one teacher chose outstanding students each week, based on their attitude, grades, and attendance. The teacher would put students' names on a bulletin board display, and students would receive a special treat on Friday. Another teacher recognized consistent performance by naming all students who had turned in all their work during the previous week as a "Student of the Week" and by placing their names on a special bulletin board display. After being named "Student of the Week" five times during a grading period, the student was entitled to claim an A for one of the four major components of the report card grade. One teacher allowed 15 or 20 minutes of free reading or game time on Friday when a class had been well behaved throughout the week. Another teacher made an "activity chain" from construction paper, adding a link when class behavior was good each day. When the chain reached a certain length, the class was permitted to have part of a period for a special activity such as free reading or a class competition.

Example 9.6 Point Systems   Point systems are useful because in addition to giving students clearly specified incentives, they can be used to have students take responsibility for keeping track of their own work. One teacher gave a handout to students at the beginning of each week with the week's assignments on it. The students recorded points they earned for each assignment, with up to 100 points awarded weekly. Some bonus points were available for extra-credit assignments, and the teacher could add extra points for good behavior and class participation. These weekly records of points were then used along with test scores to determine report card grades. A common modification of this system is to allow the summary sheet to cover a longer period of time, such as two or three weeks, instead of one week. With older and more mature students, such as those in the upper grades in high school, teachers who apply this system often use a summary sheet for the grading period rather than for each week.

MyEducationLab *Self-Check 9.1*

MyEducationLab *Self-Check 9.2*

MyEducationLab *Self-Check 9.3*

MyEducationLab *Self-Check 9.4*

MyEducationLab *Application Exercise 9.1*   Using what you've learned in this chapter, view the video and respond to the questions.

MyEducationLab *Application Exercise 9.2*   Using what you've learned in this chapter, read and respond to this scenario.

MyEducationLab *Application Exercise 9.3*   Using what you've learned in this chapter, read and respond to this scenario.

MyEducationLab *Application Exercise 9.4*   Using what you've learned in this chapter, read and respond to this scenario.

MyEducationLab *Application Exercise 9.5*   Using what you've learned in this chapter, read and respond to this scenario.

MyEducationLab *Classroom Management Simulation 9.1*   Engage with the Classroom Management Simulation *Responding to Mildly Disruptive Behavior.*

Shutterstock

CHAPTER 10

Communication Skills for Teaching

Good communication skills are an essential part of most occupations and, indeed, of living and working in society. Individuals who communicate well are able to seek or give assistance, provide leadership, and maintain cordial relations. Because so much of our lives are spent working with others, good communication is extremely important.

Perhaps more than any other profession, teaching requires excellent communication skills. Teachers interact constantly with children, parents, school administrators, and other teachers. Several different contexts for communication are common to teaching, such as delivering instruction, solving a problem, or managing behavior. The focus of this chapter is on communication skills that are used when teachers encounter problems and need to engage with students (or parents) in order to better understand what is occurring, to seek a workable solution, or to effect a change in behavior. Consider the following example:

> During the past several days, Debra and Diane have been increasingly inattentive in Ms. Harris's fifth-period class. Their off-task behavior has included whispering with other students and each other, teasing boys seated nearby, and displaying exaggerated boredom with class discussions. Ms. Harris first asked the girls to stop bothering the class, and when that had no effect, she moved the girls to different seats. However, Debra and Diane continue to disrupt by passing notes and calling out loudly to one another.

We will not second-guess Ms. Harris by wondering whether she had communicated expectations clearly or had taken action promptly enough; let us suppose that she had in fact practiced good preventive management skills but that the students misbehaved anyway. No strategy works all the time. What options are now available to Ms. Harris to deal with the situation? Possible approaches include the following:

- Ignore the problem and hope it goes away.
- Refer the students to an assistant principal.
- Call the students' parents and ask for their help.
- Apply a consequence such as detention or some other punishment.

Each of these approaches has advantages and limitations. For example, ignoring the problem requires little effort and might work if the students are mainly seeking teacher attention. The description does not, however, suggest that this is a likely reason for the behavior, and ignoring the problem may only allow it to intensify and spread to other students. Referral has the advantage of demanding little of the teacher's time, at least in the short run; it also temporarily removes the disruptive students, and it can have deterrent value. However, it may do nothing in the long run to deal with the problem the students are causing in the class, and although referral may sometimes be a reasonable approach to serious misbehavior, it can easily be overused.

A telephone call to parents sometimes works wonders and is usually worth a try. Unfortunately, parents cannot always stop misbehavior. They do not, after all, accompany their child to your class, nor do they control the cues that are eliciting the misbehavior. Punishing the students by assigning detention or withholding some desirable activity or privilege is another possible reaction. As we discuss in Chapter 11, punishment can stop misbehavior at least temporarily, and it can deter other students. But punishment can have the disadvantages of creating hostility or resentment, and it may trap the teacher and the students in a cycle of misbehavior-reaction that leads to power struggles. By itself, punishment does little to teach the student self-control and responsibility.

Because each of these approaches has limitations, you will need additional means of coping with problems. This does not mean that other approaches such as ignoring, referral, applying consequences, or involving parents will be supplanted. It does mean that communication strategies should be *added* to your repertoire to deal with problems that cannot be corrected with minor interventions and to help students learn to take responsibility for their own behavior.

In addition to being helpful when dealing with students whose behavior is creating a problem for the teacher or for other students, communication skills can be used to assist students who are themselves experiencing problems. Teachers frequently become aware of students' problems caused by factors both inside and outside the classroom. Teachers can help these students by being good listeners and by encouraging them to consider alternative ways to solve problems or to adapt to difficult situations.

We use the label *communication skills* for the set of strategies described in this chapter to emphasize that the approach focuses on communicating clearly and effectively with students to help bring about a change in their behavior, in their thinking, or in the situation that has caused the problem. Communication also means being open to information, so teachers need to be good listeners and try to understand the student's (or parents') concerns and feelings. To become an effective communicator, you need three related skills:

1. **Constructive assertiveness.** This includes communicating your concerns clearly, insisting that misbehavior be corrected, and resisting being coerced or manipulated.
2. **Empathic responding.** This means listening to the student's perspective and reacting in ways that maintain a positive relationship and encourage further discussion.
3. **Problem solving.** This involves following several steps for reaching mutually satisfactory resolutions to problems; it requires working with the student to develop a plan for change.

The three elements are derived from a variety of publications, including *The Skilled Helper* (Egan, 2014); *Teacher Effectiveness Training* (Gordon, 2003); *The Art of Helping in the 21st Century* (Carkhuff, 2010); *Teacher as Counselor* (Kottler & Kottler, 2006); *Reality Therapy* (Glasser, 1975); *Helping Skills* (Hill, 2014); *Mastering Assertiveness Skills* (Zuker, 1983); and other standard sources. These books are listed in the References. The discussion of communication skills in this chapter is intended to be an introduction; if you are interested in further reading, one or more of these books should be helpful.

Although this chapter's treatment of constructive assertiveness, empathic responding, and problem solving focuses on their use with students, the skills are very helpful when dealing with parents—especially during parent conferences—and other adults. Thus, the skills described in this chapter have a variety of applications and will improve your effectiveness in handling many classroom and school-related situations.

■ Constructive Assertiveness

Assertiveness is the ability to stand up for one's legitimate rights in ways that help ensure that others will not ignore or circumvent them. The adjective *constructive* implies that the assertive teacher does not tear down or attack the student. Constructive assertiveness can be thought of as a general characteristic or attribute that is used in a wide variety of settings or as a set of skills that are more situation specific. Some individuals are assertive in an array of situations (e.g., interacting with strangers, on the job, at parties, in school), whereas others lack assertiveness in many of these settings. Constructive assertiveness in the classroom is likely a characteristic of teachers who are referred to as "warm demanders" (see Chapter 2). Such teachers communicate high expectations for behavior and performance in supportive yet insistent ways.

Even if you are not generally assertive, you can learn to use assertive behaviors while you are teaching. In fact, doing so may help generalize your behaviors in other situations as you become more confident of your skills. People who are very unassertive (who feel nervous whenever they are expected to lead a group, who are unable to begin conversations or to make eye contact with others, who accede to inappropriate demands readily, and who are unable to ask others to respect their rights) will find teaching uncomfortable and will have particular difficulty with discipline. Such persons can help themselves in several ways, especially by reading about assertiveness and practicing some of its skills, preferably in situations that are not too uncomfortable, until they begin to develop confidence. It is also possible to obtain professional help, such as from a counseling center, or to enroll in a course or workshop on assertiveness training. A good assertiveness training program usually includes anxiety-reduction exercises, skills training and practice in developing more effective behaviors, and cognitive restructuring to reshape negative thought patterns that interfere with appropriate social interaction.

The elements of constructive assertiveness include

- A clear statement of the problem or issue
- Unambiguous body language
- Insistence on appropriate behavior and resolution of the problem

Assertiveness is not

- Hostile or aggressive
- Argumentative
- Inflexible
- Timid or apathetic behavior

Assertiveness lies on a continuum between aggressive, overbearing pushiness and timid, ineffectual submissiveness or apathy that allow students to trample on the teacher's and other students' rights. By using assertiveness skills, you communicate to students that you are serious about teaching and about maintaining a classroom in which everyone's rights are respected.

Assertiveness has three basic elements:

1. A clear statement of the problem or concern. Student misbehavior usually causes problems for teachers by making it difficult to conduct lessons, by slowing down activities, and by subverting routines that help a class run smoothly. When misbehavior persists, it is time for the teacher to let the student know what the problem is from the teacher's point of view. Sometimes a simple description of the problem is enough to produce behavior change because the student becomes more aware of the behavior and begins to self-monitor better. Stating the problem has two parts: (1) identifying the student behavior and (2) describing its effects if they are not obvious:

> "Talking and passing notes during discussion distracts other students from the lesson."

"Calling out answers without raising your hand prevents others from participating."

"Wandering around the room disturbs the class."

"Calling other students names causes hard feelings."

By focusing on the behavior and its effects, you can reduce the potential for student defensiveness and keep open the opportunity for achieving a satisfactory resolution. Conducting the conference privately (e.g., at a table separate from the class, after class, or during a conference period) lessens the potential for embarrassing the student in front of peers and reduces the likelihood of a confrontation or power struggle that challenges the teacher's authority. However, sometimes you will be forced to act immediately.

Notice that the preceding problem descriptions avoid labeling either students or their behavior (e.g., accusing them of being bad, rude, annoying, inconsiderate, or infantile). Labeling causes resentment and invites challenges from adolescents. Labeling also should be avoided because it interferes with behavior change by communicating a negative expectation that the student might accept as valid. When describing the problem, try to use statements rather than questions. Quizzing students ("Why are you talking?" "Do you think you should be calling someone that name?") invites defensive, sarcastic, or argumentative responses.

2. Body language. Constructive assertiveness with students needs to be reinforced by appropriate body language in three areas. The first is making eye contact when addressing the student, especially when describing the problem and when calling for behavior change. Note that there is a difference between eye contact that communicates seriousness and resolve versus an angry glare that emits hostility. In the former case, breaking eye contact from time to time relieves tension. A second area of assertive body language is maintaining an erect posture, facing the student (but not so close as to appear to threaten) to communicate your attention and involvement in the conversation. The third area is matching your facial expressions with the content and tone of your statements (e.g., not grinning when making serious statements).

3. Obtaining appropriate behavior. Assertiveness requires that the teacher not be diverted from insisting on appropriate behavior. Students may engage in diversionary tactics by denying involvement, arguing, or blaming others (including the teacher). When dealing with such diversionary tactics, remember: There are many reasons, but no excuses, for misbehavior. Although it is possible that others contributed to the problem, the student needs to accept responsibility for his or her behavior. It is important to listen carefully to and understand the student's situation, but in the end, if the student's behavior is interfering with your ability to teach, the behavior must change. Thus, if a student begins to argue or to deny responsibility for the behavior, you should avoid being sidetracked. The bottom line is that the student's behavior is not acceptable, whatever the reason for it.

When working with students who are evasive or who are not taking matters seriously, a little dramatic emphasis may help them reconsider the situation. Consider Ms. Harris during a conference with Debra and Diane:

"I've asked you to stay after class because I'm very concerned with the behavior in the fifth period. Please sit down." (Pauses, looks at the girls.) "I had to stop class three times today because of your loud talking." (Rises from behind desk, voice slightly louder.) "I cannot teach when noise interferes with our discussions." (Sits down, looks at the girls.) "This cannot go on anymore." (Calmer.) "I would like us to work out a solution to this problem. Do you think we can?"

Being an assertive teacher means that you let students know your concerns and needs in a manner that gets their attention and communicates your intent to carry through with consequences and to deal with the situation until it is resolved. It is not necessary that you lose your sense of humor or treat students impolitely; a little humor can reduce tension, and treating students with courtesy models the kind of behavior that you expect of them. Developing a level of assertiveness that is comfortable for you and understanding how your behavior is perceived by others are important. Working through the activities at the end of this chapter will help develop your skills and self-awareness.

■ Listening and Empathic Responding

Additional important communication skills are the ability to listen to and to respond with empathy to students. Use of these skills allows you to show that you are aware and accepting of the student's perspective as well as to seek clarification of it when necessary. Empathic responding helps keep the lines of communication open between you and students so that problems can be understood and resolved in mutually acceptable ways. Such skills are especially appropriate when students express their concerns, show stress, or display other strong emotions. As a teacher, you have to be able to respond in a manner that helps the student deal constructively with those feelings or at least avoids adding to the student's discomfort or distress. Listening and empathic responding can also be used as a part of the problem-solving process when dealing with students who must change their behavior. In such situations, students can be resistant and express negative feelings; the teacher's acknowledgment of students' feelings and concerns can help defuse these reactions and increase the acceptance of a plan for change.

Listening and empathic responding complement constructive assertiveness. Whereas assertiveness allows teachers to express their concerns, listening and empathic responding solicit and affirm the student's viewpoint. The use of empathic responding skills does not imply that misbehaving students are entitled to do their thing without regard for others; rather, the implication is that the student's views should be taken into account in order to reach a satisfactory solution. When the teacher shows openness to the student's perspective, there is a better chance that the student will make a commitment to change. Conversely, a teacher who shows no interest in the student's feelings is more likely to encounter defiant behavior and an unwillingness to cooperate or to accept responsibility.

Compare these two episodes:

Episode A

STUDENT: I'm not staying. You can't make me.
TEACHER: You'll have to stay after school. You've been tardy three times.
STUDENT: Oh man, I can't stay.
TEACHER: That's life. If you don't serve your time now, it's doubled. That's the rule.
STUDENT: (*Angry*) I'm leaving.
TEACHER: You'd better not.
STUDENT: Buzz off! (*Student leaves.*)

In this episode, the teacher's response does nothing to resolve the situation. It's likely that the student is aware of the consequences of skipping detention, so the argument only provokes a confrontation—which the student wins, at least temporarily, by leaving.

Consider another way to handle the situation.

Episode B

STUDENT: I'm not staying. You can't make me.
TEACHER: I agree. It's up to you.
STUDENT: I can't stay.
TEACHER: Staying after school is a problem for you?
STUDENT: I can't be late to practice.
TEACHER: Oh, I see. The detention would make you late for practice.
STUDENT: Right, and if I'm late one more time, I'll have to sit out the next game.
TEACHER: That's a difficult situation. What are your options?

In Episode B, the teacher avoids arguing with the student and instead acknowledges the student's concern and invites further discussion. The student responds to the teacher's approach by stating his or her concern more explicitly. Notice that the teacher's role in this conference is that of listener or helper rather than opponent. Notice, too, that the teacher does not offer to solve the student's problem by dropping the detention penalty. Instead, the student is led to consider what options are available. Of course, there is no guarantee that the situation will be resolved to everyone's satisfaction. Yet the approach at least offers the possibility of resolution, and it avoids the confrontation that occurred in Episode A. Further, it maintains the student's responsibility for dealing with the situation rather than giving the student yet another excuse for avoiding responsibility.

Empathic responding has several advantages. It allows the teacher a way to deal with strong emotions without taking the responsibility for solving the student's problems. At the same time, the strategy helps defuse emotionally charged situations: Intense feelings are often transient and persist only when fed by an intense response. By not responding with similar emotional intensity, the teacher avoids fueling the fire. Also, the calm, empathic teacher serves as a good model for constructive problem solving.

Empathic responding has two components: listening skills and processing skills.

Listening Skills

Listening skills acknowledge or accept the student's expression of feeling or ideas and are intended to encourage the student to continue discussing the situation. At a minimal level, the listener merely indicates attention. Sometimes just an interested look will encourage the student to continue speaking. Other examples of nonverbal listening behaviors are nodding, making eye contact with the speaker, and other body language that communicates openness to discussion. Verbal encouragement is indicated by such utterances as "Um-hm," "I see," "Go on," and "That's interesting." At other times, a little more encouragement may be needed. In such a case, the teacher can invite more discussion with phrases such as "Tell me more," "I'm interested in hearing your ideas about this," "Would you care to comment?" "What do you think?" and "You've listened to my opinion. I'd like to listen to yours."

Processing Skills

Processing skills are an extension of listening skills that allow you to confirm or clarify your perception of the student's message. At the simplest level, you can repeat or summarize what the student says. When the student has given multiple messages or a confusing array of statements, you can select what seems most important and paraphrase it. You can then "reflect" or "bounce back" this paraphrase as a question. Often, the student will acknowledge the correctness of your perception or offer clarification. Consider this interchange from a short after-school conference.

STUDENT: I hate this place. School is stupid!
TEACHER: Would you like to talk about it?
STUDENT: I just don't like it here.
TEACHER: School really turns you off.
STUDENT: No. Not school, I mean here, this place.
TEACHER: You like some schools, but not this high school?
STUDENT: Right, there's too many rules, no one listens to you, you can't talk to your friends. You know, it's just do this, do that, shut up.
TEACHER: You feel too restricted here, like you can't do what you want and no one cares?
STUDENT: It's always teachers telling you to be quiet, do your work. There's never time to be with friends and to have fun.
TEACHER: It sounds like you'd like more opportunities to socialize and hang out.
STUDENT: Right. If I could only have some things to look forward to, that I'd feel like coming here for, it'd be more bearable.
TEACHER: I wonder if you're aware of the activities we have after school . . .

In this example the teacher uses a variety of responses with a turned-off student and progresses to a point where the student can express, at least partially, some of the basis for his or her feelings. Note that as the discussion unfolds the student becomes more communicative and reasonable. Although one cannot expect that major problems will usually be resolved via a single empathic interchange, it is not unusual for the sharp edge of negative emotions to be blunted and for the conversation to end on a positive note. At least the student learns that an adult cares enough to listen, and the teacher establishes a better position for guiding the student in the future.

The skills of empathic responding—both listening and processing—have been presented so far in the context of interaction with individual students, but they are also helpful when problems arise in group settings. Using these skills helps prevent teachers from responding defensively when students react emotionally or express a problem during class. They also "buy time" for the teacher to consider alternatives for dealing with a problem. In addition, listening and processing skills are useful for leading group discussions or for interacting with parents.

Although empathic responding skills are very helpful in some situations, they are not the primary means of dealing with students who are acting out, breaking class rules, or interfering with other students. Such misbehavior needs to be dealt with using approaches discussed in Chapters 9 and 11 and in the next section on problem solving. However, listening and processing can be used to support these other measures.

One limitation of these skills is finding the right time and place to use them. It would be awkward to respond empathically to every expression of emotion or opinion during class activities; such reactivity would cause slowdowns and might undermine your students' attention to lessons. The frequency and circumstances in which you choose to use these skills will depend on a variety of factors, including opportunities, your goals and values, and how competent you feel.

■ Problem Solving

Problem solving is a process used to deal with and resolve conflicts. Conflicts arise between teachers and students because different roles give rise to different needs and because individuals have different goals and interests. In a crowded classroom, diverse paths can cross, and individuals can find themselves at odds with one another. When conflict arises, teachers need a way to manage it constructively so that teaching and learning can continue in a supportive classroom climate. An effective means of accomplishing this is the problem-solving process, in which the teacher works with the student to develop a plan to reduce or eliminate the problem. Steps in the process include (1) identifying the problem, (2) discussing alternative solutions, and (3) obtaining a commitment to try one of them. Depending on the circumstances, a problem-solving session may include attempts to identify the basis for the problem and may specify the consequences of following or not following the plan. Because it generally requires more than a brief intervention, a problem-solving session is usually conducted during a conference with the student. Often, the skills of constructive assertiveness and empathic responding are helpful in reaching a workable agreement.

Problem-solving conferences are usually reserved for chronic situations that have not yielded to simpler remedies. Some action needs to be taken to stop the behavior because allowing it to continue would interfere with your ability to teach, with other students' opportunities to learn, or with the student's long-term functioning in your class or school. Consider the following examples.

1. Brad likes to be the center of attention. Whenever you ask a question, he calls out the answer without raising his hand and with no regard for the fact that you have already called on another student. Although you have reminded him of correct behavior and have tried to ignore his call-outs, the behavior continues to interfere with your class discussions.

2. Alice and Alicia always seem to be in a hurry to leave your room at the end of the fourth period. Unfortunately, they do not clean up their art supplies, and they fuss and argue when you have them return to finish their jobs. Then they complain that they will be late to their next class. Their foot dragging seemed trivial at first, but it has become a daily source of irritation that disrupts the last several minutes of the class each day.

3. Terrence has not turned in his last three assignments, even though you allowed ample time in class to work on them. He seems to have a lackadaisical attitude about academic work, and he uses his time in class for goofing off whenever he can get away with it. During the previous grading period he was within one point of failing your course, and not turning in his work is sure to drop him below the failing point.

Each of these examples illustrates a situation that has reached a stage at which a problem-solving conference might be useful. In each case, routine intervention has not altered the student's behavior, and more of the same teacher response will result only in a continuing power struggle or in a deterioration in the student's ability to behave constructively.

What is evident in each example is that the students are not accepting responsibility for their behavior. Perhaps what is needed is a stronger consequence (e.g., a penalty) that is clearly contingent on a repetition of the misbehavior. In fact, this strategy can be an alternative discussed with students during a problem-solving conference. Until the students make a commitment to change the offending behavior, however, the use of punishment may be perceived as coercive and controlling rather than as a logical consequence, and thus it may do little or no good. It also appears that the basis of the problems in each of the three examples is not clear. Why won't Brad wait his turn? Why can't Alicia and Alice follow a simple cleanup procedure? Doesn't Terrence understand or care about what will happen to his grade? Giving the students a chance to discuss their situations might produce insights that would lead to better solutions. It would also permit the teacher and the students to become better aware of each other's perceptions and possibly prevent additional problems.

A problem-solving conference has three steps.

STEP 1: Identify the problem. You can begin the discussion by stating the purpose of the meeting and asking the student to express his or her viewpoint. Obtaining the student's view provides useful information for later steps, and it enables you to gauge the student's understanding of the situation and willingness to cooperate. An alternative opening is to describe the problem yourself and ask the student for a reaction; this alternative is especially needed when you are dealing with young children, with students having limited verbal skills, and with evasive and dissembling students. Unless the student's attitude is very cooperative, you must be assertive about expressing your concerns. As explained earlier, being assertive about expressing your concerns is done by describing, without labeling, the behavior of concern and the problem it is causing. You may also need to stress that the problem will not be allowed to continue and that something must be done to solve it.

In his Reality Therapy model, Glasser (1975) (cf. Bassin, Bratter, & Rachin, 1976) recommends asking students to evaluate whether the behavior is helping or hurting them or has good or bad effects. A student who understands and admits that a behavior has negative consequences will be more likely to participate in the search for and commitment to a solution. A student who denies responsibility or who sees no harmful effects seldom makes a meaningful commitment to change. It may be helpful to ask such a student what the consequences might be if the behavior continues.

During this initial phase of the conference, a student may react defensively or emotionally and may try to avoid responsibility by blaming others, arguing, citing extenuating circumstances, and so forth. When such behaviors occur, you must decide whether the student's reaction is primarily for the purpose of evading responsibility or if it has some validity. If the latter is the case, you can use listening and processing skills to respond; this communicates a willingness to hear the student's point of view and may increase subsequent cooperation. There is considerable reciprocity in interaction, and if you model desirable behavior, you encourage its use by the student. A disadvantage of using empathic responding during this phase of problem solving is that the student's excuses, arguments, and extenuating circumstances may simply be a means of avoiding responsibility. Because you do not want to be sidetracked from the issue that brought the student to the conference in the first place, be sure to return the focus to the main problem after student concerns have been expressed. When the problem has been identified and agreed on, the conference can move to the next step.

STEP 2: Select a solution. One way to begin this phase is to invite the student to suggest a solution to the problem. If the student is unable to do so, you can offer one. Whenever possible, it is best to have two or more alternatives so that options can be compared and the most desirable one chosen. Frequently, the student's solution is stated negatively, focusing on simply ending an undesirable behavior. Although this is a step in the right direction, it is best to include a positive focus as well by including a plan for increasing desirable behavior. Thus, you should be ready to work with the student's idea and to suggest modifications.

If you are the one who suggests a solution, seek the student's reaction to check on whether the plan is understood and accepted. Also, evaluate the plan's appropriateness: Is it realistic? Will it significantly reduce the problem? Does it call for changes in other students or in the classroom environment, and are such changes feasible? Can it be evaluated readily? Occasionally a student may try to avoid responsibility by proposing a solution that places the burden for change on the teacher or other students—for example, to design more interesting lessons or to get other students to "leave me alone." Consider such changes to the extent that they are appropriate and reasonable, but don't allow a student to shift responsibility to others unless that is where the responsibility for the problem lies. A reasonable response is, "Yes, such changes might help, but what will you contribute?" When a mutually agreeable solution is reached, you are ready for the third stage.

STEP 3: Obtain a commitment. In this step, the teacher asks the student to accept the solution and to try it for a specified period of time, usually with the understanding that it will be evaluated afterward. The student's commitment can be given orally or in written form, as in a "contract." Sometimes such contracts are printed with an official-looking border, seal, and script, with space for student and teacher signatures and for listing contract terms and consequences if the plan is or is not followed.

Whether or not consequences are specified depends on the severity of the problem and whether it is a first conference or a follow-up for a broken contract. Some teachers like to give students a chance to correct their behavior without resorting to penalties; the rationale is that long-range cooperation is better when the teacher uses the least controlling or coercive approach. However, if the student is not making a reasonable effort to comply with the plan, or if the misbehavior is dangerous or too disruptive to be allowed to continue, spelling out the consequences may well be needed to get the student's attention and to communicate the seriousness of the situation: "You must either follow our agreement or discuss your behavior with the assistant principal—Mr. Dreadnaught—and your parents."

If the plan fails to solve the problem, you'll have to follow through with whatever consequence was stipulated or work with the student to alter the plan and produce a more workable solution. A major consideration is how much time and energy you can or should devote to pursuing the plan versus using a referral, detention, or some other consequence available in your school. To get another perspective on the problem, you might consult with a counselor, assistant principal, or another teacher before taking further action.

When problem-solving conferences fail to make progress (e.g., the student does not make a sincere commitment to a plan or simply does not cooperate), the teacher should evaluate his or her assertiveness and empathic responding skills before concluding that a problem-solving approach does not work with that student. Poor assertiveness skills—hostile, critical, or attacking behaviors or timid, tentative responding—interfere with the problem-solving process. An overly assertive, hostile style reflects a reliance on the teacher's power and cuts off communication. An unassertive style is easily ignored; the teacher is not seen as credible, and students simply

"In fact, the work's been so good that we question whether it's Will's own."

Paul Noth / The New Yorker Collection / The Cartoon Bank

won't believe that the teacher will insist on correct behavior or will follow through with consequences if they push past the limits. A constructively assertive teacher, however, captures the students' attention and communicates serious intent to change the situation. Empathic responding communicates a willingness to listen to the student's point of view and permits the teacher to clarify and react to a student's statements without closing off further discussion. Such skills are especially needed during problem-solving discussions because they allow the teacher to deal constructively with defensive student behavior. They also help to clarify solutions as they are discussed and improve the chances of obtaining a sincere commitment to change.

When you use these skills, be patient and give them a chance to work. Often teachers use a problem-solving approach only after a situation has reached a flashpoint or for behavior that has been established over a long period of time. In such cases you cannot expect miracles; change may occur gradually and imperfectly. However, problem-solving conferences can be helpful in many cases and should be a component of your set of management and discipline skills. Exercises on problem solving are presented in activities at the end of the chapter.

■ Communicating With Parents

Walker and Hoover-Dempsey (2015) examined research on the ingredients of successful interactions between home and school. They note that one of the universal goals of families across cultures is to ensure that children "develop an understanding of, and appreciation for, and commitment to the basic values, goals, and practices of the family's culture" (p. 462). An implication is that in order to work successfully with parents, school personnel should learn about the values and goals underlying parents' concerns for their children's schooling experiences. Walker and Hoover-Dempsey recommend that schools attempt to involve parents in their children's schooling in multiple ways. One of the key features should be two-way sharing of information and support for learning. Thus, teachers need to learn about community life and parents' goals for their children, and parents need to learn about what teachers are doing in the classroom and how the teacher's efforts can be supported in the home. The skills described in this chapter—empathic responding and listening, constructive assertiveness, and problem solving—will be very important to use when interacting with parents. They will keep lines of communication open, help further the information sharing process, and help teachers work with parents to support their children's schooling as well as the teacher's classroom management plan. Additionally, we offer the following suggestions to help conferences with parents go more smoothly.

- Express your appreciation for parents' efforts to rearrange their schedules to meet with you. Use their time wisely by being prepared and organized.
- Schools and teachers may intimidate parents who had difficulty in school. Their anxiety may be expressed as anger, avoidance, or defensiveness, so realize that parental reactions may be more a reflection of the parent's state of mind than something you said or did.
- Parents whose child is exhibiting behavioral or academic problems are especially sensitive to being blamed. Focus on the choices the student is making and what can be done to encourage better decisions.
- Approach parents as team members. You have a common goal: the best interests of their adolescent. The objective of the conference is to find ways to work together.
- Whenever possible, document your concerns. Have examples of the student's work available or have notes regarding behavioral issues. If the student is not turning in assignments, give parents the assignment sheet with the due dates or make sure they have access to your assignment schedule on the class website.
- Stick to descriptions of behavior rather than characterizations of students ("Antoine calls other students names" rather than "Antoine is a bully"). Characterizations are more likely to put the parent on the defensive.
- Respect parents' knowledge of their adolescent. Parents will often have insights about what behavior is typical for the student, and they may be able to suggest alternative ways of dealing with a problem.

The secret to successful parent–teacher conferences is planning. If you have back-to-back conferences, provide a place for the next arrivals to sit and wait. Arrange chairs for all participants in a circle, a semicircle, or around a table. Decide which issues need to be addressed with the parent(s). Bring documentation and a collection of the student's work over time to support those issues. If the goal of the conference is to resolve the issue (instead of, for example, simple information sharing), use a problem-solving approach to move toward solution.

Begin the conference by describing some of the adolescent's strengths. During the meeting, avoid "teacher talk," acronyms, or technical terms the parents may not understand. Listen carefully, and encourage comments and questions. If possible, include the student in all or part of the conference. Keep a written record of suggestions, concerns, and plans of action. End the conference by reiterating any responsibilities that have been assumed. Thank the parents for supporting their child's education.

■ Who Will I Teach? Culturally Responsive Communication

Schools in most urban locations serve culturally diverse populations of students. In rural and suburban schools, increasingly diverse backgrounds are common with respect to ethnic origin, socioeconomic status, language, and cultural expectations for appropriate behavior. When teachers work with students from backgrounds different from their own, lack of understanding of the students' culture can hamper their communication with both the students and their parents. Following are some examples of the impact of cultural differences:

- Levinson and Sparkes (2005) observed Gypsy children in schools and interviewed community members to assess the basis for their frequent school problems. Cultural practices in the use of space, in-group identification, and the relationship between Gypsy culture and the larger society significantly influenced the children's behavior in school, resulting in behavior problems and conflict between the Gypsy and non-Gypsy children.
- Children from Puerto Rican families who were receiving special education services in a U.S. school district were studied by Harry (1992). She found substantial evidence for a lack of communication between school and home. The parents' cultural characteristics (e.g., deference to authority) and limited English, combined with formal bureaucratic language used by the schools caused misunderstandings and dissatisfaction among the parents, and impacted the children's schooling.
- McCarthy and Benally (2003) identified how classroom management and instructional practices that were inconsistent with Navaho cultural norms led to disruption and low student engagement. Improved student behavior occurred after modifications were made that were more in keeping with cultural practices.

These modifications included improving teacher knowledge of their students' culture, using more cooperative learning groups with hands-on materials, incorporating Navaho history and culture into lessons, and developing disciplinary interventions for chronic offenders that emphasized traditional values and reconnected the students with their cultural norms.

Fallon, O'Keefe, and Sugai (2012) reviewed research related to culture and student behavior, focusing on what features support positive behavior. Important areas they identified were culturally relevant interaction, activities, and behavior; using interventions that are consistent with culture; and including students' culture and language in instruction. Similarly, other scholars who have examined the literature on the impact of culture on classrooms have highlighted the importance of teacher characteristics and behaviors such as caring, openness to learning about other cultures, awareness of the teacher's own culture and biases, and ability to use culturally appropriate communication (Cartledge & Kourea, 2008; Weinstein, Tomlinson-Clarke, & Curran, 2004).

Brown (2003) examined literature on teaching in urban settings and interviewed 13 teachers (elementary through high school) from seven cities. Culturally appropriate classroom management strategies were identified in three key areas: demonstrating caring for students, being assertive and acting with authority, and communicating effectively. For these teachers, *caring* involved establishing trusting and respectful relationships, listening to students, and creating a classroom climate that is psychologically safe. Caring for students did not mean that the teachers were permissive about behavior. On the contrary, *assertiveness* was a key component of their communication style. Teachers made expectations for behavior clear and they followed through. A quote from one of the teachers interviewed by Brown makes this clear: "I'm here to help you. I'm not going to let you slide. You're not going to get away with acting the wrong way or not doing the work" (p. 279). Effective teaching for these urban teachers included knowing about the different *communication* styles and needs of their students and adapting classroom activities to take them into account.

These examples from research teach us that communication, culture, and classroom management are intertwined. Notice how important it is to assume an attitude of listening to students and parents in order to demonstrate caring and respect. The skills also give teachers opportunities to acquire information about the needs, perspectives, and concerns of individuals from other cultural backgrounds. By staying open to the cultures of others, the teacher can gain insights and limit the negativity associated with being an outsider. Empathic responding in conjunction with listening offers the opportunity to make connections with parents and students. Failure to make use of listening skills and empathic responding will limit a teacher's effectiveness when working with individuals from different cultural groups because the teacher will remain suspect as an uncaring and uncommitted outsider.

As helpful and important as listening skills and empathic responding are for effective communication, they are not sufficient. Constructive assertiveness is also needed. Teachers have a responsibility to establish a classroom environment that is orderly and promotes learning. Students must feel safe in the classroom and confident that the teacher is in charge. As the teachers in the studies by Brown (2003) indicated, this involves direct communication about expected student behavior and a commitment to follow through. The purpose of this assertiveness is not to project the teacher's power, but rather to ensure that the classroom culture protects opportunity to learn, tolerance for differences, and respect for all.

■ Chapter Summary

Good communication skills are essential when working with students, parents, and colleagues. Three types of skills were presented in this chapter: constructive assertiveness, listening and empathic responding, and problem solving. Uses were described for these skills, including dealing with inappropriate student behaviors, responding to students when they are encountering problems, communicating effectively with parents, and developing sensitivity to cultural differences. Guidelines were provided for good communication practices with parents. A final section examined culturally responsive communication in the classroom.

■ Further Reading

Berger, E. H., & Rojas-Cortez, M.R. (2012). *Parents as partners in education: Families and schools working together* (8th ed.). Englewood Cliffs, NJ: Prentice Hall.

This handbook provides a comprehensive look at parent–school relationships and offers practical suggestions to aid collaboration between teachers and parents. Topics include diverse families, the exceptional child, programs to enrich the parent–school environment, and communication necessary for partnerships.

Hill, C. E. (2009). *Helping skills: Facilitating exploration, insight, and action* (3rd ed.). Washington, DC: American Psychological Association.

This textbook outlines a three-stage model of helping and presents basic skills used at each stage, emphasizing the role of affect, cognition, and behavior in the change process.

Kottler, J. A., & Kottler, E. (2009). *Students who drive you crazy: Succeeding with resistant, unmotivated, and otherwise difficult young people* (2nd ed.). Thousand Oaks, CA: Sage (Corwin Press).

This book blends theory and research with examples from practicing teachers, counselors, school administrators, and students. It offers tools for dealing with frustrating, hostile interactions.

Raczynski, K. A., & Horne, A. M. (2015). Communication and interpersonal skills in classroom management: How to provide the educational experiences students need and deserve. In E. T. Emmer & E. J. Sabornie (Eds.), *Handbook of classroom management* (2nd. ed., pp. 387–408). New York: Routledge.

This chapter summarizes the literature on communication skills that foster supportive relation-ships and solve problems. The authors emphasize how important these skills are for both teachers and students in order to build healthy and productive classroom environments.

www.scholastic.com/teachers, www.edutopia.org, 712educators.about.com

These websites are good resources for teachers. For topics related to this chapter, try searching with the terms "teaching social skills," "communication skills," "parent communication," and "parent conferences."

■ Suggested Activities

ACTIVITY 10.1 : PUSHING BUTTONS

Everyone is sensitive to or self-conscious about some aspect of personal image or background. Height, weight, appearance, content knowledge, experience, ethnicity, marital status, accep-tance, and respect are among the areas that may be a source of insecurity or concern. Because teaching is so public, and because children and adolescents are astute observers of teachers' reactions, teachers often reveal much about themselves as they react when students find the right "button" to push. Think about a characteristic that represents a source of insecurity for you, and discuss your responses to the following questions with a partner: What area of teaching represents a source of insecurity to you? What can you do to minimize the negative effect of that insecurity or, better still, turn it into a plus? How might your communication with students be affected if a student "pushes your button" in that area? What insecurities might students be indicating with their misbehaviors?

ACTIVITY 10.2 : DEVELOPING ASSERTIVENESS SKILLS

This activity provides situations for practicing assertiveness skills. For each situation described, prepare an assertive response. Use the following sequence of steps with each situa-tion until you are comfortable with the approach. Then combine the steps so that you have the experience of responding to situations "on your feet."

STEP 1: Write out a statement that describes the problem clearly or that insists that your rights be respected. Compare and discuss your statements with other participants. Revise your statement if you wish.

STEP 2: Use role-playing to portray the situation, with you as the teacher and someone else as the student. During the role-play, try to use appropriate body language (includ-ing eye contact and facial expression) to support your intervention.

STEP 3: Get feedback from observers regarding your use of assertiveness skills. Use the Assertiveness Assessment Scales to assess your own behavior, and check out your per-ceptions by comparing your self-ratings to those of observers. Be sure to discuss any discrepancies and any problems you experienced enacting an assertive role. Repeat Step 2 until you feel comfortable with your handling of the situation.

It is not necessary to continue the role-play to a complete resolution of the situation; the purpose is only to provide experience in enacting assertive behaviors. The person playing the student role should respond as naturally as possible.

- *Situation A.* Bubba has been sliding by lately, doing the minimum and barely passing. At the end of class today, he asks you if it would be all right to turn in his project a few days late. He knows that you have already given similar permission to two other students who had difficulty obtaining needed materials.
- *Situation B.* Allyson and Maria are supposed to put the equipment away, but they have left much of it strewn about the gym. Now they are heading for the door in anticipation of the end-of-period bell.
- *Situation C.* Victor has not been working on his assignment. You caught his eye, but he looked away and has continued to talk to nearby students. As you move around the room checking other students' progress, he pulls his coat over his head pretending to sleep.
- *Situation D.* As you walk down the hallway, you hear two students trading insults: "Your mama . . ." and so forth. The students are not angry yet, just "fooling around," but several other students are gathering and you think they may encourage the two students to fight.
- *Situation E.* As you begin class, you observe Donalda eating a cookie in violation of the rule prohibiting food in the room. When she sees that you notice her, Donalda stuffs the cookie into her mouth and gets another one out of the package.
- *Situation F.* During your current events discussion, Jack and Jill trade notes and laugh inappropriately. You sense that other students' attention is being captured by the duo's antics, and you begin to be annoyed at having to compete for class attention.
- *Situation G.* When you were absent yesterday, your fourth-period class gave the substitute teacher a hard time. According to the note the sub left for you (with a copy sent to the principal), many students refused to work at all, four or five left for the bathroom and never returned, and a paper-and-spitwad fight raged all period. As the tardy bell rings, you enter the room to greet the fourth-period class.

ASSERTIVENESS ASSESSMENT SCALES

When using the following scales, note that a mid-range rating represents an appropriate degree of assertiveness. When rating your own or another teacher's behavior as either nonassertive or hostile, circle the descriptive term that best reflects the basis for your judgment, or write a note on the scale if the descriptors don't adequately capture your perception.

	Unassertive	**Assertive**	**Hostile**
	1 _____ 2 _____	3 _____	4 _____ 5
Eye contact	Teacher avoids looking at student.	Teacher maintains eye contact with student.	Teacher glares at student; stares student down.
	1 _____ 2 _____	3 _____	4 _____ 5
Body language	Teacher turns away, gestures nervously, trembles, fiddles with papers or pen.	Teacher faces student; alert posture but not threatening. Gestures support statements.	Teacher crowds student, points, shakes fist threateningly.

	1 _____	2 _____	3 _____	4 _____ 5
Message	Obsequious, self-denigrating; excuses student behavior; pleads with student; apologizes.		Clearly states the problem or insists that the behavior stop. Makes own feelings known, may use humor to relieve tension.	Name calling, labeling, blaming, threatening, sarcastic, long lecturing.

	1 _____	2 _____	3 _____	4 _____ 5
Voice features	Tremulous, whiny, hesitant, broken, or too soft.		Appropriate volume, natural-sounding, varied for emphasis.	Too loud; shouts, screams.

	1 _____	2 _____	3 _____	4 _____ 5
Facial features	Smiles inappropriately; nervous twitches and tics.		Expression suits message.	Excessive affect; contorted, disgusted, enraged expression.

ACTIVITY 10.3 : RECOGNIZING LISTENING RESPONSES

Each of the following dialogues depicts a statement and a variety of teacher responses to it. In each case, decide which one is closest to a listening response. In other words, which one invites further discussion or best reflects the idea or feeling. Compare your answers to the key in the Appendix.

1. STUDENT: School sucks.

   a. Don't use that type of language.
   b. You seem upset about school.
   c. Come on, things aren't that bad.
   d. That attitude will get you nowhere.

2. STUDENT: I can't understand algebra. Why do we have to learn this stuff?

   a. You'll need it to get into college.
   b. Just keep at it. It'll make sense after a while.
   c. Something isn't making sense to you?
   d. Would you like to come in for extra help after school?

3. STUDENT: I don't want to sit near those boys anymore.

   a. Sorry, but seats have been assigned for the semester.
   b. If they're bothering you, I can move you.
   c. Can you handle this on your own?
   d. What's the situation?

4. PARENT: My child is very upset and needs more help or she won't be able to pass. She says she doesn't understand anything.

   a. Please go on. I'd like to hear more about this.
   b. She needs to pay closer attention in class.
   c. She's very anxious but actually she'll do just fine. She only needs to review more before tests.
   d. Most students find my explanations to be quite clear. Perhaps she isn't listening.

(continued)

5. TEACHER NEXT DOOR: That fifth period is going to drive me up a wall. They have been impossible lately!

   a. Have you considered being more assertive with them?

   b. I know, everyone in this wing can hear them.

   c. They are really a handful!

   d. You think they're bad, you should have my sixth period.

ACTIVITY 10.4 : PRODUCING EMPATHIC RESPONSES

You will need to work with a colleague during this activity. Take turns role-playing the student and the teacher. The person role-playing the teacher should practice empathic responding skills, and the student should try to behave as naturally as possible. Note that it is assumed that the dialogue is occurring at a time and place that permits this type of interchange and that the teacher is interested in allowing the student to describe the problem. In this exercise you should avoid giving solutions to the student's problem; instead, concentrate on using listening and processing skills to encourage the student to talk about the situation and think through the problem.

Situation A. Teresa is an ESL student who is doing well in math and science; however, she has difficulty with writing. With tears in her eyes, she approaches you after class with an essay on which you have given a failing grade. "I thought that I did okay on this assignment."

Situation B. David, a capable student, offers you some advice: "This class would be a lot more interesting if we didn't have to do all these worksheets. Couldn't we choose our own work sometime?"

Situation C. While the rest of the class is at work on an assignment, Barry closes his book, throws away his assignment sheet, and slinks down in his seat disgustedly.

Situation D. For the second time this week, Katie has not turned in an assignment. Last week she "forgot" to bring her homework twice. After class, you remind Katie that assignments count for half the grade. "I don't care," she responds.

Situation E. Armand, a new student, has been having trouble making friends. Lately, he has been getting into arguments with some of the more popular boys and has been teasing a few girls, apparently to gain some attention. He has not, however, succeeded in breaking into the social scene. After class one day, he says to you, "I wish I could transfer back to my old school."

ACTIVITY 10.5 : PROBLEM-SOLVING EXERCISES

Use role-playing to practice the problem-solving steps (identify the problem and its consequences, identify and select a solution, obtain a commitment to try it out) with the following situations. In situations in which it is mainly the student who is experiencing the problem, assume that the teacher's initial listening response is received positively by the student so that there is a basis for continuing the discussion and for the teacher to assist the student in thinking through a solution. If the student's behavior is affecting the teacher's ability to teach or interfering with other students' rights, the student may initially be reluctant to participate in a discussion, and the teacher will have to use assertiveness skills to overcome this resistance. In addition to the situations listed here, you can use some of the situations presented in Activities 10.2 and 10.4 for more practice.

Situation A. Bob and Ray are noisy and distracting when they clown around and vie for other students' attention. Reminders and penalties have only fleeting effects on their behavior. You decide to have them come in for a conference.

Situation B. Loukas is good-natured as long as no demands are placed on him. However, when reminded that class time is for learning and for working on assignments, he becomes defiant and insists that it is his right to do whatever he wishes, as long as "I don't hurt no one."

Situation C. Lucy is a bright student who often turns in work late; frequently, it is incomplete. She is able to pass your tests, however, and she could easily be a top student if she were prompt and better organized. Recently, you sent her parents a progress report because of missing assignments, and Lucy and her mother have come in for a conference to discuss the situation. As things now stand, Lucy will fail your course this grading period. Her mother wonders whether you will allow Lucy to make up the missing work to avoid the failing grade.

Situation D. Tina has been off task during class, not turning in her assignments, and showing disrespect to you when you try to discuss her work with her. You've scheduled a conference with her mother, and now the two of you are sitting together to decide how you can work together to help Tina.

■ Case Study 10.1

TWO DIALOGUES

Discuss the following two dialogues. To what extent do the teachers use the problem-solving steps as well as constructive assertiveness and empathic responding? Are they appropriately used? What other approaches might the teachers try for dealing with these problems? What are their advantages and disadvantages?

Dialogue 10.1: Brad

TEACHER:	Brad, I asked you to stay to talk with me because of a problem we've been having during discussions. Often, when I ask a question, you call out the answer without waiting to be called on. Do you agree that this is happening?
BRAD:	I guess so.
TEACHER:	Can you tell me why that is a problem?
BRAD:	I suppose that doesn't give others a chance.
TEACHER:	That's absolutely right. I have to be able to find out whether other students understand what we are discussing.
BRAD:	What if they don't know?
TEACHER:	You mean, if nobody raises a hand or tries to answer?
BRAD:	Yeah, then can I answer?
TEACHER:	Do you suppose that some people might need more time to think about what they are going to say?
BRAD:	I guess so. But it's boring to just sit and wait for someone to think if I already know it.

TEACHER: It is hard to wait and be patient, but I must be able to teach the whole class and to conduct the discussions for everybody. Can you think of any way that we could handle this so that I can call on others when I want to and you can still have your fair turn?

BRAD: I suppose I could raise my hand.

TEACHER: That would be a big help. I would really appreciate that. I think you have some good ideas and should have plenty of chances to answer. Brad, how often would you like to speak during our discussions?

BRAD: I don't know. (*Pauses.*) Three or four times, I guess.

TEACHER: That would be fine. How about if I guarantee you four times during each discussion? You keep track of the times you answer, and I'll call on you when your hand is raised. If I don't call on you sometimes, you know you'll get your chances later.

BRAD: Okay.

TEACHER: How about our trying this for the rest of the week, and then we'll talk again and see if it solves our problem?

BRAD: Okay.

Dialogue 10.2: Alice and Alicia

TEACHER: Girls, I asked you to stay for this conference because I've been having to take more and more of my time to get you to clean up and to keep work areas neat. I wonder what you both think about this problem.

ALICE: I don't know.

ALICIA: I don't think we're so bad about it.

TEACHER: It has become very frustrating to me. Do you remember that I had to remind you and wait for the jobs to be done?

GIRLS: Yes.

TEACHER: Whose job is it to pick up materials and put things away?

GIRLS: Ours.

TEACHER: Do you think we can find a way for those jobs to get done? (*Girls nod affirmatively.*) Do you have any suggestions?

ALICIA: I could just do it without being asked.

TEACHER: Okay. That is a good idea. Do you have any other suggestions?

ALICE: We could ask someone to help us.

TEACHER: That is an interesting idea. Do you know someone who wants to clean up your things?

ALICE: I don't know. Probably.

TEACHER: Would you like to help someone else clean up or put things away?

ALICIA: Sure, it'd be fun.

TEACHER: How about you, Alice?

ALICE: Okay.

TEACHER: Well, then I have an idea. How about if I let you both be my room helpers this next week. As soon as you finish your own cleanup, you can help me with jobs that I need to have done. How would that be?

GIRLS: Yeah!

TEACHER: Okay. Let's try this out. Tomorrow when you have cleaned up, let me
know. Then I'll tell you what you can do to help me. How does that sound?

GIRLS: Sure! Okay.

TEACHER: I'm glad we had a chance to plan this, because now I have two room helpers and we will have our problem solved.

MyEducationLab *Self-Check 10.1*

MyEducationLab *Application Exercise 10.1*   Using what you've learned in this chapter,
read and respond to this scenario.

MyEducationLab *Application Exercise 10.2*   Using what you've learned in this chapter,
read and respond to this scenario.

MyEducationLab *Application Exercise 10.3*   Using what you've learned in this chapter,
read and respond to this scenario.

MyEducationLab *Application Exercise 10.4*   Using what you've learned in this chapter,
read and respond to this scenario.

MyEducationLab *Application Exercise 10.5*   Using what you've learned in this chapter,
read and respond to this scenario.

MyEducationLab *Application Exercise 10.6*   Using what you've learned in this chapter,
read and respond to this scenario.

MyEducationLab *Application Exercise 10.7*   Using what you've learned
in this chapter, view the video and respond to the questions.

Farina3000/Fotolia

CHAPTER 11

Managing Problem Behaviors

In this chapter we describe strategies for dealing with problem behaviors that you may encounter as you teach. Although in previous chapters we described preventive measures as well as tactics that can be used to manage inappropriate behavior, we think it will be helpful to consider a full range of approaches. Of course, we hope that you will not encounter problems, especially serious ones. But as you work with adolescents, you will undoubtedly face difficult situations that must be dealt with to preserve the climate for learning or to assist a student in developing behaviors more compatible with group life and learning. The aim of this chapter is to pull together and organize a wide array of strategies from which you can select. By having a number of approaches to draw on, you can choose one that fits specific conditions. Having alternatives in mind is useful, too, in case your first plan doesn't work.

This chapter's focus is on problem behaviors rather than problem students. Only a small percentage of students exhibit maladaptive behaviors with such consistency and to such a degree that they warrant being labeled *emotionally disturbed* or *behaviorally disordered*. Adolescents do, however, behave inappropriately on occasion; we think that it is much more constructive in the long run to help students learn how to behave rather than assume that the student's capacity to make good choices is impaired.

At times, problem behaviors result from substance abuse or stressors (e.g., abuse, bullying, a death in the family, parental unemployment, serious illness, or divorce) the student is experiencing at home or elsewhere. If a student's behavior changes or if inappropriate behavior persists after reasonable attempts to deal with

210

it have been made, a discussion of the situation with a school counselor, assistant principal, parent, or guardian is in order. Often, the student's current or previous teachers can provide additional insights. When you talk with the student about what is happening, use listening skills (see Chapter 10) to try to understand the situation. Be empathic, but help the student understand that acting out (or whatever the problem behavior is) is not a solution. By all means, follow up if you discover that a situation outside the classroom is affecting the child's behavior.

■ What Is Problem Behavior?

The concept of problem behavior is very broad. Rather than enumerate all possible behaviors that might occur in classrooms, we think it more helpful to consider categories of behavior.

Nonproblem

Brief inattention, some talk during a transition between activities, small periods of daydreaming, and a short pause while working on an assignment are examples of common behaviors that are not really problems for anyone because they are of brief duration and don't interfere with learning or instruction. Everyone is the better for such behaviors being ignored. To react to them would consume too much energy, interrupt lessons constantly, and detract from a positive classroom climate.

Minor Problem

Minor problems are behaviors that run counter to class procedures or rules but do not, when occurring infrequently, disrupt class activities or seriously interfere with student learning. Examples are students calling out or leaving seats without permission, doing unrelated work during class time, passing notes, eating candy, scattering trash around, and talking excessively during independent or group-work activities. These behaviors are minor irritants as long as they are brief in duration and are limited to one or a few students; we would not give them much thought except for two reasons. Unattended, they might persist and spread; further, if the behaviors have an audience, not to respond might cause a perception of inconsistency and potentially undermine an important aspect of the overall management system. If students engage in such behavior for an extended period of time, their learning is likely to be adversely affected.

Major Problem, but Limited in Scope and Effects

The third category includes behaviors that disrupt an activity or interfere with learning but whose occurrence is limited to a single student or perhaps to a few students not acting in concert. For example, a student may be chronically off task. Another student may rarely complete assignments. Or a student may frequently fail to follow class rules for talk or movement around the room or may refuse to do any work. This category also includes a more serious, but isolated, violation of class or school rules, such as an act of vandalism or cheating on a test.

Escalating or Spreading Problem

In the most serious category we include any minor or major problem that has become commonplace and constitutes a threat to order and to the learning environment. For example, many students roaming around the room at will and continually calling out irrelevant comments make content-development activities suffer; social talking that continues unabated even when the teacher repeatedly asks for quiet is distracting to others; and talking back and refusing to cooperate with the teacher are frustrating and may lead quickly to a poor classroom climate. Frequent violations of class guidelines for behavior cause the management and instructional system to break down and interfere with the momentum of class activities.

■ Goals for Managing Problem Behavior

When we begin to address problem behaviors, we need to judge the short-term and long-term effects of any management strategy we choose. In the short term, the desired results are that the inappropriate behaviors cease and the students resume or begin appropriate behaviors. In the long run, it is important to prevent the problem from recurring. At the same time, we must be watchful for potential negative side effects and take steps to minimize them. Effects on the individual student or students causing the problem as well as the effect on the whole class should be considered.

Behavior Vignettes

- During independent work activities Joel talks and shows off. Nearby students are drawn in and lose their focus on their work.
- Hariri gets up to throw away trash at any point during the day, including during instruction.
- D'Andre is quite the bookworm and reads constantly, even when his attention should be on instruction or assigned independent work.
- Deidre decides to talk with the school counselor and leaves class without first seeking permission.
- Antonio gets into his backpack during a lesson to retrieve a needed tissue for his nose.

Pause and Consider

1. How would you categorize each of these behaviors (nonproblem, minor, major, escalating/spreading)?

2. What types of responses might a teacher make in each of these situations?

Vignette Reflection

Discuss with a partner your responses to the following questions: What happens next if the teacher uses a sarcastic put-down? Stands close to the student(s)? Asks for the student(s) to return to work? Yells at the student(s)? Ignores the behavior? How might the combination of some of these responses play out?

The ideal strategy is one that maintains or restores order in the class immediately without adversely affecting the learning environment; in addition, such a strategy should prevent a repetition of the problem and result in the student accepting responsibility for the behavior. In reality, classrooms are very busy places, and we rarely have sufficient time to mull over our options and their effects whenever a problem arises, especially in the midst of a crisis. If only there were a "pause" button for classroom events! The need for prompt reaction should not, however, deter us from evaluating the results of our efforts and from seeking alternative approaches, especially when our initial efforts do not meet with success. It is, therefore, useful to have a repertoire of strategies to apply to various problem situations.

■ Management Strategies

In this section we present useful strategies for dealing with a variety of classroom behavior problems. The first several strategies can be utilized during instruction without much difficulty, require little teacher time, and have the great virtue of being relatively unobtrusive. They have much to recommend them because they do not give undue attention to the misbehavior, and they do not interfere with the flow of instructional activity. As we move down the list, we encounter strategies that involve direct attempts to stop the behaviors and to do so quickly; these strategies, however, have more negative features: They demand more teacher time, they may have unintended consequences for students, or they interrupt class activities. A general principle that is helpful in selecting a strategy is to use an approach that will be effective in stopping the inappropriate behavior promptly and that has the least negative impact. A corollary is that minor problems should usually be dealt with by the use of limited interventions. As problems become more serious, the limited interventions may be ineffective in quickly ending the disruptive behavior, and a more time-consuming or intrusive intervention may be required.

It should be emphasized that most secondary schools have prescribed procedures to deal with certain types of major problems and sometimes even minor ones. Teacher responses to events such as fighting, obscene language, stealing, vandalism, and unexcused absence are likely to be directed by school (or district) policies. Therefore, the beginning teacher must learn what policies are in force and follow them. When no specific policy is established for particular problems or when teachers are given latitude in their response, the following alternatives will be helpful in guiding teacher action. It's also important to stay aware of which students have been identified as needing special education services. Such students *may* have specific disciplinary interventions identified in their individualized education plan (IEP). If so, then of course you must follow that plan.

It is a given that preventive measures are more desirable than reactive ones. Thus, earlier chapters have been devoted mainly to establishing a classroom environment that greatly reduces the need for frequent recourse to major interventions. Notwithstanding such efforts, reactive strategies are needed at times. However, when teachers find themselves frequently using major interventions to deal with problems, it is time to reevaluate the overall management and instructional plan and make needed modifications. To this end, reviewing the suggestions for management presented in prior chapters and using the checklists from those chapters to provide a focus may result in changes that can help reduce the problems. Teachers should also be sensitive to the possibility that the source of the problem lies in frustration with content that the student does not grasp or with tasks that the student lacks skills to perform. When the problem is one of a poor fit between student capabilities and academic demands, the teacher must address the source by developing more appropriate class activities and assignments or by giving the student more assistance.

Here, we describe classroom strategies that have a wide range of application, but our list is not exhaustive. Readers interested in additional ways of coping with behavior problems can find more resources listed at the end of the chapter.

Minor Interventions

Use Nonverbal Cues.   Make eye contact with the student and give a signal such as a finger to the lips, a "no" head shake, or a hand signal to issue a desist. Sometimes lightly touching a student on the arm or shoulder helps signal your presence and has a calming effect. Never touch a student when you are angry, though, and avoid touching students when they are angry. Touch in those cases may cause the situation to escalate. Touching is often covered by school or district policy. To avoid the appearance of inappropriate physical contact, keep touch within appropriate contexts (e.g., celebrating student success with a high five), on appropriate body parts (e.g., hands, shoulders), and in appropriate locations (e.g., not behind closed doors with an individual student).

Get the Activity Moving.   Often, student behavior deteriorates during transition times between activities or during dead time when no apparent focus for attention is present. Students leave their seats, talk, shuffle restlessly, and amuse themselves and each other waiting for something to do. The remedy is obvious: Move through the transition quickly and reduce or eliminate the dead time. This entails planning activities so that all materials are ready and adhering to a well-conceived lesson plan. Trying to catch and correct inappropriate behaviors during such times is futile and misdirected. Just get the next activity under way and cue students to the desired behaviors.

Use Proximity.   Move closer to students. Combine proximity with nonverbal cues to stop inappropriate behavior without interrupting instruction. Be sure to continue monitoring the students at least until they have begun an appropriate activity.

Use Group Focus.   Use group alerting, accountability, or a higher participation format (see the discussion in Chapter 7) to draw students back into a lesson when attention has begun to wane or when students have been in a passive mode for too long and you observe off-task behavior spreading.

Redirect the Behavior.   When students are off task, remind them of appropriate behavior. "Everyone should be writing answers to the chapter questions," "Be sure that your group is discussing your project plan," "Everyone should be seated and quiet." To avoid giving attention to inappropriate behavior, it is best to redirect behavior by stating what should be done. If only one or two students are engaged in inappropriate behavior, a private redirection will be less likely to interrupt the activity or to direct attention toward the incorrect behavior. General acknowledgment of appropriate behavior can also be effective if it's not overused: "I appreciate everyone who has picked up around their desks" will encourage a few students who have not followed the procedure to do so.

Provide Needed Instruction.   Especially during individual or group work, off-task behavior may reflect poor comprehension of the task. Check student work or ask brief questions to assess understanding; give necessary assistance so that students can work independently. If many students can't proceed, stop the activity and provide whole-class instruction. Next time be sure to check comprehension before starting the independent work activity and consider using a classwork activity before assigning independent work.

Issue a Brief Desist.   Tell the student(s) to stop the undesirable behavior. Make direct eye contact and be assertive (see Chapter 10). Keep your comments brief and then monitor the situation until the student complies. Combine this strategy with redirection to encourage desirable behavior.

Give the Student a Choice.   Tell the student that he or she has a choice—either to behave appropriately (be sure to state the desired behavior) or to continue the problem behavior and receive a consequence. For example, suppose a student has refused to clean up properly after completing a project: "You may choose to clean up now; if not, you are choosing to stay after class until your area is clean." To a student who continues to distract nearby students: "You may choose to work quietly on your assignment at your seat, or you will have to sit by yourself to do your work." The purpose of stating the consequence as a choice is to emphasize the student's responsibility for his or her behavior. Also, making the consequence clear increases the chance of the student's choosing to self-regulate.

Use an "I-Message."   An I-message is a statement that describes the problem and its effects on the teacher, the student, or the class; it may include a description of the feelings produced by the problem. The formula for an I-message is as follows:

- When you (state the problem)
- Then (describe the effect)
- And it makes me feel (state the emotion)

For example, to a student who constantly calls out comments, the teacher might say, "When you talk without permission, it interrupts the lesson, and I get frustrated and resentful." It isn't necessary to follow the formula exactly; the main idea is to communicate clearly what the problem is and why it's a problem ("It's very distracting to me and to others when you wander around the room during seat work"). The I-message can be combined with a brief desist or with redirection. A rationale for using an I-message is that students often act without much awareness of the effects of their behavior on others, and they will change when they realize that they are causing someone a problem. Also, by communicating directly with the student about the effects of the behavior, the teacher implies that the student is capable of controlling the behavior if he or she understands its effects. These messages need to be delivered assertively. A whiny, pleading I-message will be ineffective.

Moderate Interventions

The moderate intervention strategies are more confrontational than limited interventions, and thus they have greater potential for eliciting resistance. In cases in which the student's behavior has not become disruptive, it is desirable to use a minor intervention first or to issue a warning to the student before using these interventions. Doing so permits the student to exercise self-control and may save teacher time and effort.

Withhold a Privilege or Desired Activity.   Students who abuse a privilege (being allowed to work together on a project, sitting near friends, moving freely around the classroom without permission) can lose the privilege and be required to earn it back with appropriate behavior. Sometimes teachers allow quiet talking during independent work activities, and removing this privilege can be an effective way to limit unproductive behavior. Other teachers allow a class to choose a favorite activity or a short period of free time on one or more days each week as an incentive. Time lost from such activities can then be a strong deterrent to inappropriate behavior at other times. Although withholding a privilege is a form of punishment, it usually has fewer side effects than punishment that requires directly applying an aversive consequence.

Isolate or Remove Students.   Students who disrupt an activity can be removed to an area of the room away from other students. It is helpful to have a carrel with sides or at least a desk at the back of the room facing away from other students to discourage eye contact from the time-out area. If no suitable place is available, the student may need to have time-out in the hall outside the door, although not if your school has a policy prohibiting it because of the problem of adequately supervising the student.

Time-out is a variation on the preceding consequence in that it takes away the student's privilege of participating in the classroom activity. It is a good idea to allow excluded students to return to the activity in a short time, as long as their behavior during time-out is acceptable. Some teachers prefer to let the student retain some control over the return, using a direction such as "You may come back to the activity in 5 minutes if you decide that you can follow our class rules." Other teachers prohibit the student from returning until the activity is completed or until they have had a brief conference with the student.

A problem with time-out is that some students may find it rewarding. They receive attention when it is administered, and it allows them to avoid an activity they dislike. When this occurs, you should switch to another strategy. Another problem is that a student may refuse to go to the time-out area. Usually, this is a temporary problem; if you are firm, ignoring the student's protests and continuing with the activity, the student will go eventually. One way to move a recalcitrant body is to offer a choice: "You can either take time-out or you can take a walk to the principal's office. It's your decision."

Time-out has another risk. Its use clearly identifies a student as someone who is excludable, and it may result in implicit labeling by the teacher, by other students, or by the excluded student. If used frequently with an individual student, it may cause resentment and anger. Therefore, be sure to provide opportunities for the student to resume full participation in the class and use other strategies to promote appropriate behavior at the same time.

Use a Fine or Penalty.   Sometimes a small amount of repetitious work is required as payment for inappropriate behavior. In physical education, students may be required to run an extra lap or do push-ups. In math, students may have to write multiplication tables or work extra problems. In a language class, students can write verb conjugations. The advantage of this type of consequence is that it can usually be administered quickly with a minimum of teacher time and effort. A disadvantage is that a learning task is being defined as punishing, and therefore the student's attitude toward the content may be negatively affected. This effect can be mitigated by choosing the penalty assignment from a neutral or noncontent area. For example, the assignment for students paying a small penalty for a minor infraction might be to look up and copy the definitions of ten words from the dictionary. Another problem with the use of fines or penalties is that their ease of use can lead to overuse, detracting from the overall climate.

Assign Detention.   Another commonly used penalty is detention, either at lunch or before or after school. Because of the logical relationship between the problem and the consequence, this penalty is often used for misbehaviors that involve time (tardiness, extended goofing off, and time wasting; behavior that interferes with instruction or student work time). Other common uses of the penalty are for repeated rule violations and for frequent failure to complete assignments. You may need to supervise the detention in your room, or your school might have a detention room with an assigned monitor. The time in detention need not be lengthy, especially for misbehaviors that are not severe or frequent; a 10- or 15-minute detention is often sufficient to make the point.

An advantage of detention as a penalty is that it is disliked by most students and they want to avoid it; at the same time, it is administered away from other students in the class and thus does not give undue attention to the behavior. Because it is a common punishment, extensive explanations and unusual procedures aren't needed. Finally, the teacher can sometimes use a little of the detention time to hold a conference with the student and perhaps work out a plan for improving the situation.

One disadvantage of detention is that it does take teacher time, especially when the teacher must supervise it. Even when the school has a detention area, the teacher still will have to write a referral. Another disadvantage is that students might be able to avoid detention, at least in the short run, simply by not showing up. Thus, the teacher or the school must have a backup plan, such as doubling the time; moreover, records must be kept, and additional time will be required to deal with such students.

Referral to the School Office.   Many schools have a system of referral to an assistant principal, who then deals with the misbehaving student. Sometimes referrals are built into the school's discipline plan for specific behaviors such as fighting and vandalism, but teachers also have wide latitude to refer a student for noncodified transgressions such as disrespect, rudeness, and insubordination. Often a first referral consequence is limited to detention or a warning, with subsequent referrals resulting in further detention, a parent conference, or, for serious or persistent infractions, suspension for one or several days. In order to deal with the student fairly and appropriately, the administrator must be made aware of the basis for referral. Thus an office referral form is usually filled out by the teacher or sent via e-mail to the assistant principal who is handling the referral.

Advantages of the office referral are that it can be an effective limit for students who do not respond to other approaches, and it does not take much teacher time, at least in the short run. It may also allow the teacher to short-circuit an escalating confrontation that is awkward or difficult to settle in the midst of 25 or 30 adolescents. Disadvantages are that its usefulness depends on others for its effectiveness, and frequent external support for handling in-class problems is not a realistic option in most schools.

Another concern with disciplinary referrals is their potential for discriminatory use. Extensive research (Skiba & Rausch, 2015; see also www.Indiana.edu/~equity/resources.php or http://ies.ed.gov/ncee/wwc/pdf/practice_guides/behavior_pg_092308.pdf) has shown that African American students are more likely than white students to receive disciplinary referrals, an effect that is evident even after controlling for student socioeconomic status. In addition, the research indicates that teachers are more likely to refer African American students for behaviors that are subject to interpretation, such as disrespect and excessive noise; white students are more often referred for behaviors that violate clearly defined prohibitions, such as vandalism or obscene language. Other researchers who have examined disciplinary practices in multicultural schools (Gay, 2006) have noted that African American students' communication styles tend to be more dramatic, animated, and confrontational than those of students from other racial and ethnic groups. Teachers may sometimes misinterpret these students' communications as rude and inappropriate for the classroom, and attempts to correct the students may lead to resentment and misunderstanding. It is plausible, therefore, that some portion of the higher disciplinary referrals received by African American students is a function of overreaction by teachers to their communication styles.

Research by Gregory and Weinstein (2008) examined discipline data in high school classrooms over a year's time. They found that African American students who were referred for defiance often were referred by only one or a few teachers, indicating that the behaviors were not general across all their teachers and classes. Comparisons of the students' perceptions of referring and nonreferring teachers showed that the teachers who did more referring were perceived as less caring and as having lower expectations. Thus, there is a strong possibility that these students are responding to situational differences among their classrooms and their teachers. It was also the case that a small number of the students received a referral from a majority of their teachers, suggesting that some of the students may be exhibiting a pattern of oppositional behavior.

We suggest that you be sparing in your use of office referrals. Try to use other, less impactful interventions and use a referral only if the problem is becoming more serious and intrusive. When you do use a referral, pay attention to the possibility that you are reacting to a student's communication style rather than to a specific type of misbehavior. After you have made the referral, be sure to follow up with the appropriate administrator and the student to be sure there has been a satisfactory resolution to the problem.

More Extensive Interventions

When students do not respond to minor or moderate interventions and their behavior continues to disrupt classroom activities or interfere with their own and others' learning, one or more of the following strategies can be helpful in reducing the inappropriate behaviors and allowing the teacher to reestablish a focus on learning. This section describes strategies that are more involved and more time-consuming but may be more effective with the given student(s) and problem.

Use Problem Solving.   A problem-solving conference with the student can be an effective way to get information about the source of the problem and to redirect the student to more appropriate behavior. Because this strategy was described in Chapter 10, it will not be addressed here. Following are descriptions of several other ways to intervene when inappropriate student behavior has become chronic and/or interferes with the student's learning or the overall class climate. Several of these strategies utilize problem solving as part of their overall approach.

Create an Individual Contract With the Student.   When a student's inappropriate behavior has become chronic or a problem is severe and must stop immediately, try an individual contract. You will have to discuss the problem with the student and try to understand the student's perspective. Then you and the student can identify appropriate solutions and agree on what course of action to take. Typically, the contract specifies changes the student will make, but it might also call for the teacher to alter some behavior or activity. You should make clear the consequences that will occur if the plan is not followed, and you can identify some incentive to encourage the student to follow through with the contract. The plan and consequences are written by the teacher (prototypes can be found on most websites for teachers) and signed by the student. Contracts can also be used with other strategies, such as problem solving or reality therapy and the daily report card (described later).

Use a Five-Step Intervention Procedure.   Jones and Jones (2016) recommend following five steps (see Figure 11.1) when dealing with disruptive student behavior.

> STEP 1: Use a nonverbal signal to cue the student to stop.

> STEP 2: If the behavior continues, ask the student to follow the desired rule.

> STEP 3: If the disruption continues, give the student a choice of stopping the behavior or choosing to develop a plan.

figure 11.1 ■ Five Steps in Responding to Students' Behavior that Fails to Support the Learning Process

Step	Procedure	Example
1.	Nonverbal cue.	Raised index finger.
2.	Verbal cue.	"John, please follow our classroom rules."
3.	Indicate choice student is making.	"John, if you continue to talk while I am talking, you will be choosing to develop a plan."
4.	Student moves to a designated area in the room to develop a plan.	"John, you have chosen to take time to develop a plan."
5.	Student is required to go somewhere else to develop a plan.	"John, I really wish we could solve this here. If we cannot, you will have to see Mrs. Johnson to develop your plan."

Source: Jones, Vern & Jones, Louise, *Comprehensive Classroom Management: Creating Communities of Support and Solving Problems, Loose Leaf Version*, 11th Ed. © 2016. Reprinted and electronically reproduced by permission of Pearson Education, Inc., New York, NY.

STEP 4: If the student still does not stop, require that the student move to a designated area in the room to write a plan.

STEP 5: If the student refuses to comply with Step 4, send the student to another location (another classroom or the school office) to complete the plan.

The use of the five-step intervention process requires a form for the plan (Figure 11.2). When the approach is introduced to the students, preferably at the

figure 11.2 ■ Problem-Solving Method

Choose to Be Responsible

Name_____

Date _____

Rules we agreed on:

1. Speak politely to others.
2. Treat each other kindly.
3. Follow teacher requests.
4. Be prepared for class.
5. Make a good effort at your work and request help if you need it.
6. Obey all school rules.

Please answer the following questions:

1. What rule did you violate?_____
_____

2. What did you do that violated this rule?_____
_____

3. What problem did this cause for you, your teacher, or classmates?_____

4. What plan can you develop that will help you be more responsible and follow
   this classroom rule?_____
_____

5. How can the teacher or other students help you?_____
_____

I, _____, will try my best to follow the plan I have written and to follow all other
rules and procedures that we created to make the classroom a good place to learn.___
_____

Source: Jones, Vern & Jones, Louise, *Comprehensive Classroom Management: Creating Communities of Support and Solving Problems, Loose Leaf Version*, 11th Ed. © 2016. Reprinted and electronically reproduced by permission of Pearson Education, Inc., New York, NY.

beginning of the year, the teacher explains its purpose and how to fill out the form. Role-playing the use of the five steps is recommended, both to teach the procedures and to provide a positive model of their application. It is helpful to laminate a couple of examples of appropriate plans so that students have models.

Advantages of this approach include its emphasis on student responsibility and choice. Also, a graduated response to the problem allows the teacher to intervene nonpunitively at first and thus provides a means of settling the matter quickly with a minimum of disturbance to the ongoing activity. The steps are simple and straightforward, which promotes consistency in their use by the teacher; students in turn are aided by the structure and predictability.

A disadvantage of the system is that movement from Step 1 to Step 5 can occur rapidly and intermediate strategies may be necessary to avoid excessive reliance on sending students out of the classroom. In addition, some students will have difficulty writing an acceptable plan by themselves. Finally, setting up the system, meeting with students to discuss their plans, and monitoring implementation require at least a moderate investment of time.

Use the "Think Time" Strategy.   Designed to help students learn self-control and to prevent a reciprocally escalating sequence of student noncompliance–teacher warnings and reprimands, the Think Time strategy removes a noncompliant student to another teacher's classroom to provide time for the student to gain focus and composure and then to reenter the classroom only after making a commitment to change the behavior (Nelson & Carr, 2000). Using the Think Time strategy requires the cooperation of another teacher whose classroom is in close proximity. The partner teacher reserves a location in the room that is not in a high traffic area and that will minimize attention to the entering student. After arriving at the receiving classroom, the student waits quietly in the designated area and thinks about what happened. As soon as is practicable (e.g., 3 to 5 minutes), the receiving teacher makes contact with the student and gives him or her a debriefing form to fill out that asks, "What was your behavior?" and "What behavior do you need to display when you go back to your classroom?" The student is asked if he or she can do it or if a conference is needed with the teacher. If the student completes the form acceptably, the receiving teacher sends the student back to the original class.

If you use this strategy, you'll partner with another teacher. After preparing a location in your rooms to receive Think Time students, you'll each need to teach your students about think time. Nelson recommends treating this task as you would any other complex procedure. You'll need to explain the purpose of the strategy (to help students learn self-control and to minimize disruption to learning) and what behaviors might result in think time. You'll also need to describe the signal you'll use to send someone to think time (e.g., hand the student a pass card) and model how students will be expected to leave the room and enter the other teacher's room. The students should also be shown an example of the debriefing form with examples of appropriate responses. For high school applications, Nelson recommends having a backup administrative sanction such as an office referral if a student becomes disruptive. Likewise, if a student is required to use Think Time more than once in a class period or after the third time in a semester, then an office referral or in-school suspension (ISS) assignment is used along with a parent contact.

One advantage of Think Time is that it gives the teacher a way to manage students who don't respond to simpler desist techniques; at the same time, it short-circuits the reciprocal escalation of hostile interaction that can develop when a student resists a teacher's attempt to stop misbehavior. Another advantage is that think time provides a cease-fire opportunity in which students acknowledge their part in the problem and identify a solution. In this respect, it is similar to other problem-solving strategies. Limitations in the use of the strategy are that it takes the cooperation and commitment of another teacher, and it requires planning and systematic application to be successful.

Use the Reality Therapy Model. William Glasser's (1975, 1997, 1986) ideas, including reality therapy, have been widely applied in education, and we consider now some of his recommendations for dealing with disruptive or maladaptive behaviors in a classroom setting.

The essential features of using a reality therapy strategy when working with an individual student include establishing a caring relationship with the student, focusing on the present behaviors, getting the student to accept responsibility, developing a plan for change, obtaining a commitment to follow the plan, and following up. Glasser believes strongly that students choose behavior depending on their perceptions of its consequences. Most students choose appropriate behaviors when they believe these behaviors will lead to desirable outcomes, and they avoid behaviors that they perceive will lead to undesirable consequences. Glasser's plan can be put into effect by following these steps.

STEP 1: Establish involvement with the students. If students believe the teacher cares for them and has their best interests in mind, they will be more likely to follow the teacher's guidance when evaluating and changing their behavior. Teachers can show commitment to and caring for students in numerous ways: commenting favorably to the students about their work; being friendly; and showing an interest in students' activities, families, likes and dislikes, and hobbies. Teachers can also get involved by demonstrating school spirit, joking, being good listeners, and taking time to talk with students about their concerns. The best time to establish involvement is before a student becomes disruptive, but even if a student has begun to exhibit problem behavior, it is not too late to begin. When a teacher makes a special effort to have two or three friendly contacts a day with such a student, it can be helpful in creating a more positive climate for change.

STEP 2: Focus on behavior. When a problem has occurred, Glasser recommends that a brief conference be held with the student. The initial concern should be to determine what the problem is. To this end, the teacher should ask only questions about "what happened" or "what's going on" and avoid trying to fix blame. Even if the teacher knows exactly what the problem is, it is wise to obtain the student's perspective.

STEP 3: The student must accept responsibility for the behavior. This means that the student acknowledges that he or she did engage in the behavior. No excuses are accepted. Admitting responsibility is difficult, especially when there are so many other handy things to blame. Of course, it is possible that more than one individual is responsible for the problem, but that should not be an excuse for irresponsibility or denial.

STEP 4: The student should evaluate the behavior. If students have difficulty perceiving their part or if they minimize it, Glasser suggests asking, "Has the behavior helped or hurt you? Has it helped or hurt others?" The teacher may have to point out the negative consequences of continuing the behavior. Unless the student sees that it will lead to negative consequences and that changing it will produce desirable consequences, there isn't much reason to expect a change.

STEP 5: Develop a plan. The teacher and the student must identify ways to prevent the problem from recurring and the new behaviors that are needed. The plan can be written as a contract.

STEP 6: The student must make a commitment to follow the plan. Progress will be limited at best if students do not seriously intend to make a change. It may help if the teacher makes clear the positive and negative consequences of following or not following the plan. The plan must be doable in a reasonable time.

STEP 7: Follow up and follow through. If the plan doesn't work, it should be modified with the student; if a negative consequence was called for in the plan, it should be used. Glasser proposes several additional steps beyond the classroom if a student continues to be a problem. For example, use of in-school suspension could be a consequence of continuing misbehavior; before the student is allowed to return to the classroom, an acceptable plan would have to be agreed on. Only after several attempts to obtain a change have failed should the teacher refer the student to an assistant principal.

The reality therapy approach to dealing with individual discipline problems has much to recommend it. It is a systematic way for teachers to deal with many kinds of individual student problems, and it provides a simple yet effective process for getting right at the issues without being sidetracked by fault finding, conning, or excuse making. Research on the effects of this aspect of reality therapy supports its effectiveness when used with individual students (Emmer & Aussiker, 1990).

Use Time Away. Time Away is a three-step strategy that is used to help students whose problem behaviors have become chronic or who escalate their conflicts with the teacher or fellow students (Albrecht, 2008). Use of this strategy requires a trained professional (facilitator) to work with the student outside of the classroom. The three steps in the Time Away process are the following:

1. **Time-Out.** The teacher sends the student to a designated area in the school where the facilitator supervises a brief time-out period. The purpose of the time-out is to remove social reinforcement that maintains the behavior and to give the student time to calm down.

2. **Redirection.** At the end of the time-out period and after the student has regained self-control, the facilitator works with the student on an academic task. Doing so provides an opportunity for the facilitator to establish rapport with the student; it also provides an activity that redirects the student's cognitive process to be more rational and cooperative.

3. **Conflict Resolution.** The facilitator works nonjudgmentally with the student to develop an understanding of what led up to the problem or event and what consequences ensued. The process is similar to the steps described for problem solving in Chapter 10. The facilitator and the student then summarize the understanding of the problem and plans for addressing it on a conflict resolution worksheet. At the end of this process, the student is returned to the classroom.

The Time Away strategy has several advantages. It provides a way to target specific problems in an efficient and timely manner, and it allows the teacher to continue teaching the rest of the class. It also de-escalates rather than exacerbates conflict. An obvious limitation of the approach is the requirement to use a trained facilitator. Also, the teacher is not directly involved in the problem-solving process, so follow-up with the teacher might be needed to enact changes that would help the student address classroom issues that may have instigated the process.

Hold a Conference With a Parent. Sometimes a telephone call to a parent can have a marked effect on a student's behavior, signaling to the student that accountability for behavior extends beyond the classroom. Parents react best if they don't feel that they are being held responsible for their child's behavior in school (after all, they aren't there), so don't put the parent on the defensive. Describe the situation briefly and say that you would appreciate whatever support the parent can give in helping you understand and resolve the problem. Acknowledge the difficulty of rearing adolescents as well as teaching them. Be sure to use listening skills (see Chapter 10) during the conversation and be alert for information that might help you determine an appropriate strategy for dealing with the student. Have grade information available so that you can give the parent specific information about the student's progress if the information is requested or needed.

Rather than a phone conference, you might need to schedule a face-to-face conference with a parent. Sometimes, but by no means always, when such conferences are arranged it is because a problem has become quite severe and other school personnel (a counselor or a principal) may have to be present. If you have initiated the meeting, you should try to brief the others and plan your approach ahead of time; also, inform parents about who will attend the meeting.

The chief drawback to parent conferences is the time and energy they require. The effort is frequently worth it, however. Even though not every conference is successful, many times the student's behavior will improve. Another potential problem is identifying ahead of time the best strategy to follow with the parent. Occasionally, parents overreact and punish children excessively; other parents may be defensive and unable to provide support. As the year progresses, you will get to know parents better and be able to gauge the probable effects of your call or conference.

Daily Behavior Report Card.   This technique is focused on improving an individual student's behavior when simpler interventions have not worked. Also referred to as a Home-Note program (Adams, Womack, Shatzer, & Calderarella, 2010), the components of this strategy include:

- Identify one or more target behaviors to increase or decrease. For example, the student may need to increase the rate of homework or assignment completion, hand raising, or asking permission to move about the room. Alternatively, the student may need to reduce the amount of interrupting or moving around the room without permission.
- Develop a form (or "behavior report card") to be used to record the student's behavior on a daily basis. This form can be a *checklist* of the target behaviors (e.g., Turned in homework/assignments: yes or no, or a *rating* (e.g., Raised hand and waited to be called on: Always, Most of the Time, Sometimes, Never). The teacher completes the Behavior Report Card (BRC) at the end of the day or period and the student takes it home to be signed by the parent and returned to the teacher the next school day.
- The parent provides approval and a reward for the student when the BRC indicates that the student's behavior was satisfactory (met target goals) that day. Examples might be participating in a desirable activity such as having extra computer or TV time, a treat, a privilege, or selecting a reward from among several available.
- Arrange for a discussion with the student and with the student's parent(s). It's important to agree on target behaviors, and to get buy-in from the parents.

The BRC strategy has many advantageous features. It can be applied to a range of target behaviors and modified easily when necessary. Once the plan is in place, the amount of teacher time and effort needed to implement it is not great, and the involvement of the parents can be especially helpful. It has been used successfully in conjunction with IEP plans for students receiving special education services (Fabiano et al., 2010; DuPaul, Laracy, & Gormley, 2014). Evaluations have shown the BRC strategy to be effective for a variety of age/grade levels and target behaviors (Vannest, Davis, Davis, Mason, & Burke, 2010).

A limitation of the BRC strategy is that parents might not follow through with checking and signing the report or providing a contingent reward. If parental follow-through is a chronic problem, then the teacher can provide a school-based reward. Alternatively, some other individual at school might become involved in monitoring the daily BRC. Another possible limitation involves the length of time that the BRC strategy should be used before the desirable behaviors become sufficiently established so that daily monitoring and feedback are no longer required. A vignette illustrating the use of the BRC strategy is presented in the Who Will I Teach? section later in this chapter.

Use Peer Mediation.   Conflicts between students can be disruptive and may engender resentments that spill over into the classroom. At some schools, conflicts between students in the community, sometimes resulting from gang affiliation, contribute to tension, ill will, and fighting at school. In response to such problems, some schools and teachers have implemented peer-mediation programs. The goal of these programs is to resolve conflicts peacefully, enabling all students to learn constructive approaches to handling problems. Students receive training on how to use the mediation process, and the entire school community must be educated about the process. Peer mediation is used to handle conflicts when simpler problem-solving interventions by adults have failed to resolve the problem (Johnson & Johnson, 2013).

Mediation utilizes a process in which the parties in conflict are assisted by a mediator to negotiate a solution to the problem. The procedure has four steps: (1) stop the hostilities, (2) obtain a commitment from both parties in the conflict to participate in the mediation process, (3) help them negotiate a solution, and (4) formalize the agreement (Johnson & Johnson, 1995). The negotiation process itself involves the participants in deciding what they want to accomplish, describing their feelings, and explaining the basis for both. They must also understand the other party's point of view and help generate alternative solutions that will be acceptable to all individuals involved in the conflict. Finally, they must choose a particular solution to implement.

The role of the mediator is to listen to each side in the dispute, to clarify issues, to help generate and negotiate possible solutions, and to write up the agreed-on solution. If an agreement is not reached, the mediator helps the participants decide on the next step in resolving the dispute (Cutrona & Guerin, 1994; Stomfay-Stitz, 1994). The mediator is not an arbitrator who passes judgment on the merits of the sides and who imposes a solution. Instead, the mediator attempts to facilitate an understanding of the problem and the development of a solution by the parties involved in the dispute. Research indicates that peers can be effective mediators and that use of the approach can help reduce schoolwide conflict and the use of suspensions and other exclusionary discipline (Burrell, Zirbel, & Allen, 2003).

Becoming a mediator requires learning the goals and rationale for the approach and receiving systematic training in each of the steps in the process. When peer mediation has been adopted as a schoolwide strategy, such training is typically provided to students by a school counselor or by a teacher who has received such training. If you would like to use peer mediation in your classroom and it is not being used schoolwide, you might start by reading the references on mediation cited earlier and listed at the end of this chapter; additional information about training activities and materials is included in these references.

■ Special Problems

In addition to the general types of problems described at the beginning of this chapter, some specific types occur commonly enough and are severe enough that it is worthwhile to describe additional strategies for managing them. Previously described approaches can also be applied to these behaviors.

Chronic Avoidance of Work

You may have students who frequently do not complete assigned work. Sometimes they fail to complete assignments early in the school year; more often a student will begin to skip assignments occasionally and then with increasing regularity. This behavior can be minimized by having in place efficient procedures for managing student work and by an accountability system that clearly ties student work to grades (review Chapter 5 for details). However, even in classrooms with good procedures, some students may try to avoid work. It is much easier (and much better for the student) if you deal with this problem before the student gets so far behind that failure is almost certain. By catching the problem early, you will be able to provide some incentive (i.e., passing the course) for the student to get back on track. To be in a position to take early action, you must collect and check student work frequently and you must maintain good records. Then, when you see that a student has begun to skip assignments, you can talk with him or her to identify the problem. It is possible that the student is simply unable to do the work; if so, you may be able to arrange appropriate assistance or modify the assignments for that student. It is also possible that the student feels overwhelmed by the assignments. In this case, break the assignments into parts whenever possible. Have the student complete the first part of the assignment within a specified period of time (e.g., 5 or 10 minutes); then check to see that it has been done. Sometimes you can provide a list of assignments for the student to check off. This can serve as a self-monitoring device and can provide a sense of accomplishment.

If ability is not the problem, the following procedures can be used in addition to talking with the student. Call the student's parents or guardian and discuss the situation. Often, the home can supply the extra support needed to help motivate the student, or, after conferring with the parents, you might decide to use a Behavior

Report Card with assignment completion as the target. If the student participates in athletics or other extracurricular activities, the coaches or other supervising faculty may be able to support your efforts. Many schools have a system (e.g., a weekly checklist) for monitoring the academic progress of students who are involved in extracurricular activities or who need extra support in completing assignments. Finally, apply the consequence, usually a failing grade, for repeated neglect of work. There is no purpose served in softening the penalty because the student promises to do the work during the next grading period or because you think that he or she could do better by just working harder. Leniency only teaches the student to avoid responsibility. Instead, monitor the student's progress on assignments, give recognition and approval for good effort, and consider providing added incentives for good effort and promptly completed work.

Fighting

Fighting is rarely a classroom problem; usually it occurs in hallways or in other areas of the school. Whether or not to intervene directly depends on your judgment as to whether you can do so without undue risk of injury. If you do not intervene directly, you should alert other teachers and administrators so that action can be taken. If you do intervene, try to do so with the assistance of one or several adults. It is hard for one adult to stop a fight, and attempting to do so may be dangerous. The difficulty increases especially when a crowd has gathered. Dispersing the crowd, calling the school office, and instructing a student to summon an administrator or another teacher may be the wisest first step. Your school will undoubtedly have a procedure to deal with fighting, so you should familiarize yourself with your

"*Pi what squared? Long John, you should be able to get this.*"

Pat Byrnes / The New Yorker Collection / The Cartoon Bank

responsibility (e.g., to file a report with the office). Typically, students are questioned by an assistant principal who will contact the parent, perhaps call the police, arrange a conference, and mete out any prescribed penalty, such as suspension.

Other Aggressive Behavior

Students engage in other aggressive behaviors besides fighting, such as name-calling, bossiness, rudeness toward other students, and physically aggressive—but "playful"—pushing, shoving, or slapping. Offending students should be told that such behavior is not acceptable, even if it is just fooling around. It can easily escalate. Refer to whatever class rule fits the situation, such as "Respect others." Give no more than one warning, then assess an appropriate penalty. Students engaged in such behavior should be separated and seated apart if they give any indication of intending to persist.

Once you are aware of aggressive tendencies in a student, you will need to be especially alert in your monitoring to recognize when the student is becoming agitated. Intervene with a quiet talk or allow the student to sit away from the group if that might help him or her to stay calm. Seat the student away from others who tend to provoke anger. Assume that the student wants to maintain self-control and communicate that in words and actions. When having a conference with such a student, point out how it is in his or her best interest to control this behavior, and when appropriate, help the student set up a time to meet with a school counselor. Consider coping with these behaviors in two phases: the immediate response and a long-range strategy. At the time the behavior occurs, your immediate concern is to bring it to a halt with the least disruption possible. Because these behaviors are annoying or dangerous and can arouse your anxiety or anger, be careful not to exacerbate the problem. By staying calm and avoiding overreaction, rather than becoming overbearing or dictatorial, you are more likely to bring the situation to a successful conclusion. You may tell the student how you feel, but by avoiding an argument or an emotional confrontation you will be in a better position to deal with the student and the problem. Thinking about ways to handle disruptive behavior ahead of time and consulting with more experienced teachers will help you to act rather than react.

Long-range goals are to prevent a recurrence of the behavior and to help the student learn a more constructive means of dealing with others. Preventing a recurrence of the behavior is best accomplished by (1) finding out what triggered the incident and resolving the cause if possible and (2) having a predictable classroom environment with reasonable and consistently used rules, procedures, and consequences. Aggressive behavior is less likely in such classrooms. Helping these students acquire better behavior may require much individual attention from you over a period of time. The extent to which this goal is feasible is, of course, affected by many factors, including your time constraints and the severity of the student's problem. In dealing with students who have chronic problems, you may need consultation and assistance from the student's parents, the school counselor, a behavior specialist, a special education resource teacher, or the principal. You will need to document the student's behavior, your responses to the behavior, and the outcomes.

Bullying

Bullying is repeated acts of aggression by one or more students directed toward a victim who often appears weak or isolated and is thus more vulnerable. The bully's intention is to receive peer approval and to assert power by dominating the victim. Bullying behaviors can take several forms: direct physical aggression (hitting, shoving), verbal and nonverbal aggression (name calling, threats, intimidation), relational aggression (ostracizing, isolating, spreading rumors about the victim), and cyberbullying, which utilizes technology (e.g., email, social networks) to attack, taunt, expose, threaten, or hurtfully entice a victim. Male students are more likely to engage in physical bullying, and female students are more likely to engage in relational aggression.

Bullying has been identified as a serious problem in many schools and communities in the United States as well as in other countries (e.g., Athanasiades & Deliyanni-Kouimtzis, 2010; Gini, 2006), and its prevalence has resulted in extensive research being conducted on the topic (Espelage, 2015). It is certainly contrary to a climate of respect and caring, and it can lead to serious, long-term emotional consequences for both the victim and the bully. For these reasons, schoolwide programs to address bullying are often adopted, and strategies for dealing with it are incorporated into school and district discipline codes. A widely used schoolwide program is the Olweus Bullying Prevention Program (see www.clemson.edu/olweus for material based on this approach). This and other programs' treatment components may include development of a school (or community) anti-bullying policy, consequences for bullying behaviors, education of all students about the problem, social skills training, and more monitoring by adults of locations and activities in which bullying occurs.

Strategies most frequently used in schools include talking with bullies following bullying incidents, disciplinary consequences, and increasing adult supervision. Additional strategies that are regarded as effective by school psychologists include schoolwide positive behavior support, modifying space and schedules, and immediate response to bullying incidents (Sherer & Nickerson, 2010).

If your school has adopted a special program to address bullying, it is likely that you will receive materials for classroom use, and you may participate in a workshop for teachers that will help you to implement the program. As part of your school's overall program, there are specific actions each teacher can take. First, be sure you are familiar with your responsibility concerning student safety. Typically, this topic will be addressed in your school's discipline policy statement. Also, realize that teachers are often unaware of bullying because they may not be present where it occurs (in hallways, lunchroom, bathrooms). When it occurs in the classroom, teachers may not notice its subtler forms—gestures, staring down, threatening notes—unless the victim complains. One action you can take is to do your part in monitoring student behavior in hallways and other nonclassroom spaces during transition times. Cooperate with other teachers and building administrators to cover the building so that there is an adult presence throughout.

If you become aware of bullying behavior that involves students in your classes, you should talk with the affected students about the problem. Lead a discussion of the causes and effects of bullying and make sure to emphasize the crucial role of the audience. Tell students you admire student onlookers who have the courage to give support to the victim and say that bullies who seek to assert their power need to find constructive ways to gain the approval of peers. In general, a problem-solving approach can be used when speaking privately with the bully and the victim. Be aware, though, that if the bullying involves physical contact or threats, your school's discipline code will likely require a referral of the aggressor to an assistant principal and a prescribed consequence. In addition, a school counselor may become involved in working with both students to develop appropriate behaviors.

Teaching students social skills is one strategy that can be used to help prevent bullying or to keep it from developing further. Social skills, which help students communicate and resolve conflicts more effectively and also promote friendship and working together, include learning about other students' perspectives, listening, negotiation and problem solving, asking for and giving help, taking turns and waiting, and dealing with disagreement. Students with pronounced social skills deficits can be referred to a school counselor, who may schedule group counseling sessions to work on skill development. Another possibility is to incorporate social skills training into selected classroom activities throughout the year. For example, when students engage in small-group activities or in whole-class discussions, various social skills are needed. Depending on the age and skill level of your students, one or more skills might be selected for emphasis on different occasions.

Power Struggles

Dealing effectively with power struggles requires understanding what motivates this behavior and using techniques that de-escalate any negative emotions. What drives people to attack others generally arises from needs for power, belonging, and/or respect. For students who act out hostile and aggressive feelings, one or more of these needs is unmet in their lives. Mendler and Mendler (2011) provide a number of suggested strategies for handling this problem.

Defiance or hostility is understandably very threatening, particularly when it occurs in front of other students. The teacher feels, and rightfully so, that if the student is allowed to get away with it, such behavior may continue and other students will be more likely to react in this way. Yet the student who provoked the confrontation, usually publicly, feels that backing down would cause a loss of face in front of peers. The best way to deal with such an event is to try to defuse it. This can be done by keeping it private and handling it individually with the student if possible.

If an incident occurs during a lesson and is not really extreme, deal with it by trying to depersonalize the event and avoid a power struggle. "This is taking time away from the lesson. I will discuss it with you in a few minutes when I have time." Then leave the student alone and give him or her a chance to calm down. Later, when you have time, have a private talk with the student and assess a penalty if it seems warranted. Should the student not accept the opportunity you have provided and instead press the confrontation further, you can instruct the student to leave the group and wait at a pre-arranged time-out area. After the student has had time to cool off, you can give your class something to do and discuss the problem privately with the student.

When presented with this type of behavior, you should try to stay objective. Don't engage in arguments with the student. Point out that the behavior was not acceptable, and state the penalty clearly. Listen to the student's point of view; if you are not sure how to respond, say that you will think about it and discuss it later. In an extreme (and rare) case, the student may be totally uncooperative and refuse to keep quiet or to go to the time-out area. If this happens, you can escort the student out of the room yourself, or in the case of an older and larger student, you can call the office or send another student for assistance. In almost all cases, however, as long as you stay calm and refuse to get into a power struggle with the student, the student will take the opportunity to cool down.

A Final Reminder: Think and Act Positively

Some of the strategies presented in this chapter for dealing with problem behaviors involve some form of punishment, such as use of penalties, withholding desired activities, detention, and the like. This is especially the case for strategies in the moderate and extensive categories. A drawback to punishment is that, by itself, it doesn't teach students the behaviors that should be practiced, and so it may not teach the student the behaviors that you intend. Consequently, it is important to communicate clearly what behaviors are desired; that is, the focus should remain on teaching appropriate behaviors. Furthermore, a classroom in which the main consequences are negative ones will not have a positive climate. Thus, teachers using strategies in the moderate and extensive categories more than occasionally may wish to incorporate additional incentives or a reward system into their overall classroom management to help mitigate the negative effects of using punishment. If you find yourself frequently in negative interactions with a student, find something positive to say to him or her each day: "I saw you working hard on your assignment," or "You did a good job of participating in your group," or "That answer shows good thinking." Try to smile when you say it, even if it is forced. If you stay with the strategy you may be able to make some progress with the student. Finally, after correcting student behavior, the teacher who supplies a generous measure of warmth and support reassures students that they have been restored to good grace.

■ Who Will I Teach? Using a Behavior Report Card to Reduce a Student's Problem Behaviors

In this chapter we presented a range of interventions for managing different kinds of problem behaviors. In practice, each situation and student will present unique features as well as common ones, so identifying an effective intervention will need reflection, especially for more severe or persistent problems. We will now look at a vignette in which a teacher uses a Behavior Report Card strategy to address some significant problem behaviors. As you read the vignette, you might think of alternative approaches; if you do, consider what might cause you to prefer them.

Michael is a 13-year-old student in Mrs. Brown's seventh-grade math class. His behavior has become a matter of concern during the second month of the school year. In class his work on assignments is satisfactory as long as he's supervised and able to receive assistance, but if left alone for very long he loses focus and rarely finishes his work. Michael talks to other students, fidgets, wiggles, or annoys. Homework and occasional projects that must be done at home are also rarely completed. During seat-work and group-work activities, Michael frequently wanders around the room and engages in off-task behavior. When told to return to his seat, Michael delays responding; when reprimanded or placed at a separate desk for a short time, he becomes defiant and sulks; after such episodes he rarely re-engages with the assignment or activity. His performance on content tasks other than math are in the average range and indicate that he should be able to perform at grade level.

Mrs. Brown was aware that Michael had been identified in elementary school as having a mild learning disability in math, and in sixth grade he received resource room assistance for 45 minutes each day. The decision to use a resource room placement was due to Michael's diagnosed ADHD status along with the LD diagnosis; the resource room environment, with fewer distractions and more immediate teacher attention and assistance, was considered a more suitable placement for math instruction. When Mrs. Brown checked Michael's IEP to see if there were any recommendations that might be helpful in planning how to manage Michael in the regular classroom, the only information was that Michael responds to rewards and that behavior modification is suggested. It was also noted that Michael has been on stimulant medication for a year for the ADHD condition, but that it is only moderately helpful for reducing his symptoms. At the end of his sixth-grade year, Michael's special education teacher, his regular math teacher, and Michael's parents, along with Michael himself, agreed that he should transition to a regular classroom without resource room support, since his math skills were assessed as at or just below grade level.

Pause and Consider

1. How would you categorize (minor, escalating or spreading, intense, etc.) Michael's off-task behaviors during the second month of the school year?
2. What are some ways that Mrs. Brown might address Michael's behaviors?

Mrs. Brown decided that Michael's poor record of completing assignments and out-of-seat behaviors were most concerning to her. She discussed the situation with Michael's sixth-grade resource teacher, who suggested that some incentives might help with assignment completion. Mrs. Brown also called Michael's mother to discuss the situation. Because Michael's issues were behavioral and not specifically the result of his learning disability in math, all parties agreed that it was too soon to revert to a resource room placement for math. Mrs. Brown found Michael's mother to be very cooperative and she agreed to implement a home incentive (extra game or TV time) as part of a daily Behavior Report Card. Only two target areas were identified on the report form: satisfactory completion of daily work and acceptable in-seat behavior. Mrs. Brown then had a problem-solving conference with Michael to explain the daily BRC process. During the conference, Michael expressed anxiety about being able to complete all the work. Mrs. Brown explained that he needed to make a reasonable effort but that perfect performance was not required to get a "check" for satisfactory completion. To manage the out-of-seat behavior, Mrs. Brown started by asking Michael to keep track for one day of how many times he left his seat. She gave him a check-off sheet to use to keep the record. Later, she asked Michael to judge how many times he needed to leave his seat during the math period, and they settled on a number as an acceptable amount. Mrs. Brown explained that she wanted Michael to take responsibility for this behavior, but that she would remind him; however, if she had to remind him more than two times in a period, then he would not get a check.

During the first two weeks after implementing the plan, Michael's assignment completion rate rose and his out-of-seat behavior dropped to acceptable levels on most days. On the two days that he received "unsatisfactory" checks on his card, Mrs. Brown called Michael's mother to be sure that she withheld game or TV time. Although Michael was unhappy, the united front was successful and he grudgingly accepted the consequence. Thereafter Michael settled into the routine and maintained his mostly acceptable performance and behavior. Both Mrs. Brown and Michael's mother took advantage of the BRC feedback to acknowledge Michael's efforts and good behavior, which was reinforcing and also helpful to Michael's belief about his ability to do well in school. Not only did Michael's behavior in the two target areas improve, so did his on-task behavior because working on assignments and staying in his seat reduced the opportunities for getting into trouble.

■ Chapter Summary

Not all inappropriate behaviors can be prevented, so teachers need strategies for managing problems when they occur. Principles underlying the choice of strategy are described. Strategies are grouped according to how much time and effort are required to use them. Some seemingly inappropriate student behaviors need not be defined as "problems" and are best ignored. When minor inappropriate behaviors cannot be ignored, they are usually managed with strategies that can be carried out without interrupting the ongoing activity. When inappropriate behavior persists or interferes with learning, more extensive interventions may be called for. A repertoire of alternative strategies is presented. Most teachers find some combination of these strategies helpful as they work with a range of adolescent behaviors. We also discussed some special problems that occur in secondary classrooms and schools and typical approaches to managing them. Finally, an example of using a Behavior Report Card to correct a student's escalating problems was presented in the Who Will I Teach? section.

■ Further Reading

Damiani, V. B. (2011). *Crisis prevention and intervention in the classroom: What teachers should know* (2nd ed.). Lanham, MD: Rowman & Littlefield.

Schools and teachers must deal with extreme problems—crisis events that can occur in the schools and in the community at large, such as violence, suicide, and natural catastrophes. This book explains how teachers can work with students to help them cope when a crisis occurs; it also provides information about how crisis response teams work in schools and communities.

Espelage, D. L. (2015). Emerging issues in school bullying research and prevention. In E. T. Emmer & E. J. Sabornie (Eds.), *Handbook of research on classroom management* (2nd ed., pp. 76–93). New York: Routledge.

This chapter provides an up-to-date and authoritative summary of research on bullying.

Kottler, J. A. (2009). *Students who drive you crazy: Succeeding with resistant, unmotivated, and otherwise difficult students* (2nd ed.). Thousand Oaks, CA: Corwin.

This brief book provides insightful suggestions about dealing with challenging students. The author emphasizes the importance of the teacher's understanding of the source of the conflict with the student, as well as his or her reactions.

Mendler, A. N., & Mendler, B. D. (2011). *Power struggles: Successful techniques for educators* (2nd ed.). Bloomington, IN: Solution Tree.

This short, readable book outlines specific steps teachers and other school staff can take to de-escalate the cycle of hostility that can occur when students are confrontational. It includes checklists and other aids to help identify causes of power struggles and other hostile behavior.

Shukla-Mehta, S., & Albin, R. W. (2003). Twelve practical strategies to prevent behavioral escalation in classroom settings. *Preventing School Failure, 47,* 156–172.

The authors describe ways to avoid or de-escalate confrontations with students. For example, the teacher should reinforce calm and on-task behavior, recognize what sets off a student, avoid responses that add to the escalation, and intervene early.

Sprick, R. (2012). *The teacher's encyclopedia of behavior management: 100+ problems/500+ plans* (2nd ed.). Eugene, OR: Northwest.

This book addresses individual and classwide problems common to schools. It includes model plans along with specific interventions.

Sugai, G., & Simonsen, B. (2015). Supporting general classroom management: Tier 2/3 practices and systems. In E. T. Emmer & E. J. Sabornie (Eds.), *Handbook of research on classroom management* (2nd ed., pp. 60–75). New York: Routledge.

The authors present a continuum of behavior supports with an emphasis on more intensive interventions. Integration with schoolwide practices is illustrated by an extended example.

www.apa.org/about/gr/issues/cyf/bullying-school-climate.aspx

This website offers strategies for bullying prevention and social skills training programs to help students recognize and counter occurrences of social, emotional, and mental abuse.

www.apa.org/ed/schools/cpse/activities/class-management.aspx

This website offers a set of modules to assist teachers with practical strategies for helping students behave individually and as a class, as well as interventions for emotional and behavioral problems.

www.cecp.air.org

This is the website for the Center for Effective Collaboration and Practice, whose goal is to improve services for children and youth with emotional-behavioral problems.

www.cfchildren.org

Committee for Children is an international organization committed to social, emotional, and academic learning. Special topics include bullying, youth violence, and emergent literacy.

www.pbisworld.com

This website hosts a variety of resources for responding to student problem behaviors. Tabs on the site allow visitors to select from a variety of problem behaviors (e.g., impulsive, anxious, tardy) and locate appropriate Tier 1, 2, and 3 interventions.

■ Suggested Activities

1. Teachers' reactions to the problem behaviors described in this chapter are often affected by the adult models they have observed and the type of discipline they received as children, both at home and at school. Recall your early experiences in this area, and consider their implications. To what extent do these earlier models provide a positive guide for managing problems of varying severity? Would the strategies that were effective for you be equally appropriate or effective for the varied kinds of students you may teach? Are there current behaviors or environmental problems that you did not experience (e.g., drug culture, poverty, single-parent/guardian homes, bullying)? Where should you add to or modify your approach?

2. Review the descriptions of problem types presented at the beginning of the chapter. Then decide which interventions would be best suited for each type. Given several alternative interventions for a type of problem, how would you decide which to use?

3. Within each type of intervention—minor, moderate, or extensive—are there any that you distinctly prefer? Do you reject any? Discuss your reasons for liking or disliking particular approaches.

4. Listed here are several problem situations. Decide on a strategy for dealing with each and an alternative response if your first approach does not produce good results. Indicate any assumptions you are making about the teaching context as you choose your strategy.

    Situation 1. Ardyth and Melissa talk and pass notes as you conduct a class discussion. Several other students whisper or daydream.

Situation 2. Desi and Bryce talk constantly. They refuse to get to work and argue with you when you ask them to open their books.

Situation 3. Dwayne manages to get most of his work done, but in the process he is constantly disruptive. He teases the girls sitting around him, keeping them constantly laughing and competing for his attention. Dwayne makes wisecracks in response to almost anything you say. When confronted, he grins charmingly and responds with exaggerated courtesy, much to the delight of the rest of the class.

Situation 4. When someone bumped into Marc at the drinking fountain, he turned around and spit water at the other student. Later, Marc ordered a boy who was standing near his desk to get away, and then he shoved the boy. On the way back from the cafeteria, Marc got into a name-calling contest with another boy.

5. Make a list of student behaviors, such as defiance, rudeness, aggression, and unresponsiveness, that are the most likely to embarrass, annoy, anger, or otherwise make you uncomfortable. Write down how you might handle the behaviors. For a group activity, compare notes and see if the members can agree on a preferred approach to common problems.

6. Learn about your school's bullying policy and how it is communicated to students and parents. Alternatively, read about a bullying prevention or social skills training program at a website such as www.clemson.edu/olweus or www.nasponline.org/resources/factsheets/ or www.apa.org/topics/topicbully.html. What is the teacher's role in implementing the policy or program?

MyEducationLab *Self-Check 11.1*

MyEducationLab *Application Exercise 11.1*   Using what you've learned in this chapter, read and respond to this scenario.

MyEducationLab *Application Exercise 11.2*   Using what you've learned in this chapter, read and respond to this scenario.

MyEducationLab *Application Exercise 11.3*   Using what you've learned in this chapter, view the video and respond to the questions.

MyEducationLab *Application Exercise 11.4*   Using what you've learned in this chapter, read and respond to this scenario.

MyEducationLab *Application Exercise 11.5*   Using what you've learned in this chapter, view the video and respond to the questions.

MyEducationLab *Application Exercise 11.6*   Using what you've learned in this chapter, view the video and respond to the questions.

MyEducationLab *Classroom Management Simulation 11.1*   Engage with the Classroom Management Simulation *Responding to Students' Failure to Follow Classroom Expectations.*

MyEducationLab *Classroom Management Simulation 11.2*   Engage with the Classroom Management Simulation *Dealing with Situations Where Students Are Being Bullied/Harassed.*

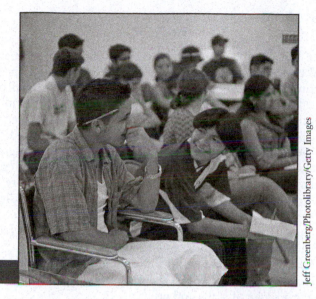

Jeff Greenberg/Photolibrary/Getty Images

CHAPTER 12

Managing Special Groups

This chapter is concerned with variations in student characteristics and their impact on classroom management. While teaching, we encounter differences among students constantly. From the teacher's perspective, the individual differences of most concern tend to be the ones that impact student learning and engagement or that influence cooperation with and among students. But let's take a more personal view of individual differences for a moment. Think of a time when you were a student and you felt fulfillment, pride, or satisfaction from some accomplishment or achievement at school. It could have been receiving a high grade in a course or on a project; perhaps you did well in an athletic event or other competition. It may have been a private moment that came with a feeling of competence or efficacy, or it might have been signaled by recognition or approval from peers or a teacher. Think about how such moments energized and motivated you, perhaps gave purpose and meaning to school then or for the future.

Now switch gears and think about moments in school when you felt dejected, alone, isolated, incapable, or rejected. What gave rise to those feelings? Did you feel different from others? Less a part of the school scene and disengaged from school? To what extent did or could teachers have mitigated those negative feelings, either by their response to your discomfort or in the ways that they provided encouragement, direction, or support to you? As teachers, our decisions can have lasting impact on the students we teach. Thoughtful reflection on student characteristics, particularly student differences that impact learning in the classroom setting, can help frame our decisions in ways that empower, rather than alienate, our students.

In this chapter we consider the classroom management actions that teachers can take to provide support for students who possess individual differences that often impact achievement or behavior. The goal is to provide opportunities for achievement and accomplishment that create efficacy and sustained effort, while minimizing feelings of isolation and disengagement. The ages, academic ability levels, goals, interests, culture, and home backgrounds of students influence their classroom behavior. Consequently, adjustments in management and instructional practices are sometimes needed to meet the needs of different groups. Among the students who present special challenges are those who are working below or well above grade level and those who are academically or physically challenged, as well as those whose predominant language is not English. Classrooms can include all of these types of students. Effectively working with students having such diverse needs and abilities requires thoughtfulness and flexibility.

This chapter presents information and suggestions that, combined with the principles laid out in previous chapters, will help you organize and manage classes that have a range of skills and needs.

■ Teaching Heterogeneous Classes

Many secondary school classrooms contain students with a wide range of entering achievement levels. A highly heterogeneous eighth-grade English class may include students who score at fourth-grade levels on reading and language usage achievement tests and students with grade-equivalent scores of eleventh grade or higher. In middle school mathematics classes, students' entering achievement levels may be spread across five or more grade levels. Required science and social studies courses often reflect extremes of student heterogeneity, with students' entering achievement levels in reading comprehension, mathematical reasoning, and content knowledge varying greatly. In any class, some or many of your students may be English language learners. The language spoken in their homes is probably not English, and they and their parents may have a different cultural identity than students whose first language is English. Of course, any group is to some extent heterogeneous: No two students are alike. Ideally, every student should receive instruction tailored to his or her needs, abilities, interests, and learning style. In practice, the pupil–teacher ratio in most secondary schools makes large-group instruction the most common and efficient means of teaching the standard curriculum.

In highly heterogeneous classes, however, a whole-class assignment may be unchallenging or repetitious for some students and too difficult for others. Students who are bored or frustrated are not likely to stay involved in activities, and inappropriate or disruptive behavior may result. Extreme heterogeneity may therefore have an impact on the management of student behavior as well as on instruction. Attempting to cope with heterogeneity by using many different assignments, providing an individualized and self-paced program, or using small-group instruction extensively in secondary classrooms increases the complexity of classroom management, requires a great deal of planning and preparation, and may require instructional materials that are not readily available. Rather than completely alter their instructional approach, many effective teachers provide for different student abilities and interests by supplementing their whole-class instruction with the use of special materials, activities, assignments, and small-group work. The following instructional procedures will help you cope with very heterogeneous classes.

■ Assessing Entering Skills

To identify the extent of differences in needs and achievement levels (i.e., the degree of heterogeneity) in your classroom, you should use several sources of information. These sources include your tests (printed and digital), your own observation of each student, and indicators of performance available in each student's file, including assessments from prior teachers, samples of the student's work, and standardized achievement test information. If one of your students is identified as having special needs, you will certainly consult the inclusion teacher or special education coordinator. Be cautious about forming a hasty impression of a student's abilities based on any single source of information. Forming and communicating low expectations to students can cause them to achieve below their potential. Also, be wary that a bias resulting from an initial assessment might cause you to discount later information that does not support the initial evaluation.

Other ways to obtain preliminary assessments of students may be found in teacher's editions of your course texts and from other teachers in your field. Often, departmental chairpersons or curriculum coordinators have a file of classroom assessment materials, including checklists that can be used to keep a record of participation or other observable behaviors. In some academic areas, students build a portfolio of performance on a variety of tasks and achievement milestones that carries forward from one year to the next. The availability of such records from prior years will help identify students who need review, extra assistance, or enrichment in particular areas or topics.

In addition to the information available from student performance on assignments, you can gain valuable insights from performance on specially designed classroom exercises. For example, in many courses the ability to follow a presentation and take good notes is important. If note taking is a necessary skill, do a preliminary assessment by giving a short presentation, then collect and check student notes. This assessment will not only help you identify students who are likely to need special assistance, but it will also indicate the overall level of note-taking skills of all the students. Similarly, requiring that students read a short section of written material, outline it, and answer some comprehension questions in class will give you an idea of the range of students' abilities to learn from the print materials you will be using.

Information on student needs, interests, and backgrounds can also affect learning and instruction and should be considered whenever possible as you plan instructional activities and set goals. Such information can be used to plan extra-credit projects and alternative assignments and to identify small groups for instruction, to pair students for peer tutoring, or to create cooperative groups for learning activities.

■ Models for Identification

Students who have been identified as needing special education are a source of heterogeneity encountered in general education. Because their education is regulated by federal law, it will be important to understand how such students are identified. The instruction of students with special needs in the United States is covered under federal law: the Individuals with Disabilities Education Improvement Act, 2004 (also referred to as IDEA 2004). This law includes two models for determining student eligibility for special education services: IQ-achievement discrepancy and response to intervention. School districts and states vary in their designation of which model(s) to use. The IQ-discrepancy model utilizes standardized testing to determine if a student has a discrepancy between his or her ability to succeed in a subject (IQ) and his or her performance in that subject (achievement). The classroom teacher serves as the catalyst for a student's testing when that teacher suspects that a learning disability is preventing a student from learning and hence refers that child for testing by a school psychologist or other assessment professional. Criticisms of this model include these: The range of discrepancy that qualifies a student for services is arbitrary, even standardized tests can have unreliable results, and identification of students for special services does not consider the possibility of poor instruction as the cause of a student's learning difficulties.

The *response to intervention* (RTI) model is a "multi-tiered method for delivering instruction to learners through increasingly intensive and individualized interventions" (www.iris.peabody.vanderbilt.edu, Online Dictionary). Inherent in RTI is the classroom teacher's collection and analysis of data on students' academic progress on a consistent and frequent basis. Within Tier 1, the classroom teacher provides high-quality instruction (defined by IDEA 2004 as research validated) and assesses all students (i.e., universal screening) to see if any are at risk for failure. In Tier 2, the classroom teacher and/or another educational professional (e.g., Title I teacher, classroom aide) provides interventions for alternative or additional support to the students at risk (individually or within small groups) and monitors their progress. When a student is still at risk for failure after the Tier 2 interventions, Tier 3 is designed to provide more intensive instruction (which may still involve the classroom teacher) and to utilize the collected data to identify if and what special education services are needed. The qualification for services depends on a district's or state's policies as well as the results from any evaluations requested to identify specific learning disabilities. (See iris.peabody.vanderbilt.edu for a number of instructional modules on RTI.)

Criticisms of the RTI model include these: There is no specific timing, number, or type of interventions designated as sufficient; and the time and expertise required of the classroom teacher can be prohibitive, considering the teacher's other instructional responsibilities. In particular, the classroom teacher must rule out poor instruction (or a poor instructional environment) as the cause of a student's learning difficulties.

The multi-tiered approach of RTI has also been applied to student difficulties with classroom behavior. Positive behavioral interventions and supports (PBIS) involves a universal Tier 1 in which all students are provided high-quality instruction on behavioral expectations. Classroom teacher monitoring (including the collection of data) identifies students at risk for failure to meet these expectations. In Tier 2, classroom teachers provide interventions for these students and continue to monitor. Students still struggling to meet expectations are recommended for additional assistance through Tier 3. The Office of Special Education Programs of the U.S. Department of Education hosts a website to provide information and assistance to schools concerning PBIS: www.pbis.org.

Most students who receive special education services are identified before they reach secondary grades. Nonetheless, you may be involved in an annual reassessment of eligibility and need for services as well as helping plan accommodations for the student(s) in your class. Of course, you also will want to learn about any specific strategies for instruction or behavior management that are a part of a student's individualized education plan.

■ Strategies for Individual Differences

In the next sections we describe strategies frequently used to adjust for individual differences, and we examine management concerns associated with them.

Modifying Whole-Group Instruction

When you know how heterogeneous your classes are, you can plan appropriate adjustments of your instruction. Begin by considering ways that you can accommodate varying student needs simply by modifying your whole-class activities. Rather than completely alter your instructional approach, you can provide for different student abilities and interests by supplementing your whole-class instruction with the use of special materials, activities, assignments, and small-group work.

Interactive Instruction.   Try to involve all students in presentations, discussions, and recitations by making a conscious effort to call on everyone, not only those who are eager to respond. It is important to learn the names of your students quickly. Sometimes using individual cards or a classroom app such as Stick Pick to select respondents at random can help you be inclusive. Allow students who have limited access to the content because of reading difficulty the opportunity to restate the main idea or summarize another student's response. Students with a special ability or an obvious interest in a topic can be encouraged to complete special projects and to organize their ideas in oral reports to the class. These opportunities allow the students to advance their understanding and receive recognition. Guard against a tendency to focus only on the higher- (or lower-) achieving students and allowing them to set the pace for the lesson.

Procedures for Managing Student Work. In extremely heterogeneous classes, carefully planned and implemented student work procedures become especially important. When you give directions, require all students' attention, and provide both oral and written versions when feasible. Some students have difficulty remembering and following a long series of verbal directions, so break them into manageable chunks and use visual cues. Also consider asking students to repeat or rephrase the directions to check what was heard. Verify that they understand, help them practice the steps, and monitor carefully to provide corrective feedback. Be sure to check in regularly with students who have problems following directions. If you have seated them near you, you will be able to provide them with quick assistance.

Assessment and grading practices are also important to consider. Your system for managing student work should accommodate extra-credit or enrichment assignments, and it must be designed so that lower-achieving students who work diligently and make progress can make a satisfactory grade. Consider your grading system carefully. Avoid systems that give very large weights to single tests or assignments. Also, realize that using a zero for missing assignments results in "catastrophe" grading (Carifio & Carey, 2009) in which one or a few such scores makes a failing grade inevitable. The grading system should permit students to stumble occasionally but still be able to recover sufficiently to succeed overall. Three common ways to limit catastrophe grading are to drop a lowest grade, use a "basement" score of 50 for individual components when computing average grades, and/or to permit students to complete extra credit assignments.

Seating Arrangement. Students who need closer supervision or more than the usual amount of explanation should be seated near the front of the room (or wherever you usually conduct whole-class presentations). Their proximity to you will enable you to check for understanding more readily and make it easier to monitor their behavior and progress.

Assignments. If you give the same assignments to all students in a highly heterogeneous class, the work may be much too easy for some students and much too difficult for others. One size will not fit all. Look for ways to give students choices on assignments, so that individual interests can be pursued. Consider giving some assignments in two parts: a basic assignment for all students to complete and a second part that can be completed for extra challenge. When assignments are the same for everyone, the students will complete them with different degrees of proficiency and speed. In such cases, use a grading or credit system that, at least in part, emphasizes individual progress rather than competition among students. Enrichment or extra-credit material for students who finish class work early should be work related and should not distract other students. The use of technology for such activities needs to be consistent with school policies. Avoid free-time activities that are so attractive that slower-working students will feel deprived or attempt to quit or rush through their work. Set up a system for giving credit, feedback, or recognition for the completion of enrichment activities. If you allow students to read when they finish their work, be sure to provide supplementary reading material at a variety of reading levels.

Supplementary Instruction

Small Group Instruction.   In some classes or in some content areas, the preceding suggestions for modifying or supplementing whole-class instruction may not be adequate to solve the heterogeneity problem. In these classes, teachers might need to use small-group instruction, forming relatively homogeneous subgroups. This commonly occurs in reading courses, in English classes for spelling instruction, and in mathematics classes, when some students lack the skills in basic operations necessary to do more advanced work. In many subjects, small-group instruction might be used as a temporary measure with a group of students who have failed to pass a criterion-referenced test covering material that is prerequisite to subsequent units. The following are examples of how small-group instruction might be conducted in secondary classes.

> *Once a week, the teacher of an eighth-grade English class uses small-group instruction for spelling only. She has three groups: 6 students using spelling materials at the fourth-grade level, 16 at the eighth-grade level, and 5 using advanced materials to prepare them for interscholastic competition. After opening class, the teacher goes over general seat-work directions with the whole class. Seat-work directions are written on the board. They include one or two assignments (e.g., journal writing) that students can do without further explanation from the teacher. Groups 1 and 3 begin seat work while the teacher meets with the middle spelling group for content development and more seat-work directions. The teacher then meets with the first group of students for checking and content development and gives them another assignment. She checks on the middle group again before moving to content development with group 3. In the time remaining in the period, after she finishes with the last group, she gives individual help to students and monitors seat work.*
>
> *In eighth-grade math, the teacher uses whole-class instruction for approximately the first half of the lessons in each chapter. Then students are divided into two groups: one containing 6 students and one with 22 students. The smaller group, which has students who are highly deficient in math skills, uses a supplementary workbook covering essentially the same content and receives a second sequence of presentation, review, and practice similar to that for the material previously covered. The larger group continues in the textbook chapter until it has been completed.*

Although small-group instruction can help cope with extreme heterogeneity, it presents more problems than modifying whole-class instruction. It requires more extensive planning and more materials—important considerations when you must prepare for five or six different class sections. Monitoring student behavior and work is more difficult because you are instructing the groups for much of the period. The availability of an aide or classroom volunteers will make monitoring and providing ongoing assistance to individuals much easier than if the teacher has to go it alone. Another important consideration is that when small-group instruction is used, students frequently spend relatively shorter periods of time interacting with you in content development and longer periods of time in seat work. Consequently, independent work must be planned so that students can work with little assistance from the teacher. Despite all these problems, small-group instruction may sometimes be necessary to meet your students' needs, and it can be managed well with careful attention to instructional planning and classroom procedures. Some of the procedures you will have to decide on and explain to your students when you use small-group instruction follow.

Group Location.   Be sure the location of the group allows you to observe the rest of the class while you work with the small group. Other considerations include minimizing distractions and making efficient use of classroom space and time.

Decide whether you will rearrange student seating according to group or, if you have space, whether you will set up a group instruction area. Rearranging seats by group has the advantage of eliminating student movement when you change groups; you will move from one group to the other, and the students need not leave their desks. Also, you may be able to plan small-group seating so that each group is close to a different board, screen, or display area for assignments and to different storage areas (e.g., bookshelves) for materials. A disadvantage of rearranging seats according to small-group assignment is that it may have the effect of segregating students by achievement level and emphasizing differences among students. A good alternative, if you have the classroom space and workable numbers of students in each of your small groups, is to set up a table for small-group instruction at one end of your room.

Student Movement.   If you are able to set up a small-group instruction area to which your students can come, you will have to decide what procedures, rules, and signals you will use for student movement into and out of the group. Smooth and efficient transitions will depend on you explaining these procedures clearly and seeing that students follow them.

Out-of-Group Procedures.   Before using group work, you must communicate your expectations for students not in the group.

- Will students be allowed to whisper or talk, or must they maintain silence?
- Under what circumstances may they leave their seats?
- What should they do if they need assistance on the assignment and you are not available?
- What should they do when they finish their work?

In-Class Aides.   Sometimes teachers are fortunate enough to have parents or other adult volunteers, teacher aides, or university education students who help out in their classrooms. Other aides may help with materials and administrative tasks and have little contact with the students. If you have one or more aides, there are several things you can do to promote smooth functioning in your classroom. Be specific when informing the aide of his or her responsibilities for teaching or working with students and for disciplining students. Aides should enforce your rules consistently when they are in charge of students. If you must leave the room, inform students that the aide will be in charge of the class and will enforce the rules as you do. If the aide will be working with individual students or small groups, create a space that will not cause distractions for the rest of the class, particularly if you are instructing simultaneously. Students should be told whether and when they may go to the aide for help.

Inclusion

Inclusion programs for students with special needs provide support that lets them participate in as many general education classes as possible. Typically, a special education teacher works with general education teachers of designated students, both to help modify assignments and written material as specified on the students' individualized education plans (IEPs) and to work as a co-teacher within the classroom itself. Regularly scheduled planning meetings between the special education teacher and general education teachers are crucial to the success of inclusion programs because only by knowing the activities planned by the general education teachers does the special education teacher know how best to provide support. The special education teacher may need to be in the regular classroom at times, such as when students are working on assignments or projects in class. At other times, the special education teacher may give the general education teacher copies of modified assignments needed by certain students and then leave to participate in another class. Both the timing and the nature of the special education teacher's participation in class will have to be specified during planning sessions, as will the extent of lesson modifications needed to accommodate the special students' conditions. Case Study 12.2 at the end of this chapter illustrates an inclusion program at a middle school. Inclusion practices and research are described in McLeskey, Waldron, Spooner, and Algozzine (2014) and Mitchell (2008).

Content Mastery

A Content Mastery Classroom (CMC) is one to which students may come from a core subject class for extra help on assignments, new material, or projects, or to have extra time to take or study for tests. In some school districts, both a general education teacher and a special education teacher are available in CMC to help students; thus, the program serves both special and general education students who need extra assistance. In other districts, this is solely a special education option. An advantage of CMC, compared to a resource or self-contained class, is that it allows the integration of students who require special education into regular classes but provides support for them when they need more help. Also, the regular teacher, who may have 30 other students, does not have to provide as much supplemental instruction. Another advantage is that students may be sent as needed or may request to go when they feel they need extra help.

It is important to coordinate with the CMC teacher(s) about the students who may be sent, when they may be sent, and what kind of information and materials they will need to take with them. For younger students, a laminated assignment card with the student's name and grade level printed on it may be helpful. When a student is to go to CMC, you might write a brief description of the help the student needs, page numbers in the text that the student will take along, and the time the student leaves your room. The CMC teacher may also have routines for getting information about the students' assignments, work, and so on.

When you have one or more students who use CMC regularly, you must provide assignments ahead of time (e.g., weekly) so that appropriate planning can be done by the CMC teacher. When students take your tests in CMC, be sure you have discussed expectations for assistance with the teacher. The IEP written for each student with special needs should be reviewed to identify desirable instructional and assessment accommodations. Because the CMC teacher will have worked with your students individually, he or she may have suggestions for adapting instruction or management that will aid you in teaching the student. The CMC teacher may be reluctant to give unsolicited advice, so be sure to ask if you have questions about how best to work with particular students.

Individualized Instruction

When each student receives instruction, is given assignments at a level established by a careful assessment of entering skills, and is encouraged to progress at whatever pace his or her abilities and motivation allow, the instructional program is said to be individualized. Proponents of both Universal Design for Learning (www.cast.org) and Differentiated Instruction (www.differentiationcentral.com) utilize some level of individualization, often offered through flexibility and choice. Digital resources and technology greatly enhance the ability to provide both choice and instructional support on an individual level. Some educators consider individualized instruction the best means of coping with heterogeneity because it offers, at least in principle, instruction tailored to the needs of each student. However, individualized instruction can be difficult to implement. It requires (1) careful and continuous assessment of individuals' progress, (2) management of time so that all students receive adequate interactive instruction from the teacher, (3) sufficient resources that include materials suitable for all ability levels in the class, and (4) time for the teacher to plan and develop appropriate activities. The absence of one or more of these features limits the effectiveness of individualized instruction. Therefore, such programs should be implemented gradually, allowing adequate time to develop the necessary resources.

Sometimes the teacher's role in individualization diminishes to the point that almost all of the time is devoted to making assessments, giving assignments, keeping records, and checking. When this occurs, students receive little interactive instruction from the teacher and do little except complete assigned tasks, and they soon begin to equate *learning* with *finishing*. The teacher's diminished instructional role may be partly due to the incorrect perception that because instruction is individualized, the teacher can instruct only one student at a time. In fact, it is far more efficient if the teacher presents information to and conducts instruction with groups of students, supplementing the group lessons with individual instruction for students who require extra help.

Areas of management that require attention during individualized instruction include the following:

Transitions.   Students engaged in individual rather than group activities generally finish their work at different rates. If the next activity is also individually based, many transitions will occur throughout the period of instruction, with a potential for causing confusion and lost time. Some students may not know what to do next; others may delay starting the next activity. A routine for students to follow will be helpful. For example, post written assignments somewhere to move students to the next task, or have students signal the teacher when their work is ready to be assessed.

Monitoring Behavior.   Different expectations for students doing different activities, along with a variety of simultaneous activities, make monitoring student behavior during individualized instruction difficult. Because the teacher often instructs individual students or performs other tasks associated with individualized instruction (such as assessment), monitoring becomes complex. To overcome these problems, consider the following key behaviors:

- Be organized. Know what all students are supposed to be doing at any given time so that you can support their efforts and prevent problems.
- Be sure students know what they are expected to do and what conduct is appropriate in different activities.
- Be alert for students who are having trouble getting started or finishing an activity so that you can provide help. Don't be engrossed in helping one or a few students, and don't wait until students quit working or become disruptive before providing assistance.
- Circulate among the students, and look at their work periodically. Scan the room frequently to detect early signs of frustration or task avoidance.
- Usually a few students require more supervision than others. When possible, be sure these students are seated where you can observe and assist them readily.

Encouraging Student Responsibility for Work.   Using an individualized instruction program does not guarantee that students will accept responsibility for completing assignments and participating in learning activities. In fact, some students take advantage of the more complex instructional arrangements and limitations on the teacher's monitoring capability to avoid responsibility and to expend minimal effort. To avoid these problems, make sure directions for assignments and other activities are clear. Many teachers prefer to review directions with students at the beginning of the period devoted to individualized instruction. List a basic set of activities on the board, and review them; or give students activity or assignment folders that list what is to be done, and check off completed work. This system helps both you and the students keep track of progress. Utilizing technology tools, such as online spreadsheets and documents, can also provide a means for tracking progress as well as an additional source for teacher–student communication. Setting time limits for work on one activity before students proceed to the next will help them pace their efforts.

Students should expect their work to be checked frequently. If they become accustomed to simply completing one activity and starting a new one without feedback, they may practice errors, and their performance will deteriorate. Develop monitoring procedures that include periodic progress checks and evaluation, as well as formative assessment on completed assignments and other work. It is also important to review overall student progress and decide whether the pace and scope of work are adequate. Some teachers prefer to do this in weekly or every-other-week reviews and a short conference with individual students.

Additional Strategies

Student Cooperation: Help From Peers.   Another method for coping with heterogeneity is to have students help other students. Examples of such peer-helping arrangements include the following:

- Students work in pairs on the content objectives, comprehension, or problem solving activities assigned as independent work.
- When the teacher is busy with small-group or individualized instruction, students who need help are encouraged to get assistance from another student before interrupting the teacher.
- A capable, mature student is assigned as a helper for another student who needs frequent assistance. The helper's responsibilities are to answer questions and explain directions.
- Students may be permitted to help or seek help from a neighbor on some independent work activities.

When using student helpers, recognize the potential for excessive noise, poor attention to the task, or excessive reliance on the helper by the "helpee." Also, not all students are amenable to this type of arrangement or will work well together. Negative effects can be averted by communicating clearly what is and is not permitted and by monitoring the helping arrangements and relationships to prevent undesirable side effects. For all of these variations from regular instruction patterns, gradual introduction of new arrangements gives the best opportunity for managing their implementation and for correcting problems.

Peer Tutoring.   An extension of the preceding instructional modification, peer tutoring provides an opportunity for an individual to receive one-on-one assistance. When time permits, it can be done on a short-term, ad-hoc basis during class time by asking a student who has achieved a certain level or learned a concept to work with another student who has not. The student who receives assistance benefits from individualized instruction. The helper, or peer tutor, benefits from planning for and providing instruction.

Teachers sometimes make arrangements to have volunteer tutors available before or after school, or during lunchtime. Students who want to tutor or be tutored can sign up ahead of time, and the teacher keeps the classroom open or arranges for another location for the tutoring to take place.

Effective peer tutoring requires that certain management issues be addressed. You must decide when tutoring is and is not acceptable. There may be topics for which peer tutoring is not appropriate. And peer tutors must have enough knowledge of the content to be able to provide assistance. When tutoring occurs during class time, you must determine where tutoring will occur. Some teachers provide a special location within the classroom where peer interactions are less likely to interrupt other classroom activities or disturb students who are working unassisted. Others may allow students to work quietly side by side at their desks or tables.

If you are going to use peer tutors frequently, it is a good idea to discuss with them the behaviors their role requires. Potential peer tutors should be shown how to model desired behaviors (e.g., demonstrate a skill or explain a concept), instructed in how to ask questions to assess the other student's understanding, and counseled on interpersonal behaviors. For long-term peer tutors, you may be able to provide brief training during class or before or after school. Other directions can be given as part of the instructions for an activity.

Cooperative Work Groups.   For many activities, using small work groups or learning teams with mixed ability levels and/or diverse backgrounds provides a good opportunity for all students to help and learn from each other. Often, such groups are used as an alternative to independent work after the teacher has provided whole-class instruction. Sometimes groups are used extensively to organize instructional activities in a class, as in project-based learning. There is considerable evidence (see reviews in the Chapter 8 reading list) that working in mixed-ability teams can benefit both higher- and lower-achieving students in many subject areas. Benefits of cooperative groups can include increased student achievement, positive race relations, and increased student self-esteem. Not all researchers or educators agree that learning teams are as effective as their proponents have argued. We believe, however, that the weight of the evidence supports the use of cooperative groups as helpful in addressing many of the issues created by heterogeneity. Chapter 8 presents guidelines for managing cooperative groups, so we will not pursue the topic further here.

■ Teaching Remedial Classes

In many secondary schools, especially in core academic subjects, students are assigned to classes on the basis of their prior academic record, standardized test scores, teacher recommendations, diagnostic placement tests, or some combination of these factors. This process of homogeneous ability grouping results in the formation of several sections of a subject (e.g., AP/honors/high, average, and low sections) or, possibly, in special remedial classes for students deficient in basic skills. Remedial level classes are frequently smaller in size because administrators recognize that their students need more individual assistance and technology support for instruction. Such grouping practices are carried out on the assumption that they help schools provide instruction that meets the needs of all students. Whether homogeneous grouping accomplishes this putative goal or instead results in a harmful segregation of lower-achieving secondary students is a topic that has been debated and researched for some time (Hallinan, 1990; Loveless, 1999; Oakes, 2005; Slavin, 1990). As can be inferred from this chapter's extensive presentation of strategies for managing heterogeneous classes, we believe that it is possible to accommodate substantial individual differences in a regular classroom setting. It is also the case that many teachers, other educators, and the communities they serve believe that teaching and learning at the secondary level can be accomplished more efficiently when the range of achievement in a class is not too great. The practice of homogeneous grouping is therefore likely to continue, even where there is an emphasis on accommodating diversity.

"My mom told me to tell you that I am the educational challenge you were told about in college."

Betty Heiser Zedonek

Concentrating lower-achieving students in homogeneous groups can exacerbate management problems. Poor classroom management and organization in a remedial class can result in a classroom climate in which any student would have difficulty learning. It is possible, however, to manage such classes effectively and to maintain student involvement in learning activities with little disruption. When such classes are effectively managed, students can make progress in the subject and complete the course with positive attitudes. Most students will do their work if they have a reasonable chance of success, and they will pay attention and cooperate with the teacher. Obtaining good results with a lower-track class requires extra effort both in managing behavior and in organizing instruction. The following sections describe how to use that effort efficiently.

Learner Characteristics

Students in remedial classes are usually achieving two or more grade levels below average students at their grade and age levels. Their grades in the subject have usually been low in the past, and some may have failed the subject in a previous year. These students bring with them more than their share of problems, some resulting from their lower achievement and some contributing to lower achievement. Absence and tardiness rates are often higher in such classes. The completion rate for assignments, particularly for homework, may be lower than in other classes. The students are likely to view grades as arbitrary, failing to see a connection between their class work and homework and the grades they receive in a course. Frequent failure in school in the past has caused some of these students to become very discouraged, and they may react by giving up easily or by fighting back. Teachers may encounter these reactions in the extremes of apathy, belligerence, or clowning around in class. Some of these students are very poor readers, which causes them problems in all subject areas. Others may have poor memory abilities. Most have poor study skills (in taking notes, outlining, being organized and methodical, and pacing efforts on long-term assignments). Maintaining their attention for long periods of time is often difficult, particularly when they encounter a demanding or frustrating task.

When considering these general characteristics, keep two important points in mind. First, a homogeneous low-level class is not homogeneous at all. Such a class contains students with a range of achievement levels, academic aptitudes, other talents, learning disabilities, goals and aspirations, attitudes toward school, and family backgrounds. Avoid making assumptions about individual students just because they have been placed in a remedial class. Second, the preceding description of general characteristics of students at low academic levels might be interpreted as a list of reasons that teaching such classes effectively is difficult (or impossible). It is not intended as such. Instead, it is a description of needs that should be addressed by the management and organization plan for such a class. These general characteristics suggest some special considerations with regard to monitoring student behavior and work; establishing classroom procedures, rules, and grading and accountability procedures; and organizing and presenting instruction.

Establishing Your Management System

Establishing good working relationships with students is important. In Chapter 2, we examined this aspect of classroom management in detail, describing a two-dimensional model of relationships consisting of *influence* and *affect*. Both of these dimensions are relevant in remedial classes. Teachers of such classes need to take charge, provide clear guidelines for behavior, follow through consistently with their expectations, and establish caring, respectful connections with the students.

In low-track classes, particularly in the early secondary grades, extra class time and attention may be required to teach students classroom procedures, rules, and routines at the beginning of the year. There may be more absences, shorter student attention spans, less ability to remember, and more testing of limits in such classes than in other class sections. Consequently, you need to give extra attention to explaining, demonstrating, reviewing, and reminding students about your expectations. Do not limit your discussion of rules and procedures to only the first day or two of school; plan to introduce and reinforce classroom procedures and routines gradually and systematically. Do not assume that students understand everything the first time you explain it; question them, provide practice, and give them feedback. A "fun" written quiz on classroom procedures, routines, and requirements at the end of the first week of classes can be helpful in solidifying students' understanding of your expectations.

Monitoring and Guiding Behavior

An absolutely essential ingredient of management is monitoring: You must be aware of what is occurring in your room. Keep your eyes on the students and scan the room frequently. If you see inappropriate behavior, deal with it promptly; when possible, use unobtrusive measures to stop it. Simple interventions work best, such as eye contact, proximity to the students, and refocusing the students' attention on their academic tasks. For example, "If you have questions about this work, raise your hand and I'll come help you" or "You should be working on the first five problems, not talking. When you finish number 5, raise your hand and I will check your work." Prompt handling minimizes the number of students involved and thus avoids creating peer pressure to resist the teacher or show off. Finally, you give the correct impression of fairness and consistency in handling problems. When these simple, relatively unobtrusive interventions are not effective, the additional strategies described in Chapter 11 are available.

Managing Student Work

The cornerstone of managing student work in lower-level classes is an emphasis on daily and weekly grades. Such a system provides students with frequent feedback; it increases students' chances of success by making it difficult for individuals to fall far behind; it allows you to monitor student progress closely; and it helps develop good student work habits. When students experience success, it's very reinforcing and improves motivation. Additionally, receiving some kind of grade or credit for effort and performance each day helps students accept responsibility for their schoolwork, especially if you have them keep a record sheet. You must allow time in class to show them how to follow this procedure. Have each student compute a weekly grade by calculating an average each week. You may have to teach them how to do this. Once established as a regular class procedure, it will help your students keep track of their progress.

Consider making appropriate participation in class a part of your grading system. Participation includes answering when called on, volunteering questions, bringing appropriate materials to class, being on time, raising one's hand before speaking, and not calling out to other students or being out of one's seat. Rewarding participation encourages involvement, learning, and attendance. There are several ways to include participation in your grading system. You can give weekly or daily points for each student to add to his or her daily assignment score. You can minimize bookkeeping time by giving participation scores as a closing activity. If your system is simple (e.g., 3 points = good participation; 2 points = some; 1 point = a little; 0 = none, or disturbed class), you can award and record points to 20 or so students in a minute or two at the end of class.

You can also help keep students accountable by making it clear that everyone is expected to participate in class discussions. To achieve this, use a system that ensures that you call on every student at least once or twice. You might also keep a weekly answer sheet. Put each student's name on it and give checks for good answers during recitation. You can then award points at the end of the week or when figuring weekly averages.

Planning and Presenting Instruction

More student learning and better classroom behavior are likely to result if you (1) organize classroom instruction into short activity segments with frequent assessments of student understanding, (2) pay extra attention to presenting directions and instruction clearly, and (3) build the teaching of study skills into your lessons. When planning classroom activities, avoid activity plans requiring that students attend to a presentation or work continuously for 25 or 30 minutes in the same seat-work activity. Instead, use two or more cycles of content development and classwork or independent work, as described and illustrated in Chapter 7. There are two distinct advantages to using several cycles instead of one. One advantage is that it is easier to maintain student involvement in shorter time segments. Another advantage is that by careful monitoring, you can more easily observe the extent to which students are able to complete the assignments. This allows you to pace instruction appropriately and to give corrective feedback and repetition during a later content development activity.

Clear communication is important in all classes, but in remedial classes, clear directions and instruction are especially important; careless, overly complex communication is likely to result in student confusion and frustration. Pay careful attention to the amount of information presented at one time and use appropriate vocabulary and concrete or specific examples to illustrate new concepts. Check for understanding frequently. Avoid overlapping many procedural directions. Get everyone's attention and then present directions in a step-by-step fashion, waiting for students to complete each step before going on to the next. Finally, as you teach, watch for opportunities to help your students improve their study and school survival skills. For example, assume that you must teach all your students how to take notes in your class. Provide demonstration, assistance, practice, monitoring, and feedback. Use content presentations or discussions of written material as vehicles for teaching students how to identify main ideas and supporting evidence. Include in your course instructional activities that will help students build their vocabularies and improve their computation or memorization skills.

■ Working With Students With Special Needs

This section deals with students who have special needs because they are physically or cognitively challenged, because they have language differences, or because life circumstances or some emotional or behavioral characteristic affects their classroom functioning. Some of these students may have been identified as eligible for special education services, whereas others may fall outside the perimeter of these classifications. According to the Digest of Education Statistics (Auld, Wilkinson-Flicker, Nachazel, & Dziuba, 2013) approximately 13% (6.4 million) of public school students receive special education services. Around 60% of these students are in regular education classrooms most of the time (80% or more). The special education category with the largest number of students is Learning Disability (36%), followed by Speech and Language Impaired (21%), Other Health Impaired (12%), Autism (7%), Intellectual Disability (7%), Developmental Delay (6%), and Multiple Disabilities (2%). Visually Impaired, Hearing Impaired, and Orthopedic are 1% or less.

Students with a diagnosed disability in one of these categories are covered by the Individuals with Disabilities Education Act (IDEA). Specific rules must be followed by school districts to assure that they receive an appropriate education. One of these rules is that each student has an IEP that identifies the services the student will receive and that sets annual goals for the child. Not all students who need instructional modifications or assistance will be identified as requiring special education services and an IEP. For example, students with attention deficit hyperactivity disorder (ADHD) *might* receive special education services under the Other Health Impaired category. However, some students with ADHD will receive services or instructional modifications under a 504 Plan, which is also used for other conditions and health problems that do not fall within the specific categories of special education noted previously. The 504 Plan gets its name from Section 504 of the Rehabilitation Act of 1973 and is used to address the educational needs of individuals who may not be covered under IDEA. For more information about the specifics of IEP and 504 plans or about the policies established by IDEA and Section 504, refer to www.iris.peabody.vanderbilt.edu or www.understood.org/en/school-learning/special-services.

Students who are identified as special education students are, by law, provided instruction in the least restrictive environment. As a result, more and more students with special needs are being served in the regular classroom with some outside help from specialized teachers. Meeting the needs of these students presents special challenges to teachers with a classroom full of other students. Large class sizes and the push to cover prescribed content in regular education greatly limit the amount of individualized planning and instruction for students with special needs. At the secondary level, teacher planning and instruction generally focus on the whole-class and group levels. Research indicates that these factors, along with classroom management concerns, limit the amount of attention teachers give to individual students' knowledge acquisition (Vaughn & Schumm, 1994; Vaughn, Schumm, Jallad, Slusher, & Saumell, 1996). It therefore requires conscious effort to take special needs of students into account and especially to keep abreast of their degree of understanding and progress.

Fortunately, research offers specific guidelines to help teachers work with these students in ways that promote their peer acceptance and their self-esteem as well as their academic achievement (Kauffman & Hallahan, 2014; Swanson, Harris, & Graham, 2013; Mitchell, 2008). Although the sections that follow are focused on students with special needs and instructional formats to serve them, many of the strategies are also appropriate for all students who have difficulty with learning and whose academic work is below grade level. The goal of many of these procedures is to increase the students' degree of participation. Such active engagement is an important condition for learning that many struggling students may lack.

Students With Learning Disabilities

Although there is still no consensus on a concise definition of *learning disability*, certain characteristics are commonly seen. One primary feature is more difficulty with and lower achievement in certain academic areas than would otherwise be expected, based on these students' overall ability levels. Other common problems experienced by these students are disorganization and a disconcerting tendency to forget something they seemed to have understood thoroughly just a short time earlier. Often accompanying these difficulties are the students' natural sense of frustration and the potential for anger or hopelessness, along with a negative view of themselves.

Students with learning disabilities generally respond well to a positive and structured approach with predictable routines. They may forget steps even in familiar routines, however, and require much patience and repetition. These students need more help than others in learning to identify and pay attention to relevant cues. Point out cues and relevant directions, and have students repeat directions out loud to be sure they understand what to do. Emphasize what is correct rather than what they are doing wrong. Model the appropriate behavior or actions to ensure that they are transferring positive learning rather than reinforcing negative learning. Avoid trial-and-error activities in which students may spend too much time doing the wrong thing, thus adding to their confusion. Overlearning is important for these students, especially because of their retention problems. It is more helpful to distribute numerous short sessions over a period of time than to have fewer and longer sessions. Students with learning challenges also benefit from a wide range of multisensory experiences to assist them in learning concepts and to help them overcome problems of inexperience.

Be aware that although social praise may help motivate, it may also interfere with the development of independent decision-making skills. When praising a student, be conscious of its feedback function, so that you identify specifically what was praiseworthy. Give recognition for accomplishment, for good effort, and for improved performance. Avoid generalized, nonspecific praise, which may only direct attention elsewhere and miss getting the desired result.

A learning disability by itself does not make behavior problems more likely. However, students with a learning disability who do not receive effective intervention for their learning problems are apt to experience frustration with their schoolwork and lower performance, which may contribute to a variety of behavior problems. Such problems may be addressed by strategies that have been presented elsewhere in this book, in addition to interventions directed at the student's specific learning problems (see the Who Will I Teach? section of Chapter 11).

Students With Emotional and/or Behavioral Problems

Students with a diagnosed emotional or behavioral disorder (Walker & Gresham, 2014) are often different from others mainly in the degree of emotionality they exhibit and in their ability to regulate their behavior in response to these emotions rather than in the types of feelings they have. Such students may be in the average or above average range on intellectual ability. Any psychological report available can be quite informative (it must, of course, be treated confidentially) both in shedding light on why the students are having such problems and in providing recommendations for working with them. You might also obtain useful information from the school psychologist, the special education teacher, the student's parents, therapists, or anyone else who knows the student well. A behavior management plan may have been developed through the special education department; becoming familiar with it and clear on how to follow it may prevent many problems.

If externalizing, acting-out behavior is a serious issue, be sure you are familiar with the steps laid out in the student's behavior intervention plan. In general, overlook minor inappropriate behavior, reinforce acceptable behavior, and reduce known stressors. This may include lowering your expectations temporarily when the student is having an especially bad day. Be careful about threatening to punish the student ("Do this or else I'll . . .") in the heat of the moment. Such statements undermine your credibility if you don't follow through or will intensify a power struggle if you've stated an unreasonable consequence or demand. A positive, supportive, structured, and predictable environment is always a help to these students, who benefit from feeling safe and accepted.

If you have students who sometimes have temper outbursts or become easily frustrated and angry, reinforce all of their attempts toward self-control. Learn to recognize behavioral cues that may precede an outburst so that you can intervene to prevent their losing control. Maintain a balanced perspective about such students; for them, getting through the day without an outburst may be more important than following instructions to the letter or completing assignments perfectly. Offering structured choices can be helpful, especially with students who have a strong need to control and who thus often appear noncompliant and oppositional (e.g., "Would you prefer to do the odd-numbered problems or the even-numbered?" "Would it be helpful for you to work awhile in the study carrel, or do you think you can concentrate well enough at your own desk?").

Work with the principal and special education staff to devise a plan to carry out if students with emotional problems become angry or aggressive in your classroom and no plan has been developed. These students may need to leave the classroom for a while to regain control in a safe time-out area. They will have to be supervised as they cool down. If there is an adult on the grounds who has good rapport with the students (e.g., a special education teacher or aide), try to have that person talk with them.

These students often do not know why they lose control, although they frequently tend to blame something or someone else if required to explain. They do not generally understand how their feelings relate to what has happened and have not yet learned to discern the subtle inner changes that trigger such outbursts. Helping them recognize the signs of increasing tension and suggesting ways to defuse before they have an outburst increases their sense of control and self-esteem. After an incident, a student may be remorseful or embarrassed; when both you and the student have regained your composure, it is important that you reestablish your relationship. Other than attempting to learn from each incident in an effort to prevent future occurrences, it is best if the teacher leaves each incident behind and does not remind the student of past failures.

One crucial reminder: When students lose control and are verbally or physically abusive, the abuse is rarely directed at you personally, even though it may sound and feel as though it is. If you have learned about the backgrounds of these students, logic will tell you that you are merely the convenient target, not the root cause, of their pain or rage. Logic and feelings do not always mesh, however, so you may need a listener who can give you support and feedback when you are dealing with extremely volatile students.

Students who frequently lose self-control are not good candidates for inclusion in a regular education classroom. Their status should be reevaluated by the special education multidisciplinary committee that deals with the student's IEP and makes placement decisions.

Students With Serious Social Deficits, Often Diagnosed With Autism Spectrum Disorder

Increasing numbers of students who have odd or severe social skills problems are being diagnosed as having *autism spectrum disorder (ASD)*, also known as *pervasive developmental disorder (PDD)*. The reason for the increasing numbers has been debated and is not clear (Leonard et al., 2010). A milder form of the disorder is called *Asperger syndrome* (www.nimh.nih.gov/health/topics/autism-spectrum-disor-ders-asd/index.shtml). Research-based National Standards from the National Autism Center will help teachers plan effectively to interact with students along this spectrum (www.nationalautismcenter.org/national-standards-project/). As very young children, some of these students appear to be especially bright because of their ability to learn, remember, and recite facts. As they grow older, however, it becomes apparent that they have limited understanding of these facts and cannot generalize or apply any of the things they relate so accurately. Another severe deficiency becomes apparent: Although highly verbal, they have extremely poor communication skills. They tend to stand too close, avoid eye contact, talk too long and loudly in a preaching or robotic manner, and talk in great detail about factual matters that do not interest their peers.

Further, individuals with ASD may be quite rigid in their outlook and develop set ways of doing things. They escalate quickly into extreme and visible anxiety when a routine is changed or when their expectations are not met. They may also have an acute sensitivity to sounds, with loud noises causing pain to their ears. Frequently, they have concomitant learning disabilities and poor gross and fine motor skills. When emotionally aroused, some individuals may engage in repetitive stereotyped movements such as hand flapping.

When students have had such problems to a severe degree, it is very likely that they have already been referred for special education services, and you can be fairly sure that during elementary school various interventions have been tried. Some attempt has probably been made to teach them adaptive ways to cope with their strong need for regularity and skills for coping with anxiety. When these students have at least average intellectual abilities, they can usually succeed in regular education classes and can thrive on the intellectual stimulation. However, their unique reactions and behaviors, despite the coping mechanisms they have learned, require that you understand their difficulties and use strategies to help them tolerate anxiety-provoking situations such as unanticipated change, movement, or noise. The following teaching strategies can help support these students in the regular classroom.

1. Use visual cues and prompts. Because students with ASD are visual rather than verbal learners, demonstrate physically how you want things done and use manipulatives and visual cues (e.g., timers, written schedules, pictures, labels) whenever possible.
2. Avoid giving both an auditory and a visual task at one time. Often these students cannot process both inputs simultaneously—they cannot both look and listen at the same time.
3. Make instructions brief. Students with ASD often have trouble remembering sequences, especially how they are to apply instructions. Write instructions for them, or check to be sure they have written them correctly. Focus on giving only one or two instructions at a time.
4. Do not insist that they maintain eye contact with you. Eye contact is extremely difficult and anxiety-producing for them, but you may insist on their attention in other ways.

5. Use "social stories" or "social scripting" techniques, which can be effective in helping these students prepare for new events, experiences, or changes in routine. Scripts and stories are most often used in elementary schools, but they may be helpful in middle and high schools to prevent an escalation of anxiety and facilitate a smooth transition through new experiences or changes in routine. The teacher may write out a story or help the student do so before the event. The goal is to familiarize the student with the change in routine ahead of time. Example: "On Thursday, I am not going to math class from homeroom. I am going with my homeroom class to an assembly in the auditorium. After the assembly, I will go to math class."

6. Capitalize on students' strengths and interests. Students with ASD may be skilled at computer work or drawing; or they may become absorbed with a particular topic such as maps, weather, trains, or electronics. Reward them for completing assignments and provide ways for them to develop their talents and contribute positively in class.

7. Give them specific social feedback and step-by-step instructions. These students do not learn social skills readily by observing others, so be alert to awkward situations and be ready to step in. If you cannot provide needed instruction in the social areas, ask the special education teacher or counselor about any problems you see. Consider using the social scripting technique to help these students when they are in extensive peer interactions.

Students With Attention Deficit Hyperactivity Disorder (ADHD)

Behavioral characteristics of students with ADHD include distractibility, short attention span, impulsiveness, an inability to organize, and a high level of movement. These symptoms vary in degree as well as combination. Some students with ADHD are mainly distractible, with short attention spans. Others are also very impulsive and disorganized. When the features of the disorder are mild and students' academic skills are average or above average, these students usually manage to compensate and function reasonably well. When academic abilities are weak and/or when impulsive and distractible behaviors are frequent, however, students experience considerable adjustment problems in most classrooms. Frequent communication with parents may be necessary to ensure that school and home techniques and expectations are compatible.

It is important to remember that these behaviors are not deliberate and that even highly motivated students can find it very difficult to learn ways to compensate for or control these problems. By the time these students have reached middle or high school, many have experienced much failure and have become discouraged and negative. Fortunately, there are ways of working with these students that increase the likelihood of success (Rooney, 2014; DuPaul, Laracy, & Gormley, 2014).

1. A positive and low-keyed, relaxed approach with much predictability and structure is almost imperative. Simple routines and clear rules and guidelines for behavior, along with friendly but consistent application, help these students.

2. Early in the year, ask other adults who know these students what works best for them. Consider consulting with the students themselves, their parents, and previous teachers or special education teachers.

3. Be sure you have the students' attention before giving oral instructions.

4. Make directions clear and brief.

5. When instructions involve a series of steps, provide them in written as well as oral form, or have the students copy down the steps and mark each one as it is completed.

6. Observe these students as they begin working on any new assignment; be willing to go over directions again individually.

7. Remind the students that accuracy is more important than speed; encourage checking over work before handing it in. Reinforce effort and, when feasible, do not penalize for messy work or errors that are not directly pertinent to the objectives of the activity.

8. During long periods of seat work, have a plan for these students to move around at least occasionally—for example, by bringing up their papers after they have completed part of the assignment. During whole-class activities, use eye contact and response opportunities to keep the students engaged.

9. Adjust the amount of work required within a time period to be compatible with the attention span of these students. The amount may be increased gradually as their ability to concentrate increases.

10. Find a spot with few distractions, and offer these students the option of doing independent work there.

Students who are highly impulsive and distractible may quickly attract your negative attention. If you find yourself frequently correcting such students and are drawn into arguments and power struggles with them, try to refocus your attention on their positive characteristics and behaviors, and try to find things to praise and support. Whenever possible, use redirection, choices, and other unobtrusive interventions to keep the students on task.

Students Who Are Deaf or Hearing-Impaired

Students with a serious hearing loss may be able to function in regular classes if some crucial modifications are made. Should you have such a student, consult with a teacher specializing in auditory handicaps to learn about your particular student's needs and about techniques that might benefit him or her. If assistive devices are available (e.g., FM auditory systems, caption decoders for videos), the specialist can show you how to use them.

It is usually best to seat these students near the center of the room, close to the front. If possible, project instructional content on a screen when presenting so that students can see your face. Have the room well-lit so that they can clearly see your lips and face to lip-read. Do not stand in front of windows or a bright doorway while talking; if you do, the glare behind you will make your face difficult to see.

Students with a hearing loss often miss out on important information, being able to catch only portions of words or phrases. Because understanding is more complex than just hearing or responding to a name and because these students are often reluctant to ask you to repeat, you must make a habit of repeating and rephrasing important information or instructions. When possible, provide written backup as well. The amount of new content vocabulary introduced routinely may be overwhelming to these students. The support of an auditory specialist in preteaching vocabulary may be necessary to help them succeed in a regular classroom. Content Mastery may be used to assist or to reteach, especially with written language assignments.

During classroom discussions, you should restate other students' questions and responses when feasible because students who are deaf or hearing impaired are often unable to lip-read them. Check frequently for understanding during guided practice by asking them questions. They will require close monitoring as they begin written work. If note taking is required, you may be able to provide a copy or enlist the assistance of a good student with legible handwriting who is willing to take notes. Students cannot take notes and lip-read at the same time. You might also assign buddies to cue these students when it is important to watch the teacher, to locate information in the text being discussed, and so on.

Increasingly, students who are deaf or hard-of-hearing are being assigned interpreters to accompany them to regular classes. Interpreters may serve as oral or sign language interpreters and provide a communication bridge between teacher and student. As such, they relay information both from the teacher to the student and vice versa. An interpreter should not function as a teacher's assistant in the classroom but should support the assigned student. A consultation with the specialist on your campus can be helpful in clarifying the interpreter's role.

Middle and high school students with an auditory impairment may need to have contact with a resource teacher, not only for assistance with written language and content vocabulary, but also to explore the social and emotional impact of being teenagers with a hearing loss. The time spent with a resource person learning coping strategies and/or assistive technology provides important information and skills, allowing older students to gain more independence in managing their hearing loss in light of the changing social contexts of adolescence and adulthood.

Students Who Have Visual Impairments

Students who are blind or visually impaired may be able to function well in regular classes with your help. Suggestions for adaptations of teaching methods and materials should be available in the students' functional visual assessments, written by a teacher of these students. The following suggestions may provide direction.

1. Remember to read aloud anything that is written/displayed on a board or screen.
2. Allow the students to record or to have fellow students make copies of their notes for parents to read aloud at home. Large type, dark print, and good contrast are easier to see.

3. When possible, use tactile models and hands-on activities along with oral descriptions to demonstrate concepts. These students often miss gestures, facial expressions, and details in demonstrations.
4. Encourage students to ask for help. If you are in doubt about how you can help, ask them directly, and do not hesitate to discuss their vision problems with them.
5. Remember that students with partial vision may tire more quickly, in part because of the concentration and effort required to perceive material close to their eyes. Frequent changes in the focus of activities may alleviate the strain.
6. Seat these students with their backs to the windows. Glare on materials, on someone who is speaking, or on the boards and displays interferes with their ability to use partial vision.
7. Allow these students to walk up to boards or other displays as needed.
8. Students with visual impairments may have limited knowledge of spatial relationships and directionality. They may miss social cues and thus need assistance in peer interactions and personal adjustment.

Students Living in Extreme Poverty

Some schools have increasing numbers of students who live in significant poverty, requiring adjustments and understanding on the part of school staff. It is well known that childhood poverty is linked to lower academic achievement, and there is evidence that the stress resulting from chronic childhood poverty causes lower cognitive functioning (i.e., working memory) in young adults (Evans & Schamberg, 2009). A key to success for these students is a strong, trusting relationship with a teacher in an environment in which they feel safe, not threatened or stressed (see the Who Will I Teach? section in Chapter 2). You may be the one to help them understand how school can ultimately benefit them and why it is worth the trouble for them to attend regularly and work hard. Although by the time they reach secondary schools such students probably understand the kinds of things that get them into trouble and make teachers angry, they may not be able to articulate why they have such difficulty meeting school expectations or the specific differences between the culture of the school and the equally strict but more informal culture of their neighborhood. Talking with them respectfully, finding out what they are thinking, and listening and responding thoughtfully and without criticism will help build this trust and provide insights into their life and perceptions.

Adolescents coming from a culture of poverty are likely to present themselves differently from those brought up in a culture more compatible with school expectations. They may talk more loudly than other students and be quicker to defend themselves against perceived threats. When an adult is talking to them, they are more likely to read body language and to interpret tone of voice and facial expressions because they may have learned hypervigilance and sensitivity to such cues as vital survival skills. In impoverished neighborhoods, great emphasis is placed on saving face. Although this is important to most adolescents, it is of paramount importance to those living in extreme poverty. When being disciplined, therefore, these students may shrug or laugh off a teacher's reprimand, or they may talk back in a manner the teacher interprets as insolent, because they are willing to get into more trouble to keep from appearing weak to their peers. In their neighborhoods, the slow and weak may be exploited and victimized. Take great care not to overreact to or humiliate these students, and whenever possible, discipline them in private. This protects their dignity, reduces their need for defiance, and shows your sensitivity to their well-being even as you require that they follow the rules.

Practical approaches to working with these students can be found in Payne (2013). Because such students are often at risk for educational disadvantage, strategies suitable for this population (Hargis, 1997) are also applicable. The following suggestions will be helpful when working with students from impoverished backgrounds.

1. Have extra supplies and materials on hand for these students to use when they don't have them. Determine whether the school or district has a fund for such items or whether there are community organizations that provide assistance.
2. Teach procedures step by step. Encourage self-talk that focuses on the steps.
3. Because they are often preoccupied with problems at home, help them "bracket" their anxieties, to put off worrying about something until a specific later time. Obviously, you will not do this if the problem needs to be addressed immediately.
4. Assign a peer buddy and encourage them to discuss problems and solutions together. These students benefit from interaction with peers, so when you use cooperative groups, monitor their groups' behavior and progress to be sure they are participating fully.
5. Because these students often need a guide to the underlying assumptions for behavioral expectations, use a three-step approach: (1) point out what they are supposed to do; (2) give meaning (reasons); and (3) provide a strategy (how to do it).
6. Encourage positive self-talk that will enhance their feelings of self-control: "I do this for myself. Not for the teacher, not for my parents, but for myself."
7. Teach goal setting. Have them write down a concrete plan for class today, and at the end of class, see what goals have been met.
8. Allow them to help another student with something they do well.
9. Work on developing positive relationships with the student's parent(s). Make the topic of your first parent contact something the student has done well. When you meet with a parent of the student, your ability to demonstrate your enjoyment of and caring for her or his child will go a long way toward establishing a cooperative and mutually supportive working relationship. If the purpose of the meeting is to discuss a problem, you should set a pleasant and cordial tone. Keep the focus on taking positive steps to address problems.
10. Keep your expectations positive. It's easy to lapse into "deficit thinking" when considering the obstacles the students face, but research has shown that a focus on positive outcomes helps build resilience. Celebrate the successes and let the students know that you believe in them.

Students With Limited English Proficiency

English is not the first language of many students in our schools. Some of these students have acquired sufficient English language skills to perform successfully in English-only classes; others do not have sufficient skills in speaking, understanding, reading, or writing English, and they need additional assistance to participate successfully in school activities.

Some of these students need bilingual classes, where school content is presented in their native language and direct instruction is provided for learning English as a Second Language (ESL). Such classes serve as a support while students make the transition from the exclusive use of a first language to the use of English. For many students, learning English occurs in conjunction with learning content in a regular classroom, ideally with the support of an ESL teacher or bilingual aide.

In many classes, including PE and electives such as art, home economics, and music, bilingual support may not be available. Even in core academic classes it may be very limited, especially for students whose English acquisition has progressed but who are not yet fluent. Here are suggestions for communicating with students whose English is limited (see also the Who Will I Teach? sections in Chapters 3, 4, and 10).

1. Find out from the bilingual or ESL teacher the extent of the students' understanding of English so that your expectations will be fair and realistic. If there are no bilingual or ESL teachers on your campus, identify the specialist who services your school and ask how to contact that person. Have the specialist evaluate the student and make suggestions.

2. Learn what the students prefer to be called, and be sure to pronounce their names correctly.

3. If their English skills are extremely limited, you will have more success if you learn some key words in their native language (e.g., listen, pay attention, good, look). When possible, use a translation program to communicate.

4. Use your creativity when communicating, speaking naturally and grammatically but not too fast. Use gestures, facial expression, and body language. Point to things when appropriate and limit your vocabulary when working one-on-one with the student.

5. Reinforce key points with visual aids and demonstration when possible and restate in clear and concise words. Help students learn basic vocabulary words needed for your class. These are the instructional words you use regularly, along with words needed to understand the content of your class. Provide the bilingual or ESL teacher with an ongoing list of these words to reinforce with the students.

6. Remember that a long receptive period is normal for students with limited proficiency in English. During that time they will respond with gestures, nods, and so on before they feel confident enough to speak.

7. Be careful not to ignore or marginalize these students; include them in class activities as much as possible. For example, assign them to cooperative small groups with their peers. They may not be able to participate fully at first, but the interactions with their peers are important.

8. Keep in mind that even students who appear fairly proficient in day-to-day English may not be able to pick up the nuances of the language easily and thus may misunderstand directions, complex assignments, or difficult content. At times, these students may need after-school help or peer tutoring, when available.

9. Consider assigning peer "buddies" who are outgoing and warm to communicate what you cannot and to let you know when the students need your help and are reluctant to ask.

10. Note variations in the cultures of home and school, and demonstrate respect in handling these differences (see Weinstein, Tomlinson-Clarke, & Curran, 2004).

Very High Achieving Students in Heterogeneous Classes

Higher-achieving students may present special challenges in heterogeneous classes. The need to keep these students productively involved in learning activities requires that they have assignments and activities at the appropriate level to avoid boredom or disruption of the rest of the class. Research has shown that students with higher levels of achievement learn more when they are challenged, specifically when their instruction is accelerated (Hattie, 2009) and/or they participate in curriculum compacting (see www.gifted.uconn.edu/general/faculty/reis/Compacting_for_at_Risk.html). Their level of success on activities can sometimes be lower than that needed for students with less ability; that is, they may not become as frustrated if they do not perform with an extremely high level of success. Effective teachers tend to work at a faster pace than normal with these students and introduce more variety in their teaching methods and materials.

It bears noting that not all of your higher-achieving students will function in your classroom in the same way. Some may be well-socialized, independent workers who have developed positive attitudes toward school and learning. Others, however, can appear very different. They may be highly creative, highly divergent, gifted thinkers who approach every problem you present in your classroom differently from their peers, or they may create behavior problems. You must be careful not to confuse compliant behavior with academic ability or misbehavior with lack of ability. Classrooms with more open-ended assignments, where each student pursues a project or a problem to the extent of his or her ability, may provide more support for divergent thinkers and may help to avoid behavior problems that arise out of boredom or frustration with the limitations of highly structured assignments.

Have resource materials available for these students to use for bonus questions or extra projects. Develop a file with a variety of ideas for projects. Include extra or bonus questions on assignments and tests, and encourage these students to attempt them. Create a home page with links that provide enrichment for areas you cover in class. Involve these students in activities that can benefit others, such as peer tutoring, peer counseling, and school improvement projects. Encourage the students to keep up with current events (as appropriate for their age) and to send their written questions or opinions to the newspaper or to people in the news.

Higher-achieving students can contribute greatly to the learning environment in your classroom. Their contributions to class discussions and activities may encourage creativity and divergent thought in your other students. Your positive response to the special groups that make up your class signals to all students that their range of abilities, interests, and skills is welcomed and appreciated.

■ Chapter Summary

Middle and high school students commonly present a very wide range of achievement levels, behaviors, and special needs. It is typical practice in our schools to accommodate such differences by modifying the way classes and curricula are organized and taught. Modifying whole group instruction, using cooperative groups, or using small instructional groups are suggested for heterogeneous classes. Managing remedial classes requires a focus on teaching appropriate behavior and effectively addressing students' learning difficulties. A variety of modifications for students with special needs have been described. Some suggestions were targeted to particular groups, including students with emotional or behavioral problems, autism spectrum disorder, attention deficit hyperactivity disorder, deaf or hard-of-hearing, blind or visually impaired, students living in extreme poverty, students with limited English proficiency, and higher-achieving students.

■ Further Reading

Buzzell, J. G., & Piazza, R. (1994). *Case studies for teaching special needs and at-risk students.* Albany, NY: Delmar.

More than 20 cases, written by teachers, chronicle their experiences in teaching students with special needs. The cases cover the full range of physical, mental, and emotional disabilities and provide grounding for analysis and problem solving.

Cobb, B., Sample, P. L., Alwell, M., & Johns, N. R. (2006). Cognitive-behavioral interventions, dropout, and youth with disabilities. *Remedial and Special Education, 27,* 259–275.

Effects are reported for 16 studies of interventions for youth with behavioral disorders or emotional disturbance. Interventions were effective in reducing inappropriate aggressive and disruptive behavior. Typical interventions taught problem solving and conflict management, emotion awareness, self-management, and other social skills; instructional techniques included praise and recognition, point systems, and contracting.

http://cecp.air.org

Supported by the Center for Effective Collaboration and Practice, this site provides an extensive collection of links to sites having information about effective practices and programs for youth at risk for emotional disorders.

iris.peabody.vanderbilt.edu/

The home site of the IRIS Center at Peabody College, Vanderbilt University, is supported by the U.S. Department of Education's Office of Special Education Programs. It promotes awareness of the needs of special learners and provides course materials, interactive training modules, case studies, and a resource library. Click on "Resources."

Lane, K. L., & Menzies, H. M. (2015). Classroom management for inclusive settings. In E. T. Emmer & E. J. Sabornie (Eds.), *Handbook of classroom management* (2nd ed., pp. 205–219. New York: Routledge.

The authors of this chapter draw attention to low-intensity behavioral supports and instructional considerations for working in inclusive settings. Included in the chapter are descriptions of the zone of proximal development, differentiation, choice, opportunities to respond (OTR), and reinforcement.

Lotan, R. A. (2006). Managing group work in the heterogeneous classroom. In C. Evertson & C. Weinstein (Eds.), *Handbook of research on classroom management: Research, practice, and contemporary issues* (pp. 525–539). Mahwah, NJ: Erlbaum.

This chapter explores the effective use of groups in classrooms having students who are academically and linguistically diverse. The emphasis is on redefining the teacher's role and creating conditions for broadened participation among students.

O'Toole, J. C. (2013). *The Asperkid's (secret) book of social rules: The handbook of not-so-obvious social guidelines for tweens and teens with Asperger's Syndrome.* Philadelphia: Jessica Kingsley. Pub.

Written by a mother of three children with Asperger's Syndrome, who herself has the condition, this book provides an insider's view.

Milner, H. R. (2010). *Start where you are but don't stay there.* Cambridge, MA: Harvard Education.

In this book, Milner presents the idea of "opportunity gaps" that children experience when coming to learning from a place of diversity or poverty that limits their potential with the learning. He challenges educators to develop their knowledge base for teaching and their relationships with these students in order to bridge the gaps.

Swanson, H. L., Harris, K. R., & Graham, S. (Eds.) (2013). *Handbook of learning disabilities* (2nd ed.). New York: Guilford.

Considered a key resource in the instruction of students with learning disabilities (LD), this handbook describes research, identification processes, and instructional strategies, and provides examples of best practices in action.

Walker, H. M., & Gresham, F. M. (Eds.) (2014). *Handbook of evidence-based practices for emotional and behavioral disorders: Applications in schools.* New York: Guilford.

This handbook provides evidence-based approaches to working with students with emotional and behavioral disorders (EBD). Included in this resource are discussions on screening, intervention, exemplary programs, and specific disorders along the spectrum.

www.ccbd.net

The website of the Council for Children with Behavior Disorders includes up-to-date information concerning issues and research related to behavioral difficulties.

www.nagc.org

The National Association for Gifted Children provides links to a number of resources for higher-ability students.

www.parentcenterhub.org

This is a comprehensive site with in-depth coverage of issues, including learning disorders and behavioral problems. Fact sheets and additional resources for specific disabilities are provided at www.parentcenterhub.org/resources.

■ Suggested Activities

1. Case Study 4.2 (in Chapter 4) deals with procedures for small-group work in a science class. In addition to procedures for laboratory activities, the case study describes small-group procedures that will help plan for the use of mixed-ability work groups in your class. Reread this case study and identify five practices that will be helpful for mixed-ability groups.

2. Read Case Study 12.1. Identify five practices used by the teacher to manage the small-group classroom activities and student behavior. Compare your list to that of another student.

3. Read Case Study 12.2. Compare the roles of the two teachers before and during instruction. Identify three ways coteaching might be helpful in managing an inclusion class. What other teacher responsibilities or roles might be useful in this classroom?

4. Two scenarios at the end of this chapter describe problems frequently faced by teachers of heterogeneous or lower-level classes. After reading each description, review appropriate parts of this and other chapters. Decide what strategies you would recommend to deal with the problems. Compare your list with those included in the keys in the Appendix.

■ Case Study 12.1

USING SMALL GROUPS IN ENGLISH

Ms. Hanson uses small-group instruction during portions of each class period two days a week for instruction and testing in spelling. On Tuesdays, she meets with each of her three spelling groups for content development and introduction to seat work on the new words for the week. Students in each group are seated together; this facilitates posting assignments, distributing or collecting papers, and group oral work.

The assignment for each group is posted near its area of the room. Each group's assignment includes at least one simple introductory task that students can do with no help from the teacher (e.g., copying each word five times, looking up words in the dictionary or online, and/or writing sentences with them). After the general instructions are given, all students begin work. The teacher works first with one group, going to its seating area to preview the words, work on pronunciation, and review the assignment. She then moves to another group. During the group activity with Ms. Hanson, each student is included in some question-and-answer exchanges.

At the end of the week, Ms. Hanson uses small groups to administer spelling tests. As the students are entering the room, she tells them to get out their journals and prepare a sheet of paper for a spelling test. After the bell rings, the teacher introduces two activities that will be proceeding simultaneously: spelling tests for three groups and a composition (journal) assignment. Ms. Hanson explains the composition assignment and then reminds the students that she will be going around the room administering spelling tests. When students are not taking the test, they are to work on the journal assignment. Students in each group are seated together. As they begin work, the teacher begins administering the test to the first spelling group. She stands near the group's desks and uses a low voice. While she gives the test, she also monitors the rest of the class to make sure they remain on task. After she finishes giving the test (about 5 minutes), the teacher collects the papers, puts them in a specially marked file folder, and goes to the next group. She begins giving the test to the next group but continues to monitor the remainder of the class and signal for quiet when there is noise from another area.

When Ms. Hanson finishes with the second group, she answers questions for students, files the papers, and then goes to the next group to give the test. She does not allow students to interrupt her while she is working with another group. When she finishes administering the test to the third spelling group, she collects the papers, files them, and lets the students know how much time they have to finish and to proof their journal assignment.

■ Case Study 12.2

AN INCLUSION PROGRAM IN A MIDDLE SCHOOL

Teachers in this school are on grade-level teams, with a teacher from each of five subject areas at one grade level on each team, along with a special education teacher. Days are divided into seven periods, allowing teachers to have one conference period and one period for team planning. Although this district has a continuum of special education programs—including self-contained classes, resource classes, and Content Mastery—the emphasis is on inclusion to the extent possible. General education teachers make necessary modifications for students who need them, and the special education teacher helps with this. General teachers give the special education teacher their lesson plans so that he or she can make up study guides, do highlighting, and identify areas in which the special students will need supplemental instruction or modification. This teacher determines which class to work in depending on what the general teachers indicate during planning sessions. If a class will be working on a written assignment for most of the period, the special education teacher may modify directions for specific students and give them to the classroom teacher for the designated students to do on their own during class. When more unstructured work will be done in class, the special education teacher usually provides on-the-spot support to some students. Often this teacher assists other students in the class as needed, although the identified students are the first priority.

How the teachers work together during instruction can be illustrated with a lesson on latitude and longitude in a seventh-grade social studies class. One week, the class worked on a project involving plotting a route for traveling around the world. The social studies teacher introduced the concepts with examples and some initial practice. At the beginning of one period, instructions were given to students, who were to work in pairs to plan their route. Students had most of one period to complete the assignment, and they had access to a variety of materials, including atlases, laminated maps, rulers, string, and so on. The special education teacher entered the room about 10 minutes after the class started, shortly before the social studies teacher had finished talking with the students about how they were to work on the assignment. Both teachers monitored the students as they worked, answering questions and offering suggestions. Although the special education teacher's attention was not limited to the identified students, she did provide them with more explanation when it was apparent they had not mastered the concepts needed to perform the assignment.

In this inclusion program, the general education teacher is responsible for planning daily lessons and grading. The special education teacher provides and/or modifies material as appropriate for special students, develops IEPs for the students, and is the main contact person for administrative meetings. On occasion, the special teacher might take students to another area to reteach new or complex material or to give a retest if needed. During planning periods, the teachers work out the details of what is needed and how they will work together on it.

■ Problem Scenarios

SCENARIO 12.1: HETEROGENEOUS CLASSES

Never before has Ms. Garcia had to deal with students of such different entering achievement levels in her seventh-grade class. She feels frustrated in her efforts to provide instruction at appropriate levels when some students are several years below grade level and others are above grade level. The brightest students finish independent work far ahead of the rest of the class, while the slowest students seldom complete an assignment successfully.

So far, Ms. Garcia has tried two things: She provides extra-credit activities for students who finish work early, and she helps slower students individually more often during class and after school. Both steps seem to help, although each has also created management problems. What else might Ms. Garcia do?

SCENARIO 12.2: UNCOOPERATIVE STUDENT BEHAVIOR IN A REMEDIAL CLASS

Mr. Oliver is concerned about behavior in his class. Several students are always late, and others frequently forget their books, paper, pencils, or assignments. During content presentations, students call out answers or comments, leave their seats to throw away paper or sharpen their pencils, and often talk or write notes. During independent assignments, students work the first problem or two while the teacher is watching but then turn to their neighbors as soon as the teacher turns his back to work with individual students. Mr. Oliver tried to establish order by using a system of penalties, in which students had to write out and turn in definitions of problems if they were caught misbehaving. This system had worked well with his other classes, but in this class he found he was constantly assigning penalties and was unable to keep track of whether they were turned in. What other ideas could Mr. Oliver try?

MyEducationLab *Self-Check 12.1*

MyEducationLab *Self-Check 12.2*

MyEducationLab *Self-Check 12.3*

MyEducationLab *Application Exercise 12.1* Using what you've learned in this chapter, view the videos and respond to the questions.

MyEducationLab *Application Exercise 12.2* Using what you've learned in this chapter, read and respond to this scenario.

MyEducationLab *Application Exercise 12.3* Using what you've learned in this chapter, view the video and respond to the questions.

MyEducationLab *Application Exercise 12.4* Using what you've learned in this chapter, view the video and respond to the questions.

MyEducationLab *Application Exercise 12.5* Using what you've learned in this chapter, read and respond to this scenario.

MyEducationLab *Application Exercise 12.6* Using what you've learned in this chapter, view the video and respond to the questions.

MyEducationLab *Application Exercise 12.7* Using what you've learned in this chapter, view the video and respond to the questions.

APPENDIX

Answer Keys for Selected Chapter Activities

CHAPTER 1

Activity 1

Answers may vary, but should highlight differences in the following areas:

- Their approaches to managing activities and students. Ms. Robert's clear guidelines and consistency in following through with her expectations has produced a classroom in which students follow procedures and engage in activities appropriately. Mr. Smith's inconsistent application of expectations for behavior in different activities and his difficulty in insisting on appropriate behavior has resulted in many students pushing against boundaries and not participating constructively in learning activities.
- How these activities might play out over time. Students in Ms. Robert's class will spend more time engaged in learning and are likely to make better progress on their course's learning objectives. Students in Mr. Smith's class will be less engaged in learning and are less likely to take it seriously. Also, the poorer behavior in Mr. Smith's class will ultimately lead to more conflicts between the teacher and his students.
- How their differences might affect student learning, motivation, and attitudes. Numerous students in Mr. Smith's class have shifted their focus away from learning and are exhibiting attitudes of disrespect or indifference toward the teacher resulting in an overall class climate that is not conducive to motivation for learning. Students in Ms. Robert's class are more focused on learning tasks and more likely to accomplish them, resulting in better attitudes toward learning and greater self-efficacy.

CHAPTER 2

Activity 1

Mr. Sahedi should be characterized as having high *influence* because of his energy when engaging students, his immediacy and enthusiasm when instructing the whole class, his use of eye contact, his insistence on appropriate behavior and his follow through. His *affect* would also be characterized as *high* because of his openness to student input, his frequent use of sincere compliments and approval statements, and his expressions of trust and respect for students.

Mrs. Harrison definitely rates high on the *affect* dimension, as indicated by her receptivity and listening to student concerns; by building opportunities for students to address issues and concerns in assignments; by giving students attention, support, and recognition; and by her above-and-beyond involvement in establishing a tutoring program. The vignette has less information about her *influence*, but based on the description of her demeanor as businesslike, her sensitivity to boundary issues, and her frequent contacts with parents, it would be safe to say that she is at least moderate on this dimension. A more definitive classification on the *influence* dimension would require more information about Mrs. Harrison as she interacts with students, leads lessons, and addresses problems.

CHAPTER 3

Activity 1

The room arrangement shown in Figure 3.2 will contribute to classroom management problems in a number of ways.

- Students at the rear of the row farthest left will have difficulty seeing the projector screen.
- When the teacher stands at the projector, six students will be seated behind her.
- Desks are arranged so that students face other students. Although this formation may be useful during class discussions for encouraging students to respond to one another, it may produce a high level of distraction during other activities.
- Some student desks face windows, which might be a source of distraction. The same desks face away from a chalkboard.
- The group of four desks on the right side of the room is in front of the bookshelf and impedes movement in that area of the room. Students at those desks are likely to be distracted by students using materials or equipment at that end of the room.
- The wastebasket is not conveniently located; a place nearer the door would be better.
- The table is too near the teacher's desk and crowds several student desks.
- Students working at the table might disturb others nearby. Traffic flow in the area around the teacher's desk and table is poor.
- The major instructional area by the projector has no table, desk, or other storage space to hold materials needed in presentations.

CHAPTER 4

Activity 4

Answers may vary, but could include the following procedures for Mr. Smith to put into place:

- Students need a beginning-of-period routine that defines what is expected of them before, at, and after the bell.

- A reasonable consequence should be used for students who arrive late without a valid excuse (e.g., a warning for the first tardy, detention thereafter).
- Mr. Smith needs his own beginning-of-period routine to enable him to take care of administrative tasks and make a quick transition to a content activity.
- Procedures are needed to define how assignments are communicated and what materials to bring to class.
- Out-of-seat and out-of-room students need to be minimized by having clear expectations in place for behaviors and procedures to manage them.
- Mr. Smith needs to monitor students better so that he can redirect them before large numbers of students are off task.
- Expectations for student talk need to be explained and reinforced consistently so that class activities can proceed with fewer interruptions.

CHAPTER 5

Activity 3

It would be useful for Ms. La Rosa to establish one or more interim checkpoints for this major project. She also should clarify her expectations for the components of the assignment, including types of information to be included and the number and types of acceptable sources. A rubric for students to reference that identifies the criteria for different letter grades on the final report would also provide guidance for students and would make grading more predictable and less subjective. The notebook and short-term assignments need quick turn-around so students receive feedback. Ms. La Rosa should consider working through some of these assignments as classwork exercises so that students do more of the work while supervised. Failing a large number of students is probably not a good option for Ms. La Rosa or the students. Instead, she can redefine her grading criteria and give students an opportunity to resubmit the work.

Activity 4

Some positive examples of ideas for good work procedures are summarized here.

- Case 5.1: Ms. Clark makes the basis for her assigned grades very concrete by having students keep a record. There is a procedure in place for informing parents of the student's scores. Ms. Clark provides a clear roadmap for class activities and assignments, and she involves many students in class activities. Procedures for absent students are clear. Checking/feedback is frequent and tied to the grading system.
- Case 5.2: Mr. Richard has a clear set of components for his grading system, with provision for students to receive prompt feedback. His procedures for managing the paperwork appear to be efficient. He has students keep records of their work, which tends to encourage self-monitoring and responsibility. Allowing students to drop a low grade probably reduces anxiety and allows individuals to occasionally do poorly on an assignment without destroying their overall grade.

- Case 5.3: Ms. Curry has the requirements for the long-term assignments clearly organized and available for students on handouts. Due dates are identified for both students and parents. Examples of the assignments are presented along with criteria. Interim checkpoints are given to the students, and provisions for feedback are made. Ms. Curry also provides students a check-sheet rubric for their presentations.

CHAPTER 6

Activity 2

Case Study 6.1

a. Use of beginning-of-year principles

- Mrs. James resolves student uncertainties in numerous ways, including the clarity of her expectations for behavior and work requirements, and her consistency in the use of the procedures.
- The initial lessons are uncomplicated and they engage the students in the content; they also allow Mrs. James to introduce systematically some of her procedures for group work.
- Although students work in groups during the initial lessons, a whole class focus is maintained by the use of the same group activity as well as by Mrs. James's monitoring of and feedback to the whole class.
- Mrs. James is clearly in charge. She directs activities, monitors, gives feedback, and keeps students focused.
- Both the influence and affect dimensions of relationship building are evident. Mrs. James's structured organization and her interactive style indicate a high degree of influence during the initial class activities. She also shared personal information, reassured students, and expressed support for students' efforts, all of which are indicators of positive affect.

b. Critical beginning of year planning and preparation activities for Case 6.1 include

- Room arrangement suitable for group activities and other formats
- Identifying expectations for desired student behavior
- Planning procedures in key areas such as talk and movement, transitions, independent student work and group activities, and handling administrative matters such as tardiness and out-of-room policies
- Identifying appropriate consequences
- Planning initial content activities along with activities to orient students and teach them behavioral expectations; arranging activities into a workable sequence

c. Similarities between Mrs. James and Ms. Holly

Although their content areas are different and Mrs. James makes extensive use of group work, the two teachers' approaches to beginning the year have many similarities. Both teachers are very organized, make their expectations for behavior explicit, and have uncomplicated initial lessons that allow them to monitor students and manage administrative matters. Both teachers give students an uncomplicated introduction to their classes, provide information about grading practices and other work procedures, and utilize initial assignments that are easy to complete.

Activity 3

Case Study 6.3

a. Actions or omissions contributing to the problems

Mr. Davis needed to be specific with his students about his expectations for their behavior. His only rule is too general to serve for all situations. Because he used one general rule, Mr. Davis must constantly interpret concrete instances of infractions as they relate to the rule. Furthermore, he has not been specific about consequences and has mentioned only one penalty—that of going to the office. Mild misbehaviors at the beginning of the year have now escalated into more serious misbehaviors as students test the limits. At this stage, Mr. Davis is receiving poor cooperation both in obtaining written work from students and in the area of class participation.

b. Suggestions for improving the situation: Mr. Davis might begin to establish better behavior in his class in several ways.

- Reevaluate the rules and procedures with the intent of making them more specific and introduce rules and procedures for areas that were previously not covered.
- Select a time, such as a Monday or the day after a vacation period, to reintroduce and explain the rules and procedures, providing students with rationales for the desired behaviors and eliciting their cooperation in following them.
- Review procedures for participating in class discussions and for times when talking and working together is allowed and when it is not.
- After the rules and procedures are introduced, state clear and specific consequences for infractions. The consequences should be tied to the behaviors themselves; trips to the office should be used only for the most serious offenses. Positive as well as negative consequences should be considered and communicated to students.
- Monitor the class constantly with the goal of anticipating and preventing misbehavior and noting appropriate behavior.
- Make sure students have enough work to do and that they understand it and are able to complete it. Require student attention during presentations and allow only relevant materials and books to be out on desks.

Have students take notes during important parts of the presentation. Be explicit and teach them how to take notes. Require them as part of a notebook.

- Break longer activities into shorter ones and vary the sequencing and routine for the sixth-period class. Students are tired at this time of the day; maintaining their attention is not easy, even in well-behaved classes.
- Pace students through their work with statements such as "You should be halfway through with this assignment by now" and "We will check the first part of the assignment in 5 minutes."
- Reward academic performance and other desirable classroom behavior regularly. For students of this age, extra-credit points or privileges may be more reinforcing than public praise.

CHAPTER 7

Case Study 7.1

The following suggestions for Ms. Liu would help improve her students' comprehension.

- Outline the lesson sequence, breaking down complex lessons into smaller, easier to understand parts or steps. Be sure to define words that students may not know.
- During presentations, let students know what they are expected to write in their notes by underlining important points as they are written on the whiteboard or by displaying them on a screen. Another way to structure note taking is to give students an outline with space for additional notes.
- During content-development activities, obtain frequent work samples by having students do problems or answer questions. Circulate during these times, checking for areas of confusion, common problems, and students who are not participating. Based on feedback from these samples, adjust instruction by slowing down, increasing the pace of the presentation, or repeating content where necessary.
- Be sure students know the purpose of the lesson. At the end of presentations, always restate major objectives or else quiz students on important points.
- Give students step-by-step instructions for assignments. Check to be sure they understand what they are to do, then help them pace their work by telling them how long the assignment should take to complete and warning them when there is a short time left.
- Circulate while students are doing seat-work assignments. Check to be sure that they are working on the assignment, that they are doing it correctly, and that they are using their time wisely.
- If it becomes apparent during a seat-work or review activity that some students do not understand the material, have them join you in a small group after the general presentation. At that time you can review the points of the lesson and answer questions.

Case Study 7.2

The following approaches could reduce the amount of time wasted by Mr. Miller's class.

- Create an academic warm-up as part of the beginning-of-class routine. Write the warm-up on a whiteboard or display it on a screen and require that students complete the task in a set period of time (e.g., 5 minutes). Be sure that warm-up activities are checked and that they count toward the students' grades.
- Use established routines as much as possible for beginning and ending lessons, passing and collecting papers and supplies, and exchanging papers to grade. Monitor to be sure students follow routines.
- Teach students exactly what behaviors are expected during transitions: voice level, pencil sharpener use, procedures for passing papers, and so on.
- Give instructions for transitions before beginning them, not during them.
- Post assignments where all students can see them. Begin independent-work assignments together as a class, doing the first problems or answering the first question as a group. Then monitor at the beginning of independent work to be sure that everyone gets off to a good start.

Case Study 7.3

Ms. Jackson can work on improving student behavior in whole-class discussions and small-group activities in the following ways.

- Students may need more direction about appropriate behaviors during group work and discussion. Because these activities require extensive interaction, students may need guidance about taking turns, listening, and speaking out. Ms. Jackson could lead a discussion in which students are asked to reach a consensus about procedures for group work or discussion activities, perhaps after students have discussed the topic in small groups.
- Poor transition management could be contributing to the problems. Ms. Jackson should be sure to give instructions for the group or discussion activity before it begins, and she should start the activity promptly. Assigning a specific task to perform or a question to address at the start of these activities will also help engage students right away.
- Instead of chasing problems around the room, Ms. Jackson should concentrate on getting students involved in the activity. Students should have a specific task to accomplish during group work, so that if a group loses focus, Ms. Jackson can redirect the group. She may also find it helpful to assign a group member the responsibility for keeping the group on task. During discussions, Ms. Jackson can display a list of discussion topics and use these to maintain focus.

Case Study 7.4

Note: Kounin's concepts are identified in parentheses after the relevant segment.

As his fourth-period class begins, Mr. Case makes eye contact with two students who are exchanging notes; the students quickly get out their class materials. (**Withitness**)

"Let's begin by working some of the exercises at the end of the chapter; you'll need your notebooks." As students begin to get out their materials, Mr. Case calls out, "Oops, I forgot to tell you to bring money tomorrow for the field trip. How many of you will be going?" (**Jerkiness or lack of smoothness**) After a brief discussion, students finish getting out their materials. Mr. Case says, "We'll go through these exercises orally, but I also want you to write the answers in your notebooks as part of today's classwork. I'll come around and check your notebook work later in the period. (**High participation format and accountability**) Now, who can answer the first question? Hands please. Tyrone?" Mr. Case conducts the lesson by calling on various students, some with hands up, others seemingly at random from the non-volunteers. (**Group alerting**) About halfway through the exercises, a student enters the room and says that he is new to the school and has been assigned to the class. Mr. Case goes to his desk, sits down, and says, "OK, come here. I'll check out a text to you. (**Absence of overlapping**) I wish the school office wouldn't send people in the middle of a period. Where are you from, anyway?" (**Jerkiness or lack of smoothness**) After giving the student a syllabus and a text, Mr. Case leaves his desk and says to the class, "Now, where were we? Oh yes, question 7. Say, where did Kim and Lee go? I didn't give them permission to leave." (**Poor withitness**) After several minutes more, Mr. Case calls a halt to the activity and says, "Now I'd like us to discuss the test coming up this Thursday. Let's make sure that you are all clear on what will be on the exam and what you will need to study to get ready for it." After a pause, he adds: "I almost forgot. Get out your questions from before and look at the next to the last one. We need to add an important point that was left out." After finishing the item, Mr. Case turns the topic back to the upcoming test. (**Jerkiness or lack of smoothness**) "Now, where were we? Oh yes, I need to show you some items that will be similar to those on the test. Here's one." He writes it on the chalkboard, then pauses: "Well, I don't want to give away the test, do I?" Without discussing the test further, he turns to another topic. (**Jerkiness and loss of lesson momentum**) "Just wait until you hear about the videotape we will be viewing tomorrow. I borrowed it from another teacher, and she said that her students thought it was one of the most thought-provoking, exciting stories they had ever seen!" (**Group alerting**)

Case Study 7.5

Diagnosis

Ms. Grant has made a common mistake. She assumes that students will be able to follow her directions with a minimum of structuring or explanation on her part. In this lesson, she assigns lab work that requires students to work in groups but does not prepare them for the activity. Group assignments are handed out but not explained clearly, nor do students attend to the directions. When students move to their groups, transitions are disorderly and directions are vague as to how the groups of students are to pursue the question, "What is in the box?" The pace of the activity slows down, and several groups sit in dead time while others finish. Groups are expected to report their findings, but no directions are given about how to do this. At the end of the activity, Ms. Grant provides no wrap-up or evaluation, and she assigns a textbook reading on a different topic.

Suggestions

Ms. Grant might achieve more success with her class if she presents information systematically.

- State major goals and objectives, and tell students what they will be responsible for knowing.
- Call for attention; do not proceed without it. Require that students listen to directions and presentations. Have them respond to questions and demonstrations.
- Explain precisely what behaviors are expected when students work together in groups on an assignment. Have each group select a recorder who will be responsible for presenting the group reports to the rest of the class.
- As groups are working, monitor and circulate to make certain they are on the right track. If widespread problems seem to be occurring, reteach the material. Allow students to begin work only when satisfied that they can complete the tasks satisfactorily.
- Provide additional activities for groups who finish early so that unnecessary dead time is avoided.
- Constructively evaluate the individual reports rather than accept poor or incomplete answers.
- Follow the group activity with relevant discussion and a summary of the lesson.

CHAPTER 8

Activity 8.4

a. The following concepts from Chapter 8 are evident in Mrs. James's first three days:

- The room is arranged for group activities, with desk arrangement and a folder system for materials supporting the use of groups.
- Mrs. James is very clear about the procedures she wants students to follow for talk and movement, and she gives students feedback consistent with her expectations.
- Mrs. James differentiates her expectations for talking according to type of activity, and makes the distinction clear to students.
- She introduces her procedure for rotating roles among students in groups clearly, using a simple task to begin the process of teaching students desired behavior in groups.
- At the beginning of the second day, Mrs. James reintroduces her group role procedure and uses it again, consistent with day 1.
- Mrs. James does not assume that students understand how to work in groups; she engages them in discussing characteristics of good group membership, and she is explicit about her expectations.
- The initial group tasks are simple and easy for students to complete successfully.

b. The following areas were not described in the case study of the first three days in Mrs. James's class. Although it was not necessary to include them in the first three days, they should be dealt with during the next several weeks of using groups.

- Teaching students signals to gain their attention when they are in groups
- Determining group composition
- Establishing both interdependence and individual accountability in group activities
- Teaching and reinforcing effective group work skills

CHAPTER 9

Activity 4

Example 9.1

a. These award and recognition systems can encourage both extrinsic and intrinsic motivation. When students perceive the recognition to be a reflection of accomplishment, then intrinsic sources should be activated. If the reward or recognition is done only for approval, then extrinsic motives are activated.

b. The systems may be somewhat competitive, but because the described rewards appear to be abundant and not restricted to only a few students, they don't seem unduly competitive.

c. The award and recognition systems are intended to foster student engagement, a focus on academic accomplishment, and students' anticipation of good outcomes.

Example 9.2

a. Competitions can induce intrinsic motivation, but their emphasis is usually extrinsic because they focus on winning and the accompanying prizes and attention.

b. The individual systems are competitive; the group-based systems encourage cooperative behavior within the class or group.

c. These systems are intended to be fun, to produce excitement and to encourage commitment to achieving the best outcome.

Example 9.3

a. The motivation will be intrinsic when the student is focused on accomplishment; it is extrinsic if the emphasis is mainly on reaching the standard or just getting through the task.

b. In itself, a mastery system is neither competitive nor cooperative.

c. By allowing students the opportunity to master material, there is less anxiety during testing or other assessment. The focus is on accomplishing learning.

Example 9.4

a. Extra-credit systems often appeal to extrinsic motivation, in that students complete them in order to receive a higher grade or to avoid a failing grade. Sometimes such assignments engage students sufficiently that they are done for the learning and sense of accomplishment that accompanies completion of an interesting task. Teachers hope for the latter motivation, of course.

b. Extra-credit systems are neither competitive nor cooperative in themselves, but they may be used in that manner. They are competitive when credit is limited to "the first 10 solving the problem," as in the example. They may be cooperative if the teacher permits students to work together to submit a joint extra-credit project.

c. Extra-credit assignments may be used as extensions of learning, and thus arouse interest and engagement with content. They are also designed as a safety valve in the grading system to take pressure off students; thus, they may reduce anxiety and fear of failure.

CHAPTER 10

Activity 10.2

Step 1 of the activity asks you to write an assertive statement in response to the situation. Here is just one example of an assertive initial verbal response to each situation. You'll need to work with someone to finish steps 2 and 3.

Situation A: "It sounds like you're running late on your project, Bubba. I did list the project requirements and due dates when we started. What seems to be the problem?"

Situation B: "Girls, the gym must be picked up before anyone leaves."

Situation C: "Victor, this time is to be used for completing the assignment independently."

Situation D: "Hey guys, what's going on here? I know you're just joking around, but have you noticed that you're drawing a crowd? It's time to break it up and get to class. . . ."

Situation E: "Donalda, you know that we don't eat in class unless everyone is eating in class. Put the food away and out of sight."

Situation F: "Jack and Jill, I'm feeling annoyed by the interruptions. You can either participate appropriately or sit apart."

Situation G: "Class, I'm extremely disappointed and shocked by the substitute's report about your behavior yesterday. Your uncooperative, out-of-control actions were inappropriate and disrespectful. Who is ready to take some responsibility for what you did?. . ."

Activity 10.3

1. b;   2. c;   3. d;   4. a;   5. c

Activity 10.4

For each situation, an initial listening response is given. Work with a colleague to role-play a continuation of the dialogue.

Situation A: "It sounds like you are really disappointed with your grade, Teresa. Would you like to discuss it?"

Situation B: "The worksheet assignments are boring to you and you've got some ideas for others?"

Situation C: "Barry, it looks like you've stopped working. What's the problem?"

Situation D: "Katie, I noticed that you have been missing some assignments lately. Do you want to talk about what's going on?"

Situation E: "It's hard to start over again in a new school, for sure. What do you miss about your old school?"

CHAPTER 11

Activity 11.2

Answers may vary; the following comments address some of the key factors in choosing interventions. Behaviors listed as **nonproblems** don't usually require an intervention, unless they persist, in which case they are no longer nonproblems. **Minor problems** should usually be addressed by the strategies listed under the category "minor interventions". Factors to consider when deciding which specific intervention to choose include their potential for allowing the content activity to continue uninterrupted, the likelihood of stopping the problem promptly, and ease of use. The ideal strategy for minor problems must be unobtrusive and straightforward to implement, must keep the momentum of the activity flowing, and must stop the problem. Problems that are **major, but limited in scope** will generally require an intervention beyond the minor category. Often, teachers will have attempted to deal with such behaviors (e.g., off-task behavior, call-outs, wandering) using minor interventions but with limited or only temporary success. When the behavior is a rule violation that has a prescribed consequence (e.g., office referral for vandalism; detention for unexcused/excessive tardiness), it should be used, of course. When the problem behavior is more than a minor problem (e.g., excess talking, wandering, off task), a moderate intervention such as withholding a privilege or time out may suffice.

If the problem verges on becoming habitual but more information is needed to understand why the student is engaged in the behavior, then a more extensive intervention can be used. For example, a problem-solving conference or the Reality Therapy approach can be useful for getting the student's perspective and causing the student to accept responsibility for her or his actions. More time-intensive interventions involving parents, such as a parent conference or use of a Behavior Report Card, can be considered for excessive behaviors that interfere with class activities. Choices for interventions are affected by time requirements, suitability for the identified problem and student, and likelihood of bringing about lasting changes.

Escalating or spreading problems, such as widespread off-task behavior, frequent disregard of class rules and procedures, or refusal to complete assignments by more than one or a few students will require more extensive interventions, but first, the teacher needs to be sure that the course content and assignments are appropriate for the students. If the latter is the source of the problems, then appropriate modifications in the course content, assignments, and activities should be made. Assuming that the problems are not the result of student frustration with failure to learn, then the teacher must evaluate whether minor and moderate interventions have been applied in a timely manner. It may also be that the class procedures need modification or that the teacher's use of withitness and other group management skills, as well as relationships with students, need addressing. To address escalating problems, one or more interventions in the "extensive" category will be needed. For example, a problem-solving conference with the involved students, coupled with a contract that addresses the behavior of concern, could be helpful. Considerations in choosing an intervention should be based on an estimate of appropriateness for the specific problem and its potential for restoring order in the class and eliciting cooperation from students.

Activity 11.4

Answers may vary. For each situation, a good first response is identified, then a follow-up intervention in case the first one is unsuccessful.

Situation 1 (Ardyth and Melissa): Make eye contact and move closer to the two students. Don't let the discussion get interrupted. Pick up the pace of the discussion by asking some more questions of nonparticipating students. Follow up intervention: Tell Ardyth and Melisa to stop passing notes and/ or use a more interactive strategy such as think-pair-share to involve more students in the discussion.

Situation 2 (Desi and Bryce). Move the two students to separate locations; don't argue, end of discussion. Get the activity going in the whole class and check back to see that each has begun. Follow-up intervention: If either (or both) of the boys doesn't participate, give him time. At a suitable time (e.g., when the rest of the class is in an independent work or group-work activity) when it won't interrupt an ongoing activity, check with the student to ascertain reasons for his lack of engagement and to develop a plan.

Situation 3 (Dwayne): Assuming that Dwayne's behavior is chronic and disruptive, and also that the teacher has addressed it with less extensive interventions that have not been successful, a problem-solving conference can be used. During the conference the focus should be on Dwayne's accepting responsibility and making a commitment to change or accept the consequences. Follow-up intervention can be a conference with Dwayne's parents.

Situation 4 (Marc): Marc's aggressive behavior calls for an office referral, since it could easily escalate into a fight. It's likely the physical contact is governed by school policy and that Marc should have been referred immediately after that incident. Assuming these behaviors are typical of Marc, follow-up intervention should include a combination of strategies, including monitoring Marc and redirecting him at early signs of conflict; a Behavior Report Card might be used to provide home consequences for appropriate behavior; and Think Time could be a useful way to de-escalate Marc during stressful situations. Group or individual counseling may also be an appropriate long-term strategy.

CHAPTER 12

Activity 12.1

Answers may vary. Five practices helpful for Case 4.2 are listed.

- The handout describing lab procedures will help keep all students aware of the teacher's expectations.
- The use of student pairs will provide needed support.
- The pacing guidelines and teacher reminders will help keep students on target to complete the activity.
- The use of assigned group roles helps assure that all students participate.
- The student self-evaluation activity will encourage all students to monitor their participation and effort, and it will reduce the likelihood that some students will avoid engagement in their group's tasks.

Activity 12.2

Answers may vary; five practices to manage the use of teacher-led small group instruction in Case 12.1 are listed.

- Students are seated in their instructional groups; they stay in place while the teacher—not the students—moves from group to group.

- Students who are not in the teacher-led small group are given clear directions and tasks to complete.
- The teacher monitors the whole class, not just the students with whom she is working.
- The teacher's procedures during the assessment phase allow her to manage the paperwork and keep the process organized.
- The teacher's routines limit interruptions and maintain the pace of the activities so that they are completed on time.

Activity 12.3

Comparison of teacher roles for inclusion classrooms:

- Both the special education and general education teachers participate in team planning sessions.
- The general education teachers take the lead in planning overall instruction and lessons; the special education teacher identifies needed modifications for identified students.
- During lessons, the general education teachers take the lead, and the special educator assists individuals. Sometimes the special education teacher instructs groups.
- The special educator identifies needed modifications in directions for students and provides assistance as needed.
- The special education teacher rotates among classes based on student needs for assistance and modifications. The special educator also develops the IEPs (presumably with input from the general education teachers) and is the contact person for administrative matters concerning the identified students.

Some other roles that are important but were not mentioned in this case are grading responsibilities, contacts with parents, assessment practices, and technology integration.

There are numerous ways co-teaching could be helpful; here are three:

- More opportunities for assistance for identified students
- Improved instruction for struggling students
- Shared information and resources to improve instruction for all students

Activity 12.4

Answers may vary; in each situation, multiple strategies should be considered.

Scenario 1: To deal with very diverse ability levels, Ms. Garcia can try the following approaches.

- If one or two students are especially likely to have trouble with whole-class assignments, these students can be seated where the teacher can easily keep an eye on them during instruction and seat work. As soon as seat-work instructions have been given to the whole class and the teacher has monitored to be sure that the students have begun work, she can check with slower students privately to go over instructions again or to modify the assignment as necessary. These instructions and directions can be done as a small-group activity if more than one or two students need the extra assistance.

- Enrichment or extra-credit material for students who finish class work early should include work-related activities that will not distract other students. Feedback, credit, and recognition for the completion of enrichment activities should be a part of the system.
- All students in the class should be involved in discussion or recitation sessions. Systematically calling on each student gives everyone an opportunity to participate.
- If the preceding suggestions are not sufficient for a given class, small-group instruction might be used for part of the course work. Procedures for group work must be planned and then taught carefully. When two or three work groups are established in a class, instruction and monitoring will be simpler if seat-work assignments are planned so that there is a basic assignment that all students complete, with additional activities at appropriate levels for each group. Some instruction can then be with the whole class, with a smaller amount reserved for each group.
- When using differentiated assignments, adjustments in the grading system should be made so that lower-ability students can attain satisfactory grades.

Scenario 2: Mr. Oliver should reconsider his classroom rules and procedures to determine whether they cover the misbehaviors that are causing him a problem. If adjustments are needed, the relevant rule or procedure should be restated and introduced to the students again. Mr. Oliver should also consider whether his monitoring is adequate or whether students are getting away with too much misbehavior before he deals with the problem. Further measures to correct or prevent specific problems described in the scenario are the following:

- Mr. Oliver may be overrelying on the penalty system to respond to misbehavior. If so, it would be better to use such penalties only for a limited number of situations (e.g., forgetting materials or disturbing the class).
- Compliance with procedures can be rewarded by awarding points toward a participation grade or a favorite activity. Give students daily points or checks for having appropriate materials, being in their seats and ready to work when the bell rings, and staying on task throughout the period.
- There are several ways to help students remember to bring materials. A supply of pens or pencils may be kept on hand for emergency loans, with some penalty imposed when students have to borrow supplies. Students can be allowed to leave pencils and papers in the classroom so that they will always be available. (They can be labeled or kept in a folder with the students' names and class period listed on it.) If different materials are needed on different days,

Mr. Oliver can have students keep a record of materials and assignments needed for the class so that they can refer to it as necessary. He can also post a list of books and other materials above or next to the door so that students can see it before they enter the room.

- Before content presentations, Mr. Oliver might remind students that he will call on them to answer and that they should not call out except when he signals that it is appropriate.
- Inappropriate behavior during presentations should be stopped by a simple procedure such as eye contact or reminding students of the procedure or rule, without interfering with the flow of the lesson. If the behavior persists, a penalty can be imposed.
- It is always helpful to move around the room during presentations and while students are engaged in independent-work activities. Mr. Oliver should walk by every student in the room, looking at papers to be sure that students are working on the right assignment and doing it correctly. He should avoid staying too long with any one student, and if a student needs additional help, he or she can come to a table or desk from which Mr. Oliver can monitor all students. Frequent circulating tends to discourage inappropriate use of electronics, note writing, and other off-task behavior.

REFERENCES

Adams, M. B., Womack, S. A., Schatzer, R. H., & Caldarella, P. (2010). Parent involvement in school-wide social skills instruction: Perceptions of a home note program. *Education, 130*(3), 513–528.

Albrecht, S. F. (2008). Time Away: A skill-building alternative to discipline. *Preventing School Failure, 53*(1), 49–55.

Allison, H., & Harklau, L. (2010). Teaching academic literacies in secondary school. In G. Li & P. A. Edwards (Eds.), *Best practices in ELL instruction* (pp. 129–150). New York: Guilford.

Arlin, M. (1979). Teacher transitions can disrupt time flow in classrooms. *American Educational Research Journal, 16*, 42–56.

Athanasiades, C., & Deliyanni-Kouimtzis, V. (2010). The experience of bullying among secondary school students. *Psychology in the Schools, 47*, 328–341.

Auld, S., Wilkinson-Flicker, S., Nachazel, T., & Dziuba, A. (2013). *The condition of education 2013.* National Center for Education Statistics, Institute of Educational Sciences. Washington, DC: Government Printing Office.

Aultman, L. P., Williams-Johnson, M. R., & Schutz, P. A. (2009). Boundary dilemmas in teacher-student relationships: Struggling with "the line." *Teaching and Teacher Education, 25*, 636–646.

Bassin, A., Bratter, E., & Rachin, R. (Eds.). (1976). *The Reality Therapy reader: A survey of the works of William Glasser.* New York: Harper & Row.

Battistich, V., Solomon, D., & Delucchi, K. (1993). Interaction processes and student outcomes in cooperative learning groups. *Elementary School Journal, 94*, 19–32.

Battistich, V., Solomon, D., Watson, M., & Schaps, E. (1997). Caring school communities. *Educational Psychologist, 32*, 137–151.

Baumrind, D. (1971). Current patterns of parental authority. *Developmental Psychology, 4*(1, Part 2), 1–103.

Bear, G. G. (2015). Preventive and classroom-based strategies. In E. T. Emmer and E. J. Sabornie (Eds.), *Handbook of classroom management* (2nd ed, pp. 15–39). New York: Routledge.

Berger, E. H., & Rojas-Cortez, M. R. (2011). *Parents as partners in education: Families and schools working together* (8th ed.). Upper Saddle River, NJ: Prentice-Hall.

Bicard, D. F. (2000). Using classroom rules to construct behavior. *Middle School Journal, 31*(5), 37–45.

Boonstrom, R. (1991). The nature and functions of classroom rules. *Curriculum Inquiry, 21*, 193–216.

Borich, G. (2014). *Effective teaching methods* (8th ed.). Upper Saddle River, NJ: Pearson Education.

Bransford, J. B., Brown, A. L., & Cocking, R. R. (Eds.). (1999). *How people learn.* Washington, DC: National Academy Press.

Brophy, J. E. (1996). *Teaching problem students.* New York: Guilford.

Brophy, J. E. (2006). History of research on classroom management. In C. M. Evertson & C. S. Weinstein (Eds.), *Handbook of classroom management: Research, practice, and contemporary issues* (pp. 17–43). Mahwah, NJ: Erlbaum.

Brophy, J. (2009). Connecting with the big picture. *Educational Psychologist, 44*,147–157.

Brown, D. F. (2003). Urban teachers' use of culturally responsive management strategies. *Theory into Practice, 42*(4), 277–382.

Burnett, P. C. (2002). Teacher praise and feedback and students' perceptions of the classroom environment. *Educational Psychology, 22*(1), 5–16.

Burrell, N. A., Zirbel, C. S., & Allen, M. (2003). Evaluating peer mediation outcomes in educational settings: A meta-analytic review. *Conflict Resolution Quarterly, 21*(1), 7–26.

Buzzell, J. G., & Piazza, R. (1994). *Case studies for teaching special needs and at-risk students.* Albany, NY: Delmar.

Cameron, J. (2001). Negative effects of reward on intrinsic motivation—A limited phenomenon: Comment on Deci, Koestner, and Ryan. *Review of Educational Research, 71,* 29–42.

Capizzi, A. M. (2009). Start the year off right: Designing and evaluating a supportive class-room management plan. *Focus on Exceptional Children, 42*(3), 2–12.

Carey, S. (2007). *Working with English language learners: Answers to teachers' top 10 questions* (2nd ed.). Portsmouth, NH: Heinemann.

Carifio, J., & Carey, T. (2009). A critical examination of current minimum grading policy recommendations. *The High School Journal, 93*(1), 23–37.

Carkhuff, R. R. (2010). *The art of helping in the 21st century* (9th ed.). Amherst, MA: Human Resource Development.

Cartledge, G., & Kourea, L. (2008). Culturally responsive classrooms for culturally diverse students with and at risk for disabilities. *Exceptional Children, 74*(3), 351–371.

Chang, H. N., & Romero, M. (2008). *Present, engaged, and accounted for: The critical importance of addressing chronic absence in the early grades.* National Center for Children in Poverty, Columbia University. New York: Mailman School of Public Health. 31pp.

Charles, A. S. (2012). Cell phones: Rule-setting, rule-breaking, and relationships in classrooms. *American Secondary Education, 40*(3), 4–16.

Clewell, B. C., Campbell, P. B., & Perlman, L. (2007). *Good schools in poor neighborhoods: Defying demographics, achieving success.* Washington, DC: Urban Institute Press.

Cobb, B., Sample, P. L., Alwell, M., & Johns, N. R. (2006). Cognitive-behavioral interventions, dropout, and youth with disabilities. *Remedial and Special Education, 27,* 259–275.

Cohen, E. G. (1994). *Designing groupwork: Strategies for the heterogeneous classroom* (2nd ed.). New York: Teachers College Press.

Committee for Children. (2012). SecondSTEP: Bullying prevention in schools starts with social-emotional learning. Accessed 1/27/15 at www.cfchildren.org/Portals/0/SS_BPU/BPU_DOC/SEL_Bullying_Paper.pdf

Cook, B. G., McDuffie-Landrum, K. A., Oshita, L., & Cook, S. C. (2011). Co-teaching for students with disabilities. In J. M. Kauffman & D. P. Hallahan (Eds.), *Handbook of special education* (pp. 147–159). New York: Routledge.

Cooper, J. L., & Robinson, P. (2000). Getting started: Informal small group strategies in large classes. *New Directions for Teaching and Learning, 81,* 17–24.

Cornelius-White, J. (2007). Learner-centered teacher student relationships are effective: A meta-analysis. *Review of Educational Research, 77*(1), 113–143.

Cutrona, C., & Guerin, D. (1994). Confronting conflict peacefully: Peer mediation in schools. *Educational Horizons, 71*(2), 95–104.

Damiani, V. B. (2011). *Crisis prevention and intervention in the classroom: What teachers should know* (2nd ed.). Lanham, MD: Rowman & Littlefield.

Deci, E. L., Koestner, R., & Ryan, R. M. (2001). Extrinsic rewards and intrinsic motivation in education: Reconsidered once again. *Review of Educational Research, 71,* 1–27.

Delpit, L. (1995). *Other people's children: Cultural conflict in the classroom.* New York: New Press.

Dieker, L. A., & Hines, R. A. (2014). *Strategies for teaching content effectively in the inclusive secondary classroom.* Boston: Pearson.

Domenici, K., & Littlejohn, S. W. (2006). *Face-work: Bridging theory and practice.* Thousand Oaks, CA: Sage.

Doyle, W. (1986). Classroom organization and management. In M. Wittrock (Ed.), *Handbook of research on teaching* (3rd ed., pp. 392–431). New York: Macmillan.

Doyle, W. (2006). Ecological approaches to class-room management. In C. M. Evertson & C. S. Weinstein (Eds.), *Handbook of classroom management: Research, practice, and contemporary issues* (pp. 97–125). Mahwah, NJ: Erlbaum.

Dunkin, M., & Biddle, B. (1974). *The study of teaching.* New York: Holt, Rinehart, & Winston.

DuPaul, G. J., Laracy, S. D., & Gormley, M. J. (2014). Interventions for students with attention-deficit/hyperactivity disorder: School and home contexts. In H. M. Walker & F. M. Gresham (Eds.), *Handbook of evidence-based practices for emotional and behavioral disorders: Applications in schools* (pp. 292–306). New York: Guilford.

Eccles, J. S., & Roeser, R. W. (2011). Schools as developmental contexts during adolescence. *Journal of Research on Adolescence, 21,* 225–241.

Egan, G. (2013). *The skilled helper: A problem management and opportunity-development approach to helping* (HSE 123 Interviewing Techniques) (10th ed.). Cengage Learning.

Eilam, B. (2001). Primary strategies for promoting homework performance. *American Educational Research Journal, 38,* 691–725.

Elden, R. (2013). *See me after class: Advice for teachers by teachers* (2nd ed.). Naperville, IL: Sourcebooks.

Emmer, E. T. (1988). Praise and the instructional process. *Journal of Classroom Interaction, 23,* 32–39.

Emmer, E. T., & Aussiker, A. (1990). School and classroom discipline programs: How well do they work? In O. Moles (Ed.), *Student discipline strategies: Research and practice.* Albany, NY: SUNY Press.

Emmer, E. T., & Gerwels, M. C. (2002). Cooperative learning in elementary classrooms: Teaching practices and lesson characteristics. *Elementary School Journal, 103,* 75–91.

Emmer, E. T., & Gerwels, M. C. (2006). Classroom management in middle and high school classrooms. In C. Evertson & C. Weinstein (Eds.), *Handbook of classroom mangement* (pp. 407–437). Mahwah, NJ: Erlbaum.

Emmer, E. T., & Sabornie, E. J., (Eds.). (2015). *Handbook of classroom management* (2nd ed.). New York: Routledge.

Espelage, D. L. (2015). Emerging issues in school bullying research and prevention. In E. T. Emmer, & E. J. Sabornie (Eds.), *Handbook of research on classroom management* (2nd ed.) (pp. 76–93). New York: Routledge.

Evans, G. W., & Schamberg, M. A. (2009). Childhood poverty, chronic stress, and adult working memory. *Proceedings of the National Academy of Sciences, 106*(16), 6545–6549. Doi: 10.1073/pnas.0811910106 [retrieved from www.pnas.org/106/16/6545.full]

Evertson, C. M. (1994). Classroom rules and routines. *International Encyclopedia of Education* (2nd ed.). Oxford: Pergamon.

Evertson, C. M., & Emmer, E. T. (1982). Effective management at the beginning of the school year in junior high classes. *Journal of Educational Psychology, 74,* 485–498.

Evertson, C. M., & Poole, I. R. (2004). *Effective room arrangement.* Nashville, TN: Vanderbilt University, Peabody College, The IRIS Center for Faculty Enhancement.

Evertson, C. M., & Poole, I. R. (2008). Proactive classroom management. In T. Good (Ed.), *21st century education.* Thousand Oaks, CA: Sage.

Evertson, C. M., & Weinstein, C. S. (Eds.). (2006). *Handbook of classroom management: Research, practice and contemporary issues.* Mahwah, NJ: Erlbaum.

Fabiano, G., Vujnovic, R., Pelham, W., Waschbusch, D., Massetti, G., Pariseau, M., Naylor, J., Yu, J., Robins, M., Carnefix, T., Greiner, A., & Volker, M. (2010). Enhancing the effectiveness of special education programming for children with attention deficit hyperactivity disorder using a daily report card. *School Psychology Review, 39*(2), 219–239.

Fallon, L. M., O'Keefe, B. V., & Sugai, G. (2012). Consideration of culture and context in school-wide positive behavior support: A review of current literature. *Journal of Positive Behavior Interventions, 14*(4), 209–219.

Fenwick, D. T. (1998). Managing space, energy, and self: Junior high teachers' experiences of classroom management. *Teaching and Teacher Education, 14,* 619–631.

Fournier, M. A., Moskowitz, D. S., & Zuroff, D. C. (2010). Origins and applications of the interpersonal circumplex. In L. M. Horowitz & S. Strack (Eds.), *Handbook of interpersonal psychology: Theory, research assessment, and therapeutic intervention* (pp. 57–73). New York: Wiley.

Freiberg, H. J. (Ed.). (1999). *Beyond behaviorism: Changing the classroom management paradigm.* Boston: Allyn and Bacon.

Gay, G. (2006). Connections between classroom management and culturally responsive teaching. In C. Evertson & C. Weinstein (Eds.), *Handbook of classroom management* (pp. 343–370). Mahwah, NJ: Erlbaum.

Gay, G. (2010). *Culturally responsive teaching: Theory, research, and practice* (2nd ed.). New York: Teachers College Press.

Gillies, R. M. (2007). *Cooperative learning: Integrating theory and practice*. Los Angeles: Sage.

Gillies, R. M. (2015). Small-group work: Developments in research. In E. T. Emmer & E. J. Sabornie (Eds.), *Handbook of classroom management* (2nd ed., pp. 261–280). New York: Routledge.

Gillies, R. M., & Ashman, A. F. (Eds.). (2003). *Co-operative learning: The social and intellectual outcomes of learning in groups*. New York: Routledge.

Gini, G. (2006). Bullying as a social process: The role of group membership in students' perception of inter-group aggression at school. *Journal of School Psychology, 44,* 51–65.

Glasser, W. (1975). *Reality therapy: A new approach to psychiatry*. New York: Harper & Row.

Glasser, W. (1977). 10 steps to good discipline. *Today's Education, 66,* 60–63.

Glasser, W. (1986). *Control theory in the classroom*. New York: Harper & Row.

Good, T. L., & Brophy, J. E. (2008). *Looking in classrooms* (10th ed.). New York: Longman.

Gordon, T. (1974). *Teacher effectiveness training*. New York: Peter H. Wyden.

Gorski, P. C. (2013). *Reaching and teaching students in poverty: Strategies for erasing the opportunity gap*. New York: Teachers College Press.

Gregory, A., & Weinstein, R. S. (2008). The discipline gap and African Americans: Defiance or cooperation in the high school classroom. *Journal of School Psychology, 46,* 455–475.

Gruman, D. H., Harachi, T. W., Abbott, R. D., Catalano, R. F., & Fleming, C. B. (2008). Longitudinal effects of student mobility on three dimensions of elementary school engagement. *Child Development, 79*(6), 1833–1852.

Hallinan, M. T. (1990). The effects of ability grouping in secondary schools: A response to Slavin's best-evidence synthesis. *Review of Educational Research, 60,* 501–504.

Hamre, B. K., & Pianta, R. C. (2001). Early teacher-child relationships and the trajectory of children's school outcomes through eighth grade. *Child Development, 72,* 625–638.

Hargis, C. H. (1997). *Teaching low achieving and disadvantaged students* (2nd ed.). Springfield, IL: Charles C. Thomas.

Harry, B. (1992). An ethnographic study of cross cultural communication with Puerto Rican American families in the special education system. *American Educational Research Journal, 29,* 471–494.

Hattie, J. (2009). *Visible learning: A synthesis of over 800 meta-analyses relating to achievement*. New York: Routledge.

Higgs, C. (2014). *Connecting with students: Strategies for building rapport with urban learners*. Lanham, MD: Rowman & Littlefield Education.

Hill, C. E. (2009). *Helping skills: Facilitating exploration, insight, and action* (3rd ed.). Washington, DC: American Psychological Association.

Hill, J. D., & Miller, K. B. (2013). *Classroom instruction that works with English language learners* (2nd ed.). Alexandria, VA: ASCD.

Holubec, E. J. (1992). How do you get there from here? Getting started with cooperative learning. *Contemporary Education, 63*(3), 181–184.

Jackson, P. (1968). *Life in classrooms*. New York: Holt, Rinehart & Winston.

Jerome, E. M., & Pianta, R. C. (2008). Teacher-student relationships. In T. L. Good (Ed.), *21st century education: A reference handbook* (Vol. 2, pp. 158–164). Los Angeles: Sage.

Jeynes, W. H. (2005). A meta-analysis of the relation of parental involvement to urban elementary school student academic achievement. *Urban Education, 40,* 237–269.

Johnson, D. W., & Johnson, R. T. (1995). Why violence prevention programs don't work—And what does. *Educational Leadership, 52*(5), 63–68.

Johnson, D. W., & Johnson, F. P. (2013). *Joining together: Group theory and group skills* (11th ed.). Boston: Allyn & Bacon.

Johnston, B. D. (1995). "Withitness": Real or fictional? *The Physical Educator, 52,* 22–28.

Jones, V. F., & Jones, L. S. (2007). *Comprehensive classroom management: Creating communities of support and solving problems* (8th ed.). Boston: Allyn and Bacon.

Kauffman, J. M., & Hallahan, D. P. (Eds.). (2014). *Handbook of special education*. New York: Routledge.

Klem, A. M., & Connell, J. P. (2004). Relationships matter: Linking teacher support to student engagement and achievement. *Journal of School Health, 74,* 262–273.

Kottler, J. A. (2009). *Students who drive you crazy: Succeeding with resistant, unmotivated, and otherwise difficult young people* (2nd ed.). Thousand Oaks, CA: Corwin.

Kottler, J. A., & Kottler, E. (2000). *Teacher as counselor: Developing the helping skills you need* (2nd ed.). Thousand Oaks, CA: Corwin.

Kounin, J. S. (1970). *Discipline and group management in classrooms.* New York: Holt, Rinehart & Winston.

Kounin, J. S., & Gump, P. (1974). Signal systems of lesson settings and the task related behavior of preschool children. *Journal of Educational Psychology, 66,* 554–562.

Kounin, J. S., & Obradovic, S. (1968). Managing emotionally disturbed children in regular classrooms: A replication and extension. *Journal of Special Education, 2,* 129–135.

Lambert, N. M. (1994). Seating arrangements in classrooms. *The International Encyclopedia of Education* (2nd ed., Vol. 9, pp. 5355–5359). New York: Pergamon.

Lane, K. L., & Menzies, H. M. (2015). Classroom management for inclusive settings. In E. T. Emmer & E. J. Sabornie (Eds.), *Handbook of classroom management* (2nd ed., pp. 205–219). New York: Routledge.

Le Maistre, C., & Paré, A. (2010). Whatever it takes: How beginning teachers learn to survive. *Teaching and Teacher Education, 26,* 559–564.

Leonard, H., Dixon, G., Whitehouse, A. J. O., Bourke, J., Aiberti, K., Nassar, N., et al. (2010). Unpacking the complex nature of the autism epidemic. *Research in Autism Spectrum Disorders, 4,* 548–554.

Lewis, T. J., Mitchell, B. S., Trussell, R., & Newcomer, L. (2015). School-wide positive behavior support: Building systems to prevent problem behaviour and develop and maintain appropriate social bevhavior. In E. T. Emmer & E. J. Sabornie (Eds.), *Handbook of classroom management* (2nd ed., pp. 40–59). New York: Routledge.

Lotan, R. A. (2006). Managing groupwork in the heterogeneous classroom. In C. Evertson & C. Weinstein (Eds.), *Handbook of classroom management* (pp. 525–540). Mahwah, NJ: Erlbaum.

Loveless, T. (1999). Will tracking reform promote social equity? *Educational Leadership, 56*(7), 28–32.

Lyman, Jr., F. T. (1992). Think-Pair-Share, thinktrix, thinklinks, and weird facts: An interactive system for cooperative thinking. In N. Davidson & T. Worsham (Eds.), *Enhancing thinking through cooperative learning* (pp. 169–181). New York: Teacher's College Press.

Mackenzie, R. J. (1997). Setting limits in the classroom. *American Educator, 21*(3), 32–43.

Malone, B. G., & Tietjens, C. L. (2000). Re-examination of classroom rules: The need for clarity and specified behavior. *Special Services in the Schools, 16,* 159–170.

Mariage, T. V., & Englert, C. S. (2010). Constructing access and understanding in inclusive middle-grade content classrooms. In G. Li & P. A. Edwards (Eds.), *Best practices in ELL instruction* (pp. 151–185). New York: Guilford.

Marks, L. U., Shaw-Hegwer, J., Schrader, C., Longaker, T., Peters, I., Powers, F., & Levine, M. (2003). Instructional management tips for teachers of students with autism-spectrum disorder (ASD). *Teaching Exceptional Children, 35*(4), 50–54.

McCafferty, S. G., Jacobs, G., & DaSilva Iddings, A. C. (2006). Cooperative learning and teaching in the second language classrooms. In Language Education Series, J. C. Richards (Ed.). New York: Cambridge University Press.

McCarthy, J., & Benally, J. (2003). Classroom management in a Navaho middle school. *Theory into Practice, 42*(4), 296–304.

McConnell, B. M., & Kubina, R. M. (2014). Connecting with families to improve students' school attendance: A review of the literature. *Preventing School Failure: Alternative Education for Children and Youth, 58*(4), 249–256.

McLeskey J., Waldron, N. L., Spooner, F., & Algozzine, B. (Eds.) (2014). *Handbook of research on effective inclusive schools: research and practice.* New York: Routledge.

McMillan, J. H. (2001). Secondary teachers' classroom assessment and grading practices. *Educational Measurement, 20,* 20–32.

McNally, J., I'anson, J., Whewell, C., & Wilson, G. (2005). "They think that swearing is okay": First lessons in behaviour management. *Journal of Education for Teaching, 3*(3), 169–185.

Mendler, A. N., & Mendler, B. D. (2011). *Power struggles: Successful techniques for educators* (2nd ed.). Bloomington, IN: Solution Tree.

Metts, S. (1997). Face and facework: Implications for the study of personal relationships. In S. Duck (Ed.), *Handbook of personal relationships* (pp. 373–390). New York: Wiley.

Metts, S., & Grohskopf, E. (2003). Impression management: Goals, strategies, and skills. In J. O. Greene, & B. R. Burleson (Eds.), *Handbook of communication and social interaction skills* (pp. 357–402). Mahwah, NJ: Erlbaum.

Milner, H. R. (2015). Classroom management in urban classrooms. In E. T. Emmer & E. J. Sabornie (Eds.), *Handbook of classroom management* (2nd ed., pp. 167–185). New York: Routledge.

Milner, H. R. (2010). *Start where you are but don't stay there.* Cambridge, MA: Harvard Education Press.

Mitchell, D. (2008). *What really works in special and inclusive education: Using evidence-based teaching strategies.* New York: Routledge.

Nattiv, A. (1994). Helping behaviors and math achievement gain of students using cooperative learning. *Elementary School Journal, 94,* 285–297.

Nelson, J. R., & Carr, B. A. (2000). *The think time strategy for schools.* Longmont, CO: Sopris West.

Oakes, J. (2005). *Keeping track: How schools structure inequality* (2nd ed.). New Haven, CT: Yale University Press.

O'Connor, R. E., & Jenkins, J. R. (1996). Cooperative learning as an inclusion strategy: A closer look. *Exceptionality, 6*(1), 29–51.

O'Toole, J. C. (2013). *The Asperkid's (secret) book of social rules: The handbook of not-so-obvious social guidelines for tweens and teens with Asperger's Syndrome.* Philadelphia: Jessica Kingsley Pub.

Pace, J. L. (2003). Revisiting classroom authority: Theory and ideology meets practice. *Teachers College Record, 105,* 1559–1585.

Palinscar, A. (2013). Reciprocal teaching. In J. Hattie & E. M. Anderman (Eds.), *International guide to student achievement* (pp. 369–371). New York: Routledge.

Palinscar, A., & Brown, A. (1988). Teaching and practicing thinking skills to promote comprehension in the context of group problem solving. *Remedial and Special Education, 9,* 53–59.

Payne, R. (2013). *A framework for understanding poverty: A cognitive approach* (5th ed.). Highlands, TX: aha! Process.

Perron, J., & Downey, P. J. (1997). Management techniques used by high school physical education teachers. *Journal of Teaching in Physical Education, 17,* 72–84.

Pianta, R. C. (2006). Classroom management and relationships between children and teachers: Implications for research and practice. In C. M. Evertson & C. S. Weinstein (Eds.), *Handbook of classroom management: Research, practice, and contemporary issues* (pp. 685–709). Mahwah, NJ: Erlbaum.

Poole, I. R., & Evertson, C. M. (2013). Elementary classroom management. In J. Hattie & E. M. Anderman (Eds.), *International guide to student achievement* (pp. 188–191). New York: Routledge.

Popp, P. A., Grant, L. W., & Stronge, J. H. (2009). *Classrooms with revolving doors: Recommended practices for elementary teachers of at-risk and highly mobile students.* National Center for Homeless Education, University of North Carolina at Greensboro. Retrieved from center.serve.org/nche/downloads/eff_teach_elem.pdf

Putnam, J. W. (Ed.). (1998). *Cooperative learning and strategies for inclusion* (2nd ed.). Baltimore: Brookes.

Raczynski, K. A., & Horne, A. M. (2015). Communication and interpersonal skills in classroom management: How to provide the educational experiences students need and deserve. In E. T. Emmer & E. J. Sabornie (Eds.), *Handbook of classroom management* (2nd ed., pp. 387–408). New York: Routledge.

Reeve, J. (2006). Extrinsic rewards and inner motivation. In C. Evertson & C. Weinstein (Eds.), *Handbook of classroom management* (pp. 645–664). Mahwah, NJ: Erlbaum.

Reeve, J. M. (2015). Rewards. In E. T. Emmer & Sabornie, E. J. (Eds.), *Handbook of classroom management* (2nd ed., pp. 496–515). New York: Routledge.

Renninger, K. A. (2009). Interest and identity development. *Educational Psychologist, 44,* 105–118.

Rooney, K. J. (2014). Attention-deficit/hyperactivity disorder. In J. M. Kauffman & D. P. Hallahan (Eds.), *Handbook of special education* (pp. 198–208). New York: Routledge.

Roorda, D. L., Koomen, H. M. Y., Spilt, J. L., & Oort, F. J. (2011). The influence of affective teacher student relationships on students' school engagement and achievement. *Review of Educational Research, 81*(4), 493–529.

Rumberger, R. W. (2003). The causes and consequences of student mobility. *Journal of Negro Education, 72(1),* 6–21.

Ryan, R. M., & Deci, E. L. (2000). Self-determination theory and the facilitation of intrinsic motivation, social development, and well-being. *American Psychologist, 55,* 68–78.

Saenz, L. M., Fuchs, L. S., & Fuchs, D. (2005). Peer-assisted learning strategies for English language learners with learning disabilities. *Exceptional Children, 71(3),* 231–247.

Schwab, Y., & Elias, M. J. (2015). From compliance to responsibility: Social-emotional learning and classroom management. In E. T. Emmer & E. J. Sabornie (Eds.), *Handbook of classroom management* (2nd ed., pp. 94–115). New York: Routledge.

Seiter, E. (2007). *The internet playground: Children's access, entertainment, and mis-education* (2nd ed.). New York: Peter Lang.

Sexson, S. B., & Madan-Swain, A. (1993). School reentry for the child with chronic illness. *Journal of Learning Disabilities, 26*(2), 115–125.

Sheldon, S. B. (2007). Improving student attendance with school, family, and community partnerships. *The Journal of Educational Research, 100*(5), 267–275.

Sherer, Y. C., & Nickerson, A. B. (2010). Anti-bullying practices in American schools: Perspectives of school psychologists. *Psychology in the Schools, 47,* 217–229.

Shukla-Mehta, S., & Albin, R. W. (2003). Twelve practical strategies to prevent behavioral escalation in classroom settings. *Preventing School Failure, 47,* 156–172.

Skiba, R. J., & Rauch, M. K. (2015). Reconsidering exclusionary discipline: The efficacy and equity of out-of-school suspension and expulsion. In E. T. Emmer & E. J. Sabornie (Eds.), *Handbook of classroom management* (2nd ed., pp. 116–138). New York: Routledge.

Skinner, E. A., & Belmont, M. J. (1993). Motivation in the classroom: Reciprocal effects of teacher behavior and student engagement across the school year. *Journal of Educational Psychology, 85,* 571–581.

Slavin, R. E. (1990). Achievement effects of ability grouping in secondary schools: A best evidence synthesis. *Review of Educational Research, 60,* 471–500.

Slavin, R. E. (1995). *Cooperative learning: Theory, research, and practice* (2nd ed.). Boston: Allyn and Bacon.

Slavin, R. E., Karweit, N. L., & Wasik, B. A. (1994). *Preventing early school failures: Research on effective strategies.* Boston: Allyn and Bacon.

Slavin, R. E., & Lake, C. (2008). Effective programs in elementary mathematics: A best-evidence synthesis. *Review of Educational Research, 78,* 427–515.

Smaldino, S. E., Lowther, D. E., Mims, C. D., & Russell, J. D. (2014). *Instructional technology and media for learning* (11th ed.). Upper Saddle River, NJ: Pearson.

Spady, W. G., & Mitchell, D. E. (1979). Authority and the management of classroom activities. In D. L. Duke (Ed.), *Classroom managment: The 78th yearbook of the National Society for the Study of Education* (pp. 75–115). Chicago: University of Chicago Press.

Sprick, R. (2012). *The teacher's encyclopedia of behavior management: 100+ problems/500+ plans* (2nd ed.). Eugene, OR: Northwest.

Stairs, A. J., Donnell, K. A., & Dunn, A. H. (2012). *Urban teaching in America: Theory, research, and practice in K-12 classrooms.* Thousand Oaks, CA: Sage.

Stomfay-Stitz, A. M. (1994). Pathways to safer schools. *Childhood Education, 70*(5), 279–282.

Sugai, G., & Simonsen, B. (2015). Supporting general classroom management: Tier 2/3 practices and systems. In E. T. Emmer & E. J. Sabornie (Eds.), *Handbook of classroom management* (2nd ed., pp. 60–75). New York: Routledge.

Swanson, H. L., Harris, K. R., & Graham, S. (Eds.). (2013). *Handbook of learning disabilities* (2nd ed.). New York: Guilford.

Thorson, S. A. (2003). *Listening to students: Reflections on secondary classroom management.* Boston: Allyn and Bacon.

Tudge, J. R. H. (1992). Processes and consequences of peer collaboration: A Vygotskian analysis. *Child Development, 63,* 1364–1379.

Vannest, K. J., Davis, J. L., Davis, C. R., Mason, B. A., & Burke, M. D. (2010). Effective intervention for behavior with a daily behavior report card: A meta-analysis. *School Psychology Review, 39*(4), 654–672.

Vaughn, S., & Schumm, J. S. (1994). Middle school teachers' planning for students with learning disabilities. *Remedial and Special Education, 15,* 152–161.

Vaughn, S., Schumm, J. S., Jallad, B., Slusher, J., & Saumell, L. (1996). Teachers' views of inclusion. *Learning Disabilities Research and Practice, 11*(2), 96–106.

Vavrus, M. (2008). Culturally responsive teaching. In T. L. Good (Ed.), *21st century education: A reference handbook* (Vol. 2, pp. 49–57). Los Angeles: Sage.

Vermette, P. (1994). Four fatal flaws: Avoiding the common mistakes of novice users of cooperative learning. *The High School Journal, 77*(3), 255–260.

Villa, R. A., Thousand, J. S., & Nevin, A. I. (2004). *A guide to co-teaching: Practical tips for facilitating student learning.* Thousand Oaks, CA: Corwin.

Walker, H. M., & Gresham, F. M. (Eds.). (2014). *Handbook of evidence-based practices for emotional and behavioral disorders: Applications in schools.* New York: Guilford.

Walker, J. M. T., & Hoover-Dempsey, K. V. (2015). Parental engagement and classroom management: Unlocking the potential of family-school interactions and relationships. In E. T. Emmer & E. J. Sabornie (Eds.), *Handbook of classroom management* (2nd ed., pp. 459–478). New York: Routledge.

Wang, M. C., Haertel, G. D., & Walberg, H. J. (1993). Toward a knowledge base for school learning. *Review of Educational Research, 63,* 249–294.

Webb, N. M., & Farivar, S. (1994). Promoting helping behavior in cooperative small groups in middle school mathematics. *American Educational Research Journal, 31,* 369–397.

Weinstein, C. S., Tomlinson-Clarke, S., & Curran, M. (2004). Toward a conception of culturally responsive classroom management. *Journal of Teacher Education, 55*(1), 25–38.

Wentzel, K. R., & Brophy, J. E. (2014). *Motivating students to learn* (4th ed.). New York: Routledge, Taylor Francis.

Whicker, K. M., Bol, L., & Nunnery, J. A. (1997). Cooperative learning in the secondary mathematics classroom. *Journal of Educational Research, 91,* 42–48.

Wubbels, T., Brekelmans, M., den Brok, P., & van Tartwijk, J. (2006). An interpersonal perspective on classroom management in secondary classrooms in the Netherlands. In C. M. Evertson & C. S. Weinstein (Eds.), *Handbook of classroom management: Research, practice, and contemporary issues* (pp. 1161–1192). Mahwah, NJ: Erlbaum.

Wubbels, T., Brekelmans, M., den Brok, P., Wijsman, L., Mainhard, T., & van Tartwijk, J. (2015). Teacher-student relationships and classroom management. In E. T. Emmer & E. J. Sabornie (Eds.), *Handbook of classroom management* (2nd ed., pp. 363–386). New York: Routledge.

Zepeda, S. J., & Mayers, R. S. (2001). New kids on the block schedule: Beginning teachers face challenges. *High School Journal, 84*(4), 1–11.

Zuker, E. (1983). *Mastering assertiveness skills: Power and positive influence at work.* New York: AMACOM.

INDEX